Elizabeth Gundrey was well known as editor of this country's first consumer magazine (*Shoppers' Guide*) long before she turned her keen eye for quality and value-for-money to the subject of travel. Her articles in the *Observer* won her the Jubilee Award of the British Guild of Travel Writers. Of all her books this one has been far the most popular, re-appearing each year in new enlarged editions, of which this is the eighth. She is also the author of *England by Bus & Coach* (Sphere); and, coming soon, *Running your own Bed and Breakfast* (Piatkus) for people who want to start doing this themselves.

Staying Off the Beaten Track reached the best-seller listings last year for months on end.

VOUCHERS WORTH £15

(by courtesy of the houses concerned)

This voucher is worth £5 at any establishment starred in the list on pages **ix–xviii** provided it is presented **ON ARRIVAL** and not later. It is valid throughout **1989**, and may be used if you stay **3** or more nights. Only one voucher usable per establishment.

This voucher is worth £5 at any establishment starred in the list on pages **ix–xviii** provided it is presented **ON ARRIVAL** and not later. It is valid throughout **1989**, and may be used if you stay **3** or more nights. Only one voucher usable per establishment.

This voucher is worth £5 at any establishment starred in the list on pages **ix–xviii** provided it is presented **ON ARRIVAL** and not later. It is valid throughout **1989**, and may be used if you stay **3** or more nights. Only one voucher usable per establishment.

OFFER OF NEXT EDITION

Using an out-of-date edition can lead to costly disappointments. A new edition appears every December, updated, with fresh entries added, some deleted and others revised, and with vouchers valid for the next year. Make sure you are not using an out-of-date edition by sending a stamped self-addressed envelope to Explore Britain, Alston, Cumbria, CA9 3SL, for an order form (UK only) on which you can apply for the 1990 edition even before it reaches the shops. No need for a letter: just put SOTBT 1990 on top left corner of the envelope you send. **New in 1990: Channel Islands; and more entries for Warwickshire, Dorset, Bath (Avon), Surrey, Sussex, the Cotswolds, Worcestershire, Suffolk, the Yorkshire Dales, Lancashire, the Lake District, Oxfordshire and other areas.**

STAYING OFF THE BEATEN TRACK

ELIZABETH GUNDREY

*A personal selection of moderately priced
inns, small hotels, farms and country houses
in England, Scotland and Wales.*

EIGHTH EDITION
1989
Over 100 more entries

NEW THIS YEAR: WALES

ARROW BOOKS

To Andrew, with love

Arrow Books Limited
62–65 Chandos Place, London WC2N 4NW

A division of Century Hutchinson Limited

London Melbourne Sydney Auckland
Johannesburg and agencies
throughout the world

First published in Great Britain 1982
by Hamlyn Paperbacks
Second edition 1983
Third edition 1984
Fourth edition 1985
Fifth edition 1986
Arrow edition (Sixth edition) 1986
Seventh edition 1987
Eighth edition 1988

Set in Linotron Plantin by
Rowland Phototypesetting Limited
Bury St Edmunds, Suffolk
Printed and bound in Great Britain by
The Guernsey Press Co. Limited, Guernsey, C.I.

Cover picture: **Coombe Farmhouse**, Widegates,
Cornwall
(*see page 76*)

British Library Cataloguing in Publication Data

Gundrey, Elizabeth
    Staying off the beaten track: a personal
    selection of moderately priced inns, small
    hotels, farms and country houses in England,
    Scotland and Wales. – 8th ed.
    1. Great Britain. Hotels – Visitors' guides
    I. Title
    647′.944101

ISBN 0-09-958720-3

The author and publishers would like to thank all those
owners who allowed us to use their drawings. Additional
line drawings by David Mostyn, Peter Gregory, Matthew
Doyle, Nicole Tedder, Jeremy Ford and Leslie Dean.

CONTENTS

The hotels and houses in England appear in alphabetical order later. For convenience in locating them, they are grouped in the following list according to counties. On the left is the nearest town (sometimes distant), with its map reference (see page vii), followed by the house or hotel and its nearest village.

✻ Establishments marked with a star will accept the discount vouchers from page ii. Other discounts to readers are described in the text.

NOTE: The houses in this book have been personally visited by Elizabeth (or in some cases Walter) Gundrey. **Over two-thirds charge £14 or less for bed-and-breakfast; and the rest little more, particularly when bargain breaks are available.** But owners, and prices can change overnight; so check before you book. At many places, you can dine or lunch without staying: see entries under 'dinner'. Entries added since the previous edition are marked '*New*'.

COMPLAINTS: I will investigate if you have first taken the matter up with the owners, who are normally anxious to put right anything that is wrong. E.G.

COUNTY LIST OF HOUSES & HOTELS IN ENGLAND

Nearest town	Map reference (*see page vii*)	Address	Page
AVON			
Bath	F.11	Oldfields ✶	214
		The Orchard, Bathford	216
		Paradise House ✶	222
		Somerset House ✶	266
		Strathavon	278
		Parkside ✶	278
Bristol	F.11	Cameley Lodge, Temple Cloud	45
BEDFORDSHIRE			
Bedford	J.10	Church Farm, Roxton	59
		The Grange, Ravensden ✶	119
BERKSHIRE			
Hungerford	G.11	Marshgate Cottage, Marshgate ✶	170
Maidenhead	H.11	Inverlodden, Wargrave	142
Newbury	G.11	St Mary's House, Kintbury	254
Reading	H.11	Boot Farm, Bradfield	30
		Bridge Cottage, Woolhampton	30
Windsor	H.11	Bear Farm, Binfield ✶	17
BUCKINGHAMSHIRE			
Aylesbury	H.10	Foxhill, Kingsey ✶	115
		Poletrees Farm, Brill	232
		Wallace Farm, Dinton	298
Beaconsfield	H.11	Old Jordans, Jordans	195
Milton Keynes	H.10	Castlethorpe Lodge	213
		White House, Olney	314
CAMBRIDGESHIRE			
Cambridge	J.9	The Coach House, Dry Drayton ✶	70
		The Watermill, Hildersham	302
Ely	K.9	Warden's House, Wicken	301
CHESHIRE			
Chester	E.7	Castle House	49
		Duddon Lodge, Tarporley	271
		Hatton Hall, Hatton Heath	130
		Stapleford Hall, Tarvin	271
Nantwich	F.7	Burland Farm, Burland	41
CORNWALL			
Bude	C.12	Manor Farm, Crackington Haven	167
		St Christopher's, Boscastle	251

Nearest town	Map reference (see page vii)	Address	Page
Plymouth	C.13	Modbury Poppin, Modbury	180
		Sloop Inn, Bantham	264
		The Wood, Salcombe ✳	322
Tiverton	D.12	Bark House, Oakford Bridge ✳	13
		Bickleigh Cottage, Bickleigh	23
Torquay	D.13	Tor Haven Hotel, Brixham ✳	284
Totnes	D.13	Buckyette, Littlehampton	38
		Cott Inn, Dartington ✳	77
		Ford Farmhouse, Harberton	111
		Preston Farm, Harberton	238
Two Bridges	D.13	Cherrybrook	55
Yelverton	C.13	Overcombe Hotel, Horrabridge ✳	221

DORSET (east)

Nearest town	Map reference	Address	Page
Bere Regis	F.13	Appletree Cottage	7
Blandford Forum	F.12	Courtney Cottage, Iwerne Courtney ✳	81
		The Fox, Ansty ✳	114
		Old Bakery, Mitlon Abbas ✳	189
		Sound o'Water, Cerne Abbas	189
Bournemouth	G.13	Mon Bijou Hotel	181
Bridport	E.13	Chimneys, Chideock ✳	56
Corfe Castle	F.13	Scott Arms, Kingston	256
Dorchester	F.13	The Court, Frampton	80
		Old Vicarage, Affpuddle	206
		Yoah Cottage, West Knighton ✳	80
Lyme Regis	E.13	Red House	242
		Springfield ✳	242
Shaftesbury	F.12	Stourcastle Lodge, Sturminster Newton	276
Swanage	G.13	White Lodge	315
Wareham	F.13	Old Granary	193
		Trent Vale Farmhouse, Hyde ✳	286
Weymouth	F.13	The Beehive, Osmington	19

DURHAM (COUNTY)

Nearest town	Map reference	Address	Page
Bishop Auckland	G.4	Grove House, Hamsterley Forest ✳	122
Stanhope	G.4	Pennine Lodge, Weardale	226

ESSEX

Nearest town	Map reference	Address	Page
Chelmsford	K.10	Blackwater Hotel, West Mersea ✳	28
Colchester	K.10	Dedham Hall, Dedham ✳	95
		Elm House, Earls Colne	104
		Upper Park, Dedham ✳	95
Saffron Walden	K.10	Old School House, Castle Hedingham ✳	205

GLOUCESTERSHIRE

Nearest town	Map reference	Address	Page
(Burford, Oxon)	G.10	Lamb Inn, Great Rissington ✳	148
Cheltenham	F.10	Bouchers, Bentham	32
(Faringdon, Oxon)	G.11	Manor Farm, Kelmscott	168
Gloucester	F.10	Burrows Court Hotel, Dursley	43
		Damsells Cross and Damsells Lodge, Painswick	94

Nearest town	Map reference *(see page vii)*	Address	Page
Faringdon	G.11	Portwell House ✳	237
Oxford	H.10	Old Inn, Black Bourton	194
Thame	H.10	Upper Green Farm, Towersey	293
Witney	G.10	Morar Farm, Bampton ✳	182

SCILLY ISLES

Bryher	A.14	Bank Cottage	11
St Agnes	A.14	Coastguards ✳	71
St Mary's	A.14	Carn Vean, Pelistry Bay ✳	48
		Carnwethers, Pelistry Bay	47

SHROPSHIRE

Ludlow	E.9	Birches Mill, Clun	26
		Bucknell House, Bucknell	37
		Upper Buckton, Leintwardine	37
Shrewsbury	E.8	The Citadel, Weston-under-Redcastle ✳	62
		Fitz Manor, Bomere Health ✳	109

SOMERSET

Bridgwater	E.12	Alfoxton Cottage, Holford ✳	5
Cheddar	E.11	Penscot Farmhouse Hotel, Shipham ✳	227
Glastonbury	E.12	Almshouse, Axbridge	6
Minehead	D.12	The Cleeve, Porlock	66
		Cross Lane House, Allerford	197
		Cutthorne, Luckwell Bridge	101
		Edgcott House, Edgcott ✳	101
		Karslake House, Winsford ✳	145
		Old Manor, Dunster Beach	196
Taunton	E.12	Old Manor Farmhouse, Norton Fitzwarren ✳	198

STAFFORDSHIRE

Leek	F.7	White House, Grindon	313

SUFFOLK

Bury St Edmunds	K.9	High Green House, Nowton ✳	134
		Pykards Hall Farm, Rede	241
(Colchester, Essex)	K.10	Old Vicarage, Higham ✳	209
Framlingham	L.9	Broadwater ✳	35
Hadleigh	L.10	Edgehill Hotel ✳	102
Ipswich	L.10	Pipps Ford, Needham Market	230
Lavenham	K.10	Buttons Green Farm, Cockfield	45
Stowmarket	L.9	Old Rectory, Wetherden ✳	204
Sudbury	K.10	Bells, Clare	22
		Bulmer Tye House, Bulmer Tye	40
		Ship Stores, Clare	22
		Street Farm, Brent Eleigh ✳	45
		Western House, Cavendish ✳	306

Nearest town	Map reference (*see page vii*)	Address	Page
		Sugarswell Farm, Shenington	280
Warwick	G.9	Ashleigh House, Henley-in-Arden ✳	9

WILTSHIRE

Nearest town	Map reference	Address	Page
(Bath, Avon)	F.11	Avonside, Limpley Stoke	10
Chippenham	F.11	Church House, Grittleton ✳	61
		The Cottage, Bromham ✳	78
		Red Lion, Lacock ✳	243
Corsham	F.11	Spiders Barn, Pickwick	267
Devizes	F.11	Crookwood Watermill, Stert	85
		Etchilhampton House, Etchilhampton ✳	107
Marlborough	G.11	Ivy House Hotel	170
Salisbury	G.12	Corner Elm, Netton	176
		Enford House, Enford ✳	105
		Farthings	277
		Langley Wood, Redlynch	150
		Mill House, Berwick St James ✳	175
		Old Mill Hotel, West Harnham ✳	200
		Saint Marie's Grange, Alderbury	253
		Stoke Farm, Broad Chalke	273
		Stratford Lodge ✳	277
(Shaftesbury, Dorset)	F.12	Milton Farm, East Knoyle ✳ '	177
Swindon	G.11	Cove House, Ashton Keynes ✳	82
Warminster	F.12	West House ✳	305

WORCESTERSHIRE

Nearest town	Map reference	Address	Page
Broadway	G.10	Mill Hay House ✳	174
Malvern	F.10	Holdfast Cottage Hotel, Welland ✳	215
		One-Eight-Four	215
Worcester	F.9	The Birche, Shelsey Beauchamp	25
		Leigh Court, Leigh	153
		Pool House Hotel, Upton-on-Severn	236
		Upton House, Upton Snodsbury	295

YORKSHIRE (NORTH)

Nearest town	Map reference	Address	Page
Ampleforth	H.5	Newton Grange Farm	152
Harrogate	G.5	Alexa House	4
		Sportman's Arms, Pateley Bridge	268
Hawes	F.5	Cockett's Hotel	73
		Low Green House, Bishopsdale	159
		Stone House Hotel, Sedbusk ✳	275
Helmsley	H.5	Laskill House Farm, Hawnby	152
Leyburn	G.5	Holly Tree, East Witton	137
		Old Rectory, Patrick Brompton	202
Malton	H.5	Beansheaf, Kirby Misperton	16
		Oakdene	16
Pickering	H.5	Bramwood ✳	34
		Moorlands, Levisham ✳	164
Richmond	G.4	Gunnarsgill Hall, Gunnerside	123
		Howe Villa	140
		Old Vicarage, Muker	210

THANK YOU . . .

. . . to the hundreds of readers who write to me with comments on houses from this book at which they have stayed: very useful guidance about what readers like or don't like (on which subject, more below). As in the previous year, I will be sending a free copy of the next edition to three readers who this year send me the largest number of comments on houses visited.

And thanks also to those who write with comments on the book: praise is an encouragement, criticism useful. The latter often helps me to improve subsequent editions, although I cannot act on all suggestions – some are impractical, some cancel one another out.

And a particular thank-you to those who send me details of their own finds, for possible future inclusion in the book. Do not be disappointed if your candidate does not appear in the very next edition. I never publish recommendations from unknown members of the public without verification, and, as I am a one-woman show, it takes time for me to get round each part of Britain in turn. I use the services of others only for re-visits. My brother, Walter Gundrey, helps with some parts of the North.

Also, there is a long time-lag between my visits and the appearance of what I write in book form: editing, printing, binding and distribution take many months. The details you send are always filed, under counties, until such time as I go to the county in question; and then they are a very great help, although there is never enough space for all of them to be used. Please, however, do not send details of houses already featured in many other guides, nor any that are more expensive than those in this book.

The importance of personally verifying information received from readers cannot be over-emphasized. Here is just one example. A reader wrote with praise of a remote guest-house in one of England's most scenic counties. When I got there (a long journey), I discovered he had not mentioned that the house is alongside a quarry, with lorry-park next to it and the mechanical excavators near.

Checking also extends to any complaints or criticisms I receive – hearteningly few. Many of these are matters of taste or opinion on which two people may never agree. Here is one: 'Very disappointing, inadequate, meagre, dull meals, expensive.' *On the same day*, I received another letter about the same house. It read: 'One of the best, delightful, comfortable, food exactly to our taste. Mrs X went to endless trouble, service like a 5-star hotel.'

More factual, however, was a complaint – about a dairy-farm, of all places – that had put powdered milk-substitute on the bedroom tea-tray. When I enquired into this, I was sent the complainant's letter booking her room: it mentioned that she was unable to digest milk. The substitute had therefore been obtained specially for her.

From this you will see why I have to check the validity of every criticism I receive before being influenced by it. All very time-consuming, but necessary if *Staying Off the Beaten Track* is to be reliable. Further, by drawing hosts' attention to any valid criticisms, I can – and do – get improvements made where these are desirable. But why not voice criticisms yourself? (See page xxiii.)

Most annual accommodation guides of repute (other than some with subsidies, financial sponsors or big membership associations behind them) require a payment before anyone can get an entry in them. This is because the cost of inspection, travel and much else is exceedingly heavy and it has to be paid for somehow. The most important aspect of any accommodation guide, however, is not how it is financed but the quality of the inspection and reporting. The only way to evaluate any guide is to read, use and then judge it.

SOTBT does not require payment from proprietors in order to get into the book – and because of this another system has evolved, of voluntary contributions which proprietors make only at the *end* of each season. No bills are issued: each proprietor sends what he/she decides, and my trust is rarely exploited. The proprietors themselves – not I – recommend (through meetings and circular letters) at what level contributions might be made by each, proportionate to the benefits the book has brought them. Without such support, *Staying Off the Beaten Track* would not have survived (and I would particularly like to pay tribute to the loyalty of proprietors who helped the book in its early struggling days before it became a success). The system is a fair one because any small proprietor who receives few visitors from SOTBT gives very little, while those who make a substantial profit give more; and of course it does not affect the reliability of the book's recommendations, as those who use it testify – see readers' comments throughout the book.

Last year, for the first time in seven years, the book made a surplus for me, part of which was given to charity – most going to one which I particularly commend to the support of readers who can afford holidays, since it exists to provide holidays for those who cannot: families suffering not only from poverty, but from chronic illness, physical handicaps and other severe hardship. It is the Family Holiday Association (Hertford Lodge, East End Road, London, N3).

HOW TO HAVE A GOOD TIME

For months on end last year, this book was either first or second among accommodation guides on the weekly bestseller lists of the book trade. Good news, but it does also mean that as the readership grows so also does the diversity of readers' tastes. My detailed descriptions are meant to help each one pick out the places that suit him or her best; but I still get readers who write to complain about bar noise in inns (so why pick an inn rather than a house without a bar?), the presence of dogs (why go to a house with the code letter **D**, meaning dogs accepted, or to a farm where dogs are almost certainly kept?) and so forth.

Some people have very particular requirements; and it is up to them to discuss these when telephoning to book. Many hosts in this book are more flexible than big hotels, and all are eager to help if they can. I have in mind such things as: a bad back, needing a very *firm mattress*; special *dietary* requirements, and *allergies* to feather pillows or animals; a strong preference for *separate tables* rather than a shared dining-table – or vice versa; *fewer courses* than on the fixed menu; *twin beds* rather than double beds – or vice versa; freedom to *smoke* – or freedom from it; a particular wish for *electric blanket*, *hot water-bottle*, etc. or a dislike of *duvets*; the need to arrive, depart or eat at *extra-early* or *extra-late* hours; an intention to pay by *credit card* (this should not be taken for granted, particularly at small guest-houses). Houses which ordinarily do not admit non-residents to dine may nevertheless permit you to invite a friend – just ask.

The code letters that appear after the name of each house will help you identify houses suitable for children, dogs, handicapped people, users of public transport, etc.: for full explanation, see page xxviii.

Please also use the 'how to book' checklist on page xxi when telephoning.

And one final tip on ensuring that you get all that you hope for: at the end of each season, throw away *Staying Off the Beaten Track* and get next year's edition (you can soon recoup its cost through using the fresh set of accommodation vouchers it contains). Here's why this is so important. A reader wrote to me as follows: 'The house was dirty; room smelt damp; toilet-seat wobbly and stained; under-pillows had no cases; grubby carpets . . . (etc.)'. The house had changed hands years ago, and been dropped from my book as a consequence; but the reader was using an out-of-date edition. Prices change, so do telephone numbers and much else. Change of owner or grossly inflated prices are the two most common reasons why I drop houses; a third is that I find somewhere better – or of better value – in the neighbourhood.

My own standards (and, indeed, standards generally) have gone up over the years. Value for money remains one of my main criteria. I rate unpretentious hospitality far above outward show.

There is one other, important component in having an enjoyable experience: congenial company. I am struck by the number of readers who comment that, when they stay at a *Staying Off the Beaten Track* house, they find other visitors – from the same source – very agreeable company because they are compatible people. (Just occasionally there is an exception: the one who keeps aloof, or who loudly complains about trivia, for instance.)

At Foxhill, there is a 'Guest of the Year Award' and I asked the criteria for their idea of a perfect guest. Answer: 'Good-humoured; relaxed with other guests; conversational; appreciative; willing to speak up if there is a problem [*note that, please! and see page xxvi – suggestion slips*]; tidy their rooms and don't have secret meals in them; enjoy doing "something different", and sharing their local finds with others; recommend others to come.' I would add also those that refund the cost of any phone calls, and of postage for sending on things they have left behind; and those that **don't telephone their booking at mealtimes or late** (proprietors work long hours and deserve an undisturbed evening). Perhaps one day somebody will compile a Good Guest Guide!

TELEPHONING TO BOOK: A CHECKLIST

Book well ahead: many of these houses have few rooms. Further, at some houses rooms (though similarly priced) vary in size or amenities: early applicants get the best ones. Mention that you are a reader of *Staying Off the Beaten Track*.

1. Ask for the owner by the *name* given in this edition. (If there has been a change, standards may differ.)
2. Specify *your precise needs*: see above. (Do not turn up with children, dogs or disabilities if you have not checked that these are accepted or provided for.) Elderly people may wish to ensure that their room is not on the second floor.
3. Check *prices* – these, too, can change (particularly after spring). Ask whether there are any bargain breaks. All prices quoted in this book are minimum; and at some houses wide variations occur. Be sure that VAT is not extra.
4. Ask what *deposit* to send (or quote a credit card number). There is more about deposits on page 355.
5. State your intended *time of arrival*, and what *meals* are wanted. (If you should then be late, telephone a warning – otherwise your room may be let to someone else.)
6. Ask for precise instructions for *locating the house*, many are remote. Better still, ask for a brochure with map to be posted to you. Check where to park.

EXCLUSIVE SOTBT TOURS

On page 235 is a description of Pond Cottage whose owner, Vi Viljoen, is a fully qualified tourist guide. She has offered to organize and accompany a series of minibus tours in 1989 in and around the Cotswolds, Stratford-upon-Avon, Warwick and also, if there is sufficient demand, a gardens tour. These tours would be exclusive to SOTBT readers.

In addition to Pond Cottage there is plenty of SOTBT accommodation in the vicinity for the nights before and after each tour. Participants would gather at Pond Cottage at 9.30 or 10am and would be dropped back there about 4 or 5pm. (There is ample car parking space there for the duration of the tour.)

If you are interested, please send Mrs Viljoen a stamped, self-addressed envelope marked 'SOTBT TOURS' in the top left corner (there is no need for a letter unless you have a special request as to dates or proposed itinerary). Overseas readers should enclose an international reply coupon. Mrs Viljoen will then send you a descriptive programme of all the tours with dates and prices (these will vary according to the specific tour), together with a booking form.

. . . AND AN SOTBT CLUB

An experiment last year proved such a success that I am now not thinking of extending the idea.

What happened was that interested readers were invited (via a page of the 1988 edition) to a special weekend exclusively for them (at a Wiltshire hotel noted for its good food) with certain events laid on – a sherry party on the first evening; on the next day, a coach tour to a stately home, gardens and a prehistoric site in the vicinity; an after-dinner talk about the history of the locality; and on the last morning, a guided walk: all included in a price that represented very good value.

One of the things which particularly appealed to those who attended – a compatible group – was the pleasure of meeting one another and comparing notes on other SOTBT hotels or houses they had visited. (I too was there, to give individual advice on places at which to stay, off the beaten track.)

'*More*, please', said many who attended. And thus was born the idea of starting a SOTBT club, with an annual programme of events such as the above (and also others: Sunday lunches? wine tastings? theatre parties? who knows what else!).

One thing I feel strongly about – as always – is that 'smaller is nicer'. Therefore it would be my intention not to accept for any event more than about 40 people at a time, and much fewer at most of them.

If you are interested, please send a stamped self-addressed envelope, marked SOTBT CLUB in the top left corner (no need for a letter unless you have special requests), to me at 19 Fitzjohns Avenue, London NW3 5JY; or in the case of overseas readers, please enclose an international reply coupon. I will later – probably in Autumn 1989 – post you particulars of events planned, the subscription, and an application form (assuming enough people indicate that such a project is wanted!).

READER PARTICIPATION

1 It would be very helpful if you will let me know your opinion of places from this book at which you have stayed. Please also tell me if you experience difficulties in making bookings. Please post this to: Elizabeth Gundrey (SOTBT), 19 Fitzjohns Avenue, London NW3 5JY (no phone calls please!). If you wish for an acknowledgement please enclose a stamped addressed envelope.

Names of establishments

Your comments (with date of stay)

2 If you find other places you think I should visit, for possible inclusion in a future edition, please will you either send me their brochure or give your own description (including price and address). No expensive places, please.

Your name and address (capitals): _____

_____

Date: _____ Occupation (optional): _____

READERS' LETTERS

Our thanks and appreciation for all the help and guidance provided by your excellent book. (R. Cook, Royal Navy)

We are firm Gundrey fans – you've changed our lives! (R. I. Johnson, Wakefield)

We found your book invaluable when planning our UK vacation and will get the most up-to-date version when we next come over. (C. I. Wilkes, South Africa)

Congratulations on your book. It travels with us wherever we go and has facilitated many a happy evening away. (J. Stafford, London)

How much we have enjoyed our last two years' holidays staying at addresses we obtained from the book. (N. Ealey, London)

It's the very best guide of its kind that I've come across and I'm sure I have the largest British guidebook collection in the US. I often browse through your book just for fun, it's that good. (J. Paul, California)

Completely reliable and helpful. (C. Pugh, Southport)

Congratulations on your excellent guide. As a veteran of some 200 hotel nights a year, I have discovered at last the peace and tranquillity that the small and caring establishment can offer. (Conference organizer, London)

Your book is invaluable for our sort of holiday – thank you.
(S. Haslem, Doncaster)

How indispensable we find the book, and enjoyable.
(B. Lancaster, Market Harborough)

Your splendid book . . . all houses we have stayed at have come up to the standard which we have come to expect. (P. Engles, Sidcup)

We consider your book our bible! You really are a blessing. (D. Wood, London)

On a holiday touring England, 'Staying off the Beaten Track' proved so helpful. We stayed at 7 places and found them exactly as you described them.
(W. Harris, Canada)

Your book is excellent. I've planned several short breaks around it.
(M. Bradley, Holmfirth)

We stayed eight times 'Off the Beaten Track' and are greatly indebted to you. We shall be sampling more of your wonderful discoveries. (J. Bradley, Scarborough)

Thank you for 'Staying off the Beaten Track'. We have done just that so many times with your book as a guide and have never been disappointed.
(D. Pinian, London)

OFF THE BEATEN TRACK IN FRANCE

Some readers have suggested I should write about accommodation in France too. Answer, no! For two reasons, one of which is that it is more than a full-time job covering Britain. The second is Patricia Fenn, whose *French Entrée* series of paperbacks (Quiller Press) provides such admirable guidance to accommodation in many parts of France that the job is already well done.

Her approach is very similar to mine. She visits hotels and guest-houses herself, and writes vivid descriptions of their ambience, hosts and food. She too concentrates mainly on affordable places. Sightseeing is covered as well.

Her books are not updated annually but are nevertheless well worth getting. The *French Entrées* currently in print are nos. 3 (Normandy), 5 (Brittany) and 6 (Boulogne, Pays d'Opale, Picardy) at £3.95 each; and 7 (Calais, Champagne, Ardennes, Bruges) and 8 (Loire Valley) at £4.95. On sale at bookshops or by post from Quiller Press, 50 Albemarle Street, London, W.1.

'U3A'

This mysterious code is one that older readers of *Staying Off the Beaten Track* should certainly try to crack.

It stands for University of the Third Age, which may sound rather formidable but is in fact something likely to appeal greatly to lively-minded readers who, on retirement, have more time for satisfying leisure pursuits (such as touring around with *Staying Off the Beaten Track*).

U3A is open to retired people (now one-fifth of the population) who want to join like-minded others in all kinds of activities – not organized *for* them but *by* themselves, in groups.

As to its name, the 'third' age is that which succeeds the first (childhood) and the second (work and rearing a family); and 'university' harks back to the original meaning of this word, a co-operative of people engaged in intellectual pursuits – regardless of their educational qualifications, if any.

U3A members are not students, though learning and sharing knowledge is at the core of what goes on in each local group. Travel, here and abroad, comes into it – so do many other activities. Some groups engage in study circles or research together, some in sharing their expertise with the less skilled or disadvantaged elderly in their community; just what each does depends entirely on the personal resources of the participants – but creativity and fulfilment are what every group is about. Wine-tastings, language classes, luncheon clubs, field study trips, local history, collecting prints, writing and drama circles, a 'hobbies fair', backstage theatre visits, American quiltmaking – all sorts of fun as well as serious activities go on in different parts of the country wherever a U3A group flourishes. And there are now 140 of these in Britain (ranging in size from 12 to 1200 members!).

There are also individual U3A members who do not join any group but pay a £5 subscription to get the Third Age newspaper three times a year, and certain special offers (such as travel schemes).

Any reader who thinks U3A sounds interesting can obtain a leaflet about it (and a list of groups) by sending a large, stamped, self-addressed envelope marked SOTBT in the top left corner (no letter needed) to:

Dianne Norton, U3A, 6 Parkside Gardens, London SW19 5EY

Good hosts are always keen to know if there is anything amiss or lacking in what they provide. Some guests are too diffident to tell them!

Here are suggestion slips to fill in, cut out and leave when paying your bill, if you cannot bring yourself to speak up.

SUGGESTION

As a reader of 'Staying Off the Beaten Track', may I suggest that enjoyment of a visit to your house would be enhanced by the following improvement:

SUGGESTION

As a reader of 'Staying Off the Beaten Track', may I suggest that enjoyment of a visit to your house would be enhanced by the following improvement:

SUGGESTION

As a reader of 'Staying Off the Beaten Track', may I suggest that enjoyment of a visit to your house would be enhanced by the following improvement:

From a hotelier's letter to me:

'We still get exasperated with some visitors, like the person who wrote in our Comments Book: "Very disappointed that we had to repair our own electric plug". We find it difficult to have extra-sensory perception! If only he had asked.'

ALPHABETICAL DIRECTORY OF HOUSES AND HOTELS IN
ENGLAND

Prices are the minimum per person
in a double room, at the beginning
of the year

SPECIAL REQUIREMENTS

(see code letters after names of houses)

C D H PT S S-C X

Code letters after the names of houses indicate which ones are (in alphabetical order) likely to prove suitable for families with *children* (**C**), *dogs* (**D**) or *handicapped people* (**H**); and for those who, being without a car, depend upon *public transport* (**PT**). (In the case of children, a minimum age is sometimes stipulated, in which case this has been indicated by a numeral: thus, **C**(5) means children over 5 are accepted.) **S** indicates those that charge singles no more, or only 10% more, than half a double (except, possibly, at peak periods). Some houses additionally have *self-catering* accommodation available (**S-C**); some accept visitors at *Christmas* (**X**), but do not necessarily provide Christmas meals.

In most cases, places that accept *children* (**C**) offer reduced rates and special meals. They may provide cots, high chairs and even baby-listening; or games and sports for older children. Please enquire when booking. And do not expect a toddler to be regarded as a (free) baby.

For *dogs* (**D**) a charge is rarely made, but often it is a stipulation that you must ask before bringing one; and the dog may have to sleep in your car, or be banned from public rooms.

Handicapped people vary in their needs. Wherever I have used the code letter **H**, this indicates that not only is there a ground floor bedroom and bathroom but that these, and doorways, have sufficient width for a wheel-chair, and that steps are few. For precise details, ask when booking.

It is not necessary to have a car in order to get off the beaten track because public transport is widely available: hotels indicated by the code **PT** have a railway station or coach stop within a reasonable distance, from which you can walk or take a taxi (quite a number of hosts will even pick you up, free, in their own car). The symbol **PT** further indicates that there are also some nearby buses to use for local sightseeing, but these may be few. Ask for details when booking.

ABBEY BRIDGE INN

C(5) **D PT S X**

Lanercost, north of Brampton, Cumbria, CA8 2HG   Tel: 06977 2224

5 bedrooms (single or double) from £15. Rooms have central heating; own bathroom (two); armchairs; views of country or garden. Tea in bed is available.
Dinner A la carte. Vegetarian or special diets if ordered. Lunches, packed lunches, snacks. Coffee, tea, for a charge. Drinks can be ordered.
2 sitting-rooms with central heating, open fire, TV, books; bar.
Nearest main road A69 from Carlisle to Newcastle.

Where two rivers converge to the sound of rushing water, there is an old hump-backed bridge of red sandstone built in the time of James II. The traffic ignores it, hurrying across over a modern bridge further along. From it you can see part-ruined Lanercost Priory, or leave it to walk along riverside paths. Right here, Mr and Mrs Arthur run the Abbey Bridge Inn. Its name has been changed at least five times – once, when the reforming Countess of Carlisle made it 'dry', it was called the Temperance Hotel.

It's a snug place to stay, particularly when log fires are blazing in the lounges, or after a day's strenuous walking in the Border hills. The bedrooms are simply furnished. The Arthurs' first achievement was the renovation of what was once a blacksmith's forge, dating back to the 17th century, where meals (other than breakfast) are served to residents and non-residents. It is a barn-like building with gnarled rafters and white-painted walls. The bar (with real ale) and sitting area downstairs are made cosy by a big iron stove. Up a specially made wrought-iron spiral staircase is a gallery where one eats beneath wrought-iron chandeliers with flickering electric candles. You can have either very good bar snacks; or a dinner including home-made pâté, venison and a fruity dessert, for instance.

Drinks or coffee can be enjoyed sitting under sun-umbrellas on the old bridge itself; or in the garden, frequented by the Arthurs' Great Dane.

As well as scenic walks or drives, and the beautiful priory, there is plenty to do or see in the area: 14th-century Naworth Castle, Hadrian's Wall with Roman forts, the Saxon church at Over Denton, and historic villages like Gilsland and Bewcastle with Roman remains. Bewcastle has a decorated stone cross which is one of Britain's greatest Saxon treasures. In the river at Corby Castle on the way to Carlisle are salmon-traps built by 12th-century monks and still in use today. The road from Brampton to Alston is particularly attractive, running alongside the South Tyne River, with views of the northernmost Pennines. There is a good garden centre at Hexham. The new 'dig' at Bird Oswald Roman fort is near the inn.

Readers' comments: A wonderful stay. Very high standard, excellent food, thoroughly to be recommended. Exceptional interest in the well-being of guests; outstanding value for money. Well ordered; Mrs Arthur gives a warm welcome and caters for guests as individuals. Quite wonderful.

For explanation of code letters (**C, D, H, PT, S, S-C, X**) see page xxviii.

1

ABBEY HOTEL   C D X
Church Street, Tewkesbury, Gloucestershire, GL20 5RX   Tel: 0684 294247

16 bedrooms (single, double or family rooms) from £18 (or £15 at weekends). Less for 6 nights or bargain breaks. Rooms have central heating; bathroom; TV, phone; tea/coffee-making facilities on request. Clothes-washing facilities.
Dinner £8–£10 (Mon.–Fri.) for 3 courses (with choices) and coffee, at 7–9pm. Vegetarian or special diets if ordered. Lunches, packed lunches, snacks. Coffee, tea, for a charge. Non-residents not admitted. Drinks can be ordered.
Nearest main road M5.

Lorna Slatter having once been an antique dealer, her small hotel – parts dating from Tudor times – is interestingly furnished with period pieces in every room. She has complemented them with distinctive wallpapers and well chosen colour schemes; and with Victorian bedheads go quilted, flowery bedspreads. Even bathrooms are well carpeted, and most bedrooms have comfortable armchairs (for quiet, ask for one at the back of the house).

Lorna serves dinners, Monday–Friday only. You might start with mushrooms in wine-and-cream sauce, followed by mustard-glazed lamb, and chocolate rum crunch to finish. There is a bar (furnished in Victorian style), and a stone-flagged patio where visitors can take their coffee or drinks. There are also many restaurants in Church Street: I ate particularly well at Roger Brown's **Bell Hotel** – which also has very good (but dearer) accommodation, particularly in a former monastery building which overlooks the river at the back.

Tewkesbury is a mediaeval town boasting fine black-and-white timbered buildings, antique shops and inns, but above all the great abbey with an immense Norman tower. It lies within hilly country from which the River Severn descends to the sea, passing through the cathedral city of Gloucester (old warehouses now shelter crafts studios and antique shops; in one of its lanes is a Beatrix Potter Museum – remember *The Tailor of Gloucester*?). The Cotswolds are near.

Some hotels and even farms offer special Christmas holidays; but, unless otherwise indicated (by the code letter X at top of entry), those in this book will then be closed.

Many houses have cards, chess, Scrabble etc. – just ask. And also such things as irons, hair-dryers, maps, gumboots and bridge-tables.

Take the trouble to get free booklets about the area before you set off. Every habitual traveller should keep a copy of the booklet of local Tourist Information Centres issued free by the English Tourist Board (Thames Tower, Blacks Road, London W6; tel: 01-846 9000) for this purpose.

ABBEY HOUSE
Monk Soham, north-west of Woodbridge, Suffolk, IP13 7EN
Tel: 072882 225

3 bedrooms (double or family) from £14. Less for 7 nights. Rooms have central heating, electric heaters; bathrooms; armchairs; views of country or garden. Hair-dryer, clothes-washing facilities.

Dinner £8 for 4 courses and coffee, at 7–8pm. Vegetarian or special diets if ordered. Lunches, packed lunches, snacks. Coffee, tea, free. Drinks can be brought in.

Sitting-room with central heating, open fire, TV, books, piano.

Large garden and meadows with croquet, swimming-pool.

Nearest main road A1120 from Stowmarket to Yoxford.

'Fish, fish, do your duty!' the rector who lived here in the late 19th century used to admonish the inhabitants of his ponds (still there), which had originally provided Friday food for monks at the abbey (long vanished). This and other anecdotes of his life at Abbey House are in a book by his son which Sue Bagnall shows her visitors. It was he who planted the huge oaks, beeches and limes in the grounds.

Sue and her husband have made the old mansion comfortable and immaculate, filling it with antiques yet keeping the atmosphere informal. Among fine old features they have restored is a magnificent cast-iron fireplace in the dining-room. Colours are soft (pale buff or shell pink, for instance). Sue, a former nurse, cooks traditional English meals (using their own meat and vegetables) such as artichoke soup, steak-and-kidney pie, lemon ice cream and cheeses.

Guests are welcome to look at the livestock which includes a Jersey cow (calves sometimes), sheep, pigs, turkeys, chickens, ducks and peafowl.

The Norfolk Broads are within reach; historic Norwich and its cathedral; bird reserves along the coast; old-fashioned seaside towns like Southwold and Aldeburgh; Lowestoft with its sands and its busy fishing port. Inland are famous beauty spots like the villages of Lavenham and Kersey or Dedham Vale ('Constable country').

Other sights include Somerleyton and Helmingham halls, Framlingham and Orford castles, Bressingham Steam Museum (with gardens), the Otter Trust, wildlife or farm parks, Saxtead windmill, rural crafts, vineyards, inns and historic market towns. There's a rosarium at Claydon, and Notcutts garden centre at Woodbridge.

Nearby is **Monk Soham Hall** (tel: 072 882 358), a very pleasant Tudor farmhouse where in addition to other bedrooms Gay Clarke has created, in a beamed ground-floor room opening on to garden and moat, a bedroom and bathroom fully equipped for disabled people.

rear view

3

ALEXA HOUSE

26 Ripon Road, Harrogate, North Yorkshire, HG2 2JJ   Tel: 0423 501988   **C H PT S**

12 bedrooms (single, double or family) from £17. Much less (outside summer) for 2 nights or bargain breaks. Rooms have central heating or electric heaters; shower or bathroom; TV, armchairs; tea/coffee-making facilities.
Sitting-room with central heating, gas fire, TV, books, record-player, bar.
Small garden
Nearest main road A61 from Leeds to Ripon.

Dating from 1830, this house is typical of many such solidly built and handsome private homes which later became small hotels in Yorkshire's famous spa town. It has been furnished by Marilyn and Peter Bateson with an eye to their guests' comfort (generous armchairs in the bedrooms, for instance) more than to elegance.

In the cheerful breakfast-room, Marilyn recently uncovered a pink-and-white marble fireplace, and added silver chandeliers. As to dinner, she gives visitors a street map with nearby recommended restaurants marked on it.

Behind the house are some small new rooms (very neatly designed) ideal not only for visitors wanting quiet, but also for disabled guests – with sitz baths and grab-rails, for instance, and an emergency bell connected to the house. (Marilyn was once a teacher of physically handicapped children, and understands what is needed.) A recent addition is a ground-floor suite with its own sitting-room.

A clerical visitor wrote to Marilyn after his first stay: 'I have never fared better since I once spent a weekend at Balmoral. Both hostesses proved to be most charming and kind, but I think you have the edge over HM for you did not feel disposed to discuss my sermon with me!'

Elegant Harrogate is full of shops selling antiques and other luxuries. Its award-winning gardens and flowery parks are famous; it has a large, modern entertainments centre; and it is an ideal centre from which to explore the Yorkshire Dales and such famous sights as Fountains Abbey, Ripon Cathedral, Harewood House, Harlow Car gardens and, of course, the city of York as well as Bolton Abbey, Ripley Castle, Newby Hall and Knaresborough.

Readers' comments: Every comfort, and super food. Courteous welcome, we had an excellent time – our stay surpassed all others. Excellent food and facilities. Well furnished, comfortable; quieter at the back. Will return whenever possible; refreshingly friendly atmosphere, staff happy to please.

Prices are the minimum *per person* in a double room at the beginning of the year.

It's best to stay at least 2–3 days: you cannot possibly appreciate an area if you only stay overnight (prices per night are often less, too, if you stay on). The vouchers on page **ii** are usable for 3-night stays.

ALFOXTON COTTAGE *New* S
Holford, west of Bridgwater, Somerset, TA5 1SG   Tel: 027874 418

4 bedrooms (single or double) from £12. All have central heating and views of sea, country or garden. No smoking. (Washing-machine on request.)
Dinner £10 for 4 courses and coffee, at 7pm. Non-residents not admitted. Vegetarian or special diets if ordered. Tea, coffee, free. Wine can be ordered or brought in.
Sitting-room with central heating, open fire, books, piano, record-player. No smoking.
Small garden
Nearest main road A39 from Bridgwater to Minehead.

The cottage is truly remote, right up in the Quantock Hills with views across the Bristol Channel to Wales. You may believe you are never coming to it as you follow twists and turns up the small wooded lane to the top of the hill.

This little house is now the home of Richard and Angela Delderfield who started Little Byres in Sussex (in previous editions of this book). Rooms are small and low but pleasantly furnished – for instance, bamboo or velvet bedheads; a grandfather clock and flounced armchairs by the log fire in the white sitting-room, from which a door leads to the garden, woods, a trickling stream, donkeys and chickens.

Angela's cooking is one of the main attractions of staying here. She sometimes serves as a starter prawns in a creamy sauce containing whisky, or perhaps chilled lettuce soup. Chicken breasts will be stuffed with cashew and brazil nuts, raisins, herbs and lemon juice. Into her salads may go unusual ingredients such as spinach, sunflower seeds or hot crisp bacon with slivers of avocado. She makes flans of rhubarb and lemon, rum and almonds, or orange and almonds.

All round the cottage are the Quantock Hills and pretty hamlets, the very first area of Britain to get official designation as an area of outstanding natural beauty. Alfoxton House (now a hotel) was tenanted by Wordsworth and his sister in 1797. They frequently walked here on their way to visit Coleridge who was busy writing *The Ancient Mariner* and *Kubla Khan* at Nether Stowey (his cottage now belongs to the National Trust). Some of Wordsworth's best poems, the *Lyrical Ballads*, were inspired by the Quantocks. The area is ideal for walking and for wildlife-spotting (red deer roam here) and wildflowers are abundant. Within a short drive are Exmoor, Dartmoor, the fenland known as the Somerset Levels, and the coast – including Watchet's active little harbour, cliffs and sands (Cleeve Abbey's Norman remains are in this direction). There are idyllic finds to be made up many a secluded lane – for instance, East Quantoxhead's cottages around a duckpond. Nether Stowey has a ruined castle, prehistoric earthworks, two mediaeval mansions and a stream; beyond it is Stogursey with priory church and castle. Let Wordsworth have the last word about Alfoxton:

> Through primrose tufts, in that green bower,
> The periwinkle trailed its wreaths;
> And 'tis my faith that every flower
> Enjoys the air it breathes.

Readers' comments: A wonderful establishment. A lovely home in a beautiful area. Very hospitable, food and service excellent. Friendly and genuine people.

ALMSHOUSE *New*
off The Square, Axbridge, north-west of Glastonbury, Somerset, BS26 2AR
Tel: 0934 732493

3 bedrooms (double) from £12.50, with central heating.
Dinner A la carte from 7pm. Vegetarian or special diets if ordered. Lunches, snacks. Tea, coffee, extra. Drinks can be ordered.
Sitting-room with central heating, open fire, TV, books, bar.
Nearest main road A38 from Bristol to Bridgwater.

Not long ago this impressive 15th-century building was near collapse. Then Beverley and Victor Jenkins (an expert in restoring buildings) determined to save it, using in its restoration authentic materials and techniques. First, they had to do quite a bit of historical research into its origins. As restoration proceeded, they uncovered mediaeval hearths and a garderobe (toilet) with drains. They put in a gallery (made out of old timbers from a church), which makes it possible for visitors to get a close-up view of the superb roof timbers. They even tracked down the quarry from which stone for the pointed mullion windows had come five centuries ago, and got stone from the same place for replacement mullions – their stonemason was a man who has worked on Windsor Castle and Westminster Abbey. The window glass was hand-made, some with heraldic devices of monastic orders associated with the Almshouse. Even the heavy tables in the restaurant, which is what the Almshouse has now become, were hand-made from English oak. At the back is a small courtyard, with white iron tables and chairs for meals.

Resident visitors are accommodated in the adjoining house, which is the Jenkins' home. On its ground floor is a long, beamed sitting-room with stone walls and flagstone floor, an excellent foil to a scarlet carpet and comfortable sofas of brown velvet strewn with poppy cushions; and above are white bedrooms with Laura Ashley fabrics, brimming window boxes on every sill overlooking The Square. The house is full of very lovely arrangements of dried flowers – which, along with hand-made chocolates, are among Beverley's many skills. (The Almshouse gallery is hung with bunches of these for sale.)

Food here is well above average, with a number of flavoursome specialities such as Stilton mousse, pâté of smoked chicken, and mushrooms in a creamy basil sauce enriched with brandy. Casseroles always have an original touch: in with lamb there will be apricots and herbs; with beef, whisky and mustard; with pork, celery and cider. Venison, rabbit and guinea-fowl regularly appear on the menu. The cream cakes at tea-time are light and luscious. Dinner is served by candlelight, and sometimes by firelight too when logs burn in the big inglenook fireplace.

Pretty little Axbridge is on the edge of the Mendip Hills and very close to the Cheddar Gorge. Around its square are ancient byways, old buildings and a museum of local bygones. The Gorge (for the finest view, approach it from the north) has a number of caves with stalactites, in rich colours; Stone Age men lived in these caves and some of their tools and weapons are on show.

Readers' comments: Delightful accommodation, tastefully decorated. Superb cooking. Terrific value.

APPLETREE COTTAGE

C PT S

12 Shitterton, Bere Regis, south of Blandford Forum, Dorset, BH20 7HU
Tel: 0929 471686

rear view

2 bedrooms (double or family) from £11. Less for 4 nights. Rooms have central heating; views of country or garden. Coffee, tea, for a charge.
Sitting-room with central heating, open fire, TV, piano.
Nearest main road A35 from Dorchester to Poole.

This is a real Hansel-and-Gretel style cottage – thick cob (clay) walls and thatched roof, with honeysuckle clambering round the pink front door. It was built in the 17th century and was a tiny inn when the little lane outside was a coaching road, and is now a listed building.

Inside, all ceilings are low, and walls slope. The breakfast-table is in the sitting-room, which has silky patchwork cushions on the velvet armchairs gathered around the inglenook with log stove. The very modern bathroom (its chocolate-brown suite includes a bidet) is also on the ground floor. Bedrooms have sprigged wallpapers, beams and board doors – some overlooking the pretty garden with flagstone steps leading to the lawn. For evening meals, Beryl Wilson recommends two inns in the hamlet.

Bere is about half way between Poole and Dorchester, the environs of which are described elsewhere in this book. Lulworth Cove, T. E. Lawrence's cottage, Hardy country, good walks, pretty villages like Milton Abbas, a parachute club, seaside resorts and mellow old towns are all within easy reach as well as Bovington Tank Museum, Corfe Castle, Kingston Lacy House (and garden). Garden-lovers will enjoy Abbotsbury, Compton Acres, Athelhampton, and Galtons garden centre. The area has many antique shops, and pick-your-own farms.

Inclusive terms for dinner, bed-and-breakfast (particularly for a week) can be much lower than those quoted here for these items taken separately. For short-notice bookings you may be able to get a reduction.

No proprietor wants to have a room standing empty. This particularly applies to Sunday nights. Some hotels make a discount if you want only two courses from a three-course menu.

When writing to me, if you want a reply please enclose a stamped addressed envelope.

Book well ahead: many of these houses have few rooms. Do not expect dinner if you have not booked it.

APSE MANOR

C(4) D H PT X

west of Shanklin, Isle of Wight, PO37 7PN   Tel: 0983 866651

rear view

5 bedrooms (double or family) from £16; Bargain breaks. Rooms have central heating; own bathroom; TV, armchairs; views of country or garden; orthopaedic mattress available; tea/coffee facilities. Four-poster suite.

Dinner £8 for 5 courses and coffee, at 6.45pm. Vegetarian diets can be prepared.

Packed lunches. Coffee, tea, and drinks can be ordered.

Sitting-room with central heating, open fire, TV, books.

Large garden

Nearest main road A3020 from Shanklin to Newport.

Until recently, this fine Tudor mansion was a farmhouse but it has since been renovated – Suzanne Boynton will show you her albums of 'before' and 'after' pictures as you sit by the log fire blazing in a huge inglenook that was one of the features uncovered and restored. This is in a great room with coffered ceiling and stone-mullioned windows, the other end of which is used for dining (buttoned banquettes of cream velvet surround tables with lace over crimson cloths).

A corridor, still with a long row of bells to summon servants, leads to bedrooms which have flowery wallpapers and light colour schemes; one has a four-poster. The main entrance hall serves as a bar – you help yourself and write down what you have taken.

The choices at dinner by candlelight may include plaice goujons or home-made pâté to start with; pork cooked with cider, apples and cream; then perhaps crême caramel or profiteroles and cheeses. Suzanne, who used to do large-scale catering, says she much prefers cooking for smaller numbers to higher standards, often using produce (including eggs) straight from the garden.

The surroundings are attractive, from the flowerbeds by the drive, with cupid statues here and there, to the stone verandah with view of a stream below.

Readers' comments: Very comfortable and well appointed. Friendly hosts, strongly recommended.

About a mile northward is **The Grange, Alverstone**; an immaculate guest-house where Geraldine Watling provides good home cooking (tel: 0983 403729).

Readers' comments: Effortless efficiency. Relaxed and happy atmosphere. Imaginative cooking. Warm and welcoming. Excellent accommodation, wonderful food.

ASHLEIGH HOUSE

C(5) **D X**

Whitley Hill, Henley-in-Arden, west of Warwick, Warwickshire, B95 5DL
Tel: 05642 2315

6 bedrooms (double or family) and another 4 in a converted coach house, from £17.50. Rooms have central heating; shower or bath; TV, armchairs; phones; views of farmland or garden. Tea-making facilities on request. **Sitting-room** with central heating, and reading-room with books.
Large garden
Nearest main road A34 from Stratford to Birmingham.

This handsome Edwardian mansion, once the home of a Birmingham merchant, stands well back from the road, on top of a hill with fine views. Since Colin Eades, a retired accountant, took it over (together with his partner Francisco Garcia, who used to run a restaurant) it has been immaculately restored and filled with Edwardian – and earlier – antiques as well as flowers. On my last visit, I thought it even better than before: its hospitable owners, the immaculate and handsome rooms, the outstanding garden.

Francisco in particular enjoys spending time with visitors and giving them sound advice on where to go hunting for antiques in this well-supplied area – also on where to dine in Henley or elsewhere (I ate well at Grubb's). Only snack suppers are served.

Every bedroom is furnished in keeping with the style of this spacious, solid house and all the original features have been retained – shuttered bay windows, panelled doors, turned banisters, for example.

There is good walking country all around, an 18th-century canal for boats, historic Henley-in-Arden itself (it has the longest village street in England), Stratford-upon-Avon, great Warwick Castle, Birmingham, the National Exhibition Centre, Ragley Hall, Packwood House, Baddesley Clinton, and all the countryside associated with Edith Holden's *Country Diary of an Edwardian Lady*. Head for the Vale of Evesham if you want pick-your-own fruit farms.

Readers' comments: Very warm welcome, excellent food. Good value. Converted stables are delightful; breakfast beautifully served; congenial atmosphere. So welcoming and restful.

All prices are inclusive of any VAT or service charge. They are minimum prices: superior rooms or high-season bookings may cost more.

Houses which do *not* take children tend to have vacancies in July and August.

Many houses have cards, chess, Scrabble etc. – just ask. And also such things as irons, hair-dryers, maps, gumboots and bridge-tables.

AVONSIDE

AVONSIDE   C(10) **PT**
Limpley Stoke, east of Bath (Avon), Wiltshire, BA3 6EX   Tel: 022122 2547

2 bedrooms (double) from £14.50. Less for 4 nights. Rooms have central heating and electric heaters; armchairs, views of country and garden.
Dinner £9.50 for 3 courses, wine and coffee, at 8pm. Afternoon tea free. Non-residents not admitted. Drinks can be brought in.
Sitting-room with central heating, open fire, books, piano.
Large garden and orchard, with hard tennis court, croquet and coarse fishing.
Nearest main road A36 from Bath to Beckington.

A typical English country house, built of honey-coloured Bath stone, the Challens' secluded home stands on the banks of the River Avon: walks along it (or the nearby Kennet and Avon Canal) are one of the attractions of staying in this very scenic area.

Ursula has furnished the sitting-room with tangerine or pale lime armchairs, oriental rugs and antiques that show up well against walls painted peach, on which hang many paintings by Peter who, after serving as a major in the Gurkhas, turned to a completely different career as an artist. Through the bay window is a serene view of the well-kept lawn and landscaped grounds.

Other rooms are equally pleasing, with attractive wallpapers and leafy views. The Challens treat visitors as if they were house guests, offering them pre-dinner drinks and wine (no extra charge). Typical of the kind of meal Ursula serves: avocado pâté; roast lamb with quince jelly and vegetables from the garden; a brûlée of brown sugar, cream and yogurt over raspberries. Alternatively, visitors can go out to the excellent Nightingales restaurant in the village or to the Hop Pole inn.

At Bradford-on-Avon several steep roads converge downhill to the mediaeval bridge with domed chapel on it. It takes time to discover all Bradford's handsome houses, Saxon church, vast tithe barn and old inns. Only a mile further is Bath, and, northward, such other lovely spots as Corsham, Lacock (mediaeval abbey, and museum of photographic history) and the Chippenham-Calne area. Garden-lovers head for Stourhead, antique-hunters for Bath. Malmesbury (on a hill almost surrounded by the River Avon) has its famous Norman abbey and handsome stone houses from the 17th and 18th centuries lining its streets and market square. Longleat, Dereham Manor and the historic American Museum are popular.

Readers' comments: Wonderful people, very friendly. Elegant; lovely meals. The Challens make one feel like their house guests. Excellent accommodation and food.

Prices are the minimum *per person* in a double room at the beginning of the year.

For explanation of code letters (**C, D, H, PT, S, S-C, X**) **see page xxviii.**

BANK COTTAGE
C S PT(boat)

Bryher, Isles of Scilly, TR23 0PR   Tel: 0720 22612

5 bedrooms (double or single) from £17. Rooms have central heating or electric heaters; TV, armchairs; own bathroom; views of sea and garden.
Dinner is 4 courses and coffee, at 6.30pm. Special diets if ordered. Lunches, packed lunches, snacks. Coffee, tea, soft drinks, free. Non-residents not admitted. Wine can be ordered.
Sitting-room with TV, books.
Garden with badminton.
Closed in winter

Even a millionaire might have a long search before finding somewhere to stay in quite such an idyllic situation as this little guest-house on Rushy Bay. Visitors here have a superb sandy beach (right outside) virtually all to themselves: when I was there, I encountered only one other couple on the golden, sunny sands. And beyond it is one of England's most beautiful seascapes, dotted with 22 islets.

Mac Mace works as a diver: sometimes diving for lobsters and crabs or for archaeological finds, including Spanish doubloons, on the many nearby wrecks; sometimes for sea urchins, the decorative shells of which are exported by the thousand. He and his wife Tracy take a few guests in their cottage (built at least 300 years ago, but with later additions). The rooms are simple, with low ceilings and thick walls to keep winter's gales at bay. Bedrooms are cheerful and bright.

Many visitors are content just to sit all day in the colourful garden (facing south-west) to enjoy the view of the bay, sheltered by the pink-flowered escallonia hedges; or they can accompany Mac when he is setting nets or fishing. The sunsets are outstanding. A gate opens onto the beach, but although the climate is warm here, the sea is not. There is a badminton lawn. The garden is at its most colourful in early summer (fuchsias, flowering cherries, tulips and arum lilies abound), the islets are best in late spring, when they are smothered in pink sea-thrift and fresh green fronds of bracken.

Vegetables and loganberries are home-grown, rolls home-baked, eggs from the Maces' hens. A typical meal cooked by Tracy may start with fish or fish pâté, followed by a roast or casserole. Tracy particularly enjoys making puddings like banana mousse or sherry trifle and her vegetarian meals are imaginative. Sometimes meals are served outdoors, using the granite barbecue.

Visitors arriving by boat from St Mary's are met and their baggage taken up for them by tractor or Landrover. The boats provide a service throughout winter (which can be mild and sunny, or with dramatic storms), but less frequently. Up to Easter, there are very few visitors; but even in summer Bryher is never crowded.

Readers' comments: Wished we could stay for ever! Felt completely at home; happy and relaxed atmosphere. Comfortable room, excellent food. Simply delighted, a marvellous time. Nothing is too much trouble.

11

BANK VILLA
Masham, north-west of Ripon, North Yorkshire, HG4 4DB   Tel: 0765 89605

C(5) **D**

7 bedrooms (double) from £12.50. Less for 7 nights. Rooms have central heating; shower; armchairs; views of country or garden.
Dinner £10 for 3 courses and coffee, at 7.30pm. Vegetarian or special diets if ordered. Coffee, tea, for a charge. Non-residents not admitted. Drinks can be ordered.
2 sitting-rooms with central heating, TV, books.
Terraced gardens
Nearest main road A6108 from Ripon to Masham.
Closed in winter

Good food is the principal attraction at Bank Villa, where Phillip Gill (former administrator of York's arts festival) is an inspired cook.

The villa is a late Georgian stone house set back from the busy road, with a steep terraced garden behind it (where there are a sunny summerhouse and conservatory in which to sit). Here are grown fruit and vegetables for the kitchen.

Dinner is served in a pleasant room – pretty 'Old Colonial' china and rush mats on the pine tables contrast with the deep raspberry walls. Phillip cooks, and his partner Anton serves, such delicious menus as spinach-and-cheese soufflé as a starter, smoked pork cooked with Calvados, and iced Drambuie parfait.

Bedrooms, too, are attractive, many with floral wallpapers and pine furniture, and some with a glimpse of the River Ure at the foot of the hill.

Masham, a little market town, has a church with interesting features; and, in mid-July, a traction-engine and steam fair. It stands at the beginning of Wensleydale, in an area of great historic as well as very varied scenic interest: within a few miles are two abbeys, three castles, one cathedral and a stately home, as well as the spa towns of Harrogate and Ripon. There are scenic roads, markets, the sight of racehorses exercising, waterfalls, a beautifully restored Georgian theatre (at Richmond), and fine gardens.

Bedale, which has had a market since the 13th century, is a town of pleasing buildings with a very fine church. Don't miss Fountains, finest of all the Yorkshire abbeys. Other nearby sights are Newby Hall, Ripon's cathedral, Middleham Castle, Brimham Rocks and Harlow Car gardens.

When to go? Seaside resorts or other places suitable for children will be at their busiest (and dearest) in July–August and during half-term holidays (especially, in late May, which is also a bank holiday period). Other peak periods are, of course, Easter, Christmas, New Year and the bank holiday in late August. (The bank holiday in early May is not usually a peak, because it comes rather soon after Easter, but much depends on the weather.) There are local peaks, too (the Gold Cup races at Cheltenham or the regatta at Henley, for instance, are apt to fill hotels for miles around), and local troughs (Brighton, a conference centre, is least busy in high summer). You won't get much personal attention when hotels are full to bursting.

BARK HOUSE *New*   D
Oakford Bridge, north of Tiverton, Devon, EX16 9HZ   Tel: 03985 236

rear view

6 bedrooms (single, double or family) from £16. Less for 7 nights. Some have own bath/shower; TV; tea/coffee facilities; central heating; views of river, country, garden; balcony. (Washing-machine on request.)
Dinner £11.25 for 3 courses (with choices) and coffee, at 8pm. Non-residents not admitted. Vegetarian or special diets if ordered. Lunches, packed lunches, snacks. Tea, coffee, extra. Drinks can be ordered.
Sitting-room with central heating, open fire, books, bar.
Large garden
Nearest main road A361 from Taunton to Barnstaple.
Closed in January and February

In a wooded valley through which runs the River Exe is a stone building of unusual origin. It was used as a tannery, the oak bark for which was brought from Exmoor Forest. Today, it has been handsomely converted; and Pauline and Douglas West provide visitors with complete comfort. Books, good pictures, thick Berber carpets, antiques, pot-plants and the flicker of a cheerful log fire set the scene.

In the dining-room brown and pink tablecloths contrast with white walls; around the tables are either pews or Windsor chairs. Every bedroom is different. No. 1 has a bow window with window-seat from which to enjoy the tranquil view; No. 4, art nouveau nymphs on the ceiling – however did *they* get there! No. 6 is a huge family room with its own ancient arched door to a rock garden with pool, and leaded casements.

Dinner may begin with smoked salmon mousse or fish chowder or eggs en cocotte (there are several choices at every course). With a daube of beef will be served potato galette and other vegetables. The fresh peach Melba has an orange-and-raspberry sauce. Because the Wests once lived in Provence, Pauline has many recipes from that region. (Breakfast is continental. English breakfast extra.)

From Bark House there is a particularly scenic route over moors to Minehead in Somerset. Both Exmoor and the sea are near; and so are Exeter, Taunton and Barnstaple, all described elsewhere. The area has a great many stately homes to visit, such as Knightshayes (NT), and gardens (Killerton); as well as churches and castles. Dunster village and Dartington are other popular outings. South Molton, a market town, has a number of good 18th-century buildings and fine views; North Molton likewise (derelict copper mines here); Swimbridge, a particularly rich church; outside Rose Ash is pretty Cuckoo Mill Bridge. The area is one for quiet enjoyment, largely undisturbed by traffic: thatched villages, stone manor houses, woods, cider orchards, trickling streams and lanes that wander up and down.

Readers' comments: Beautiful setting; excellent cooking; friendly and cheerful hosts. Have stayed four times.

13

BARNFIELD FARM   S
near Charing, north-west of Ashford, Kent, TN27 0BN   Tel: 023371 2421

4 bedrooms (single, family or double) from £13. Rooms have central heating, electric heaters; armchairs; views of country or garden; tea/coffee facilities. Clothes-washing facilities. No smoking.
Dinner £7.50 for 3 courses and coffee, at 7pm or by arrangement. Vegetarian or special diets if ordered. Coffee, tea, for a charge. Drinks can be ordered. No smoking.
Sitting-room with central heating, TV, books, record-player. No smoking.
Garden with tennis; farmland.
Nearest main road A20 from London to Folkestone.

This historic farmhouse was built about the time of the Battle of Agincourt (1415). It is so remarkable that sometimes coaches of overseas visitors come to see it; and even individual visitors are given a tour round by Martin Pym, who grew up here, or his wife Phillada.

One steps into a large hall, where the oak framework of the house is exposed to view (draped with hop bines) and a cask holding shepherds' crooks stands in one corner – for outside are sheep pastures, with arable fields beyond. The main sitting-room has an exceptionally large inglenook where logs blaze in front of a Cromwellian fireback; the original pot-hooks, soot-blackened, are still in place. Along one beam hangs a set of handbells, on which Christmas is rung in every year. The dining-room, too, has an open fire and ancient beams, with one especially fine door (linenfold panels contrasting with intricately carved foliage), made from a church chest. There is another sitting/dining-room for guests' use, comfortably furnished with deep cretonne armchairs, plenty of books and – like every room in the house – attractive objects.

The bedrooms are equally agreeable, and in two one can see the construction of the house very clearly: massive treetrunks, rough-hewn to shape, curve up to support the roof.

Some of the furnishings were made by Martin's grandmother – for instance, a screen of Victorian scraps in one room, and an intricate embroidery commemorating two Pyms who died in the first world war in another. An old linen-press, chests, rocking-chairs – at every turn of the wandering corridors there is something interesting to see. Outside are lawns, herbaceous borders surrounding a pool guarded by four stone owls, and a lake visited by ducks and Canada geese.

Phillada serves such meals as egg mayonnaise, casseroled lamb cutlets and apple fool with shortbread – loading a hot-tray on the sideboard so that guests can help themselves to as much as they wish.

The most popular nearby sights are Leeds Castle, Canterbury Cathedral, Sissinghurst, Chilham and Dover castles, and Godinton Park. (Bicycles on loan.)

Readers' comments: Enjoyed our stay very much; a warm welcome.

When writing to me, if you want a reply please enclose a stamped addressed envelope.

BARROW HILL FARM
Ramsdean, west of Petersfield, Hampshire, GU32 1RW   Tel: 073087 340

rear view

3 bedrooms (single or double) from £12. Less for 4 nights or more. Rooms have central heating or electric heaters; shower or bathroom; armchairs; views of country or garden. Tea, coffee, free.
Sitting-room with central heating, open fire, TV, books.

Garden and farmland.
Nearest main road A272 from Petersfield to Winchester.
Closed in winter

A nearby hill with prehistoric burial-mound gives this beef and dairy farm its name. In the opposite direction it has a view of equally ancient Butser Hill, a windswept height well worth a visit.

The tile-hung house itself is beautifully furnished, with Victorian antiques shown at their best against well-chosen colour schemes and fabrics. The beamed sitting-rooms are divided by a see-through fireplace, and on the sills of the big windows all round is a profusion of pot-plants. Breakfast is served at a large oval table of mahogany in the dining-room. Bedrooms are excellent.

Everything is immaculate, outside as well as in, from carefully trained roses climbing up flint walls to the smooth lawns where one can sit to enjoy the setting sun amid the scent of catmint or lavender. Old chimney-pots have been used for planting petunias and lobelias. There are mementoes of Beatrix Potter – the very plates to be seen in the Tiggy-Winkle drawings; Mary's great-aunt was the little girl in the story.

Mary Luff serves only breakfast, recommending local inns (or Langish House Hotel) for other meals, including those at East Meon, described elsewhere.

Petersfield's 18th-century streets are pleasant; and at Greatham Mill is a lovely garden. All around are hills, woods and tranquil valleys of great beauty: a very agreeable area to explore by car or on foot. Jane Austen's home at Chawton and Gilbert White's at Selborne are only a few miles away. The Queen Elizabeth Country Park is an area of superb scenery.

Readers' comments: Excellent, very comfortable. A pleasant welcome.

All prices are inclusive of any VAT or service charge. They are minimum prices: superior rooms or high-season bookings may cost more.

If you want your hosts to post you things you have accidentally left behind, send them the cost of postage. (The trouble they take is free.)

BEANSHEAF *New*   C D H PT S S-C X
Kirby Misperton, north of Malton, North Yorkshire, YO17 0UE
Tel: 065 386 614

17 bedrooms (single, double or family) from £16.50. Less for 2 nights and bargain breaks. All have own bath/shower; TV; tea/coffee facilities; central heating; views of country or garden. No smoking. (Washing-machine on request.)
Dinner £8.50 for 3 courses (with choices) and coffee, at 7–9.30pm. Vegetarian or special diets if ordered. Lunches, packed lunches, snacks. Tea, coffee, extra. Drinks can be ordered.
Sitting-room with central heating, books, record-player, bar.
Large garden
Nearest main road A169 from Malton to Whitby.

Michele Sardone trained as a chef in Switzerland before bringing his skills to England. He offers a fixed price menu or a huge à la carte choice with every dish freshly cooked to order: some twenty starters (antipasta pescatore and home-made lasagne are two examples) and even more main courses (from steaks and Barnsley chops to game). Often there are unusual vegetables available – pumpkin, kohlrabi, fennel, ratatouille or cauliflower polonaise, for instance. Michele's specialities include beef with a pork-and-veal stuffing, and kid cooked in an earthenware pot with mushrooms, tomatoes and peppers. He makes his own Parmesan cheese, using milk from his goats. Meals are served in a pleasant dining-room where Tyrolean-style chairs surround tables laid with pink cloths, overlooking a patio.

The well-equipped bedrooms have good colour schemes, and outstanding bathrooms or showers with such things as navy-and-gold fitments or basins of marble inlay brought from Italy. One pink room has a pine four-poster with a curvaceous and frilly canopy. There is a sauna and a solarium. For quiet, ask for one at the back: the Beansheaf is on a road.

Readers' comments: Superb. The best Italian food we have had in Britain. Friendly service. A little gem.

In Malton itself is **Oakdene**, 29 Middlecave Road, (tel: 0653 693363), a very handsome Victorian house in a large garden, with a feeling of solid quality, peace and comfort. Some rooms have antique or four-poster beds and all are very well equipped. Elaine Harland serves four-course meals such as ham-and-onion quiche, salmon or chicken suprême, chocolate éclairs or strawberries and cream, cheeses.

rear view

Readers of this book are offered a discount.

BEAR FARM *New*
Binfield, Bracknell, south-west of Windsor, Berkshire, RG12 5QE
Tel: 0734 343286

2 bedrooms (double or family) from £15. Both have TV; tea/coffee facilities: central heating; view of garden. (Washing-machine on request.)
Dinner £10 for 4 courses, (wine etc.) and coffee. Snacks. Tea, coffee, free.
Sitting-room with central heating, open fire, TV, books, bar.
Large garden
Nearest main road M4 from Maidenhead to Reading.

This has one of the prettiest approaches of any farm in this book: a garden with roses and lily-pool; big porch smothered in honeysuckle; lawn, weeping willows and brilliant busy-Lizzies. A pantiled barn partly surrounds a sheltered court and what was once the milking-parlour has been turned into attractive and very well-equipped ground-floor bedrooms. Visitors walk across to the house for meals at which Ann Skidmore joins her guests (typically, dinner might comprise a seafood cocktail, roast joint, raspberry pavlova and cheeses – with aperitif and wine included – unless a simple supper of omelette and fruit is preferred). Afterwards, unless tempted to return to the hard tennis court, they relax in deep, cushiony sofas and armchairs around a hearth brimming with her collection of copper wine- and beer-funnels.

The house itself, low-beamed and with leaded casements, is 400 years old. Its name is a corruption of 'bere' meaning 'woodland', for once Windsor Forest covered this area. Today the farm, which concentrates on cereals and beef-cattle, is surrounded by attractive countryside; and yet it is less than an hour from London (and half an hour from Heathrow) on the motorway.

Binfield (where Alexander Pope grew up) is well placed for visiting Windsor, many Thames beauty spots, Ascot and the little market-town of Wokingham. Reading is a big shopping centre; its university has an outstanding museum of rural life, and many river trips start from here. Bagshot Heath is good for picnics and walks; there are country parks (the Wellington park houses a dairy museum, the California country park particularly appeals to children, and Windsor has its safari park). Garden-lovers particularly enjoy Cliveden, Virginia Water, the Savill Garden, and (on the rare May dates when it is open) the garden around the royal mausoleum at Frogmore – with tombs of Victoria and Albert.

Berkshire is a county of contrasts – regal at Windsor, full of Edwardian elegance in its Thames-side houses, more rural as you go further west. Its history goes back to prehistoric times, and great events have been taking place there ever since: for instance, Runnymede is where King John was forced to accept the Magna Carta. It is a particularly good choice for a winter break because there is so much to see which does not depend upon the weather and many sights remain open throughout the year.

Prices are the minimum *per person* in a double room at the beginning of the year.

BEECROFT *New*   C

Middle Drive, Woolsington, north of Newcastle-upon-Tyne, NE13 8BS
Tel: 091 2861009

2 bedrooms (single, double or family) from £15. Less for 5 nights. No smoking. (Washing-machine on request.)
Dinner £4.50 for 3 courses and coffee, at 6–8.30pm. Non-residents not admitted. Vegetarian or special diets if ordered. Packed lunches, snacks. Tea, coffee, free. Drinks can be brought in.

Sitting-room with central heating, open fire, TV, books, record-player.
Small garden
Nearest main road A696 from Newcastle to Ponteland.
Closed from December–February

Newcastle's airport was built on what was once the great Woolsington estate, of which John Beattie's grandfather was head gamekeeper.

This 17th-century sandstone lodge was his home, and John remembers seeing game hanging and pheasant chicks being reared here. No longer, alas – though there remain the bees that give the house its name and which provide honey for breakfast. John also produces leeks (for which Northumberland is famous – in early September, growers compete at innumerable leek shows throughout the county).

Sylvia's soups and pâtés are all home-made; garden vegetables accompany her roasts and casseroles; and then may follow fruit tarts, lemon meringue pie or a cheesecake. (Excellent meals at the price.) All bedrooms are on the ground floor. From the house there are pleasant woodland walks to Woolsington Hall and its lake.

This is obviously a very useful stopover for people using the airport to go to Europe or Canada (the Beatties give free lifts to and from the airport, and will let you leave your car at Beecroft while away). But it deserves a lingering stay, not least to visit Newcastle itself: ¼ hour by bus from here. No one passing through this city's one-way maze in a car can guess at its hidden splendours: it needs to be explored on foot. It has some really exceptional Georgian streets.

I recommend starting at the old Blackfriars monastery which has a particularly imaginative museum explaining the city's history, crafts and a good café. Downhill are Dean Street (antiques, crafts and bistros), the cathedral, castle (where Northumbrian bagpipes are played – different from Scottish ones), quays (markets and a lighthouse museum). All Newcastle's museums are exceptionally good: the Joicey (historical – particularly good on Bewick), the Laing art gallery, the Hancock (natural history) and the Museum of Science and Engineering. Another bus will take you to Gateshead (for the finest park in the north and an excellent art gallery), the metro to Jarrow (where Bede's monastic times are vividly brought to life again). In the Eldon Square shopping centre, Marks & Spencer's first 'penny bazaar' has been recreated.

THE BEEHIVE
C(5) D PT S X

Osmington, east of Weymouth, Dorset, DT3 6EL Tel: 0305 834095

Rooms have central heating or electric heaters; armchairs; views of country or garden; bedboard; tea/coffee facilities. No smoking.
Dinner £4 for 2 courses and coffee, or £6 for 3 courses; at 7.30–8pm. Vegetarian or special diets if ordered. Packed lunches. Coffee, tea, free. Non-residents not admitted. Drinks can be brought in.
Sitting-room with central heating, log fire, TV, books, record-player. No smoking.
Small garden
Nearest main road A353 from Weymouth to Wareham.
Closed in January

4 bedrooms (single or double) from £11. Much less for 2 nights or bargain breaks.

Mary Kempe's father was Lord of the Manor at Osmington; and this little thatched stone cottage was the holiday home of her childhood. While the manorial lands passed into other hands, she was pursuing an academic career at the universities of Nairobi and London: the former accounts for the presence of African crafts in the old cottage, which is now her permanent home.

It is tucked away – in a pocket-handkerchief garden – down a lane leading to countryside of great beauty, with some lovely walks; to the south fine coast scenery lies only a mile away (shingle beaches closest, sandy ones a little further).

The friendly sitting-room is a place of books and water-colours, lead-paned windows and old cretonne-covered sofas or chairs. Breakfast is served in the big, cork-floored kitchen warmed by a stove (you can buy jars of Mary's home-made jams). She produces, on certain nights only, imaginative dinners with many dishes based on traditional local recipes and produce – for instance, Martlemas (or Michaelmas) beef, which is marinaded in wine and vinegar then rubbed with spices before being baked, or Wessex chicken in a cider sauce. Before this might come Dorset pâté or a soup of carrots or lentils; and after it apple hedgehog, blueberry pie or buttered oranges. Or you can eat well at the nearby Smugglers' Inn. (Ask Mary for an excellent leaflet on where to buy Dorset local foods to take home.) Nearby are good nurseries and garden centres, too.

Birdwatchers go out from here to spend days at Radipole Lake, the Fleet or Studland nature reserve. Others tour the Thomas Hardy sites. Osmington, being roughly midway between Poole at one end of Dorset and Lyme Regis at the other, is a good centre from which to explore all parts of the county: see details elsewhere in this book.

Upstairs, among the cottage-style bedrooms (and bathroom decorated with African hippos), Mary has a large collection of maps and books on all aspects of Dorset history and wildlife, and is herself a willing fount of guidance on where to go.

Readers' comments: Superb; delightful haven of peace; a marvellous hostess. One of the best meals we have ever sampled.

For explanation of code letters (**C, D, H, PT, S, S-C, X**) **see page xxviii.**

19

BEGGAR BOG *New*

Housesteads, Haydon Bridge, west of Hexham, Northumberland, NE47 6NN
Tel: 04984 320

4 bedrooms (single, double or family) from £11. Less for 3 nights and bargain breaks. Some have own bath/shower; TV; tea/coffee facilities; central heating; views of country or garden. No smoking. (Washing-machine on request.)
Dinner £7 for 3 courses (with choices) and coffee, at 7pm. Non-residents not admitted. Vegetarian or special diets if ordered. Lunches, packed lunches, snacks. Tea, coffee, free. Drinks can be brought in.
Sitting-room with central heating, open fire, TV, books, record-player. No smoking.
Large garden
Nearest main road A69 from Newcastle to Carlisle.

Housesteads is one of the best-known sites on Hadrian's Wall, with the remains of a big Roman settlement and some of the most dramatic views of the Wall itself as it sweeps along the windswept hills. Almost opposite the National Trust information centre and car park stands this solitary stone farmhouse.

It is a spick-and-span house with light colour schemes and handsome new pine doors. In the sitting-room, comfortable beige velvet armchairs face a stone fireplace across a brown Axminster carpet, and there are some fine pieces of antique oak furniture about. Some bedrooms give views of the Wall, and all the windows are double-glazed. This makes them quiet, even though the house is quite close to the road. The (relatively) 'beaten track' here is itself of interest, being the Military Road built, like his better-known one across the Highlands, by General Wade to improve communications after the first Jacobite rebellion.

The house is surrounded by trim lawns, garden and the pasture the Huddlestons use for horses which are the family passion.

The typical farmhouse cooking is of a high standard: home made pâté, stuffed eggs, steak, lasagne, hazelnut meringue, and lemon pie are the sort of things visitors might get. Everything is home-made. Incidentally, despite the name of the house, there is no bog now and there never was a beggar ('beggar' is a type of ash tree).

Readers' comments: Beautifully situated. Very friendly and very good cook.

A few miles away, towards Hexham, is **The Stanegate**, Newbrough (tel: 043474 241), the Fentons' sparklingly smart restaurant where the polished à la carte menu has an excellent reputation. The airy bedrooms here cost much more than at Beggar Bog but each has an en suite bathroom (and pleasant views).

BELL INN

Smarden, west of Ashford, Kent, TN27 8PW   Tel: 023377 283

C D S

4 bedrooms (single or double) from £12; bargain breaks. Rooms have electric heaters; TV, armchairs; views of country or farmland; tea/coffee facilities.
Dinner A la carte, from 6 to 10pm. Special diets if ordered. Lunches, packed lunches, snacks. Drinks can be ordered.
Bars have central heating, open fire, TV, books, darts and bar-billiards. Children's room.
Large garden
Nearest main road A274 from Maidstone to Headcorn.

Kent has innumerable picturesque old inns, but few can be more attractive than the 15th-century Bell. Facing an apple orchard and surrounded by a beer-garden, it has a façade of chequered brickwork overhung with scalloped tiles. Inside there are three bars, two with inglenook fires and all paved or brick-floored. Here one can eat very well, seated on oak settles or Windsor chairs under beams strung with hop-bines – and Ian Turner keeps nearly a dozen different kinds of real ale to sample.

Outdoors an iron spiral staircase, wreathed in honeysuckle, leads up to the bedrooms, still with the original board ceilings and white brick walls but immaculately furnished in soft colours. (No wash basins.) Visitors are provided with the wherewithal to make their own continental breakfast.

Three times a year, Morris dancers come to the Bell; and on the second Sunday in each month there is a gathering of vintage cars or of steam engines. Popular sights near the Bell are Leeds Castle, Sissinghurst gardens, and the castles of Bodiam, Hever and Chilham.

Don't complain if –
– because you booked at short notice, you do not get the best room
– because you did not order a meal in advance, you get something plucked from the freezer
– because you do not arrive on time, your room is let to someone else
– because you bring a dog without asking, it is refused entry
– because you don't express your wishes (for more heat, a second helping, or whatever), you don't get what you want!

When writing to me, if you want a reply please enclose a stamped addressed envelope.

Families which pick establishments with plenty of games, swimming-pool, animals, etc., or that are near free museums, parks and walks, can save a lot on keeping youngsters entertained.

37 Bridewell Street, Clare, west of Sudbury, Suffolk, CO10 8QD
Tel: 0787 277538

2 bedrooms (double) from £10. TV and central heating.
Dinner £6.50 for 3 courses and coffee, at 7pm. Non-residents not admitted. Vegetarian or special diets if ordered. Wine can be brought in.
Sitting-room with books. No smoking.
Nearest main road A1092 from Baythorn End to Long Melford.

This small but historic house (once three cottages in a terrace) is filled with antiques, paintings that include family portraits which go back to the 18th century, all kinds of Victoriana and a great many books. At the back is a little paved garden frequented by the Bells' four cats and two dogs. Around the dining-room are ladderback chairs and a pine settle. Bedrooms, too, are cottage-like in their furnishings.

For many years, the Bells used to run a restaurant in nearby Cavendish so cooking here is above average: Gillian serves such meals as fish mousse, chicken Provençale and raspberries with home-made ice cream.

Clare is a place to explore on foot, to enjoy all the details of its ancient houses – plasterwork decoration, exuberant inn signs, the old priory. It is close to Cavendish, Sudbury and other attractive places in Suffolk such as Kentwell Hall and gardens, Long Melford, Clare country park, the Colne Valley steam railway, Gainsborough's house, Hedingham Castle and Melford Hall. Bury St Edmunds and its abbey gardens are worth a leisurely visit, and so is Lavenham (both described elsewhere in this book); as well as Beth Chatto's garden and the many nursery gardens of the area, Constable's Flatford Mill, and Cambridge.

In nearby Callis Street is the **Ship Stores** (tel: 0787 277834). Miles from the sea, this one-time inn was originally called the Sheep, not the Ship. Now it is a small shop run by former teacher Norman Kies, with a few simply furnished bedrooms and an upstairs sitting-room for guests. Norman is still uncovering secrets in this building, 400 years old; fireplaces long boarded up, and the original brick floor downstairs, for instance. It is a place of low beams, creaking floors, undulating roof and pink-plastered front: full of character, but very modest (as are its prices). In  the breakfast-room there is solid elm furniture locally made; and anyone who wants an out-of-the-ordinary breakfast (pâté? sardines? beans?) is welcome to select from the stock in the grocery.

If, when touring, you ask a host to book your next stop – at another *Staying Off the Beaten Track* house – remember to pay the cost of the telephone call.

BICKLEIGH COTTAGE

Bickleigh, south of Tiverton, Devon, EX16 8RJ   Tel: 088 45 230

C(6) **S PT**

9 bedrooms (single or double) from £13.50. Less for 7 nights. Rooms have central heating or electric heaters; tea/coffee facilities. Some have bathrooms and/or river views.
Dinner £6.50 for 4 courses and coffee, at 7pm. Non-residents not admitted.

2 sitting-rooms with central heating, TV, books.
Riverside garden
Nearest main road A396 from Exeter to Tiverton.
Closed in winter

This very picturesque thatched cottage, built about 1640 and later extended, has been run as a guest-house by the same family for over 50 years. It stands on a road by the banks of the River Exe, with a foaming weir a few yards downstream: everyone's ideal of a typically Devonian beauty-spot. Across the road is the mediaeval **Trout Inn** (also owned by the Cochranes) which has bedrooms too (well equipped), but is not on the riverside.

The rooms downstairs are full of antiques such as old chests and carved oak chairs, as well as a collection of blue glass and other interesting trifles including articles of Honiton lace made by Mrs Cochrane, which are for sale. The bedrooms (many with river views) are more simply furnished, though one has a four-poster bed. Outside is a pretty riverside garden with a fish-pool and glasshouses containing a collection of cacti and succulents.

Meals are of plain home cooking, a typical menu being smoked mackerel, roast lamb, pineapple meringue and cheeses.

The attractions of this area include Exeter Cathedral and maritime museum, Bickleigh and Tiverton castles, Killerton House and Knightshayes Court. (More information under other entries.)

Readers' comments: Delightful. A favourite place.

Single people may find more company in houses that have a shared dining-table, a bar, and no TV in the sitting-room. As my descriptions indicate, some owners mingle more with their guests than others do. Houses marked **S** charge singles little or no more than half a double.

Some readers tell me they have stayed at lots of places from *Staying Off the Beaten Track*. I wonder who has stayed at most? A free copy of the next edition awaits the reader who sends me his/her comments on the greatest number!

BIGGIN HALL
Biggin-by-Hartington, south of Buxton, Derbyshire, SK17 0DH
Tel: 029 884 451

C D S X

12 bedrooms (single, double or family) from £22 with dinner. Less for 5 nights or bargain breaks. Rooms have central heating and/or electric radiators; bathroom; some have TV; armchairs; views of country or garden; tea/coffee facilities in some. Clothes-washing facilities.

Dinner 4 courses (with a choice) and coffee, at 7pm. Vegetarian or special diets if ordered. Packed lunches; cream teas. Coffee, tea, for a charge. Drinks can be ordered.

2 sitting-rooms with central heating, open fire, TV, books, piano, record-player.

Extensive grounds Grassland.

Nearest main road A515 from Ashbourne to Buxton.

Charles II was on the throne when this handsome stone house with leaded windows was built, and it has changed little since his day (modern comforts apart). It is owned by an antique dealer. Logs blaze in the great stone fireplace, with cretonne-covered chairs grouped around on a quarry-tiled floor. Another sitting-room has one wall of bookshelves, and glass doors opening into the garden where children can play on the swing. Upstairs, one oak-panelled room has an oak-panelled half-tester bed (pink lilies on its blue draperies) and another a spectacular four-poster under the exposed beams – its bathroom is huge, carpeted and even equipped with a bidet. There are other rooms in an 18th-century stone annexe: no room service here.

In the dining-room (oriental rugs on flagstones, rush chairs, flowers on each table) Mrs Moffett serves such food as devilled kidneys or melon and grapefruit in port to start with; hill lamb; queen of puddings or sherry trifle; cheeses that include the local Hartington Stilton; fresh fruit. The emphasis is on wholefoods.

Breakfast is (unless you pay a little extra) continental-style, but this includes a choice of cereals, fruits and juices followed by home-made brioches, croissants and jams.

In front of the house is a small stone-walled garden with poppies and peonies, and an old laburnum bowing low over its iron gates. A serene spot (slightly marred by telephone wires and a bright green plaque) in which to take one's tea or coffee.

Biggin is near the centre of the Peak District, 1000 feet up where the air is pure and fresh. Scenery is the main attraction here, but most visitors also go to see sights like Chatsworth House, Haddon Hall, the Tram Museum at Crich. Cycles can be hired locally, to follow the 'Tissington Trail' or the famous River Dove. Arbor Low has prehistoric remains. Unfrequented walks abound.

Readers' comments: A wonderful weekend; warmly greeted, excellent food, gorgeous furniture. Superb food; the Moffetts are friendly, humorous and jovial. Warm and welcoming.

Some hotels and even farms offer special Christmas holidays; but, unless otherwise indicated (by the code letter X at top of entry), those in this book will then be closed.

THE BIRCHE C D

Shelsey Beauchamp, north-west of Worcester, WR6 6RD Tel: 08865 251

rear view

3 bedrooms (single, double or family) from £21. Less for 4 nights or bargain breaks. **15%** discount to readers of this book. Rooms have central heating; shower or bathroom; TV, phone, armchairs; views of country or garden; tea/coffee facilities.

Dinner £13.50 for 4 courses and coffee, at 7.30pm. Vegetarian or special diets if ordered. Lunches, packed lunches, snacks. Coffee, tea, for a charge. Drinks can be ordered.

Sitting-room with central heating, open fire, TV, books, record-player; bar.

Extensive grounds Cherry orchards with trout fishing.

Nearest main road A443 from Worcester to Tenbury Wells.

Previously a farm (from pre-Domesday until a decade ago), this elegant and beautifully sited house now belongs to an American manufacturing company with interests in Kidderminster (they originally bought it to accommodate their visiting directors). From the big bay window of its dining-room, yellow-curtained, one looks down to the private trout lake with Canada geese, cherry orchard beyond, and views of the Clee Hills. Green velvet chairs are drawn up to tables at which manageress Claire Sutherland (whose family farms nearby) supervises the serving of meals, which must be pre-booked. There is much emphasis on local produce – salmon, home-grown vegetables and herbs, even the horseradish which accompanies the roast sirloin. Claire records regulars' favourite dishes – from the avocado mousse with prawns or the chicken terrine through to jam rolypoly or crême-de-menthe ice cream.

In the sitting-room, William Morris armchairs cluster around the inglenook fire in a beamed and white-walled room where there are always big vases filled with fresh flowers. The bedrooms are especially attractive and original. I particularly liked one which had a jade carpet, quilted spreads in floral chintz, and cushioned seats in the bay window overlooking the lake. At no greater price, one can book a suite with rosy bedheads, duvets and valances contrasting with the celadon carpet; in the matching sitting-room is a fire, alcoves with flowers, and even a cooking-corner in which to produce your own snack meals. This, too, has window seats and lake view.

The Birche is ideally placed for visiting the cathedral cities of Worcester and Hereford, Malvern spa and hills, historic Ludlow and Bewdley, the Wyre Forest and the River Severn. Hill-climbing championships, a safari park, Royal Worcester factory and clematis nurseries at Tenbury Wells are other attractions.

Prices are the minimum *per person* in a double room at the beginning of the year.

Houses which do *not* take children tend to have vacancies in July and August.

BIRCHES MILL *New*   **C D PT X**
Clun, north-west of Ludlow, Shropshire, SY7 8NL   Tel: 05884 409

TV. All have central heating; views of river, country or garden. (Washing-machine on request.)

Dinner A la carte or £9 for 3 courses (with choices) and coffee, at 7.30pm. Vegetarian or special diets if ordered. Lunches, packed lunches, snacks. Tea, coffee, extra. Drinks can be brought in.

Sitting-room with central heating, TV, books.

Large garden

3 bedrooms (double or family) from £11.85. Less for 2 nights and bargain breaks.

Nearest main road A488 from Clun to Bishops Castle.

On the secluded valley banks of a trout river stands a 17th-century, ivy-covered watermill, its working days long over. Now it is the home of Avis and Peter Ades, beautifully converted to provide accommodation for guests. The sitting-room still has the old flagged floor and stone walls, but now with a thick Indian carpet, and deep leather armchairs drawn up around the fire. Glass doors open onto waterside lawns. The loudest sounds are the slow tick of a grandfather clock within and the frothing weir without. There is a large rock garden (with plants for sale – primulas are a speciality), and all around grow fritillaries, ragged robin, crocuses and orchids. This is an area particularly rich in wildflowers.

In the beamed dining-room there is still an old range in the stone fireplace. Here Avis serves, on handsome Royal Worcester porcelain, meals using organically-grown produce. The choice of dishes is wide and her standards are high. There might be a choice of rabbit pâté or onion soufflé soup to start with, and then saddle of lamb accompanied by an onion soubise. Puddings such as apple pie or brandied prunes (with cream) are followed by cheeses. You can buy some of her pies and cakes to take home.

Attention to detail is evident in everything from freshly squeezed orange juice at breakfast to the lace or crochet trimmed bedlinen. Altogether there is something idyllic about this isolated spot, the old mill and the Ades' hospitality.

Readers' comments: Cared for with consideration, in most congenial surroundings. Very comfortable, many amenities; the peace is so special; delicious cooking. Intend to return. Comfort standards are high, dinners most interesting. Courteous, friendly and helpful.

Take the trouble to get free booklets about the area before you set off. Every habitual traveller should keep a copy of the booklet of local Tourist Information Centres issued free by the English Tourist Board (Thames Tower, Blacks Road, London W6; tel: 01-846 9000) for this purpose.

If you want absolute quiet, avoid any place that takes children or has a bar open to non-residents. Inns sometimes get extensions to their licensing hours for late private parties; and may lack quiet sitting-rooms.

BISHOPFIELD FARM HOTEL

Allendale, south of Hexham, Northumberland, NE47 9EJ   Tel: 043483 248

C(12) **D PT S**

11 bedrooms (single or double) from £16. A barn provides more bedrooms (with bathrooms) and a sitting-room. Rooms have central heating; shower or bathroom; TV, phone, armchairs; views of country or garden. Other extras: drinks in bedrooms, icemaker, clothes-drying for walkers.
Dinner £9 for 3 courses and coffee, at 7pm. Special diets if ordered. Cream teas. Lunches, packed lunches, snacks. Non-residents not admitted. Drinks can be ordered. Help-yourself coffee or tea, free.
2 sitting-rooms with central heating, open fire, TV, books, snooker.
Grounds Farmland and woods.
Nearest main road A69 from Newcastle to Carlisle.
Closed January

Built in 1740, this stone farmhouse with clematis growing up its walls stands in 200 acres through which the River Allen runs (with trout for guests to fish). There are views of the fields, with cows and their calves. Guests have a sitting-room with snooker and an adjoining library, comfortably and prettily furnished.

Kathy Fairless serves good, homely meals – soups with cream and croûtons, fish brought direct from the North Sea, and fresh fruit salad for example. Guests eat by candlelight and log fire, with silver and Minton china.

All the guests' accommodation is now in recently converted 18th-century farm buildings. The spacious bedrooms, with traditional furniture, overlook the ground floor where the sitting- and snooker-rooms are also situated. One sitting-room is reserved for non-smokers and one dining-area for children. For children there is also a playground with swings etc. and a Shetland pony. In the newly converted conservatory is a barbecue.

Outside there is plenty to see and do. One can swim in river pools, give a hand with haymaking or herding the cattle, pony-trek, go for walks (and be collected by car) or cycle rides (bikes for hire), or just sit idle in the sunken rock garden with pool. One of the most interesting parts is the farmyard where a drama was acted out over two centuries ago. When clearing the hay-loft a few years back, an old muzzle-loading pistol was found. Experts identified it as a Jacobite pistol, and connected it with the tradition that a rebel on the run had been arrested at Bishopfield after the rising of 1745. Presumably he was hiding in the hay.

Allendale is Catherine Cookson's country. She lives nearby and many of her Mallen stories are set here. It is one of the loveliest parts of the north country, wild and rocky, in parts comparable with some Swiss scenery. Allen Banks, where two rivers converge, is a beauty spot. Not far off is the Killhope pass (nearly 2000 feet high) with a great wheel once used for crushing ore when these hills were mined for lead. In Allendale town, on every New Year's Eve costumed 'guizers' parade with blazing tar-barrels on their heads – vestige of a half-forgotten pagan fire-rite. At Hexham is a great Norman abbey, well worth visiting (and a garden centre), and a lively market every Tuesday. The Roman Wall, Kielder Forest with its vast landscaped reservoir, and the Scottish borders are not far off.

Readers' comments: Very comfortable; most helpful couple. Restful, good food, friendly atmosphere. Delightful place and people; very high standard. Comfortable, warm, pleasant service; good meal.

BLACKWATER HOTEL

C D PT X

Church Road, West Mersea, north-east of Chelmsford, Essex, CO5 8QH
Tel: 020638 3338

7 bedrooms (single, double or family) from £17. Less for 7 nights or bargain breaks. Rooms have central heating or electric heaters; shower or bathroom; TV, armchairs; tea/coffee facilities.
Dinner A la carte, at 7–10pm. Special diets if ordered. Lunches, packed lunches, snacks. Coffee, tea and other drinks can be ordered.
Sitting-room with central heating, open fire, books; bar.
Nearest main road A12 from Colchester.

The coastline here is a wilderness of creeks, islets and estuaries made colourful by the sails of small boats. A causeway now connects Mersea to the mainland, yet it still has the feel of an island with an identity all its own. There are Roman, Saxon and Norman remains – and, of course, the beds of Colchester oysters still flourish as they have done for centuries. Visitors go there, too, for all the usual seaside pleasures, for golf, sea-angling or for riding and walking. At nearby Fingringhoe Wick is an outstanding bird reserve, with hides alongside its lakes.

Down a quiet side-street is the creeper-covered Blackwater Hotel. Downstairs, beams and scarlet gingham tablecloths, copper pans and strings of onions, give the dining-room the informal air of a French bistro – these touches are Monique Chapleo's style. Here and in the small sitting-room with its tub chairs there are bowls of roses and pinks. All the bedrooms are very neat and fresh: wallpaper, curtains and bedspreads in matching sprigged patterns; bedheads of cane. Outside is a lawn with seats.

The food cooked by chef Roudesli is excellent, and the wine list is good. One might start with mushrooms champenoises or local shellfish, to be followed by pigeon pie or guinea-fowl in Marsala sauce and a pudding such as profiteroles or lemon tart. There is a bamboo-and-chintz coffee-room that serves snacks.

Although so near London, there are plenty of rural rides in this part of Essex, and many sights to see within a few miles – such as the timbered village of Coggeshall (with Paycockes, a National Trust house, and antique shops), the historic city of Colchester founded by the Romans before London (castle, museums, old churches, ancient byways and zoo), St Osyth's Priory and East Bergholt (Constable country). Maldon is very near – an old port still frequented by the great sailing-barges. Oyster fishery and museum can be visited (tastings, boat trips – phone 0206 384141).

Readers' comments: Charming hostess, excellent dinner and breakfast superb. Excellent cuisine. A real find – quite simply, perfect; charming patronne; superb meals; I don't think we have ever enjoyed a place so much.

Some readers tell me they have stayed at lots of places from *Staying Off the Beaten Track*. I wonder who has stayed at most? A free copy of the next edition awaits the reader who sends me his/her comments on the greatest number!

BLEA TARN HOUSE

D S

Little Langdale, Ambleside, Cumbria, LA22 9PG   Tel: 09667 614

3 bedrooms (small doubles) from £12. Rooms have central heating; views of country or garden.

Dinner £6 for 3 courses and coffee, at 6.30pm. Lunches, packed lunches. Coffee, tea, for a charge. Non-residents not admitted. Drinks can be brought in.

Sitting-room with open fire, books.

Nearest main road A593 from Ambleside to Coniston.

'It seemed a home of poverty and toil', said Wordsworth of Blea Tarn House, but it does not seem at all like that any more, for it is warm and cosy and prettily decorated, with an open fire in the corner of the guests' sitting-cum-dining room. Off it is Sheila Myers' kitchen: she likes to talk to guests while she prepares, as it might be, egg mayonnaise, roast beef, and apple or lemon-meringue pie. She serves classic country dishes, always with two vegetables (usually fresh, occasionally frozen, but never tinned) and two sorts of potatoes. In summer, there will be more in the way of salads, and in cooler weather hotpots and cobblers. Upstairs, the bedrooms are small, but they are quaint and pretty.

This is the very heart of the Lake District, for Blea Tarn House sits on its own, high above the Langdales, Great and Little, amid the scenery which has made the area such a draw for centuries – rugged and colourful, and punctuated by famous peaks. Reached by a narrow and twisting road, this is a popular beauty-spot, but it is never excessively crowded with the sightseers who can sometimes detract from such places. From the late afternoon onwards the peace and quiet are unbroken.

A field away from the house is the tarn (small lake) from which it takes its name, where you can bathe or fish. Within a few miles are some of the Lake District's best known villages – Grasmere, Hawkshead, Ambleside and Coniston.

Readers' comments: Comfortable atmosphere, friendliness, good food. Delightful cottage and situation: an experience we would not have missed for anything. Excellent: good food, wonderful views, nice atmosphere. Characterful.

Tongue Ghyll near Grasmere (tel: 09665 571) is more spacious: a 17th-century house once the home of the county's High Sheriff. From Mrs Dixon's rooms and pretty garden (with streams) there are mountain views – a path leads up to Helvellyn. B & b only.

29

BOOT FARM *New*   C(10) **S**

Southend, Bradfield, west of Reading, Berkshire, RG7 6ES   Tel: 0734 744298

3 bedrooms (single, double or family) from £12. Less for 3 (midweek) nights and bar-gain breaks. Some have own bath/shower; TV; tea/coffee facilities; central heating; views of country, garden. No smoking. (Washing-machine on request.)

High tea £3 served at 5.30 or 6.30pm. Non-residents not admitted. Vegetarian or special diets if ordered. Packed lunches. Tea, coffee, extra. Drinks can be brought in.

Sitting-room with central heating, open fire, books.

Large garden

Nearest main road M4 from London to Wales.

From this farm comes some of the best cream and butter there is – supplied direct to many top restaurants and hotels. Guests may enjoy these at high tea, a filling and very good value meal of ham salad, omelette or Welsh rarebit followed by home-made cakes and jams. (Patricia Dawes is prepared to cook a full dinner sometimes; otherwise visitors go to The Bladebone or the Royal Oak.)

There is a large and very comfortable sitting-room, William Morris fabrics contrasting with pale walls, a log fire blazing on cold days, casements open to the garden in summer. Bedrooms are attractive and the bathroom is exceptional; toilet as well as bath has a flowery pattern. In the dining-room hand-stitched roses on tapestry chairs are complemented by an all-pink colour scheme.

In addition to farming, the Dawes run a livery stable and riding school and so are able to offer special riding weekends or holidays, popular with Londoners who live under an hour away. Others come for the open-air theatre of Bradfield College, for the trout lakes, or for the many golf courses in the country. East Berkshire has been described under other entries; to the west lies picturesque Hungerford, famous for its scores of antique shops (many open even on Sundays). Nearby are the windswept heights of the Berkshire Downs where racehorses train, and you can walk along the prehistoric Ridgeway Path. The sites of Iron Age forts or burial mounds dot the area. The Kennet valley is in complete contrast – fertile meadows with birch and oak woods beyond, a great area for birdwatchers. The villages here have flint-and-brick cottages roofed with thatch. In and around both Lambourn and Newbury are historic buildings (the latter has a racecourse and a theatre in a converted watermill), stately homes and pretty villages. In this area is Littlecote (stately home with a Cromwellian armoury, jousting and other sights).

Further south, at Woolhampton is mediaeval **Bridge Cottage** (tel: 0734 713138), so-called because it is right beside a bridge over the old Kennet & Avon Canal. Jill Thornely has furnished the house pleasantly and from its windows you can see the boats going by (or take out Jill's canoes yourself). Breakfast is served in the low-beamed kitchen or in the walled garden. For dinner there is the nearby Rowbarge Inn.

BOSSELL HOUSE

C D H PT S X

Plymouth Road, Buckfastleigh, south of Ashburton, Devon, TQ11 0DG
Tel: 03644 3294

17 bedrooms (single, double or family) from £16.50, **less 5% discount to readers paying**

by cheque or cash. Out of season, less for 2 nights or bargain breaks. Rooms have central heating or electric heaters; shower or bathroom; TV, video, phone, armchairs; views of country/farmland/garden; tea/coffee facilities.
Dinner £10 for 4 courses and coffee, from 6.30pm. Special diets if ordered. Lunches, packed lunches, snacks. Coffee, tea, for a charge. Drinks can be ordered.
2 sitting-rooms with central heating, TV, books; bars.
Large garden with tennis, bowls, badminton, tennis trainer.
Nearest main road A38 from Exeter to Plymouth.

Bossell House is run by Sylvia and Eric Bottell with their daughter Melanie and son-in-law chef (Malcolm Wright). It is a mansion with tower, built by a wealthy woollen-mill owner in 1835. A large glass-walled dining-room was later added from which to enjoy views of the big garden (it has one of the tallest monkey-puzzle trees in Britain, a Canadian redwood and other specimen trees). The Bottells had decades of brambles and weeds to clear before they could plant flowers and vegetables. When not in the large, bay-windowed sitting-room or the damask-papered bar-lounge, guests can sit at tables with sunshades on the paved terrace outside. There is also a snug cellar bar with games.

Bedrooms are spacious, with antique or old-fashioned furniture, velvet bed-heads and striped duvets. All rooms are comfortable rather than elegant. There is also simpler accommodation (much used by fishing parties) in a coach house.

A wide choice is offered on the table d'hôte menu. Malcolm cooks such popular dishes as trout with almonds, haddock in prawn sauce, roast chicken or beef Stroganoff – all sauces are home-made, and many vegetables home-grown.

From Buckfastleigh one can readily visit Torquay and its sandy bays, Dartmoor, the River Dart (with river trips from Totnes to Dartmouth), a steam railway, Buckfast Abbey, Paignton zoo, Plymouth, Exeter and many picturesque fishing ports on the south coast of Devon. There are many fine gardens, for instance at Bickton and Dartington.

Readers' comments: Friendly; good food. Warm reception, excellent service.

Book well ahead: many of these houses have few rooms. Do not expect dinner if you have not booked it.

Prices are the minimum *per person* in a double room at the beginning of the year.

31

BOUCHERS

C(5) **PT S EH5**

Bentham, south of Cheltenham, Gloucestershire, GL51 5TZ
Tel: 0452 862373

2 bedrooms (double) from £9. Rooms have central heating; views of country or garden. No smoking.
Sitting-room with central heating, open fire, TV, books. No smoking.
Large garden
Nearest main road A46 from Cheltenham to Bath.

Once a farmhouse, Bouchers is still surrounded by hayfields just beyond the garden, where rock doves fly across the lawns and rose-beds to a graceful weeping willow. A sundial on one wall declares the date of the house, 1661, and of the old cider-house which is now the workshop of Mr Daniels (he is a carpenter).

Inside all is immaculate and very comfortable, and you will get a warm welcome from Mrs Daniels as you step through the front door straight into the big U-shaped living-room. Here plenty of velvet armchairs are grouped round the hearth where an open fire crackles in winter, and a grandfather clock ticks the time away. Round the other side of the U is the dining-room, for breakfast only (visitors eat other meals at the Cross Hands Inn nearby or at one of the innumerable restaurants in Cheltenham, which is also near).

Bentham, on the edge of the Cotswolds, is close to the route south to Bath. Gloucester with its cathedral, historic Cirencester (don't miss the Roman museum) and the Forest of Dean are all within easy reach, as are Prinknash Abbey and the Wye Valley. Also in the area are Slimbridge Wildfowl Trust, Westonbirt Arboretum, Badminton House (a Palladian mansion, where the Queen is often seen at the spring horse trials), 12th-century Berkeley Castle in its lovely grounds. Cheltenham and Tewkesbury are both near – as are the gardens at Hidcote.

Readers' comments: Service excellent – the sort for which you would expect to pay double the price. Will go there again.

Don't complain if –
- because you booked at short notice, you do not get the best room
- because you did not order a meal in advance, you get something plucked from the freezer
- because you do not arrive on time, your room is let to someone else
- because you bring a dog without asking, it is refused entry
- because you don't express your wishes (for more heat, a second helping, or whatever), you don't get what you want!

Single people may find more company in houses that have a shared dining-table, a bar, and no TV in the sitting-room. As my descriptions indicate, some owners mingle more with their guests than others do. Houses marked **S** charge singles little or no more than half a double.

BOURNE EAU HOUSE

Bourne, south of Lincoln, PE10 9LY   Tel: 0778 423621

C D PT

3 bedrooms (single, double or family) from £17.50, **with a 10% discount to readers of** **this book**. Less for 7 nights. Rooms have central heating; shower or bathroom; TV, phone, armchairs; views of garden; tea/coffee facilities. Clothes-washing facilities.

Dinner £12.50 for 4 courses and coffee, at 7.30–8pm. Vegetarian or special diets if ordered. Packed lunches, snacks. Coffee, tea, free. Non-residents not admitted. Drinks can be ordered.

2 sitting-rooms with central heating, open fire, TV, books, table tennis, piano, record-player.

Large garden

Nearest main road A15 from Peterborough to Lincoln.

There are many good reasons to visit Lincolnshire (a much underrated county), and this exceptional home is one of them. It lies, almost islanded, within a twist of a little river frequented by swans and geese (the 'eau' that gives the house its name), a mixture of Tudor and Georgian architecture. A small wrought-iron footbridge leads to a Norman abbey behind the house; at the front are public gardens and the mound which is all that is left of Hereward the Wake's castle – the last Saxon leader to hold out against William the Conqueror.

To one side of an all-white, tiled hall is a pretty sitting-room where blue velvet chairs, contrasting with aquamarine walls, are grouped around a fireplace and its shining brass fender and firedogs. Through two bay windows are views of the lovely garden, of almond blossom and immaculate lawns. In another room is a concert piano and an ornately carved 17th-century mantelpiece; while the low-beamed, flagstoned dining-room (its floor made of Stamford 'marble') has yet another distinctive fireplace with a hood (depicting a wild man of the woods) made by a fenland blacksmith. Throughout the house there are other interesting features such as lattice window-panes, a cheese cupboard built into a wall, and (in a bedroom) a little cast-iron fireplace with built-in boiler for hot water.

The best bedroom, a suite, has a carved mantelpiece that was once part of an altar – hence the symbols of alpha and omega, oats and vines. The room is decorated in soft pinks and creams, has gros-point cushions and a Kashmiri camphor chest. The carpeted bathroom is equally elegant, in peach and turquoise.

Dawn Bishop's meals fully live up to the standards of the house, and, Lincolnshire being famous for its vegetables, plenty of local produce is served. A typical menu might comprise prawn and avocado salad followed by cauliflower soup with croûtons, then chicken in a ginger and soya sauce (there are always several vegetables interestingly prepared – such as courgettes cooked with paprika), and perhaps a syllabub. Cheeses will include Stilton made in the region.

This part of the country is perhaps at its best in spring when the scudding clouds in blue skies are reflected in the many dykes that drain the land, and the fields of the bulb-growing districts are brilliant with daffodils or tulips – road verges too. Villages of stone and thatch are picturesque, and this is an outstanding area for gardeners who want to go home laden with purchases from the many nurseries.

Readers' comments: House and hosts charming. Excellent accommodation. Care, quality and hospitality can not be beaten.

BRAMWOOD *New*   **C D PT S X**
19 Hallgarth, Pickering, North Yorkshire, YO18 7AW   Tel: 0751 74066

rear view

6 bedrooms (single, double or family) from £10. Less for 7 nights and bargain breaks. Some have own shower; tea/coffee facilities; central heating. No smoking.
Dinner £6 for 3 courses and coffee, at 6.30pm. Non-residents not admitted. Vegetarian diets if ordered. Tea, coffee extra. Wine can be brought in.
Sitting-room with central heating, open fire, TV, books, record-player. No smoking.
Small garden
Nearest main road A169 from Malton to Whitby.

The best approach to this 18th-century guest-house is from the back, through an old archway built for coaches – racks for the horses' tack and an old forge still survive, but beyond what was once the stable yard there is now a pretty and secluded garden, with clematis scrambling up old walls and an apple tree; in one part vegetables are grown for the table.

All the bedrooms are immaculate, some of them spacious, and many have cane rocking-chairs – a nice touch. Ann Lane, who used to enjoy cooking 'for recreation' has put her enthusiasm to good use here, providing visitors with such meals as garlic mushrooms, pork medallions served with sage-and-apple sauce, and Yorkshire curd tart. She finds old-fashioned puddings are very popular with guests, particularly at the end of a strenuous day's walking, cycling, birdwatching or even gliding. Her home-made chutneys and marmalades are on sale.

In the vicinity are lovely Staindale and many moorland villages tucked away which are well worth seeking. Lastingham, for instance, which has fountain and crypt dating back to the 11th century. Two hundred years ago, its inn, the Blacksmiths' Arms, was run by its curate: when the bishop objected, he said he had thirteen children to support! Thornton Dale is very picturesque: trout swim in the clear stream that curves through the village and under the little footbridges that lead to each 17th- or 18th-century house and its flowery cottage-garden. Hutton-le-Hole, which has the region's folk museum, was once a refuge for persecuted Quakers. Through the middle of its cluster of pale stone houses is a ravine carved by a stream that descends, with cascades, from the high moors near Rosedale Abbey.

If you want absolute quiet, avoid any place that takes children or has a bar open to non-residents. Inns sometimes get extensions to their licensing hours for late private parties; and may lack quiet sitting-rooms.

Two-thirds of the houses in this book have bargain breaks or other discounts on offer, some exclusive to readers. Only a third raise prices at the peak of summer.

BROADWATER

C D PT S S-C

Woodbridge Road, Framlingham, Suffolk, IP13 9LL Tel: 0728 723645

6 bedrooms (single, double or family) from £13. Less for 2 nights or bargain breaks.

Rooms have central heating; shower or bathroom (some); armchairs; views of country or garden; tea/coffee facilities.
Dinner (£8) for 3 courses and coffee, at 7pm. Vegetarian or special diets if ordered. Non-residents are not admitted. Drinks can be ordered.
Sitting-room with central heating, open fire, TV, books, piano.
Extensive grounds Wood, garden, paddocks, vineyard.
Nearest main road A12 from London to Great Yarmouth.

I came away with a case of white wine – for Broadwater is a name you will find on wine labels: it consists of a vineyard and an 18th-century house, with a large garden. You can drink the wine at dinner here, in a pleasant green-and-white room. It is usually a homely meal (such as courgettes in cheese sauce; fish pie containing smoked haddock and prawns; summer pudding). Vegetables and fruit usually come from the garden. Big cretonne armchairs are grouped round a log fire in the sitting-room, which has windows all round with views of woodland, occasional rabbits, horses and Jacob sheep. Sheila Stocker's garden is sometimes opened to the public for charity.

The bedrooms are well furnished – even the single rooms, which is not always the case – and one has a four-poster bed. One of the toilets is rightly nicknamed 'the throne room': a real museum-piece!

The most popular places to visit near here are Framlingham and Orford castles, Woodbridge, Glemham Mill, Easton Farm Park and Bruisyard vineyard. Notcutts, Helmingham and Charlsfield attract garden-lovers. (Bicycles on loan.)

If you go further afield, you will find Thetford – its architecture begins with Saxon remains – and the riverside walks here are particularly attractive. Whether shopping for antiques (shops or auctions) or for farm produce, this is a good area. Near Bury St Edmunds are stately homes including Kentwell Hall, Ickworth House and Melford Hall. This area also has several very good garden centres and innumerable antique shops. Altogether, a county of great interest and variety.

If you have not arrived by, perhaps, 6pm your room may be let to someone else – unless you telephone to say you are on your way.

Unless otherwise agreed, send a 10% deposit when confirming your booking.

Book well ahead: many of these houses have few rooms. Do not expect dinner if you have not booked it.

BROOKFIELD FARM HOTEL   C D H PT X
Plummers Plain, Horsham, West Sussex, RH13 6LO   Tel: 0403 76568

rear view

16 bedrooms (single, double or family) from £17.25. Less for 7 nights or bargain breaks. (Two ground-floor bedrooms. One four-poster room with marble bath.) Rooms have central heating or electric heaters; shower or bathroom; TV, armchairs; views of country or garden; tea/coffee facilities.
Dinner £7.50 for 3 courses (with choices) and coffee, at 6.15pm onwards. Special diets if ordered. Packed lunches. Coffee, tea, for a charge. Drinks an be ordered.
2 sitting-rooms and a games-room with central heating, open fire, TV, books, billiards, darts, Star Wars, organ, record-player. Sauna and gym. There is a bar.
Garden and lake (with fishing, swimming and boats, croquet, golf-driving, children's play area), farmland and forest.
Nearest main road A281 from Horsham to Brighton.

Although this modernized farmhouse in the Sussex Weald is now a busy guest-house, it is on a very real farm with hundreds of acres of sheep and cattle. The owner is John Christian, who is well known on TV and radio farming programmes, but much of its popularity is due to its manageress, Carole. Born just down the road, John lectures on farming and travels widely to study farm methods.

When I arrived, from my bedroom window I saw him mowing the lawn which slopes down to the lake – and then running up an American flag on one of the flagpoles (a tribute he often pays to overseas visitors is to fly their national flag). Beyond lay fields and woods.

On the white walls of the beamed dining-room, made cheerful by scarlet lampshades and cushions, is a huge collection of old plates. Guests usually share tables for a meal of generous home cooking. The picture windows that look out onto the lawn slide right back on warm evenings, and there is a paved terrace with seats and lighting outside. There is a tiled, flat roof for sunbathing.

The sitting-room has sofas and armchairs of ample dimensions, a plethora of ornaments, and an open fire for chilly nights. Bedrooms vary in size.

John occasionally organizes a barbecue or barn dance, celebrates Christmas and New Year (fireworks!), and sometimes takes visitors on a tour of the neighbourhood's many old inns (though he doesn't drink himself) or to see a local cattle-market in action.

Adjoining the house is a games room (with bar billiards, darts, video games and so forth); children can ride the donkey; there are pedal-boats and a canoe on the lake (and a watersplash into it); and croquet on the lawn, as well as children's slides and swings, and a golf-driving range. A special attraction is 30-year-old Adam, a grey parrot.

Walkers can make for St Leonards Forest. Some of the most popular sights of Sussex and Kent are within motoring distance, including Arundel (castle), Chichester (cathedral), Chartwell (Churchill's house), Hever (stately home), and the gardens of Nymans and Leonardslee.

Gatwick Airport is near, and visitors can be collected from there by car. Some people going on holiday abroad spend a night at Brookfield first and then leave their car here, at far less cost than using an airport car park.

Readers' comments: Cheerful surroundings, friendly hospitality.

BUCKNELL HOUSE *New*   C(12) D
Bucknell, west of Ludlow, Shropshire, SY7 0AD   Tel: 05474 248

3 bedrooms (double or family) from £11. Less for 3 nights and bargain breaks. All have tea/coffee facilities; central heating; views of country or garden. (Washing-machine on request.)

Sitting-room with central heating, fire, TV, books, piano.
Small garden
Nearest main road A4110 from Hereford to Knighton.

In the early 18th century, the clergy lived well: this huge and handsome house, honeysuckle and wisteria clambering up its walls, was a vicarage then. The vicar would have approved of the equally handsome way in which Brenda Davies has furnished it – the dining room with Sheraton chairs, a fine wallpaper, sideboard laden with silver; the sitting-room with big velvet armchairs, curtains of pale green silk, cream brocade wallpaper and alcoves of fine china; flowers everywhere. Bedrooms are just as good, spacious and with antique furniture.

The grounds (garden and water meadows) are secluded, looking across the lovely valley of the River Teme to Wales. There are rosebeds, daffodil drive, shrubbery, croquet lawn, a hard tennis court and fishing in the river.

Woodlands and hills around here are full of wildlife; and throughout the area there are castles to be discovered, hill forts, markets in old towns, manor houses and picturesque black-and-white villages. Mediaeval Ludlow, beautifully preserved, has a Norman castle of red sandstone. The church is as grand as a cathedral; Housman is buried here. Old inns, alleyways of antique shops, and riverside walks add to its charms.

(Go to Milebrook House or the Angel at Kingsland for meals.)

Readers' comments: Wonderfully comfortable bed, breakfast an ample repast, some of the most beautiful countryside in England. Such excellence and outstanding amenities; marvellous people.

For those who require dinner there is **Upper Buckton** at Leintwardine, home of Yvonne Lloyd (tel: 05473 634). This is an 18th-century house at the peaceful centre of a large sheep and cattle farm, with croquet and other garden games, table tennis and snooker in a granary. Antiques furnish the comfortable rooms, fine china the tables; Yvonne is an accomplished cook, serving such starters as bananas

and bacon with curry sauce or stuffed mushrooms; then roasts, salmon or chicken with orange and almonds; vacherins or chocolate roulade.

BUCKYETTE *New*   C S S-C
Littlehempston, north of Totnes, Devon, TQ9 6ND   Tel: 080 426 638

6 bedrooms (double or family) from £10.25. Less for 7 nights. Tea/coffee facilities; night-store heaters in 4; views of country or garden.
Dinner £5.75 for 3 courses (with occasional choices) and coffee, at 6.30pm. Non-residents not admitted. Vegetarian or special diets if ordered. Drinks can be ordered.
Sitting-room with open fire, TV, books, piano.
Small garden
Nearest main road A381 from Newton Abbot to Totnes.
Closed from October–April

The curious name of this house appears in the Domesday Book and is believed to be a Saxon word meaning 'head of a spring': the spring is still there, and in use. The present building, made from stone quarried on the farm, dates from 1860. It is on a commanding site with far views, and is furnished with Edwardian pieces suited to the scale of the lofty rooms. In the sitting-room is a log fire for chilly days, and for sunny ones tall French doors open onto a wisteria-hung verandah. The peppermint-pink dining-room has particularly handsome tables, which Roger Miller himself made from timber on the estate, and pictures of theatrical costumes. Bedrooms are not elegant but comfortable.

Elizabeth Miller serves such meals as lentil soup, chicken in a crisp cheese-and-garlic coating and queen of puddings; with home-baked bread. The garden provides asparagus, strawberries and other produce. Everything about the house is solid, comfortable, unpretentious, and very English.

Littlehempston is well placed for a family holiday because the safe sands of Torbay are so near – as are Paignton's zoo, miniature gardens, a scenic steam railway and river trips. There are plenty of inns, theatres and concerts including those at Dartington's celebrated arts and crafts centres. Totnes has its castle and streets of ancient buildings, with interesting little shops. In the church is an especially fine rood-screen. At Buckfast Abbey the monks sell their wine and honey to visitors; Buckland Abbey was Sir Francis Drake's house. Ashburton is a pretty hill town, with all of Dartmoor beyond – its most famous beauty-spot is Dartmeet where two rivers converge and there is an old 'clapper' bridge of stones by which to cross the water, a typical Devon feature. Widecombe, of 'Uncle Tom Cobleigh' fame, still has its celebrated fair high up on the moor every September. Princetown (large, bleak and weather-beaten) is where the big Dartmoor Prison is, originally built by and for Napoleonic prisoners-of-war. Brixham, Salcombe and Plymouth are described elsewhere.

Inclusive terms for dinner, bed-and-breakfast (particularly for a week) can be much lower than those quoted here for these items taken separately. For short-notice bookings you may be able to get a reduction.

No proprietor wants to have a room standing empty. This particularly applies to Sunday nights. Some hotels make a discount if you want only two courses from a three-course menu.

BULMER FARM

C(12) **D S X**

Holmbury St Mary, south of Dorking, Surrey, RH5 6LG   Tel: 0306 730210

3 bedrooms (twin-bedded) from £11. Rooms have central heating or electric heaters; views of farm or garden; tea/coffee facilities.
Sitting-room with open fire, TV, books, record-player.
Large garden plus farm.
Nearest main road A25 from Dorking to Guildford.

In the folds of Surrey's high North Downs (most of which are so scenic that they are in National Trust protection) a number of very picturesque villages lie hidden, and Holmbury is one. Near the centre stands Bulmer Farm, built about 1680. One steps straight into the large dining-room, and through this to an attractive sitting-room – a room of pink walls and old beams, chairs covered in cretonne patterned with pink poppies, logs crackling in front of the cherubs and harps of an old iron fireback in the inglenook. It opens onto the large garden.

Upstairs are attractive bedrooms with immaculate paintwork and cottage-style furnishings.

Outdoors (where chickens run free among the old rickstones), a Dutch barn is crammed with hay; across the yard from an ancient byre, the tiles of its long, wobbly roof softened with moss, is a small farm shop from which you can take home Bulmer's own vegetables or eggs, lettuces from the glasshouses, or Gill Hill's home-made marmalade. David will show you the lake he created a few years ago, now a haven for herons, kingfishers, Canada geese, snipe and other wildfowl.

Bed-and-breakfast only, but the area is full of inns offering good meals such as the Royal Oak.

Some tourists find this a good area in which to stay while visiting London – train day-tickets cost only £3 or so, and the journey takes three-quarters of an hour (from Dorking).

The surrounding area of woodland and hills is one of the finest beauty-spots near the capital, truly rural, and dotted with stately homes to visit, footpaths to follow, historic churches and villages with craft shops, trout farms, antiques and the like. Dorking and Guildford (the latter with castle ruins, river trips and a good theatre) are each well worth a day's visit. The Royal Horticultural Society's gardens at Wisley are near, too, and so are Box Hill (viewpoint), Leith Hill (walks), Clandon and Polesden Lacey (stately homes). Several fine gardens open to view. Beautiful Shere has monthly antiques' fairs.

Readers' comments: One's every wish is catered for. So warm and friendly. Made so welcome, made to feel like one of the family.

Many houses have cards, chess, Scrabble etc. – just ask. And also such things as irons, hair-dryers, maps, gumboots and bridge-tables.

For explanation of code letters (**C, D, H, PT, S, S-C, X**) **see page xxviii.**

BULMER TYE HOUSE *New* C X
Bulmer Tye, south-west of Sudbury, Suffolk, CO10 7ED   Tel: 078729 315

4 bedrooms (single, double or family) from £10. Some have own bath; all have central heating and views of garden. No smoking. (Washing-machine on request.)
Dinner £5 for 2 or 3 courses and coffee. Served at time to suit guests. Non-residents not admitted. Vegetarian or special diets if ordered. Tea, coffee, free.
2 sitting-rooms with central heating, open fire, TV, books, piano. No smoking.
Large garden
Nearest main road A131 from Halstead to Sudbury.

One of Gainsborough's most famous paintings is of the Andrews family whom he knew when he lived in Suffolk. It was one of their sons, a parson, who in the 18th century 'modernized' this house, most of which dates back to the reign of Elizabeth I, by putting in huge sash windows and so forth.

Today its old timbers resonate to the sound of music (played by family or guests), for Peter Owen is a maker of very fine clavichords – and of much of the interesting furniture seen in the rooms. A hexagonal table with a complex pattern of end-grain triangles is his; so is a throne-like chair of elm, its joints secured with wood pegs only; and also two dolls' houses – one of which is in fact a scale replica of Bulmer Tye House itself. Little boxes here and there and eggs in decorative woods are his work too.

His wife is an authority on antique furniture, about which she writes articles for specialist magazines (under the name Noël Riley); so not surprisingly there are many unusual period pieces in the house – such as chests inlaid with ivory or with Delft tiles, and oriental rugs on the wood floors. Instead of using furnishing fabrics with a traditional look, the Owens have contrasted the antiques with strong modern patterns – a Bauhaus design for curtains in one room, an Aztec-style pattern in another, in strong colours such as tangerine and turquoise. A Japanese sunshade, inverted, makes an unusual ceiling light-shade. There is a large Bechstein in one of the sitting-rooms and log fires in both. In one bedroom, with a particularly handsome bed, 19th-century Persian curtains and a Laura Ashley pattern co-exist happily.

The quarry-tiled kitchen is decorated in brilliant primary colours and on one wall screen-printed Spanish tiles give a *trompe l'oeil* effect. Here guests eat with the family, round a huge pine table and are apt to get drawn into family life, as well as anything from duets to political debates with Peter. Garden produce often goes into the making of soups and of fruit puddings; wine, lemonade and elderflower cordial are all home-made and Peter bakes the bread. Some of the dishes guests enjoy most are beef-and-lentil flan; Roman cobbler (pork and mushrooms with a topping of semolina and cheese), fish pie and, for vegetarians in particular, a cheesy bread-and-butter pudding served with stir-fried vegetables. Only a basic continental breakfast is served.

The large garden is notable for its many fine trees (some 200 years old) which include copper beeches, walnuts, cedars and yews, as well as a number of unusual plants. There is a grass tennis court.

Readers' comments: Characterful house, beautiful garden, very informal and friendly.

BURLAND FARM *New*   **C D X**
Wrexham Road, Burland, north-west of Nantwich, Cheshire, CW5 8ND
Tel: 0270 74 210

4 bedrooms (double or family) from £15. Less for 7 nights and bargain breaks. Some have own bath/shower; TV; tea/coffee facilities; central heating; views of country or garden.
Dinner £10 for 3 courses and coffee, at about 7pm. Vegetarian or special diets if ordered. Lunches, packed lunches, snacks. Tea, coffee, free. Drinks can be brought in.
2 sitting-rooms with central heating, open fire, books, piano.
Small garden
Nearest main road A534 from Nantwich to Wrexham.

This early Victorian house, surrounded by lawn and trees, is in the pretty *cottage ornée* style that was once fashionable: windows are lozenge-paned, the gable is decorated with woodwork, hinges are of wrought iron. (The lozenge panes are to be seen elsewhere in the area – a feature of many houses on the great Tollemache estate.)

The Allwoods' furnishings complement this well. Their huge dining-table and cupboard were made by Michael's great-grandfather from oaks felled on the farm, and other antiques have been added, such as spindleback chairs. Colour schemes are pleasant – a pink and grey bedroom, for instance, with a white tapestry bedspread from Portugal.

Sandra likes having visitors as an excuse to use her talent for 'dinner party' cooking (unless they prefer a cottage-pie supper). She produces such meals as hot chicken mousse (served with a spring-onion sauce), pork fillet in mustard sauce, blackcurrant sorbet accompanied by home-made biscuits, and then cheeses. She usually bakes her own bread, and will make American-style muffins for breakfast if requested.

Nearby Nantwich is an old town where black-and-white Tudor houses jostle one another in picturesque streets such as Welsh Row (the carvings inside the church and on the almshouses are well worth seeing). Its prosperity was founded on salt-mining, salt having been deposited here millions of years ago when the sea covered Cheshire. 'Magpie' houses (timbers painted black and plaster white) are characteristic throughout the great plain of Cheshire, a vast area like an immense park, with cows grazing among buttercups, meres shining, tracts of woodland, and rivers flowing peacefully to the sea. This is a historic area which was well populated even before the Romans came here in strength: on hilltops with far views are traces of prehistoric forts. Throughout the county there are historic towns full of character, such as Macclesfield (hilly streets from which you can see right to the Peak District, and old silk-weaving mills), Knutsford (Mrs Gaskell's 'Cranford') and of course Chester itself, described elsewhere. Near Knutsford is the huge radio telescope of Jodrell Bank (there is a visitor centre here). Macclesfield Forest is a vast wild moor, with crags and narrow valleys; at Anderton a lift raises boats from one canal to another (Cheshire is criss-crossed with canals); and in nearby Northwich houses lean at odd angles because of subsidence caused by salt-mines.

Readers' comments: Warmly recommended, lovely airy room, superb meal.

BURNT WOOD *New*   **C S-C X**
Powdermill Lane, Battle, East Sussex, TN33 0SU   Tel: 04246 2459

5 bedrooms (single, double or family) from £12. Less for 7 nights and bargain breaks. Some or all have own bath/shower; TV; tea/coffee facilities; phone; central heating; views of sea (just!), country, garden; balcony. (Washing-machine on request.)

Dinner £8 for 3 courses (with choices) and coffee, at 7.30pm. Non-residents not admitted. Vegetarian or special diets if ordered. Lunches, packed lunches, snacks. Drinks can be brought in.

2 sitting-rooms with central heating, open fire, TV, books, organ, record-player.

Large garden

Nearest main road A21 from London to Hastings.

One of the most elegant swimming-pools in this book is to be found in the large garden here, with a vine-covered Ionic colonnade and steps at one end of it. A peacock frequents the rose garden, which also has its own sundial; in a sun-trapping courtyard is a grapevine from which wine is made; and there is a croquet lawn and a tennis court. Adjoining the garden is a smallholding which produces meat and fresh vegetables for the kitchen – the Rollands keep pigs, sheep and cows (as well as dogs); and all around are woods, fields and lakes.

The house was once the home of Hastings' MP (the resort is only six miles away); it was built in 1903 as a copy of an 18th-century house in Gloucestershire. One large L-shaped room with arches has windows all around, and there is a big television room with yellow panelling and sofas, warmed by a log stove in winter. Bedrooms are comfortable rather than smart: I particularly liked a big white-and-yellow room with windows on two sides which, sharing a bathroom with the adjoining single room, could be ideal for families. The Rollands run a language school for overseas businessmen who come here with their wives and children.

Jane enjoys cooking and often serves meals like gazpacho; liver cooked with mushrooms, cream and wine; and trifle. The reputation of her food has spread, and so she now does a good deal of cooking for local people as well as her own visitors.

Battle (scene of William the Conqueror's epic victory) is in the middle of a very scenic area. The magnificent South Downs end with the famous cliffs at Beachy Head and Seven Sisters and then, in complete contrast, there are the wide Romney marshes and the woodlands of Ashdown Forest. History is everywhere, with numerous great castles and fortifications (at Pevensey, mediaeval Rye, Lewes, Bodiam, Sissinghurst – with famous gardens, Hastings and Herstmonceux). Over the border into Kent there are still more. Historic houses include Batemans (Kipling's Tudor home) which is very close, Michelham Priory near one of the nicest resorts – Eastbourne, and Glyndebourne (opera). There are wildlife parks and bird sanctuaries, a number of outstanding gardens open to the public, and sophisticated entertainments, at Brighton in particular, within easy driving distance.

Incidentally, the unusual name of the house refers to the fact that charcoal used to be made on the site, once used in the making of gunpowder nearby (hence the name of Powdermill Lane).

BURROWS COURT HOTEL

Nibley Green, Dursley, south of Gloucester, GL11 6AZ   Tel: 0453 546230

8 bedrooms (double) from £17 but far less for 2 nights or bargain breaks. Rooms have central heating; shower or bathroom; TV; views of country or garden; tea/coffee facilities. Clothes-washing facilities.

Dinner £9.50 for 3 courses and coffee, at 7–8.30pm. Vegetarian or special diets if ordered. Lunches, packed lunches, snacks. Drinks can be ordered.

2 sitting-rooms with central heating, open fire, books; bar.

Large garden with croquet and unheated swimming-pool.

Nearest main road A38 from Bristol to Gloucester.

In the 18th century, this was a woollen mill: the big dining-room, with its floor of herringbone brick and a stone hearth, is where weavers sat at their looms. Now there are gay poppy and cornflower curtains at the windows and willow-pattern china on the tables. It adjoins what was the mill-owner's house, and in what is now the entrance hall his built-in bread-oven and spice-cupboards still survive. Many rooms have beams or deep-shuttered windows – an attic family room with great sloping rafters is particularly popular with children. The Rackleys have redecorated the rooms with sparkling paintwork, Laura Ashley fabrics and a good deal of stripped pine furniture; and have put in excellent bathrooms. There is a large upstairs sitting-room, with bar and log stove. The staff are helpful.

For dinner you might be served home-made mushroom soup, beef in red wine with apricots, and hot chocolate fudge cake or meringues with kiwi fruit. There are over a dozen inexpensive wines to choose from.

Outside is an attractive garden. Beyond a patio (with seats below a grapevine) and a goldfish pond is a sheltered swimming-pool (unheated). Views are of open countryside – the Cotswold Edge and Berkeley Vale, threaded by streams and small lanes. Bath, Bristol and Cheltenham are about half an hour by car. Slimbridge Wildfowl Trust, 12th-century Berkeley Castle (where Edward II was murdered) with its lovely grounds and deer park, Westonbirt Arboretum and Badminton (annual horse trials) are even nearer. Berkeley Church has a very fine stained glass window (Jenner, who discovered vaccination, is buried there); there's another good church at Wotton-under-Edge, an old market town. The Cotswold Way for walkers and 'royal' Tetbury are near, and within an easy drive are at least 40 gardens open to the public and many pick-your-own fruit farms.

Readers' comments: Idyllic situation, helpful staff.

In a very steep valley called Waterley Bottom, near North Nibley, is hidden the **New Inn** (tel: 0453 3659) and its prettily landscaped garden. It has a good play area for children, and there's a well furnished family bedroom too. Ruby Sainty sometimes serves breakfasts on the patio. Snacks and real ales are available in the bar, where her

rear view

collection of antique brewing gear is displayed. Every room is spotless.

BUTCHERS ARMS X
Woolhope, east of Hereford, Herefordshire, HR1 4RF   Tel: 043277 281

3 bedrooms (double or single) from £15.50. Less for 7 nights or bargain breaks in winter. The rooms have central heating; TV, armchairs; views of country; tea/coffee facilities; fruit.

Dinner 3-course bar meal, £5.85. Restaurant, £9.15, at 7.30–9.00pm, Wednesdays to Saturdays only. Special diets if ordered. Smoking discouraged. Lunches, packed lunches. Drinks can be ordered.

Lounge bar (open during licensed hours only), with central heating and open fire, books.

Patio garden

Nearest main road A438 from Hereford to Ledbury.

The sun streamed down from a clear blue sky onto the paved garden where I was lunching; a small stream clattered by and birds were singing. Yet it was mid-November!

The half-timbered Butchers Arms, which dates back to the 14th century, stands among fields and woods far from any other building. Nevertheless its excellence is well known to scores of people who, though they live some distance away, beat a path to its door; and the bar was crowded. Even the snacks are outstanding, and the small restaurant is of gourmet standard. Breakfasts too are excellent.

Hospitable Mary Bailey, previously a computer programmer, who took over the inn only a few years ago, has built up a wide repertoire of rather unusual dishes to complement the straightforward Herefordshire beef steaks which are also served. From a wide selection one might, for instance, choose fried clams or a terrine made from tongue, chicken livers and brandy to start with; while main courses often include rabbit-and-bacon pie, pigeon with juniper berries and beef Bourguignonne. Vegetarian dishes are imaginative.

In the bar, where an open fire crackles, you must duck to avoid low beams. Dining-room and bedrooms (quiet except over the bar) are furnished simply.

Woolhope is in the middle of a particularly scenic area: the Wye Valley and Symonds Yat are only a few miles away; so are the attractive old towns of Ross-on-Wye, Ledbury, and Hereford with its fine cathedral, big garden centre and cider museum. The Welsh borders, Black Mountains, Forest of Dean and Malvern Hills attract walkers as well as those who enjoy touring by car along traffic-free lanes. There is a falconry centre at Newent and gardens at Hergest Croft. Go in late autumn if you want to see a blaze of copper and gold foliage.

Readers' comments: Pleasant comfortable room; excellent staff; food extremely good. One of the nicest holidays in years. Excellent value. Outstanding value; excellent bar meals. Excellent food and service. Highly satisfied. Very good on all points.

Some readers tell me they have stayed at lots of places from *Staying Off the Beaten Track*. I wonder who has stayed at most? A free copy of the next edition awaits the reader who sends me his/her comments on the greatest number!

BUTTONS GREEN FARM
Cockfield, south of Bury St Edmunds, Suffolk, IP30 0JF   Tel: 0284

3 bedrooms (single, double or family) from £12; or much less for 2 nights. Rooms have electric heaters; armchairs; views of country or garden; tea/coffee facilities.
Dinner £6 for 3 courses and coffee, at 6.30pm. Special diets if ordered. Coffee, tea, for a charge. Non-residents not admitted. Drinks can be brought in.
Sitting-room with open fire, TV, books.
Garden and farmland.
Nearest main road A1141 from Lavenham to Bury St Edmunds.
Closed in winter

Behind a big duckpond and masses of roses stands an apricot-coloured house built around 1400, the centre of an 80-acre farm of grain and beet fields. A serious fire a few years ago revealed all sorts of hidden architectural features – mullioned windows and a Tudor fireplace upstairs – all now restored.

In the sitting-room, with large sash windows on two sides, a pale carpet and silky wallpaper make a light background to the antiques and velvet armchairs grouped round a big log fire. In one window is an epiphyllum which annually produces over 80 huge pink blooms. The dining-room has a log-burning stove in the brick inglenook, and leather-seated chairs are drawn up at a big oak table. Here Margaret Slater serves meals with home-grown or home-made produce, her own chutneys and marmalade. Among her most popular starters are egg mayonnaise and home-made pâté. A chicken or other roast may follow and then, for instance, chocolate soufflé or raspberries and cream.

Twisting stairs lead to big beamed bedrooms with sloping floors, which Mrs Slater has furnished attractively with flowery fabrics, pot-plants and good furniture.

The farm is only a few minutes from Lavenham, one of the county's show villages – very beautiful (but, in summer, often very crowded), with a guildhall owned by the National Trust and a spectacular church. Still further south, in beautiful countryside threaded by rivers with old bridges and water-meadows, are such other historic villages as Bures (where St Edmund was crowned King of East Anglia in 855), pretty Kersey, full of colourful half-timbered cottages, and Nayland. Within easy reach are places described elsewhere in this book: Bury St Edmunds, Sudbury, 'Constable country' (Dedham, East Bergholt, Flatford Mill). Made rich by wool, Suffolk farmers of the Middle Ages put their money into building churches for every village, many of almost cathedral-like magnificence.

Just the other side of Lavenham is Brent Eleigh and **Street Farm** (tel: 0787 247 271), its apricot walls half-timbered, its garden well-groomed. Inside are beamed ceilings and good furnishings – big velvet armchairs, and Hepplewhite-style chairs in the dining-room, for instance. Bedrooms are spacious, the L-shaped bathroom huge. Jean Gage serves breakfast only.

Bristol, Avon, BS18 5AH   Tel: 0761 52790

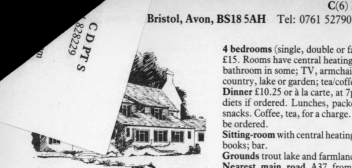

C D PT S
828229

rear view

4 bedrooms (single, double or family) from £15. Rooms have central heating; shower or bathroom in some; TV, armchairs; views of country, lake or garden; tea/coffee facilities. **Dinner** £10.25 or à la carte, at 7pm. Special diets if ordered. Lunches, packed lunches, snacks. Coffee, tea, for a charge. Drinks can be ordered.
Sitting-room with central heating, open fire, books; bar.
Grounds trout lake and farmland.
Nearest main road A37 from Bristol to Wells and Shepton Mallet.

A huge, stone barn in a superb setting was converted a few years ago into an extremely comfortable guest-house, run by John Harris whose parents own the farm on which it stands. It was built three hundred years ago for hay. Now it has a sitting-room with a bar and log fire, and an airy dining-room with windows overlooking the trout lake below, which is shared by swans, ducks and anglers. The conversion has been done with style: a red pantiled roof was put on, lattice windows inserted and panelled doors hung. Above are pleasantly furnished bedrooms, some with lake views and some looking towards the church.

Unexpectedly, Cameley Lodge is often quite full midweek but not at weekends – for Bristol businessmen find it a quiet place in which to confer, where they can offer business guests good fly-fishing afterwards (tuition bookable). Meals are based on local produce served in generous quantities (a whole 2lb trout may be offered as one serving). As a starter there might be prawn-and-apple cocktail or kidneys in brandy, before such a main course as suprême of chicken with a Madeira-and-peach sauce and to follow, a deliciously light coffee gâteau.

This is a very scenic area. The limestone Mendip Hills vary from wild ridges to gently rounded foothills, with drystone walls. Caves and gorges (at Cheddar and Wookey, in particular) add to their interest; and the stone, of course, means villages are as beautiful as many in the Cotswolds. The cathedral city of Wells is the region's greatest jewel; but Bristol now is very well worth visiting – its ancient quays restored, many good restaurants and theatres (the Welsh National Opera Company comes here), fine mediaeval church, and Brunel's SS *Great Britain* to visit. Bath is near, and the scenic Chew Valley.

Readers' comments: Good value.

Two-thirds of the houses in this book have bargain breaks or other discounts on offer, some exclusive to readers. Only a third raise prices at the peak of summer.

Some hotels and even farms offer special Christmas holidays; but, unless otherwise indicated (by the code letter X at top of entry), those in this book will then be closed.

CARNWETHERS

Pelistry Bay, St Mary's, Isles of Scilly, TR21 0NX   Tel: 0720 22415

C S

rear view

10 bedrooms (single, double or family) from £15. Discounts for payment in advance and repeat visits. Rooms have central heating or electric heaters; shower or bathroom; armchairs; views of sea, country or garden; tea/coffee facilities; and TV on request.

Dinner £7 for 4 courses (some choice) and coffee, at 6.30pm. No smoking. Packed lunches. Bedtime hot drinks can be ordered. Non-residents not admitted. Drinks can be ordered.

2 sitting-rooms with central heating, TV, books. Bar lounge opening onto patio.

Garden with heated pool (75°), croquet, putting, pool table, darts, table tennis.

Closed in winter

St Mary's, the principal island in the Scillies, is only three miles long. Even its centre of action, Hugh Town, can hardly be called busy by mainland standards (though it does receive tides of day-visitors during high summer), and so it is easy to find any number of unfrequented coves or beaches within a mere quarter of an hour or so from Hugh Town. Pelistry Bay is one of these – sheltered from wind, calm and unspoilt. Around it are pines and ferns, coastal footpaths and nature trails.

Carnwethers is more than an ordinary guest-house (and a very good one, at that): it is also a centre for marine studies. Its owner is Roy Graham, well known in the island and beyond as an underwater explorer and photographer, and a marine archaeologist – with 30 years in the Navy before he came here. Even non-experts appreciate his library of books on maritime subjects (wrecks, shipping, fish, wildlife, boats) and his immense knowledge of Scillonian history and ecology. His illustrated lectures in St Mary's twice a week should not be missed. He has assembled a number of videos about the islands which he shows to visitors, and can advise on boating or diving.

As to the house itself, this was once a farmhouse, but has been modernized. It is still surrounded by fields. Every room is as neat as a new pin. There is a bar and lengthy list of good-value wines, a heated 30-foot swimming-pool within sight of the sea itself but sheltered by granite walls and flowering shrubs, solarium, sauna, games room (for table tennis, darts, pool, etc.) and croquet lawn.

Meal times fit in with the times of the buses that take visitors into Hugh Town for evening events: not cinemas and night clubs, but slide shows which are usually packed out, concerts and the pubs.

Local produce is much used by Joyce for meals: fish (obviously), new potatoes, free-range eggs, home-grown vegetables and home-made marmalade, for example. A typical meal might comprise soup (not home-made) or fruit juice, roast turkey, and rolypoly pudding or fudge cake. Breakfasts include options like kedgeree and kippers. The dining-room has hanging plants, a stove for cold days and views of the fields with cows, flowers or potatoes in them according to season. Here and in the sitting-room, there are pictures of ships and seascapes. Bedrooms, too, are agreeably decorated; colours are pretty, cupboards have louvred pine doors, and each has at least its own shower.

The main attractions of the Scillies are their unspoilt beauty, mild climate, low rainfall and pure air. Storms are brief, sunny days long. Visitors to St Mary's get about on foot, by bus, and with hired cars or cycles (no cars on the other islands, which are reached by boats that regularly ply to and fro). Of course, the superb scenery and the solitude are the biggest attractions on all the islands; but in St Mary's, the main island, there are other things of interest: prehistoric villages and burial chambers; old fortifications and watch-tower; a clifftop golf course with arguably the most beautiful setting in England; boat-building, pottery and other crafts to watch (or learn); streams and pools, rocks and islets to explore; subtropical flowers growing wild, butterflies, and rare birds that excite the ornithologists. The excellent local museum tells the story of the innumerable wrecks in these waters and of the latest discoveries by underwater archaeologists diving to them. There is the lifeboat station to visit, and weekly races of gigs (a type of rowing-boat peculiar to the Scillies). Penninis Head is infinitely more beautiful than Land's End: just one of the many memorable walks around the varied coastline. Nearly every kind of sea sport, of course; and fish that go straight from sea to saucepan. There is a new heritage/ecology centre with shipwreck museum. Day-trips to each of the other islands are well worth taking. Among these, Tresco is world-famous for its romantic gardens planted with subtropical flowers from every continent; it contains an outdoor museum of ships' figureheads.

There is rarely any rain in summer, and so, all along the wild tracks of the islands, succulents and cacti flourish together with high, blue echiums from New Zealand and the Madeira geranium (magenta in colour, round and bushy). The island is ideal for little ones, as there are safe beaches and lanes; and island children quickly become friends with young visitors. For town children, this is a paradise of wild violets, bumblebees, pennyworts growing on the stone walls and lichens in a dozen colours. Diving, boating and shark fishing can be arranged.

Readers' comments: Happy, friendly atmosphere. Could not ask for more.

Nearby is **Carn Vean** (tel: 0720 22462) in a pleasant setting of lawn and trees. Here Laurel Deason provides inexpensive accommodation and meals, as well as running a tea-garden.

Inclusive terms for dinner, bed-and-breakfast (particularly for a week) can be much lower than those quoted here for these items taken separately. For short-notice bookings you may be able to get a reduction.

No proprietor wants to have a room standing empty. This particularly applies to Sunday nights. Some hotels make a discount if you want only two courses from a three-course menu.

There is no point in turning up with a dog or child in tow if the description does not say these are accepted; nor in expecting a garden, or alcoholic drinks, if these are not indicated.

If you want absolute quiet, avoid any place that takes children or has a bar open to non-residents. Inns sometimes get extensions to their licensing hours for late private parties; and may lack quiet sitting-rooms.

CASTLE HOUSE *New*   **C D PT S X**
23 Castle Street, Chester, Cheshire, CH1 2DS   Tel: 0244 350354

5 bedrooms (single, double or family) from £18. Less for 7 nights and bargain breaks. Most have own shower; TV; tea/coffee facilities; phone; central heating; views of garden. (Washing-machine on request.)
Sitting-room with central heating, open fire, books; bar.
Small garden
Nearest main roads A41, A51, A55.

Right in the middle of the city but in a quiet by-road, this interesting house has a breakfast-room which dates from 1540 behind an 18th-century frontage and staircase. The arms of Elizabeth I (with English lion and Welsh dragon) are over the fireplace.

It is both the Marls' own home and a guest-house with elegant bedrooms that are exceptionally well furnished and equipped. Bed-and-breakfast only, for Chester has so many good restaurants; but visitors are welcome to use the kitchen. Newspapers and local phone calls are free – as are evening refreshments: Cheshire cheese with a help-yourself drink from a small bar. Coyle Marl, a local business-man, is an enthusiast for Chester and loves to tell visitors about its lesser-known charms.

The city is, of course, of outstanding interest – second only to Bath and York in what there is to see. It is surrounded by ancient walls of red sandstone, just outside of which is a large Roman amphitheatre (fresh Roman and even older remains are constantly coming to light, the smaller artefacts displayed in the Grosvenor Museum). You can walk all round the top of the ramparts, a 2-mile trek. The most unique feature, however, is The Rows: here steps from street level lead up to balustraded galleries overhanging the pavements, serving a second level of small shops above the ones below. Many of the half-timbered houses have particularly fine carvings. Chester's cathedral of red stone dates back to the 14th century; its zoo is one of Britain's best.

From Chester many visitors head for Wales; but there is a nearby part of Cheshire which should not be ignored – the Wirral. This thumb of land is sandwiched between two estuaries: the Mersey on its industrial side, the Dee on its other, very scenic side – facing Wales. The climate here is so mild that spring comes earlier than in some southern counties, which is why (at Ness) there are such beautiful botanic gardens. Visit little Parkgate for shrimps, sea-birds and Nelson connections; the country park for tranquillity and views; the Victorian fort on a rock at the mouth of the Mersey; the Lady Lever art gallery, containing some of the world's most famous paintings; Port Sunlight – one of the first garden-cities; Ellesmere Port for the canal boat museum – all these are on the Wirral, as is Wallasey, a popular seaside resort with sand dunes, beaches and piers.

For explanation of code letters (**C, D, H, PT, S, S-C, X**) **see page xxviii.**

CATHEDRAL GATE HOTEL   *New*   C PT X
36 Burgate, Canterbury, Kent, CT1 2HA   Tel: 0227 464381

25 bedrooms (single, double or family) from £16. Some have own bath/shower; TV; tea/coffee facilities; central heating; views of cathedral. (Washing-machine on request.)
Dinner £7.50 for 3 courses (with choices) and coffee, at 7–10pm. Non-residents not admitted. Vegetarian or special diets if ordered. Packed lunches, snacks. Drinks can be ordered.
3 sitting-rooms with central heating, TV (in one); bar. No smoking (in one).
Nearest main road M2/A2 from Canterbury to London.

The cathedral has a great, sculpted, mediaeval gateway. Tucked beside it is a row of shops and restaurants, above part of which is this upstairs guest-house (which has direct access to the cathedral precincts).

Even in Saxon times there was some kind of hospice here; and when the martyrdom of Thomas Becket in 1170 began to bring pilgrims to Canterbury in their thousands, it was in these beamy rooms that many of them stayed.

The spacious bedrooms (and small residents' sitting-rooms) are reached via a maze of narrow corridors and creaking stairways which twist this way and that. All are quiet (for Burgate is now restricted to pedestrians only); and some at the top have superlative views across the cathedral precincts to the great tower and south transept – floodlit at night.

The small hotel was recently taken over by Caroline Jubber and her husband who have greatly improved the bedrooms – some of them reached via a rooftop walkway – while retaining ancient beams, leaded casements and bow windows. There are now three small sitting-rooms, too, which include a bar and a television room. Breakfast (continental, unless you pay extra) is brought to you in one of these or in your bedroom. Formal dinner is not provided because there are so many restaurants close by; but at any hour you can order meals such as spaghetti bolognese or chicken Kiev, or full afternoon teas. Bedrooms are very well equipped and some even have mini-bars. Many look across undulating old roofs and red chimney-pots where chattering starlings perch. The only inconvenience is that cars have to be parked a few minutes' walk away.

It is, of course, the cathedral which brings most visitors to Canterbury: one of Britain's finest and most colourful, with many historical associations. It is the site of Becket's martyrdom (commemorated in some of the finest stained glass in the world), houses the splendid tomb of the Black Prince, and much more.

The ancient walled city still has many surviving mediaeval and Tudor buildings, the beautiful River Stour, old churches and inns, Roman remains, a very good theatre, and lovely shops in its small lanes. It is in the middle of some of Kent's finest countryside, with a coast of great variety quite near (cliffs, sands or shingle; resorts, fishing harbours or historic ports). It would be very easy to spend a fortnight here without discovering all there is to see in one of England's most beautiful and most historic counties.

Canterbury is a useful place to stay before or after a ferry-crossing to the continent – or as a base from which to explore the historic south Kent coast, the Cinque Ports, Dover Castle and Dover's famous Roman 'Painted House' or the Kent countryside, the garden of England.

CAVENDISH HOUSE

Eastmount Road, Shanklin, Isle of Wight, PO37 6DN   Tel: 0983 862460

3 bedrooms (double) from £13.50. Less for 7 nights or bargain breaks. Rooms have central heating; shower or bathroom; TV, armchairs; tea/coffee facilities.
Nearest main road From Shanklin to Ryde and Newport.

Although this resort is full of hotels, I had difficulty in finding any with really attractive rooms. Lesley Peters' home is an exception. She has furnished the large Victorian rooms with style – Laura Ashley fabrics and well-chosen colour schemes complementing good antiques. She has made the most of handsome architectural features (for instance, picking out in blue the plasterwork vine of one ceiling and filling an old tiled fireplace with pot-plants). Every room has a table and chairs for breakfast, as there is no dining-room. For dinner, Lesley recommends The Cottage or Small's, a French brasserie; or you can take the nearby lift to the foot of the cliff and **Osborne House Hotel** where, after an excellent help-yourself buffet, prepared by Mike Hogarth, you can sit on the flowery, grass-enclosed verandah facing the sea. Bedrooms available, but hardly 'off the beaten track'.

Shanklin has sandy beaches and a beautiful chine (ravine); the picturesque village of Godshill and its smithy lie inland. In many parts of the island, there are plenty of well-marked footpaths for walkers; and sights to see are described under other entries of which the most popular are Queen Victoria's Osborne House, Carisbrooke Castle, Blackgang Chine, Alum Bay, Barton Vineyard and Arreton Manor.

Although Shanklin itself gets uncomfortably busy in high summer, this house is well away from all the bustle.

Other attractions of the Isle of Wight are described elsewhere.

In holiday areas, travel on any day other than a summer Saturday if you can. Make ferry, Motorail or coach/train reservations well in advance if travelling at such periods.

It's best to stay at least 2–3 days: you cannot possibly appreciate an area if you only stay overnight (prices per night are often less, too, if you stay on). The vouchers on page **ii** are usable for 3-night stays.

If you have not arrived by, perhaps, 6pm your room may be let to someone else – unless you telephone to say you are on your way.

CHAPEL HOUSE

C PT

Friar's Gate, Atherstone, north of Coventry, Warwickshire, CV9 1EY
Tel: 0827 718949

9 bedrooms (single, double or family) from £17.50. Rooms have central heating; shower or bathroom; TV, phone, armchairs; views of garden. Clothes-washing facilities.
Dinner £7.50 for 3 courses and coffee, at 7pm. Vegetarian or special diets if ordered. Lunches, packed lunches, snacks. Coffee, tea, for a charge. Drinks can be ordered.
Sitting-room with central heating and open fire, books and a bar.
Walled gardens
Nearest main road A5 from Dunstable to Wales.

Tucked away in a flowery corner just off the Market Square is hidden an elegant 18th-century house, now once again equally elegantly furnished by Pat and David Roberts, both highly expert cooks (David used to teach in a catering college).

It was previously the dower house of Atherstone Hall, home of Selina Bracebridge who in the 1840s was the only friend of young Florence Nightingale to encourage her ambition to become a nurse. The Bracebridges accompanied Florence to the Crimea in 1854 and were her most loyal assistants.

This is why Florence's head ornaments the pelmet in the dining-room. It is a handsome room where the marble fireplace contrasts with walls covered in cocoa hessian, the long curtains are of magnolia chintz and the shield-back chairs are upholstered in velvet. Chapel House is renowned for its gourmet meals, particularly at weekends (the Prince and Princess of Wales were lunched here when attending a civic function at Atherstone).

Through a small conservatory, hung with fuchsias, one reaches a very pretty enclosed garden with tables on the lawn. This is one of three gardens around the house. Another has a high, curved wall behind which lay the one-time friary where Henry VII prayed before he defeated Richard III at the Battle of Bosworth.

The sitting-room (pine-panelled, with an attractive colour scheme of watermelon pink, pale grey and moss green) lies beyond a stone-flagged hall, from which the staircase rises to equally attractive bedrooms – I particularly liked one with a window seat overlooking the walled garden, but even those on the second floor – under the eaves, furnished in cottage style – are very pretty.

The inclusive terms for residents allow for a 3-course meal (such as potted meat made from rabbit, pork and chicken liver; stuffed pork; chocolate, hazelnut and brandy mousse), with coffee. Five-course à la carte choice on certain evenings.

Atherstone, a pleasant town on the A5 (which is often an agreeable alternative to using the M1 as a way to get from London to the Midlands), is in the northern part of Warwickshire. There is wooded countryside, and from here you can visit Sutton Coldfield's 2000-acre natural park. Around are woods, valleys, heather moors, lakes, bird reserves and a championship golf course. The town itself has 17th-century stone houses. Mediaeval Maxstoke Castle and nearby Coleshill; Arbury Hall (near which George Eliot was born); Birmingham's art gallery (strong on pre-Raphaelites) and outstanding botanical gardens; Tamworth for its castle; Lichfield for its 3-spired cathedral and Samuel Johnson's birthplace.

Readers' comments: Beautifully furnished, food superb.

52

CHASE LODGE

C D PT X

Park Road, Hampton Wick, Surrey, KT1 4 AS   Tel: 01-943 1862

6 bedrooms (double or family) from £15. Less for 3 nights and bargain breaks. Some have own bath/shower; all have TV; tea/coffee facilities; central heating. (Washing-machine on request.)
Small garden
Nearest main road A3 from London to Portsmouth.

This is a very handy place at which to stay in order to explore the 'royal' stretch of the Thames Valley (monarchs chose nearby Richmond, Hampton Court, Kew and Windsor for their palaces). It is only half an hour from London in one direction and from Heathrow Airport in the other.

Park Road is in a quiet conservation area, a street of pretty little Victorian villas with cottage-gardens, yet only a minute or two from a railway station, buses and the excellent shops and market of Kingston.

Chase Lodge has been redecorated with interesting pieces of Victorian furniture and decorative trifles in its sitting-room and elsewhere (even a toilet has a tented ceiling of pleated silk). There are African violets and other pot-plants in the bedrooms; and attractive quilted spreads are on some of the beds.

Only breakfast is served as a rule, but there are local restaurants and take-aways. (Denise Dove encourages visitors to use the breakfast-room for snacks.)

At the back of the house is a tiny, sun-trapping patio with a few seats among the petunias and nasturtiums. One bedroom has a tented scarlet-and-green ceiling and a mural of a crusader castle in its bathroom. Another, a four-poster with lace.

I was greatly impressed by Mrs Dove's attention to detail and the immense trouble she takes. Not many far more costly hotels provide room service free, fresh towels and soap daily, fridges with milk and soft drinks in every room.

There is an enormous amount to see and do in the neighbourhood: river trips from nearby Kingston Bridge, walks among the deer and chestnut trees of Bushey Park or along the towpaths, Kew Gardens and Palace, Hampton Court – now with son-et-lumière shows at night – and its gardens (with maze), horse-racing, tennis at Wimbledon, rugby at Twickenham, and any number of regattas and festivals in summer. Richmond deserves at least a day to itself, to explore the byways and curio shops off the green, the stunning river view from the top of the hill, and the 3000 acres of Richmond Park. Windsor has its great castle, royal steam-rail show and safari park (Eton College is close by). There are Georgian villages, and Georgian or earlier mansions in fine grounds (Ham House, Orleans House, Marble Hill, Syon Park, Chiswick House, Hogarth's house and Osterley Park).

A little further west is Staines and at **Thames Side**, Penton Road (tel: 0784 52294), Geraldine Lewin not only provides bed-and-breakfast but also runs a booking service for other private houses nearby: several with gardens by the Thames; some are historic houses and others (including hers) modern; a few provide dinner. If you explain your tastes and needs to her, she will select a house suited to you. In her own house, the guest-room – with shower and toilet – is on the ground floor. Geraldine is a talkative lady and happy to draw every-one into the family's many activities.

(Do not expect *total* quiet in this part of the county. There is the sound of aircraft using Heathrow.)

CHEDGRAVE COTTAGE · C PT S

11 Langley Road, Chedgrave, south-east of Norwich, NR14 6HD
Tel: 0508 28444

2 bedrooms (double) from £11. Less for 7 nights and bargain breaks. Tea/coffee facilities; central heating; views of garden. No smoking. (Washing-machine on request.)
Dinner £5.50 for 4 courses and coffee, at 6.30–7pm. Non-residents not admitted. Vegetarian or special diets if ordered. Lunches, packed lunches, snacks. Tea, coffee, free. Drinks can be brought in.
Sitting-room with central heating, open fire, TV, books.
Small garden
Nearest main road A146 from Norwich to Lowestoft.

Anne Cornwall has furnished her part-Tudor and part 18th-century country cottage most attractively, in simple country style. Previously she provided only breakfast but now does dinners too (if ordered in advance), comprising such menus as: melon, beef Bourguignonne (with fresh local vegetables), raspberry or kiwi-fruit pavlova, and cheese.

The Tudor dining-room has its original pamment (brick) floor, pine furniture, Laura Ashley fabrics and wallpaper, and – like other rooms – many of the Cornwalls' collection of watercolours and prints, both Victorian and modern. By contrast, the sitting-room is Georgian in style and oil-paintings hang on the walls. Sofa and armchairs are grouped around an open fire where logs crackle on chilly evenings.

Bedrooms are pretty (and these too are furnished with antiques): one is pink and flowery and the other, with view of stables and the attractive garden, has brown and beige sprigged fabrics. The bathroom's blue-and-white shell patterned theme is striking.

Norfolk has a tremendous amount to see apart from the Broads, and Chedgrave is in the middle of it all. There are at least 8 famous mansions (the gardens at Bressingham and Somerleyton Hall are very good), 5 wildlife parks and 3 steam railways or museums. There's a museum of rural life, the famous shrines at Walsingham, windmills and watermills, boat trips, lavender fields, an otter reserve and above all the scenery of countryside and unspoilt coast.

When to go? Seaside resorts or other places suitable for children will be at their busiest (and dearest) in July–August and during half-term holidays (especially, in late May, which is also a bank holiday period). Other peak periods are, of course, Easter, Christmas, New Year and the bank holiday in late August. (The bank holiday in early May is not usually a peak, because it comes rather soon after Easter, but much depends on the weather.) There are local peaks, too (the Gold Cup races at Cheltenham or the regatta at Henley, for instance, are apt to fill hotels for miles around), and local troughs (Brighton, a conference centre, is least busy in high summer). You won't get much personal attention when hotels are full to bursting.

CHERRYBROOK

Two Bridges, Devon, PL20 6SP Tel: 0822 88260   **C D S**

7 bedrooms (single, double or family) from £17.50. Less for 3 nights. Prices go up from Easter. Rooms have central heating; own bathroom; armchairs; views of country or garden; tea/coffee facilities.

Dinner £8 for 4 courses and coffee, at 7.30pm. Special diets if ordered. Packed lunches, snacks. Coffee, tea for a charge. Drinks can be ordered.

Sitting-room with central heating, open fire, books; bar.

Extensive grounds

Nearest main road A38 from Exeter to Plymouth.

High up and right in the middle of Dartmoor, this little hotel is full of character. It was built by a friend of the Prince Regent when he acquired farming rights on the moor, and many of the old features are still to be seen – low-beamed ceilings and thick stone walls (now painted white). What was once a cowshed is now a sitting-room, with rugs on floors made of polished slate. On the walls. John Reynolds has hung old peat-digging tools and a pair of Canadian snow shoes (still awaiting sufficient snow to make them useful). There is a log stove and, tucked away at one end, a small bar. Pewter mugs hang from a beam; Susan's spinning-wheel stands ready for use.

Bedrooms are pleasantly furnished, with leafy views and no sound louder than the baaing of sheep. Every room is immaculate, and paintwork throughout is pristine. I particularly appreciated the huge armchairs facing the big windows of bedroom no. 2.

This remote house pumps its own pure spring water and has no TV. Truly 'away from it all'!

There are always choices at each course of dinner, from which one might perhaps choose mushroom soup, chicken casseroled in cider, chocolate sponge and then cheese. Vegetables and eggs are home-produced.

As to sightseeing, apart from the moor itself (a National Park) and all its villages, National Trust houses and gardens, nature reserves and guided walks (of one to six hours), it is possible to visit both north and south coasts of Devon as well as the historic cities of Plymouth and Exeter. Occasionally special holidays are offered with walks laid on, or visits to National Trust houses, of which there are a great many in this region.

Readers' comments: Comfortable and well fed. Wonderful host and hostess. Warm, friendly; excellent food. Decor, food and friendly atmosphere exceptional. Peace and tranquillity with exceptional views.

For explanation of code letters (**C, D, H, PT, S, S-C, X**) **see page xxviii.**

Families which pick establishments with plenty of games, swimming-pool, animals, etc., or that are near free museums, parks and walks, can save a lot on keeping youngsters entertained.

CHIMNEYS

C(4) PT

Chideock, west of Bridport, Dorset, DT6 6JH   Tel: 029789 368

5 bedrooms (double or family) from £12.50. Less for 3 nights. Rooms have central heating or electric heaters; views of country or garden; tea/coffee facilities. Continental breakfast in bed is available. Some rooms have shower. Laundering facilities available. No smoking.

Dinner £7.75–£9.75 for 4 courses and coffee with liqueur, at 7.30pm (5 days a week). Special diets if ordered. Coffee, tea, for a charge. Non-residents by prior arrangement. Drinks can be ordered. No smoking.

Sitting-room with central heating, log fire, TV and video, books; bar.

Garden

Nearest main road A35 from Dorchester to Exeter. Car washing and vacuuming facilities free.

This pretty thatched cottage in its old-fashioned garden is on the road between Georgian Bridport and the historic town of Lyme Regis. Built in the 17th century, the guest-house has been furnished in keeping with its age. The bedrooms are pretty (the ones at the back are quiet, front ones are double-glazed), the sitting-room and bar beamed and with log fires in winter. Two rooms have four-posters, and several are beamed.

For dinner you might get a home-made soup, pork chop in orange sauce, ice cream made with Cointreau, cheese, Rombouts coffee (and free liqueur), on a table with lace cloth, cut glass and Royal Worcester china. For breakfast, try the coddled eggs or one of many other imaginative options.

Mr and Mrs Hardy lend visitors Ordnance Survey maps and give advice. For example, they can tell you where to find fossils easily plucked from the Blue Lias clay (they lend fossil-hunting hammers), or where the best walks are on clifftops or through valleys – and if you want a lift back at the end of a walk, they are willing to come and fetch you in their car. They also show a film of Dorset.

Chideock itself is a very pretty village of thatched cottages, in a fold of the west Dorset hills designated an 'area of outstanding natural beauty'. The sea is close and much of the coastline hereabouts belongs to the National Trust. Within a short distance are Lyme Regis, Charmouth, Abbotsbury (swannery and subtropical gardens), Chesil Beach, Portland and Weymouth – all on the coast. Among the hills and vales, the farmlands and streams, are Sherborne (castle and abbey), Parnham House and Cricket St Thomas, Cerne Abbas (abbey and the giant cut in the chalk hills nearly two thousand years ago) and Beaminster (Georgian houses). There are fine gardens at Forde Abbey and Clapton Court.

Readers' comments: Beautifully appointed house, historic without detracting from 20th-century comforts, comfortable, friendly, good food. Very helpful and pleasant, well prepared food but not too exotic. Charming house and owners. A delight; meal was exceptionally good value, owners have warmth and humour. Comfortable room, excellent meals, many little extra touches.

If you want your hosts to post you things you have accidentally left behind, send them the cost of postage. (The trouble they take is free.)

CHISWICK HOUSE *New*   C

Meldreth, north of Royston, Hertfordshire, SG8 6LZ   Tel: 0763 60242

4 bedrooms (single, double or family) from £13.50. All have own shower; TV; tea/coffee facilities; central heating; views of garden. No smoking. (Washing-machine on request.)

Sitting-room with central heating, open fire, TV, books.

Small garden

Nearest main road A10 from Cambridge to London.

Closed in December and January

Elbourns have lived in this house for a century. When the latest generation, John and Bernice, set about renovating it, they uncovered beams with drawings and lettering from the 14th and 15th centuries. It originally had no chimney or fireplaces: these 'mod cons' came in during Tudor times. Over one fireplace is the coat-of-arms of James I: it is believed he used the house as a hunting lodge (he had a palace at nearby Royston, of which fragments still remain), and the panelling in the dining-room dates from his reign.

The house, although modernized, still has a very historic look, with old oak beams, polished woodwork and flowers in every room. Carved chairs surround a refectory table, there is a Knole sofa, and brass-studded leather chairs. One of the beamy bedrooms opens onto the garden. Bed-and-breakfast only: visitors dine at the Swan (Fowlmere), Royal Oak (Barrington) or Red Lion (Grantchester – immortalized in Rupert Brooke's poem).

Many people stay here as a base from which to visit Cambridge, but north Hertfordshire is itself worth exploring. Royston, a town of narrow streets and old inns, has a strange man-made cave beneath its streets with carvings of the Crucifixion. Baldock, with many 18th-century houses, is distinguished by a main street lined with trees and grassy banks. Ashwell's Roman origins are shown in its unusually spacious planning, and the traces of a Roman road can still be seen nearby; there are fine 17th-century houses with decorative plasterwork (pargetting) and ash trees still grow around the spring which gave it its name. (South Hertfordshire has been described elsewhere.)

From Meldreth it is no distance to the borders of three other counties – Cambridgeshire (Cambridge itself, Newmarket of racing fame, and St Neots – its market square flanked by the river Great Ouse and its church adorned with wonderful carvings; Gog Magog hills for a view of the university spires; stately Wimpole Hall); Essex (mediaeval Saffron Walden and further south the picturesque Rodings – eight waterside villages, the great 17th-century house of Audley End, much-photographed Wendens Ambo and Finchingfield, the three historic Bardfield villages); and Bedfordshire (Bedford itself, Whipsnade Zoo park, stately homes such as Luton Hoo, Ampthill's park, Houghton House ruins – Bunyan's 'House Beautiful', the water gardens of Wrest Park, Sandy's RSPB reserve, historic aircraft at Biggleswade). Altogether, this is an area of great variety and yet one which many tourists merely pass through on their way to more famous places.

Readers' comments: Unassuming, hospitable hostess; homely, comfortable rooms. How relaxed we felt!

CHITHURST FARM

Chithurst Lane, Smallfield, Horley, north of Gatwick, Surrey, RH6 9JU
Tel: 034284 2487

3 bedrooms (single, double or family) from £11. Much less for 2 nights. Rooms have electric heaters; armchairs; views of country or garden. Coffee, tea, snacks, for a charge. Non-smokers preferred.
Sitting-room with central heating, open fire, TV, books.
Garden and farmland.
Nearest main road A264 from East Grinstead to Crawley.
Closed in December and January

Despite being so near Gatwick (and even London is only 35 minutes from the nearest rail station), this farm seems truly remote, reached by a long and winding lane. Built in the 16th century, it has tile-hung walls of mellow red brick against which the japonica flowers in spring.

Inside are low beams and a twisting staircase leading to simple but spacious bedrooms. These have double-glazing so that the sound of aircraft (numerous only during the day in summer) is not disturbing, with air-conditioners providing fresh air. In the visitors' sitting/dining-room, armchairs and a rocking-chair are grouped around a huge inglenook fireplace (with log stove), its original spit-rack still in place.

Visitors are welcome to watch cows being milked, and to buy home-made jams. This is a good area for walking in the North Downs. There are several stately homes, gardens (such as Ardingly and Wakehurst), and bird or wildlife parks nearby. Even Brighton in one direction, and the Kentish Weald in the other, are soon reached. Nearby, several old towns like Horsham and Dorking are worth exploring. Churchill's house (Chartwell), the Bluebell steam railway, Hever Castle, Box Hill, Tunbridge Wells and Ashdown Forest are all very popular as are the many pick-your-own fruit farms.

Some people stay at the farm before flying from Gatwick, and if necessary Mrs Tucker will leave early breakfasts ready. A nearby garage will house your car, with free transport (24 hours a day) to and from the airport – where parking would cost you far more.

Mrs Tucker does not provide evening meals, but has a list of recommended local restaurants etc. which do, such as the Plough Inn at Smallfield. Chithurst Farm is remarkably good value for this area.

Readers' comments: Charming. Pleasant attention.

Prices are the minimum *per person* in a double room at the beginning of the year.

Book well ahead: many of these houses have few rooms. Do not expect dinner if you have not booked it.

CHURCH FARM *New*　　　　　　　　　　　　　　**C D PT X**

41 High Street, Roxton, north-east of Bedford, Bedfordshire, MK44 3EB
Tel: 0234 870234

2 bedrooms (double or family) from £12. Tea/coffee facilities; central heating; views of garden. (Washing-machine on request.)
Sitting-room with central heating, open fire, TV, books.
Large garden
Nearest main road A428 from Bedford to Roxton.

It is a surprise to find such a peaceful village (a thatched church as well as thatched cottages) so close to the busy Great North Road, the A1, and in it this house – part 16th- and part 18th-century. One bedroom has a royal coat-of-arms carved in the wall, dating from Stuart times.

A beautiful breakfast room has a Chippendale-style table and a sideboard with its original brass rails. Bedrooms in the guest wing are large (one has a particularly handsome wardrobe); all rooms are furnished with an informal mixture of family antiques. There is a pleasant sitting-room in shades of cream and brown with a log fire. (For dinner, Janet Must recommends restaurants in either St Neots or Bedford, both a few miles away, or else local village inns.)

Visitors who stay here are often surprised to discover Bedfordshire's little-publicized charms, particularly its pretty villages, many of which are sited on wandering streams. Popular outings include not only Bedford (with the John Bunyan museum, the art collection in the Cecil Higgins gallery, a church with carved angels in the roof and pretty riverside lawns) and Cambridge, but Shuttle-worth's historic aircraft collection, the Swiss Garden, stately homes (such as Luton Hoo, Woburn and Hinwick House), Grafham Water and Olney (for its antique shops and boutiques). Sandy has the RSPB's headquarters and bird reserve, Huntingdon its Cromwell associations. In 15 towns or villages of Bedford-shire there are antique shops; there are also a number of pick-your-own fruit farms.

A little further north is **Manor Farm-house**, Swineshead (tel: 0234 708126), with an exceptionally lovely garden and interior. Diana Marlow has a particular talent for decoration. She has used pink sprigged fabrics from Laura Ashley together with woven cane bedheads, or mulberry-and-white or blue-and-white colour schemes, in each bedroom to create a light effect. The luxurious bathroom is in raspberry. All this com-plements the 400-year-old house admirably, while downstairs there are a brick-floored hall (with elm staircase) and two sitting-rooms, in one of which is an inglenook. Beyond a brick patio with deep well is a landscaped garden

and Diana's chickens, geese, guinea-fowl and pony. Diana caters for bed-and-breakfast only; visitors usually dine at the Côte d'Or in Kimbolton (which has a castle) or the Fox & Hounds Inn in Riseley.

CHURCH FARMHOUSE   *New*   **C PT**
3 Main Street, East Ayton, west of Scarborough, North Yorkshire,
YO13 9HL   Tel: 0723 862102

4 bedrooms (single, double or family) from £14. Tea/coffee facilities; central heating; views of country or garden; TV (extra). No smoking. (Washing-machine on request)
Dinner £10 for 3 courses (with choices) and coffee, at 7pm. Non-residents not admitted. Vegetarian or special diets if ordered. Lunches, packed lunches, snacks. Tea, coffee, extra. Wine can be ordered.
2 sitting-rooms with central heating, open fire, TV, books, record-player.
Small garden
Nearest main road A170 from Thirsk to Scarborough.

This 18th-century farmhouse is not in the countryside but in the middle of a picturesque village. Although the house is on the road to Scarborough, rooms at the back are quiet and all of them have character. In the thick-walled pink sitting-room, there is a log fire on the brick hearth, pink and green velvet armchairs surround this, and 'country Chippendale' chairs are at the dining-table. A second sitting-room has an unusual ceiling of wood boards. There is a flowery courtyard at the back, with pool and fountain; and a landscaped garden. Another stone outbuilding houses a games room.

With the help of some young part-timers from the village, Sally Chamberlain produces excellent home-cooked dinners and sometimes bakes her own bread. Said one visitor: 'The pudding trolley fairly groans'. Cakes and tea are free on arrival. Sometimes she serves mushroom vol-au-vents as a starter or hot, spiced grapefruit as an alternative to home-made soups. The main course could be an 8-oz steak, fish straight from nearby Filey, pork in orange sauce, or lasagne accompanied by garlic bread. Popular puddings include profiteroles, Bakewell tart, strawberry mousse and a gâteau with oranges, ginger and brandy in it. Sally likes children and encourages them to join in with the cooking if they enjoy this.

East Ayton is well placed to visit both the superb Yorkshire coast, where safe sandy beaches alternate with towering cliffs, and the North Yorkshire moors (national park). There are excellent walks by the River Derwent and in lovely Forge Valley. Within an hour's drive is a choice of beaches (at Redcar, Sandsend and Whitby, for instance, as well as at nearby Scarborough); abbeys at Rosedale and Rievaulx; castles at Helmsley and Pickering; Flamingoland zoo park; and great Castle Howard. There is a steam railway right across the moors. Theatres and other entertainments are available at Scarborough which is also a good shopping centre.

Roads southward go to Flamborough, a great chalk headland the sheer cliffs of which accommodate thousands of seabirds; on the way, one passes 18th-century Sewerby Hall, and the road goes through the middle of a prehistoric promontory fort. The seaside resort of Bridlington is near here (sands, harbour and a notable priory church).

Readers' comments: Comfortable and well furnished, excellent cooking. A splendid, comfortable bedroom. Nothing was too much trouble for Mrs Chamberlain. Delighted. Food fantastic; delicious.

CHURCH HOUSE

Grittleton, north of Chippenham, Wiltshire, SN14 6AP   Tel: 0249 782562

C(12) **X**

4 bedrooms (single, double or family) from £16. Less for 8 nights or winter bargain breaks. Rooms have central heating; own bathroom; TV with remote control, armchairs; views of country or garden; tea/coffee facilities.

Dinner £10 for 4 courses, wine and coffee, at 8pm. Vegetarian or special diets if ordered. Lunches, packed lunches, snacks. Coffee, tea, for a charge. Drinks can be brought in.

2 sitting-rooms with central heating, open fire, TV, books, indoor games (including indoor boules, table skittles), piano, record-player. Sun-bed.

Garden with croquet, trampoline, swimming-pool (80°).

Nearest main road M4.

This little-known but very beautiful village lies just off the M4 midway between London and Wales: a cluster of elegant houses, a great Tudor mansion and church, all built from golden Cotswold limestone.

Church House began life in 1740 as a huge rectory, which it took six servants to run. Around it are lawns with immense copper beeches (floodlit at night), an orchard, fields of sheep and a swimming-pool, well heated in summer – as well as a walled vegetable and fruit garden which provides organic produce for the kitchen, where Anna Moore produces imaginative meals if these are ordered in advance. A typical menu might comprise sorrel soup, chicken in a creamy apricot-and-curry mayonnaise, a tart of fresh peaches, English cheeses, fruit and wine (included in the price). Anna can also cater for special dietary needs.

She and her family treat all visitors as house guests. If you want to meet Grittleton people, she will invite some to dinner – a local historian, for example – and she often escorts overseas visitors on sightseeing tours. Some she takes to the Royal Shakespeare Theatre (Stratford is 1½ hours away), with a champagne picnic supper on the banks of the Avon afterwards. The Moores are a musical family, and occasionally arrange music evenings – there is one huge room with a grand piano used for this purpose. Watching polo can be arranged.

The house has handsome and finely proportioned rooms. In the yellow sitting-room (which has an immense bay window overlooking the garden) are antique furniture, interesting paintings and a large log stove. The dining-room is equally handsome: raspberry walls, an Adam fireplace of inlaid marble and, on the long mahogany table, silver candelabra and Victorian Spode Copeland china. The most impressive architectural feature is the graceful staircase that curves its way up to the second floor, where the guest rooms are (and also a kitchen for making tea etc. at any hour). These bedrooms are furnished with antiques.

There is an immense amount to see and do in the neighbourhood. Close by is Badminton (celebrated for the annual horse-trials, attended by the royal family); Bath is only 12 miles away; and the many historic (and prehistoric sites of Wiltshire, such as Avebury, are all around. Both the west country and the Cotswolds are accessible from Grittleton. Malmesbury Abbey, Castle Combe, Westonbirt Arboretum and the gardens at Bowood, Broadleaze and Sheldon Manor are favourite sights. Antique shops abound (Swindon has monthly sales) and so do pick-your-own fruit farms.

THE CITADEL
Weston-under-Redcastle, north of Shrewsbury, Shropshire, SY4 5JY
Tel: 063084 204

3 bedrooms (double or family) from £18. Less for 3 nights. All have own bath/shower; central heating; views of country or garden. (Washing-machine on request.)
Dinner £10 for 3 courses (with choices) and coffee, at 7.30pm. Non-residents not admitted. Vegetarian or special diets if ordered. Packed lunches. Tea, coffee, free. Drinks can be brought in.
Sitting-room with central heating, open fire, TV, books, piano.
Large garden
Nearest main road A49 from Shrewsbury to Whitchurch.
Closed from November–March

The castellated turrets of this unusual red sandstone mansion have never known a shot fired in battle. Erected in 1820 when the fashion for mock-Gothic architecture was at its peak, it was built as the dower house for Lady Jane Hill – the Hills lived in nearby Hawkstone Hall.

The interior is equally striking: some rooms – including one guest bedroom – are round, windows are deep-set, and ceilings are particularly decorative. From the cobbled terrace there are views of the Welsh hills and of Hawkstone Park (now a golf course). Among its trees are follies (a tower and an obelisk) and caves.

One enters through a round hall with an inlaid octagonal table; the ceiling has decorative ribs and bosses. In the celadon-green dining-room the coffered ceiling is embellished with plasterwork vines. There is a sitting-room (chocolate and white) which houses a grand piano; as well as a billiard room with terracotta ceiling. An unusual stone staircase leads up to the turret bedrooms; one of the bathrooms is of Edwardian splendour.

Sylvia Griffiths serves such dinners as cheese and asparagus flan to start with, jugged pheasant and chocolate roulade.

Apart from the scenery of one of England's loveliest and most peaceful counties, the greatest attraction of the area is historic Shrewsbury – perched on a hill almost islanded by a great loop of the River Severn. It deserves repeated visits to explore twisting lanes (with such curious names as Dogpole, Shoplatch or Coffeehouse Passage), the castle, the main square with flower-baskets hung around an open-pillared market hall, and all the exceptionally decorative black-and-white houses with carved figures of warriors and other characters. Wealthy wool-merchants built impressive homes here, and helped to enrich the colourful church with stained glass and carved angels. Among the zigzag alleys are craft and curio shops.

The house of Clive of India is open as one of Shrewsbury's many museums (a good china collection); and between the town walls and the river are the Quarry Gardens. Percy Thrower designed these.

Other places of interest in north Shropshire include Georgian Ellesmere and its surrounding lakes (seven of them); the little market town of Wem; the curiously named Ruyton-XI-Towns (11 small hamlets decided to unite in 1301, resulting in a main street over a mile long); Hodnet, particularly rich in black-and-white houses and with fine gardens around Hodnet Hall; Market Drayton, where Clive was born and where canal cruises are now popular; and Oswestry – castle and historic houses.

CLANDON MANOR FARM

C(12) PT

Back Lane, East Clandon, east of Guildford, Surrey, GU4 7SA
Tel: 0483 222357 and 222765

3 bedrooms (twin or family) from £9.50. Rooms have central heating; TV; views of farmland or garden.
Small sitting-room with central heating, TV, books.
Nearest main road A246 from Leatherhead to Guildford.

When financial disaster struck Sir Freddie Laker, this immaculately kept farm was one of the properties he had to sell. Its purchaser, surprisingly, was Sally Grahame, who hitherto had led a typically Kensington life as an interior designer. But inside Sally the townee there was clearly a country-girl struggling to get out, and she took to this life like one of her newly-acquired ducks to water.

On the farm are a hundred cattle; innumerable pigs, free-range chickens, geese, Khaki Campbell ducks and rabbits; and fifty horses. The horses include some pale mink-coloured Norwegian Fiords, rare in this country, with manes of black-and-white – velvety to stroke, gentle and at their superb best when pulling the maroon Victorian landau which Sally hires out for weddings and suchlike, complete with green-uniformed coachman and groom. Riding lessons are available.

The black-and-white beamed cottage which contains guests' bedrooms (simply furnished and without washbasins), one downstairs, is surrounded by lawn, farmyard and flint barns hung with baskets of geraniums and often crammed with hay, oats or barley. Mrs Haines, wife of Sally's farm manager, comes in to cook breakfast. For other meals, most visitors go to the Queen's Head opposite.

East Clandon, itself a very lovely old village, is well placed for exploring the many others hidden in the folds of the North Downs – much of the landscape protected by the National Trust which also owns a large number of the stately homes near here. Beauty-spots (many accessible to motorists as well as walkers) have great variety; the spectacular summit of Box Hill, the woods of Leith Hill, the blue Silent Pool near Albury, the watercress beds (and clock with automaton) at Abinger Hammer, riverside villages such as Shere, Ranmore Common (National Trust), the Royal Horticultural Gardens at Wisley, trips on the River Wey.

Readers' comments: Very good; friendly.

Also in this area is **Hazelgrove** at West Horsley, a comfortable and well-kept 'twenties house with lovely garden and sun-room, on the road to Leatherhead. Jean Green can provide snack meals as well as breakfast. (Tel: 048 65 4467.) Visitors watch her occasional dog-training classes and buy orchids from her greenhouse. No smoking.

CLAY LANE HEAD FARM

C D PT S

Cabus, Garstang, north of Preston, Lancashire, PR3 1WL   Tel: 09952 3132

rear view

3 bedrooms (single, double or family) from £9. Less for 7 nights. Rooms have electric heaters; armchairs; views of country or garden.
Dinner £6.50 for 4 courses and coffee, at 6.30pm. Special diets if ordered. Coffee, tea, free. Non-residents not admitted. Drinks can be brought in.
2 sitting-rooms with open fire, TV, books, piano, record-player.
Garden and fields. Riding available.
Nearest main road A6 from Preston to Lancaster.

Though hardly off the beaten track – it stands on the A6 – Clay Lane Head Farm could easily be missed as one sped by, on the way to or from Scotland or the Lake District. It would be a good place to break a long journey, though it deserves more than a brief overnight visit, for both the house and the surroundings have much to offer visitors who like an easygoing atmosphere.

The stone house, which is more characterful than it appears to be from the outside, is basically 16th century, and some of the internal walls are of plastered reeds. It is a rambling, beamy old place, full of family antiques and Victoriana, with a book-lined sitting-room to sprawl in (it has a log fire); and it has not been modernized. The rooms face away from the main road.

Joan Higginson, a pharmacist, dispenses good food home-made from fresh ingredients, including plenty of cream from the Jersey cow. A typical dinner might be creamy carrot soup, steak braised with mushrooms and lemon meringue pie. There are goats too, and ponies for children to ride; and though this is no longer a working dairy farm, there are cattle, hens and sheep. Bicycles on loan.

The immediate surroundings are not exciting, but there is good reason to investigate the hinterland – notably the Trough of Bowland, which is like a miniature Lake District without the lakes. The steep, heather-covered hills here are excellent for walking and picnicking, and there are picturesque stone villages and mansions to visit. One such is Browsholme Hall, a little-altered Jacobean house still in the possession of the family which provided the hereditary Bow-bearer of Bowland. Historic towns such as Lancaster and Clitheroe are not far, and the Lake District and the resorts of the Lancashire coast are within an easy day-trip. Other popular outings include Lancaster Castle, Cockersand Abbey, Sunderland Point, Beacon Fell country park and Brock Bottom nature trail.

Readers' comments: Very enjoyable. Excellent cooking and attentive service. Concerned for our every comfort, spotless rooms, excellent dinner. Interesting place, excellent food.

Single people may find more company in houses that have a shared dining-table, a bar, and no TV in the sitting-room. As my descriptions indicate, some owners mingle more with their guests than others do. Houses marked **S** charge singles little or no more than half a double.

CLEAVERS LYNG

C D PT S

Herstmonceux, east of Hailsham, East Sussex, BN27 1QJ Tel: 0323 833131

8 bedrooms (single or double) from £12.60. Less for 7 nights. Rooms have central heating; armchairs; views of country or garden; balcony (some). Tea/coffee facilities.

Dinner £5.90 for 3 courses and coffee, at 7pm. Special diets if ordered. Lunches, packed lunches, snacks. Coffee, tea, for a charge. Non-residents admitted for lunch only. Drinks can be ordered.

Sitting-room with central heating, TV, books.

Garden with play area.

Nearest main road A271 from Horsebridge to Bexhill.

The unusual name means a woodcutter's (cleaver's) hill by a marsh (lyng). Many centuries ago this was a yeoman's house – with a tile-hung exterior typical of Sussex, and an interior given character by beams, and an inglenook fireplace in the dining-room. Marylin Holden and her sons have been running it for many years as a small hotel, and often have visitors to nearby Herstmonceux Castle – its beautiful gardens and moat can be seen in summer.

The bedrooms are prettily furnished, and have views of the garden and its apple-trees with the far distant hills beyond.

Good meals with plenty of choices – home-made soups or seafood cocktails, roasts or game pies, lemon chiffon or mincemeat tarts, are just examples. Home-made preserves are on sale. On Sundays there is always a traditional lunch with a choice of two roasts.

Herstmonceux village is the centre of Sussex trug-making (trugs are traditional garden baskets made from slats of willow), one of many pretty Downland villages around here. It is an area in which valleys alternate with wooded ridges that have panoramic views when the leaves thin out. Many craftsmen work here and wrought iron is a local speciality. Popular sights include Michelham Priory, Batemans (Kipling's home), Battle Abbey, Pevensey Castle and picturesque Alfriston.

Readers' comments: Very welcoming. Excellent, have stayed many times.

If you have not arrived by, perhaps, 6pm your room may be let to someone else – unless you telephone to say you are on your way.

Unless otherwise agreed, send a 10% deposit when confirming your booking.

Families which pick establishments with plenty of games, swimming-pool, animals, etc., or that are near free museums, parks and walks, can save a lot on keeping youngsters entertained.

THE CLEEVE

Hawkcombe, Porlock, west of Minehead, Somerset, TA24 8QW
Tel: 0643 862351

4 bedrooms (double or family) from £9. Less for 7 nights. Rooms have central heating, shower or bathroom; armchairs; views of country or garden; tea/coffee facilities.
Sitting-room with central heating, TV, books.
Grounds Woodland, terraces and lawn.
Nearest main road A39 from Bridgwater to Barnstaple.
Closed November–Easter.

Little Porlock attracts many visitors to its narrow streets, but The Cleeve is sited five minutes' walk away from all that, within its own four acres of woodland. The Victorian house perches on a hillside, facing south and sheltered from any wind. A steep drive up to it passes banks smothered with thousands of daffodils in spring, lavender and fuchsias later on; up at the top, from the terrace, lawn or wide windows there are fine, open views to the distant hills. The Fentons fell immediately in love with it all when, on Pip's retiring early from his work as a professional engineer in Bath, they came househunting here a few years ago. The best bedroom from which to enjoy the views is no. 3 (there are windows on three sides). With luck you might see Exmoor deer who trespass in the garden and eat the roses. Furnishings are homely. Many visitors dine in Porlock's restaurants such as Lapsewood or Cross Lane House.

At the Ship Inn, Southey wrote a poem to Porlock ('thy verdant vale so fair to sight, thy lofty hills with fern and furse so brown . . .'). There are fine sea views at Porlock Weir, along the coast (the road to Lynton and the little harbour at Lynmouth is one of the steepest in England), and inland to wild Exmoor, its pretty villages (such as Parracombe, Brendon and Dunster with castle) and wooded valleys. Visit the cliffs at Heddon's Mouth. From Exford there's a strenuous walk to high Dunkery Beacon. Garden-lovers make for Arlington House, Knightshayes and the Malmsmead garden centre.

Readers' comments: Splendid view, a very pleasant four days. Made us very welcome; comfortable, relaxed; beautiful garden.

All prices are inclusive of any VAT or service charge. They are minimum prices: superior rooms or high-season bookings may cost more.

Book well ahead: many of these houses have few rooms. Do not expect dinner if you have not booked it.

No one in this book insists that you stay out all day. But do not necessarily expect heating to be on, drinks available, etc.

CLEY MILL

C D PT S-C X

Cley-next-the-Sea, west of Cromer, Norfolk, NR25 7NN   Tel: 0263 740209

4 bedrooms (single, double or family) from £12. Less for 3 nights. Rooms have central heating; shower or bathroom (some); armchairs; views of sea and country; tea/coffee facilities on request. One has balcony. **Dinner** £10 for 3 courses and coffee, at 7–9pm. Vegetarian or special diets if ordered. Packed lunches, snacks. Coffee, tea, for a charge. Drinks can be brought in. **Sitting-room** with central heating, open fire, TV, books, indoor games (including table tennis, darts).
Nearest main road A149 from Wells to Cromer.

On the enthusiastic recommendation of a friend, I made my way to this most unusual of guest-houses – not, in fact, next to the sea (for centuries of silting up followed by land reclamation have left Cley a little way inland) but overlooking a rivulet winding its way through salt marshes where cattle graze.

Once Cley was a principal port of East Anglia, and great ships came to collect wool, and flour from the mediaeval windmill (the present structure dates from the 18th century). Milling ceased in 1921, since when generations of the Blount family have lived in it: one of the most celebrated visitors was the Duchess of Bedford who learned to fly when she was about seventy, and was lost flying at sea in 1937.

Only a few years ago, it was completely renovated, and the rooms are excellent. One enters through the beamy dining-room for which oak chairs and sideboard were specially made locally. The circular sitting-room has big armchairs around the brick fireplace, where Toby jugs are arranged, and window-seats overlooking the marshes. Upstairs, bedrooms are named according to the original purpose which they served: for instance, in the Wheat Chamber flour was sifted; in the Stone Room above it the flour was ground. Lace bedspreads and wildflower curtains contrast with brick walls, now painted white, and soft green carpet. One room has a balcony running all round the mill, with views on one side to Blakeney Harbour and on the other to the pantiled roofs and chimney-pots of Cley, its flint gables and its walls with hollyhocks peering over the top. Higher still are observation and information rooms, with telescope.

The Mill is run by Carolyn Hederman, who produces such meals as roast lamb, casseroles, or fish with Hollandaise sauce; followed by lemon soufflé or mousse.

Cley is in the centre of the north Norfolk coast; a shoreline of cliffs and sands now officially protected for its beauty and its wildlife. Inland are woods, heath and pretty villages of flint walls or (eastward) red carr stone, with inns where crab salads are as common as ham sandwiches. The National Trust owns a number of stately homes which, along with castles and almost cathedral-like churches, innumerable craft studios and wildlife reserves, provide plenty of opportunities for sightseeing. Blakeney's waterfront is always lively with boats; Cromer is a family seaside resort in the old-fashioned style. Holkham Hall, Felbrigg, Blickling Hall are near and the royal gardens at Sandringham a little further. At Walsingham are two famous shrines.

Readers' comments: Cooking and hospitality could not be faulted. Comfortable; food very good. Excellent. Shall return.

COACH HOUSE C D H PT S S-C

Crookham, Cornhill-on-Tweed, east of Coldstream (Scotland),
Northumberland, TD12 4TD   Tel: 089082 293

views of country or garden; tea/coffee facilities. Clothes-washing facilities available.
Dinner £9 for 4 courses and coffee with petits fours, at 7.30pm. Special diets if ordered. Tea with home-made cakes is free on arrival. Non-residents not admitted. Drinks can be ordered or brought in (£1 is charged). Occasional barbecues.
2 sitting-rooms with central heating, open fire, TV, books, record-player. Also a billiard room with darts, table tennis room, music room.
Grounds Terrace, paddock, orchard and fields. Escorted riding or birdwatching.
Nearest main road A697 from Morpeth to Coldstream.
Closed in winter

10 bedrooms (single, double or family) from £17. Rooms have central heating or electric heaters; shower or bathroom; armchairs;

This is almost on the border of Scotland, and very close to the site of Flodden Field, where in 1513 Henry VIII's armies slaughtered the King of Scotland and 10,000 of his followers: the very last mediaeval battle with knights wearing armour, and swords or arrows the principal weapons. Each August there is a tremendously emotive spectacle commemorating it, with 200 horsemen bearing down at a canter after being led by the Coldstream Guards across the old bridge at Coldstream. A piper plays that tragic lament, 'The Flower of the Forest'.

The Coach House is a group of several old farm buildings forming a square around a courtyard which traps the sun. What was the coach house itself is now a highly individual sitting-room, with lofty beamed ceiling and great arched windows where there used to be doors for the carriages. One looks onto an orchard. Colours are light and cheerful, and there is a log fire in an enormous brick fireplace. The dining-room was once a smithy and the forge still stands at one end.

An old dower house is now used as an annexe, particularly suitable for families who would like the use of its kitchen to prepare children's meals (which means that very little is charged for their accommodation) and of its games room. It has panelled doors of stripped pine, pointed 'gothick' windows, rare chestnut beams, an old Victorian kitchen-range, and an immensely high attic bedroom.

In the main part, some of the ground-floor bedrooms look onto paddocks where goats graze. All are light and airy, with interesting paintings and a file of leaflets on the many local places worth visiting. They have fridges which guests find useful for a variety of purposes (baby's feeds, dog's meat, insulin or soft drinks) and toasters: there are reduced prices for people who make their own breakfast.

The owner, Lynne Anderson, used to travel a great deal when she was a singer, and so has a lot of practical ideas about what travellers need – disabled travellers in particular. When converting the buildings, she had doorways made wide enough for wheelchairs, and unnecessary steps eliminated. She has a stack of information about local sights accessible by wheelchair.

This is the place to come for good, wholesome food and all-year warmth. Porridge is properly made from pinhead oatmeal, and breakfast includes bacon from an Edinburgh smokery, beef sausages from a local butcher, and free-range eggs. Other breakfast alternatives are 'home-toasted grains' (oats, coconut, honey), rhubarb compôte, and home-made jams (apricot and almond, rhubarb and orange and damson cheese, for instance). For dinner, she may prepare a choice of six starters (pâtés, soups, quiche); a roast or casserole; puddings like lemon meringue pie or almond ice cream with damson sauce; cheese and coffee. Steak, pheasant and salmon are often served, and garden produce. Even the wine is organically produced, as well as meat. Vegetables are imaginatively prepared.

This is a fascinating area to visit. Across the border are Scotland's ancient abbey towns (Jedburgh, Melrose, Kelso, Dryburgh). The Pennine Way ends near here, Kirk Yetholm is a famous gipsy centre, and in the Border mill towns cashmere and other woollies can be had for less than half the price charged in city shops. It's an area of wide open spaces and blue skies, breezy but hardly ever rainy. Historic Berwick-on-Tweed and the spectacular Northumbrian coast are accessible; the Cheviot Hills lie to the south. Unusual and interesting sights include Lady Waterford Hall, pretty villages like Etal and Ford, Heatherslaw Mill, and many ruined castles. Good birdwatching country. There are many gardens, garden centres and (by arrangement with Lynne) a private water garden to visit.

Readers' comments: Very friendly and welcoming, exceptionally well organized; most impressed. Warm and friendly owner; professional efficiency. A great success! Wonderful. So much room, the very best breakfast, and Lynne is exceptionally good at making guests at ease with one another. A charmer, she hums arias as she serves dinner! A very relaxing and comfortable stay; fresh wholesome food. Tip-top; service excellent. Food terrific; delightful lady!

When to go? Seaside resorts or other places suitable for children will be at their busiest (and dearest) in July–August and during half-term holidays (especially, in late May, which is also a bank holiday period). Other peak periods are, of course, Easter, Christmas, New Year and the bank holiday in late August. (The bank holiday in early May is not usually a peak, because it comes rather soon after Easter, but much depends on the weather.) There are local peaks, too (the Gold Cup races at Cheltenham or the regatta at Henley, for instance, are apt to fill hotels for miles around), and local troughs (Brighton, a conference centre, is least busy in high summer). You won't get much personal attention when hotels are full to bursting.

Don't complain if –
- because you booked at short notice, you do not get the best room
- because you did not order a meal in advance, you get something plucked from the freezer
- because you do not arrive on time, your room is let to someone else
- because you bring a dog without asking, it is refused entry
- because you don't express your wishes (for more heat, a second helping, or whatever), you don't get what you want!

For explanation of code letters (**C, D, H, PT, S, S-C, X**) **see page xxviii.**

COACH HOUSE
Scotland Road, Dry Drayton, north-west of Cambridge, CB3 8BX
Tel: 0954 82439

4 bedrooms (single or double) from £17. Rooms have central heating; own bathroom; armchairs; views of garden; tea/coffee facilities. No smoking.
Sitting-room with central heating, TV, books. No smoking. (Also a room for group meetings.)

Large garden
Nearest main road A604 from Huntingdon to Cambridge.
Closed January and February

Only a year before I visited, what is now an immaculate reception room (pink walls, chinoiserie curtains) contained mounds of dung, for it had been stables. The transformation wrought by Catherine Child and her builders was as total as it had been swift – here and in the rest of the building. In its grounds, too: now turned into a very pretty landscaped garden, with moorhens in the lily-pool.

The rector who, a century ago, stabled his horses here must have been a man of considerable substance, keeping several carriages and maintaining his own forge. The forge fire still burns, built into a corner of the entrance hall.

A new and handsome pine staircase rises to the bedrooms but offers temptations to linger on the way up, for one large window and a blocked-up doorway have been filled with shelves to display small bits of Victoriana (for sale – they are provided by antique-dealer friends of Catherine). Bedrooms are light and pretty, with excellent bathrooms (in one, a shower). The best has a Victorian brass four-poster, its valance beribboned and its Victorian white-and-pink spread hand-quilted. The tulip fabrics are matched by the wallpaper here and in its pink bathroom.

Guests have the use of a large dining-room with mahogany tables for breakfast, and of a small television room – both south-facing, with sunny views of the garden. (And there's a lovely room to hire for groups, music-making and such like.)

In the folders of local information provided for guests Catherine lists recommended eating-places (such as Trinity Foot or the Three Horseshoes inn at nearby Madingley or the Plough at Coton, and many in nearby Cambridge, of course). She can arrange for private guided tours round Cambridge. Go to Huntingdon for the Oliver Cromwell museum (this was his birthplace) and to St Ives; there are several stately homes within easy reach; and close by is the American Cemetery, which is well worth a visit. Grantchester and Duxford aircraft museum are also close. All around are wide, windswept skies and marvellously clear light.

Readers' comments: Very warm welcome, such pretty bedrooms, a lovely outlook. A lovely house. Every conceivable care given to visitors' requirements. Totally impressed by it all! Has great character, most peaceful, will stay again.

COASTGUARDS

St Agnes, Isles of Scilly, TR22 0PL   Tel: 0720 22373

2 bedrooms (double and family) at £12. **Discounts are offered to readers of this book, except in high summer.** Rooms have views of sea. Laundering facilities.
Dinner 4 courses and coffee, at 6.30pm. Special diets if ordered. Packed lunches. Coffee, tea, free. Non-residents not admitted. Drinks can be brought in.
Dining/sitting-room with open fire, books.
Small garden
Closed in winter

There are very few coastguards living in the many coastguard cottages still left around the shores of England: electronic surveillance has taken over from the man with the spyglass. Needless to say, such cottages were always well sited for sea views, on coasts where high seas and jagged rocks make spectacular scenery, but are hazards for ships, and where coves and inlets were an attraction to smugglers.

One such group of cottages stands on a high point of St Agnes, a little island in the Scillies so unspoilt that there are no cars, no hotel, no commercialism at all. It is a paradise for those who want nothing more than sunshine early or late in the year, wildflowers, walks, birdwatching, going about in boats and perfect peace.

Wendy and Danny Hick live in one of these cottages, with a couple of rooms for guests. They have furnished the rooms simply but attractively, with interesting objects around. (No washbasins.) The sitting-room has a William Morris sofa and brown tweed curtains, polished board floors, many books on the shelves and an open fire for chilly evenings. The pieces of iron-studded furniture are from Curaçao, where Danny's father was a mining engineer. The collection of old bottles (from inkwells to flasks that contained sheep-cures) are mostly local finds. Danny makes ship models sold in London's West End galleries.

The food is all of a very good, homely style: bread is home-baked, soups home-made, clotted cream is from a friendly neighbourhood cow, fish (of course) straight out of the sea, and new potatoes from the fields around.

Visitors reach St Agnes via St Mary's from which boats take them in 15 minutes to the little quay at St Agnes. (Mrs Hick will supply all the times etc. for getting to the Scillies by rail and boat or helicopter.) Luggage is conveyed for them up the steep track that leads to the few cottages; past the Turk's Head inn (for a really succulent Cornish pasty, pause here!); and past Rose Cottage, and Covean which serve Cornish cream teas and light lunches. Whatever track you follow, there is a superlative view at every turn. This is a great place for birdwatchers, particularly in autumn when rare migrants arrive. But even at other times it is a pleasure to watch the red-legged turnstones, for instance, scuttling like busy mice among the rock-pools on the shore. Around the lighthouse (built in 1680) are fields from which daffodils and narcissi are sent early in the year to mainland florists. There are strange rock formations and islets, deserted sandy coves and pools, a simple church (built from money raised by salvaging a wreck), and – a mystery – the centuries-old Troy Town maze by a remote cliff edge.

Readers' comments: Excellent in every respect. Good food, lovely scenery, such nice people. Warmly welcomed, well looked after, delicious food, excellent value; beautiful and peaceful place.

COBBLERS

South Creake, north-east of Fakenham, Norfolk, NR21 9PF
Tel: 032879 200

2 bedrooms (double) from £15. Rooms have central heating; views of garden; tea/coffee facilities. One has en suite bathroom; one a shower (and downstairs toilet).
Dinner £10 for 4 courses and coffee, at 7.30pm. Drinks included.

Sitting-room with central heating, open fire, TV, books.
Garden
Nearest main road A148 from Cromer to King's Lynn.

This U-shaped house encloses a particularly pretty little garden that comes as a surprise when one turns in from the main road. Arches and hanging baskets of flowers surround the lawn and a sun-trapping patio, stone hounds guard a lily-pool (lit up at night), there are tubs of marigolds, and one can open a narrow wrought-iron gate to watch trout and ducks in the clear stream flowing by.

Ian Dow was formerly a theatrical production manager – hence the many theatrical designs, photographs and posters around the house. The small sitting/dining-room is crammed with other interesting objects – from samplers and old jigsaw pictures to portraits of his Scottish ancestors. Here his wife Mardi serves generous meals that may comprise, for instance, avocado with smoked trout, followed by duck or another roast, and home-made ice creams, then cheeses.

The bedrooms are attractively furnished with, for instance, both furniture and walls painted dark billiardcloth green to contrast with the shaggy rust carpet in one room; ivy trellis paper in another which has fabrics striped in cobalt blue.

South Creake is centrally placed for enjoying many of Norfolk's contrasting areas – the scenic coast lies six miles north; there are bird reserves; several great houses lie near (Oxburgh, Blickling, Felbrigg – all National Trust – and also Holkham, Houghton and royal Sandringham).

Readers' comments: Lovely imaginative cooking, generous portions. Very friendly atmosphere. The Dows spoil their guests.

A little further west is Docking, where Margaret Robinson caters inexpensively for bed-and-breakfast guests in her immaculate 18th-century **Holland House** (tel: 04858 295), with peaceful garden. Most dine at the Pilgrim's Reach.

COCKETT'S HOTEL   D X
Market Place, Hawes, Wensleydale, North Yorkshire, DL8 3RD
Tel: 09697 312

7 bedrooms (double) from £14.50. Less for 3 nights. Rooms have central heating; own bathroom; TV, armchairs; tea/coffee facilities. Clothes-washing facilities. No smoking.
Dinner from £13 for 4 courses (with choices) and coffee, from 7.45pm. Vegetarian or special diets if ordered. Packed lunches. Coffee, tea, for a charge. Drinks can be ordered. No smoking.
Nearest main road A684 from Hawes to Leyburn.
Closed in winter (except for Christmas to New Year).

'God being with us Who can be against' is carved deep into the stone lintel of a door, together with the date 1668. It was the main entrance to a hostel once used by Quakers travelling to distant meeting-houses.

Things are different now. One steps from the paved forecourt into a snug little bar with leather chairs and racing-prints all over the walls – most visitors much prefer this to the larger, pine-panelled sitting-room elsewhere. Adjoining it is a dining-room where, on lace-covered tables, are served the imaginative meals cooked by Cherry Guest (cordon bleu trained). There is always plenty of choice at each of the courses, with many French specialities such as lamb Argenteuil (it is cooked with asparagus and cream), or chicken Marika (cottage cheese and green peppercorns go into the sauce), or duck-breasts stuffed then braised in lettuce leaves. The cheeseboard usually includes a rarity – local Swaledale cheese.

Brian Guest owns the adjoining art gallery, which has many examples of local painters' work. The house itself is something of a gallery, with over two hundred pictures on its walls. Every room has interesting furniture, too: one four-poster, with barley-sugar posts, is covered in a scarlet dragon fabric; another, of pine, has pale green chintz. One's eye is caught by interesting details everywhere: satinwood bedside cupboards, art nouveau fingerplates on the doors, for example.

In the annexe (over the art gallery) are the two least expensive bedrooms, which would make an ideal suite for a family wanting to be self-contained.

Hawes, its buildings clustered around a stream, is near the head of Wensleydale from which the spectacular Buttertubs Pass leads to very different Swaledale (described elsewhere): the 'butter tubs' are curious holes in the rock. The dale's crags and waterfalls, castles and history museums, attract visitors from all over the world. Hardraw Force, a 100-foot waterfall, has a footpath that goes behind the gushing torrent – take your showercoat!

I called again just as this edition was going to press and learnt that the hotel was about to be taken over by John Oddie. Readers' reports welcome, please.

For explanation of code letters (**C, D, H, PT, S, S-C, X**) **see page xxviii.**

73

COLDHARBOUR FARM

C(10)

Sutton, south-east of Petworth, West Sussex, RH20 1PR Tel: 07987 200

3 bedrooms (twin-bedded) from £13. Less for 7 nights. Rooms have central heating or electric heaters; own bathroom; TV, armchairs; views of country or garden; tea/coffee facilities.
Dinner £9 for 2 courses and coffee, at 7.30pm. Packed lunches. Coffee, tea, for a charge. Non-residents not admitted. Drinks can be brought in.
Sitting-room with central heating, TV, video, books.
Large garden and 160 acres of farmland.
Nearest main road A285 from Petworth to Chichester.
Closed December–March

Nowhere could feel more off the beaten track than this, even though London is only 60 miles away.

A seemingly endless lane, trees arching overhead, winds its way through folds in the South Downs until at the end of the trail one suddenly arrives at this large, black-and-white farmhouse, built in 1665. There is an attractive brick terrace outside with chairs and tubs of flowers, and a fine view towards the hills: the walkers' South Downs Way is only a quarter-hour away. At one side, is a large and well-tended garden with a herbaceous border running the length of a fine flint wall.

Within, there are large, low bedrooms in pretty colours, furnished with antiques; a little beamed sitting-room opening onto the garden; and a dining-room with refectory table, rush chairs and grandfather clock. Here Mrs Shiner serves dinners – two courses only. She cooks such things as pork with a sauce of wine, tomatoes and onions, and pavlovas made with fresh peaches. Vegetables in great variety come from her garden.

'Coldharbour' is an ancient term for an overnight camp without cover: very different from today's comforts!

As to sightseeing, the sea is only 12 miles away; and walks, long or short, are one of the greatest attractions of the area – as well as the many stately houses (Petworth, Uppark, Goodwood, Arundel Castle etc.), Bignor Roman villa, the Wildfowl Trust and a large number of very fine gardens.

Readers' comments: Very good food. Very welcoming and comfortable. Food excellent and generous. Fantastic situation and so peaceful. Excellent in every respect.

It's best to stay at least 2–3 days: you cannot possibly appreciate an area if you only stay overnight (prices per night are often less, too, if you stay on). The vouchers on page **ii** are usable for 3-night stays.

Take the trouble to get free booklets about the area before you set off. Every habitual traveller should keep a copy of the booklet of local Tourist Information Centres issued free by the English Tourist Board (Thames Tower, Blacks Road, London W6; tel: 01-846 9000) for this purpose.

COLLEGE FARMHOUSE

Thompson, north of Thetford, Norfolk, IP24 1QG   Tel: 095383 318

4 bedrooms (single or double) from £12. Rooms have central heating and electric heaters; TV, armchairs; views of country or garden. Coffee, tea, free.

Large garden
Nearest main road A1075 from Thetford to Watton.

Over six centuries ago, colleges (meaning residential communities) of some half-dozen priests were established in various parts of East Anglia, to serve local communities. This house was built for one of them. When these colleges were (like the monasteries) disbanded by Henry VIII, it became a private house: the new owner had his coat-of-arms put above the main fireplace. Later, carved oak panelling with fluted pilasters was put into the dining-room; a second storey was added in 1700; and then all manner of Victorian or later accretions followed. These last William and Lavender Garnier have gradually removed, revealing forgotten fireplaces and beams masked by hardboard. A tremendous task; and when they took over, the only running water was from leaks in the roof. The house is therefore full of curious architectural features – Gothic windows blocked up, walls (some three feet thick) with odd curves, steps up and down.

The Garniers have collected together interesting pieces of furniture and some ancestral portraits of their own (including a great-grandfather who took part in the first Oxford and Cambridge boat-race, and selected dark blue as Oxford's now famous colour). Bedrooms have pleasing fabrics – brilliant nasturtiums on the bed of one room, for instance; yellow linen bedheads in another white-panelled room – and in one the basin is set in a thick, handsome plank of polished elm. Each bedroom has armchairs and TV, as there is no sitting-room for guests' use.

Outside, a lovely old garden slopes down to eel ponds, and flint walls make a perfect background to the roses, herbaceous borders and a great beech.

Breakfast is the only meal served, but there is good inn food at the thatched Chequers, a mile away.

Thompson is in an attractive, leafy part of Norfolk, where the landscape undulates and villages are pretty. There are varied options for day-outings – from the very beautiful Norfolk coast to Cambridge, from Norwich and the Broads to Bury St Edmunds (described elsewhere in this book). Breckland is an area of heath and meres, with little population now but a considerable history (explained in Thetford's museum, in a Tudor house). Visit Brandon to see the variety of ways flints are used in building; and Grimes Graves where prehistoric man mined the chalk to find these, for use as tools and weapons. Castle Acre lies within Norman earthworks (the priory remains are impressive); near Denver is an unusual windmill, and the 15th-century Oxburgh Hall is moated.

COOMBE FARMHOUSE *(illustrated on cover)* C(5) **D H**
Widegates, east of Looe, Cornwall, PL13 1QN   Tel: 05034 223

8 bedrooms (single, double or family) from £12.50. Less for 2 nights half-board for families. Rooms have central heating or electric heaters; shower (some); armchairs; views of sea, country or garden.

Dinner £8.50 for 4 courses and coffee, at 7–8pm. Special diets if ordered. Lunches, packed lunches, snacks. Coffee, tea, for a charge. Drinks can be ordered.

Sitting-room with central heating, open fire, TV, books. Games room with snooker, table tennis, video films.

Grounds Lawns, meadows, woods and ponds; with croquet, swimming-pool (73° in summer).

Nearest main road B3253 from Hessenford to Looe.

Closed November–February

Built on a marvellous site with a distant sea view between hills, this very spacious and comfortable 'twenties house had long been coveted by Alexander Low, who used to bring his family regularly to Looe for holidays. When at last it came up for sale, it had deteriorated into a seedy guest-house, gaudily decorated, with barbed wire and a cow-field outside. But within a year he and Sally transformed it and its grounds, and every year sees still further improvements (a swimming-pool and a stone-walled games room for snooker and table tennis are the most recent).

Alex frequents salerooms to find additions to the already rich array of antiques, paintings and interesting objects with which he has filled the house. Some, like the collection of fans, are family heirlooms.

The dining-room extends into a glassed-in verandah from which there are views of terraced lawns where peacocks roam, and of a pond (one of several) frequented by ducks and coots. Elsewhere, geese and ponies graze, there are woods with rhododendrons, and camellias grow wild.

All rooms have an abundance of pot-plants, flowers are put on each green-clothed dining-table and in each bedroom, and on cool nights log fires crackle on two hearths: all part of the considerable attention to detail.

My bedroom (like several, very big indeed) opened straight onto the garden. Others upstairs have armchairs or, in one, a big sofa from which to enjoy the view. All are very comfortably furnished, and with thick carpets.

As a professional photographer and one-time picture editor of the *Telegraph* magazine, Alex used to travel a lot and knows what makes guests feel truly at home. They are welcome to take picnic lunches into the garden, for instance; and to help themselves to drinks, writing down in a book what they have had.

A typical dinner prepared by Sally may comprise something like home-made soup, roast duck and a fruit sponge accompanied by Cornish clotted cream – freshly cooked from local produce, and served in generous quantities.

As to sightseeing, there are twenty mansions and gardens within motoring distance, plenty of coast or moorland walks and river trips, a wide choice of sandy bays or coves, and such special attractions as a monkey sanctuary and another for seals. There is a huge choice of unusual museums or exhibitions: mechanical music, miniature villages, smuggling, steam rail, air history, mining, shire horses, local history, tropical birds, historic pottery and much more – such as antique shops and auctions, farm shops, etc.

Readers' comments: Excellent!

COTT INN

C(10) D PT X

Dartington, north of Totnes, Devon, TQ9 6HE   Tel: 0803 863777

6 bedrooms (double) at £18.50. Less for 3 nights, or bargain breaks. Rooms have electric heaters; armchairs; views of garden.
Dinner £15 for 3 courses or à la carte, at 7pm and 9pm precisely. Special diets if ordered. Lunches, packed lunches, snacks. Coffee, tea, for a charge. Drinks can be ordered.

Sitting-room with central heating, TV, books. Bars.
Large garden
Nearest main road A385 from Totnes to Plymouth.

This long, low inn with roses over whitewashed walls and a 200-foot thatched roof looks almost too good to be true: a once-upon-a-time kind of place. It was built in 1320, by a laborious method called cob, for which no one has time these days but which has withstood six centuries and looks like standing for another six. Cob walls are immensely thick, built up painstakingly from one lump of clay upon another, each layer left to dry before the next is added. The thick, uneven walls not only give the inn character but keep it warm in winter and cool in summer. The stone-flagged bars and dining-room, with oak settles, have low-beamed ceilings, and there are great fireplaces for logs.

Bedrooms are pretty, comfortable and, mostly, quiet. Lunch is selected from hot and cold dishes on a buffet, but dinner is served at table: salmon, duck, steaks and other local produce cooked with imagination. The Cott Inn is run by Steve Culverhouse whose career in catering began there twenty years ago.

The Cott is a good staging-post on the long journey to Cornwall, or for a holiday in one of England's most beautiful regions – south Devon. There is much to see and do in the area but the beauty of the countryside and coast are what make it so outstanding (and its mild climate, with an early spring each year). Many streams run down to coves and creeks, and the country lanes are always going up hills and down valleys as they wind between banks full of wildflowers, visiting sleepy villages on the way. To the north lies wild Dartmoor. For those who want them, resorts like Torquay and Plymouth (with its naval dockyard and its *Mayflower* associations) are easily reached, as well as many smaller towns: Totnes (full of antique shops), Brixham (fishing harbour), Dartmouth (old quays), Slapton Ley (waterfowl reserve) and Salcombe (for sailing). Dartington Hall, only a few minutes from the Cott, is an outstandingly beautiful mediaeval mansion in lovely gardens. A number of musical and artistic enterprises are connected with it, and crafts (glass, furniture, weaving). The boat trips from Totnes (to Dartmouth) are particularly well worth taking. The shire horse centre is very popular, and so is the Friday antiques market. Pick-your-own and farm shops provide organic produce to take home.

Readers' comments: Excellent meals, will go again. Attractive bedrooms, good quality food. Very helpful service. Perfect! Delightful; good value.

77

THE COTTAGE
Westbrook, Bromham, south-east of Chippenham, Wiltshire, SN15 2EE
Tel: 0380 850255

C H S-C X

5 bedrooms (double) from £14. Rooms have central heating or electric heaters; shower or bathroom; TV, armchairs; views of country or garden; tea/coffee facilities.
2 sitting/breakfast-rooms with central heating, open fire, TV, books.

Large garden and paddock with 9-hole putting and badminton.
Nearest main road A3102 from Calne to Melksham.

Converted stables, weatherboarded and pantiled, provide the accommodation here, in a quiet hamlet once the home of Thomas Moore, the Irish poet. The adjoining mediaeval cottage was originally a coaching inn.

Inside, the roof beams are still visible. The bedrooms have been furnished in keeping with the style of the building and Gloria Steed has added such decorative touches as patchwork cushions and pincushions which she made herself. Through the bedroom windows one can sometimes see deer and rabbits, with a distant landscape created by Capability Brown in the 18th century.

At breakfast (in a room with rough white walls, small William Morris armchairs and beautifully arranged flowers) there will be, in addition to the usual things, home-made muesli and some very special jams from France. For other meals, Gloria can show you a selection of menus from all the inns and restaurants within a few miles (I ate very well at the Lysley Arms). Occasionally she invites guests to a family barbecue in the garden.

This is very lovely walking country, and with lots of sightseeing possibilities too (Lacock, Devizes, Avebury and Bath are all within a few miles; and Bowood House is close – an Adam building in superb grounds, with lake and cascade). Chippenham and Calne are historic market towns, with fine churches and other buildings of golden stone. Castle Combe is a much-photographed village in a dramatic setting – woods above it, stream through it, mellow stone cottages and fan-vaulted church. Corsham Court, and the waterside at Devizes, are well worth visits. This part of Wiltshire is very rustic but with fine limestone houses built in the centuries when wool brought wealth. Riverside pastures contrast with hills and wooded dells. Sheldon Manor and Stourhead have exceptional gardens. A good area for hunting antiques, or buying farm produce.

Single people may find more company in houses that have a shared dining-table, a bar, and no TV in the sitting-room. As my descriptions indicate, some owners mingle more with their guests than others do. Houses marked **S** charge singles little or no more than half a double.

COTTESWOLD HOUSE

Market Place, Northleach, Gloucestershire, GL54 3EG   Tel: 0451 60493

4 bedrooms (single, double or family) from £12.50. Less for 4 nights. Rooms have central heating. Tea, coffee, free.
Sitting-room with central heating, TV, books.
Nearest main road A40 from Fishguard to London.

This is not strictly 'off the beaten track', being in the centre of the historic little town, but now that heavy traffic has been diverted, Northleach is quite a quiet place. The house has tremendous character, after being carefully restored by Mrs Powell a few years ago. Zigzagging passages lead to roomy bedrooms with rugged stone walls and low oak beams now exposed. She has furnished all the rooms with good carpets and folkweave or similar fabrics. Guests breakfast in a dining-room with oak furniture, including a vast carved chest, and can use the large sitting-room and its comfortable yellow armchairs – big and velvety. There are plenty of good places for dinner within a few yards, such as Wickens and the Union Inn. Plenty of antique shops in the area – and a world-famous clock restorer.

There is plenty of interest within easy motoring distance. For example, Cirencester still has a lively market (I recommend the farm cheese stall) outside its almost cathedral-like church. The Corinium Museum is one of the country's best-displayed Roman museums, and there is a flourishing craftsmen's market in a former brewery. The most picturesque villages and lanes of the Cotswolds are close – stately homes, gardens, a Roman villa, the source of the Thames, handsome Cheltenham, Gloucester's cathedral and the colleges of Oxford are all easily accessible.

Readers' comments: Eminently satisfied, thoroughly enjoyed it.

When to go? Seaside resorts or other places suitable for children will be at their busiest (and dearest) in July–August and during half-term holidays (especially, in late May, which is also a bank holiday period). Other peak periods are, of course, Easter, Christmas, New Year and the bank holiday in late August. (The bank holiday in early May is not usually a peak, because it comes rather soon after Easter, but much depends on the weather.) There are local peaks, too (the Gold Cup races at Cheltenham or the regatta at Henley, for instance, are apt to fill hotels for miles around), and local troughs (Brighton, a conference centre, is least busy in high summer). You won't get much personal attention when hotels are full to bursting.

For explanation of code letters (**C, D, H, PT, S, S-C, X**) see page xxviii.

THE COURT *New*   **D**
Frampton, north-west of Dorchester, Dorset, DT2 9NH   Tel: 0300 20242

4 bedrooms (single, double or family) from £25, including dinner. Tea/coffee facilities; central heating; views of river, country or garden. Some have own bathroom. No smoking. (Washing-machine on request.)
Dinner (see text) at 7.30pm. Non-residents not admitted. Vegetarian or special diets if ordered. Tea, coffee, extra (but free on arrival). Drinks can be brought in.
Sitting-room with central heating, open fire, TV, books.
Large garden and farmland.
Nearest main road A37 from Dorchester to Yeovil.
Closed from mid-October–April

In the 'thirties, a mansion that had belonged to Sheridan's family was demolished. Materials from it – such as the limed oak staircase and the window frames – went into the construction of this handsome house. The buff-and-white dining-room, has rush ladderback chairs around oval tables and William Morris curtains. In the conservatory bamboo sofas invite one to linger among the bougainvillaea and fuchsias. The gold-and-cream sitting-room has windows on three sides. One bedroom is huge, with a magnificent walnut suite complemented by frilled bedlinen; carved gilt pelmets top windows at each end (like others, it has a very good, carpeted bathroom). In another, there is much *trompe l'oeil* maple and gilt.

The garden is a particularly attractive spot in which to take tea. It has a long pool with weeping-willow island (reached by footbridge), once a monastic fishpond; a stream; and woods with some delightful walks. Nearly twenty kinds of ornamental waterfowl and peacocks roam at will.

Peggy Lazenby runs The Court with her friend Maureen Stephens, and they produce gourmet-class meals for visitors. A typical dinner might start with avocado mousse in a prawn dressing, followed by lamb with garlic sauce, a bavarois made with oranges and cream, and cheeses.

Readers' comments: Made to feel at home, lovely memories, cordon bleu cooking. A cosy, intimate quality; beautifully landscaped gardens, flawless meals.

On the opposite side of Dorchester is West Knighton and picturesque **Yoah Cottage** (tel: 0305 852087), all whitewash and thatch. On every windowsill are terracotta images of country life, which Furse and Rosemary Swann sculpt in their garden studio (visitors sometimes try their hand too). The garden is a romantic spot, flagged paths wandering between old junipers and a well among the cottage flowers. Rosemary produces not only imaginative dishes of her own (for instance, pork tenderloin with water chestnuts in a sweet-sour cream sauce or trout fillets with ginger and dill) but also a number of Swedish specialities.

COURTNEY COTTAGE *New*   **C D S S-C**
Iwerne Courtney, north of Blandford Forum, Dorset, DT11 8QA
Tel: 0258 860650

3 bedrooms (double or family) from £13. Less for 7 nights. All have own bath; TV; electric heating; views of country or garden. Free early morning tea served. (Washing-machine on request.)
Dinner £8.50 for 3 courses and coffee, at 7.45pm. Vegetarian or special diets if ordered. Snacks by arrangement. Tea, coffee, extra. Drinks can be brought in.
2 sitting-rooms (one with open fire); books.
Small garden
Nearest main road A350 from Shaftesbury to Blandford.

The cottage is in a village with two names (on some maps it appears as Shroton): by either, this is an attractive spot, with a large green. In the 17th century this cottage was the village school, possibly the first such in England.

Today, the ambience – and the food – are far removed from these humble beginnings. When Tacina Rae-Smith turned her home into a guest-house, it soon secured a reputation for exceptional meals and these are what bring most visitors to stay – together with the particularly attractive, old rooms with family heirlooms. Now it is her daughter Emma who does most of the cooking, to the same high standards: she used to cook for the British Minister in Paris.

For example, you might be offered for dinner cheese aigrettes, paupiettes of beef in red wine, raspberry and almond iced bombe, coffee with home-made chocolates.

This will be served in a dining-room furnished with unusual antiques (a painted Korean chest, for instance), shelves of plates and a number of family portraits. (There is a separate dining-room for families who want to be on their own.) By contrast, in the library there are Dufy prints. The pretty blue sitting-room with log fire has a bay window in its thick walls. Bedrooms, too, are very pleasant and the attic suite, under the eaves, would particularly suit a family or friends travelling together. Views are of hills, one topped by a prehistoric fort.

Eastward lies scenic Cranborne Chase, described elsewhere. Most visitors here also like exploring the area's Roman remains, and great houses such as Longleat, Montacute and Wilton. Stourhead has particularly lovely gardens and lakes. The Dorset coast is near, so are the Purbeck Hills and many picturesque Dorset villages. The nearest town, Blandford Forum, is a remarkably complete 18th-century town (because in 1731 fire destroyed earlier buildings) with an exceptionally grand church of the period. The lovely River Stour flows languidly by; on the bridge is a warning that anyone damaging this will be transported! Other popular destinations include Dorchester, Corfe Castle, Kingston Lacy house, and a famous silk and butterfly farm.

Readers' comments: Cooking superb, wonderful views and walks on the very doorstep.

Houses which do *not* take children tend to have vacancies in July and August.

COVE HOUSE

Ashton Keynes, north-west of Swindon, Wiltshire, SN6 6NS
Tel: 0285 861221

3 bedrooms (single, double or family) from £15. Less for 2 nights or bargain breaks. Discounts for repeat bookings. Rooms have central heating or electric heaters; shower or bathroom; TV, armchairs; views of garden; tea/coffee facilities.
Dinner £10 for 3 courses and coffee, at 7.30pm. Garden fruit free (when available) for picnics. Drinks can be brought in.
2 sitting-rooms with central heating, open fire, TV, books. Videos of local attractions.
Large garden
Nearest main road A419 from Swindon to Cirencester.

The narrow trickle running through this little village is in fact the infant Thames; you can walk right to its source from here. All around is a chain of large pools (originally gravel-diggings) now known as the Cotswold Water Park, which more or less encloses Ashton Keynes as if it were an island: birdwatchers come here to view the waterfowl.

Here Peter and Elizabeth Hartland live in one half of a 17th-century manor house (with later alterations) surrounded by a particularly lovely and secluded garden which has a succession of lawns and a paved carriage-yard with barbecue beside its lily-pool. One of its previous owners was Puritan John Richmond, who had a part in founding Taunton, Massachusetts.

Indoors is a large, friendly sitting-room; a dining-room that has interesting wallpaper, antiques and huge heirloom paintings; and Elizabeth's lovely flower arrangements everywhere. In the small library is an alcove lined with a large-scale, illuminated map of the area. Here Peter keeps a collection of packs for visitors, each full of carefully compiled information about various day-outings and his own 'good food guide' to local eating-places. Yet another sitting-room, upstairs, is for TV.

Bedrooms have individuality – one green-and-white sprigged; another full of roses; while a third (turquoise, with brass bedheads) has an unusual domed ceiling. Flowers are usually present.

Elizabeth uses garden produce for meals, at which the Hartlands dine with their guests. You might start with gazpacho or home-made pâté, perhaps; to be followed by a roast or salmon mayonnaise and then perhaps fruit sorbets or rhubarb-and-orange pudding.

Ashton Keynes is on the edge of the Cotswolds. Among other sightseeing possibilities the following are within an easy drive: Cheltenham, Oxford, Burford, Avebury, Bath, Stratford-upon-Avon, Marlborough, Blenheim, Cirencester, Malmesbury, Bibury village – also the gardens of Hidcote, Barnsley House and Kiftsgate. Ashton Keynes has an outstanding farm shop (meat etc.) with fruit and trout farms nearby. Antique shops are numerous.

Readers' comments: Stayed several times. Excellent in all respects.

For explanation of code letters (**C, D, H, PT, S, S-C, X**) **see page xxviii.**

CRAB AND LOBSTER INN

C PT S

Foreland, east of Bembridge, Isle of Wight   Tel: 098387 2244

5 bedrooms (single, double or family) from £11.50. Less for 7 nights. Rooms have central heating or electric heaters; shower; armchairs; views of sea or country; tea/coffee facilities.

Dinner A la carte, from 7pm. Lunches, packed lunches, snacks. Coffee, tea, for a charge. Drinks can be ordered.

Sitting-room with TV and sea views. Bars.

Nearest main road A3055 from Ryde to Shanklin.

This old inn perched on a clifftop provides simple accommodation and spectacular views over the Channel. David Hill will tell you the inn was not named after the plentiful local shellfish but a New Zealand shrub (Puniceus) which has flowers that look like crab or lobster claws and which grows by its walls. Before he took over the inn he used to have the job of advising hotels on their wine, so naturally his are good value. Good straightforward food – big lobsters straight from the sea.

The inn started in 1810 as tea-rooms, but one day the clifftop garden fell into the sea. The dining-room, with big windows is very attractively decorated (as is the adjoining bar); its walls are white-painted boards, and there are pot-plants everywhere. In the main bar are casks of sherry, peach and apricot wine, mead and scrumpy alongside more conventional drinks. There is a second bar with darts etc.

Outside are the weatherboarded watchtower of the coastguards who keep a careful eye on the reef below, footpaths along the clifftop or down to the sands, and, out in the sea, the enormous old Nab Tower that was built in Southampton and towed to its site in the days when French invasion was feared, later to be used for suspending anti-submarine nets across the approaches to the Solent. David and the coastguards who frequent the bar are full of anecdotes about such local oddities, and about some of his past visitors ('we get prince and pauper here'), who have included the French Ambassador on one occasion, and Edward Heath with the crew of *Morning Cloud* on others. The inn is very busy in high summer.

Bembridge itself is an interesting little place with a lifeboat house open to the public, sailing harbour and a particularly good maritime museum. Coast and rolling countryside are equally lovely here. Although it is at the east end of the island where most of the resorts are, it is not difficult to get to the wilder west end. There is a lot to visit here: many stately homes, fossils around Sandown (visit the geology museum to identify your finds), a first-rate wildlife park, botanical gardens with an intriguing museum of smuggling, Queen Victoria's house outside the sailing centre of Cowes, beautiful Blackgang Chine with one lovely garden after another, a centre with dozens of craftsmen at work, Carisbrooke Castle.

Readers' comments: Food excellent; service most attentive.

83

CRITERION HOTEL

CDPTSX

Cawsand, Torpoint, west of Plymouth (Devon), Cornwall, PL10 1PD
Tel: 0752 822244

8 bedrooms (single, double or family) from £15. Less for 3 nights or bargain breaks. Rooms have electric heaters; shower and wc; TV, armchairs; views of sea; balcony (one).
Dinner £10.50 for 3 courses and coffee, at 7.30pm. Special diets if ordered. Lunches, packed lunches, snacks. Coffee, tea, for a charge. Drinks can be ordered.
Sitting-room with central heating, TV, books, record-player. Bar.
Nearest main road A38 from Bodmin to Bristol.

Inconspicuous when seen from the narrow street, this little hotel occupies one of the most intriguing sites of any in this book. Originally three fishermen's cottages, it is built not just on but into the vertical cliffs behind Cawsand Bay, which faces the historic waters of Plymouth Sound. One descends from the dining-room to a cellar lounge below, and to yet another cellar (the bar, with an array of malt whiskies) below that: each with verandah hanging over the sea and steps down to what is, at low tide, a private beach of golden sand (perfect for a pre-breakfast swim). The sea here is so clear you can watch the fish swim, while not far off all the shipping going to the dockyard at Plymouth passes by.

The rooms have been furnished in keeping with the old stone buildings, their low ceilings and boarded doors, narrow and twisting corridors. I particularly liked one which has a window seat from which to enjoy the sea view. There are model ships about, local artists' paintings (for sale) and a large number of Victorian dolls beautifully dressed by Mrs Kidd, for she loves sewing as much as cooking – some of these, too, are for sale. She bakes the hotel's bread and cakes, as well as cooking such meals as bouillabaisse, beef Bourguignonne (served with interesting vegetables) and queen of puddings (accompanied by Cornish clotted cream), with cheese and coffee to follow. There is also a steak and lobster bar.

Cawsand (though so easy to reach by ferry from Plymouth) is a fishing village most tourists pass by, and so it has not been ruined like Polperro, for instance. The shops sell good pottery not trashy souvenirs, and there is no vandalism. The peninsula on which it stands is a pretty area; beyond it lies Plymouth and south Devon in one direction and the Looe area in the other. Popular sights include Mount Edgcumbe house and historic gardens, Saltram and Antony houses (NT) and Rame Head.

Readers' comments: High quality, charming and affable host, fine cooking.

Inclusive terms for dinner, bed-and-breakfast (particularly for a week) can be much lower than those quoted here for these items taken separately. For short-notice bookings you may be able to get a reduction.

No proprietor wants to have a room standing empty. This particularly applies to Sunday nights. Some hotels make a discount if you want only two courses from a three-course menu.

CROOKWOOD WATERMILL
Stert, south-east of Devizes, Wiltshire, SN10 3JA   Tel: 0380 2985

1 bedroom (double) from £10. Less for 3 nights. Central heating. No smoking.
Dinner £5 for 3 courses and coffee, served when required. Vegetarian diets or light suppers if ordered. Coffee, tea, free. Non-residents not admitted. Drinks can be brought in. No smoking.
Family sitting-room with open fire, TV, books. No smoking.
Grounds Farmland and garden.
Nearest main road A342 from Devizes to Upavon.

There has been a watermill here since Saxon times but the present pantiled building, carefully restored by Elliott Herrod-Taylor (formerly a vet), dates from about 1850. Though the mill-race is now partly filled with rushes, and the wheel awaits replacement, the mill's other surroundings have changed little through the centuries.

One finds it at the end of a very long winding track, amid pastures where Elliott's Jersey cows graze, the Wiltshire hills making a lovely backdrop to the scene. Close by is a thatched farmhouse, home of Elliott's son; and around the mill periwinkles and pansies grow.

The four floors of the mill have been converted into comfortable rooms, though still with the old joists exposed – and, in the sitting-room, the hopper down which the wheat was once fed to the turning stones that ground it into flour. One of the millstones now serves as the hearth for a log stove. On the board walls are hunting prints and bookshelves; antiques and cretonne sofas furnish the room.

The one twin-bedded room above is small but sufficient. Guests eat in the kitchen/dining-room downstairs, with the family. Denise (a wildlife expert, connected with the award-winning Devizes Museum) cooks organic produce from the farm: asparagus, pheasant, lamb, veal and pork, honey and jams, free-range eggs; above all, she uses the dairy products of the Jersey herd (not only thick cream to go with crêpes or mousses, strawberries or raspberries, but also fruit yogurts, cottage cheese and – made by her French daughter-in-law – *fromage frais*). These are also on sale.

Birdwatchers like staying at the mill in order to spot the buzzards, curlews, owls and woodpeckers which abound in this peaceful place. Denise, who has participated in the county's Flora Mapping Scheme, can point out all kinds of wildflowers. Visitors are also welcome to watch milking or the cream-separator at work.

Devizes has pleasant Georgian houses round its market square. It stands at one end of the lovely Vale of Pewsey, with Salisbury Plain to the south. This is an area of contrasts: unspoilt chalk downs, prehistoric remains (such as Avebury, Stonehenge and Silbury), river valleys, prairie-sized wheatfields, high views, boat trips, wildlife walks along the Kennet and Avon Canal, markets, museums, stately homes such as Longleat, villages of thatched cottages – it is a place that deserves a long stay. Other sights are Stourhead gardens, Marlborough, Bath and Salisbury.

For explanation of code letters (**C, D, H, PT, S, S-C, X**) **see page xxviii.**

CROSS KEYS

The Cross, East Meon, west of Petersfield, Hampshire, GU32 1NN
Tel: 0730 87251

rear view

2 bedrooms (single or double) from £11. Rooms have central heating, electric heaters; bathroom; armchairs; views of country and garden.
Large garden with river.
Nearest main road A272 from Petersfield to Winchester.
Closed November–January

In one of Hampshire's most beautiful villages, through which a trout river threads its way, is a lane where three 17th-century cottages have been united to make a very attractive family home for the young Mackinlays. The River Meon cuts across their large garden, stepping-stones and a little bridge leading from one half to the other where there is a croquet lawn (big enough for the annual village fête to be held here): a lovely scene, with hills beyond, to contemplate from wicker chairs.

Bedrooms are pleasantly furnished – crochet bedspread, rose prints and antique furniture, for instance. The informal sitting-room has an alcove of coronation and other mugs facing the leaded windows, with handsome chairs of turquoise leather, brass-studded, around a table where Rachel serves breakfast. For other meals, there are two historic inns close by – the George (where I chose an excellent game pie from their bar snacks) and the Izaak Walton, of *Compleat Angler* fame.

This green valley amid the South Downs has churches that go back to Saxon times, flint-walled houses, and prehistoric burial mounds. To the south are woodlands, remnants of the once-great Forest of Bere, and then comes Portsmouth Harbour. Despite heavy traffic on roads into the port, this is well worth a visit – to see Nelson's *Victory*, Henry VIII's *Mary Rose* and his Southsea Castle, Victorian forts up on the hills and Norman Portchester Castle down by the waterfront. There are boat trips and ferries to the Isle of Wight; excellent museums (don't miss the Royal Marines one); Dickens's birthplace; much ceremonial on Navy Days; and waterfowl on the wilder shores of the two natural harbours here. Queen Elizabeth Forest contrasts with all this (drive to Georgian Buriton, up Butser Hill, or visit the recreated Iron Age village). There's a mediaeval palace at Bishop's Waltham. Hambledon has a vineyard.

The approach to **South Farm**, East Meon (tel: 073 087 261) is delightful. There are specimen trees on a lawn (ash, viburnum, chestnut), an old granary and a grapevine under glass. In the 500-year-old house is a brick-floored dining-room with huge ingle-nook, rush ladderback chairs and a big oak table. The very large sitting-room has carved furniture and chinoiserie curtains in gold-and-blue. Bedrooms have been very agreeably furnished by Mrs Atkinson: one with poppy fabrics, for instance; in another are purple-and-

white clematis curtains and a lace bedspread. An oak-panelled room has William Morris's chrysanthemum fabric.

CROSSKEYS

Hilgay, south of King's Lynn, Norfolk, PE38 0LN   Tel: 0366 387777

5 bedrooms (double or family) from £16.90. Less for 2 nights or bargain breaks. Rooms have central heating; bathroom; TV, armchairs; views of country and river; tea/coffee facilities.
Dinner £6.50 for 3 courses (with choices) and coffee, from 7pm. Vegetarian or special diets if ordered. Packed lunches. Coffee, tea, for a charge. Drinks can be ordered.

Sitting-room with central heating, books; bar.
Large garden
Nearest main road A10 from Ely to King's Lynn.
Closed mid-December to mid-January

Long ago, this riverside house was an inn, beside a ford across the pretty River Wissey (it now has a bridge).

When it was taken over by Joan and William Lamb after he left the RAF, it was derelict: they themselves executed the transformation into an impeccably converted small hotel, with garden.

One steps straight into a small, rustic bar with copper tables, beyond which is the beamed dining-room (where Joan serves such meals as home-made soup, chicken chasseur and fruit tart with cream, for example). The bedrooms are quite outstanding for such an unpretentious little hotel: beautiful wallpapers, four-posters in two, and armchairs from which to enjoy views of river or garden (or to watch TV). I liked no. 3 best. A ground-floor suite of two rooms and bathroom would be ideal for families: children are delighted by the sight of ducks and boats on the river a few yards away and ponies grazing right outside the windows of their own bedrooms.

The area immediately around is rather flat, but soon one comes to the very fine beech and oak forest around Thetford (itself well worth a visit). Historic King's Lynn and Bury St Edmunds, the superb north coast of Norfolk, Ely, Cambridge and Newmarket are all within a short drive; Norwich and the Norfolk Broads a little further. Stately homes include Oxburgh and Houghton halls, and there are nature reserves as well as gardens (Sandringham, Blickling, Gooderstone water gardens, and an African violet centre).

If, when touring, you ask a host to book your next stop – at another *Staying Off the Beaten Track* house – remember to pay the cost of the telephone call.

For explanation of code letters (**C, D, H, PT, S, S-C, X**) see page xxviii.

CROSSWAYS FARM

C D PT

Abinger, south-west of Dorking, Surrey, RH5 6PZ   Tel: 0306 730173

3 bedrooms (double or family) from £10. Less for 2 nights. Rooms have electric heaters; armchairs; views of country or garden; tea/coffee facilities. Laundering facilities.
Dinner £5.50 for 3 courses and coffee, at 7pm. Packed lunches. Drinks can be brought in.
Sitting-room with wood burner, TV, books.
Garden with croquet and putting.
Nearest main road A25 from Guildford to Dorking.

Meredith's *Diana of the Crossways* (one of those books most people have heard of and few have read) took its title from this historic building of unusual architectural interest, which featured in a television film about the 17th-century diarist John Evelyn.

One steps through the arched door in a high wall to find a small, enclosed garden with a flagged path leading to the wide front door of the house. In its façade decorative brickwork combines with local sandstone, and Dutch-style arches curve over the small-paned windows. There is an immense chimney-stack towering above – 30 feet in circumference. But the most striking feature of all is the great oak staircase inside, its two flights leading up to large, beamed bedrooms, simply but comfortably furnished; the banisters and newels handsomely carved.

The house has had many owners since it was built about 1620. For the last quarter-century, the Hughes family have farmed here, producing beef and corn. Mrs Hughes serves homely farmhouse meals (like Irish stew, fish pie, roast chicken etc.) usually with garden vegetables; or you can eat outstandingly well at, for instance, nearby Wootton Hatch. Breakfast options include, if ordered in advance, such extras as fishcakes or kidneys.

Crossways is attractive to many people: walkers, because both the Pilgrims' Way and the Greensand Way are near (and you need no car – buses can be picked up only yards away); continental visitors, because it is a good half-way stop en route to the west country or to Wales; people making for Gatwick, because the Guildford-Gatwick-Brighton coach stops only a few steps from the door. And for Londoners, it's an ideal weekend retreat: a drive of only half an hour or so. Leith and Box hills are near; Polesden Lacey and Clandon Park; also gardens at Wisley, Chilworth and Ockley; and countless antique shops.

Single people may find more company in houses that have a shared dining-table, a bar, and no TV in the sitting-room. As my descriptions indicate, some owners mingle more with their guests than others do. Houses marked **S** charge singles little or no more than half a double.

In holiday areas, travel on any day other than a summer Saturday if you can. Make ferry, Motorail or coach/train reservations well in advance if travelling at such periods.

CROWN INN   C(14) PT
Downham Market, south of King's Lynn, Norfolk, PE38 9DH
Tel: 0366 382322

10 bedrooms (single or double) at £14. Bargain breaks. Rooms have central heating; own bathroom (most); TV, phone, armchairs; tea/coffee facilities.
Dinner A la carte, 6–10pm. Vegetarian or special diets can be prepared. Lunches, packed lunches, snacks. Coffee, tea, free. Drinks can be ordered.
Nearest main road A10 from Ely to King's Lynn.

The unassuming and small façade of this inn, facing the market square, gives no hint of what lies behind. The 17th-century building straggles far back, and when you pass under the high arch (built for coaches) you come first to the bars, with rooms above, and beyond them to what were once a considerable range of stables – since converted into restaurant and kitchens: black-and-white pantiled buildings, with hanging baskets of flowers. This was once a yeomanry centre. John Champion (formerly a civil engineer) keeps the bar more or less as it has been for the last century or so – oak-panelled, jugs hanging from its beams, a brick hearth at each end. The bar is made from sherry casks, and on the walls are wartime photographs of the famous Pathfinders air squadron who, based nearby, used this bar as their 'local'.

The stable restaurant has been discreetly converted: floors and walls are of brick, solid elm tables stand in each former loose-box. A young chef works in full view at one end, cooking griddled steaks or chops, for instance. Gâteaux, pâtés and everything else are made in the kitchens. A house speciality is Humble Pie (filled with sausage meat, potatoes and cheese). Breakfasts are served elsewhere – in a low-beamed Dickensian parlour, beyond which are two very handsome Jacobean staircases leading to the bedrooms (and a residents' sitting-room). These are spacious and furnished to a much higher standard than is usual in country inns: most have beautiful bathrooms en suite, fully tiled. (Ask for a quiet bedroom at the back.)

From Downham Market one can tour north Norfolk. Royal Sandringham is a few miles in one direction, Ely Cathedral in the other. King's Lynn itself certainly needs more than a flying visit because its mediaeval quarter alongside the river holds so much of interest. Just walking along the quays, through courts and alleys, into the cathedral-like church and to the immense market square is pleasure in itself. In addition, there are museums, art gallery, theatre in a historic building and snug inns to visit. Eastward lies one of East Anglia's finest coastlines (an area of outstanding natural beauty) with a string of bird reserves and natural shoreline. One can visit Houghton Hall and three older National Trust mansions from here, the Norfolk lavender fields, the fens, the Caithness glass factory (with bargains), Castle Rising, the cliffs of Hunstanton, Nelson's birthplace, and also the Peterborough area. The fens have a strange, wild beauty all their own. Peterborough's cathedral is one of the great splendours of the area, but its museum, riverside gardens and old byways are well worth visiting too. Go to Wisbech for a Dutch-style town (and Peckover House) and the surrounding tulip-fields in spring; to Spalding for the annual flower festival; to Thorney for its abbey and wildlife park; and to Burghley House, a great Tudor mansion.

CRYER HOUSE

Castleton, north-east of Buxton, Derbyshire, S30 2WG   Tel: 0433 20244

2 bedrooms (double or family) from £10. Rooms have central heating; TV, armchairs; views of country or garden.
Garden
Nearest main road A625 from Sheffield to Chapel-en-le-Frith.

Castleton's main claim to fame is its range of huge underground caves (several can be visited), from one of which is mined a very pretty stone, unique in the world, called Blue John – elegant trinkets made from it are lovely souvenirs to take home. Another would be a painting by actor-artist Terence Skelton, whose excellent local landscapes are very moderately priced.

Wisteria-covered Cryer House (named after a 17th-century rector who owned it) is where he lives with his wife Felicity, a former theatrical director, and their children. They have furnished the house with great flair: excellent colours and well chosen furnishings in every room. On the ground floor is a tea-room (board floor, pine tables and benches, green trellis wallpaper). Breakfast is served either here or in the new conservatory adjoining it. Packed lunches are available, but for other meals there is a choice of six eating-places in the village (I found the food at the inn next door excellent); then after dinner one can join the Skeltons' Burmese cat to relax in their little cottage garden, brimming with flowers, and watch the world go by.

The High Peak of northern Derbyshire is in complete contrast to the rest of the county. Here the crags that rise from windswept heather moors are wild and challenging. No towns – only stone hamlets sheltering below the towering ridges. This is where you will see climbers and pot-holers (hang-gliders too), and where even the less intrepid can explore winding footpaths or go down to caves of stalactites and stalagmites, some visited by boat. Some of the loveliest hamlets are Abney (with gorge), Baslow (mediaeval bridge), Castleton itself (and Peveril Castle), Edale (gorges, crags and a path up Kinder Scout, over 2000 feet high), Eyam (in wild, open country with superb views and a prehistoric circle). Eyam is 'the plague village': to prevent infection spreading, in 1666 the heroic villagers deliberately cut themselves off to die alone. Grindleford is celebrated for sheepdog trials on the moors and for Longshaw Park (1000 acres, NT). Axe Edge Moor and the Goyt valley are two areas of outstanding scenery; so is the Snake Pass; and the chain of reservoirs starting with Lady Bower.

Readers' comments: A warm welcome; comfortable, spacious rooms, lovely conservatory.

Take the trouble to get free booklets about the area before you set off. Every habitual traveller should keep a copy of the booklet of local Tourist Information Centres issued free by the English Tourist Board (Thames Tower, Blacks Road, London W6; tel: 01-846 9000) for this purpose.

CUMBERS HOUSE

Rogate, east of Petersfield, Hampshire, GU31 5EJ   Tel: 073 080 401

rear view

2 bedrooms (double) from £14. Rooms have central heating or electric heaters; showers; TV, armchairs; views of country or garden, tea/coffee facilities.

Dinner £8.50 for 3 courses and coffee, at 7.30pm. Coffee, tea, for a charge. Non-residents not admitted. Drinks can be brought in.

Sitting-room with central heating, open fire, TV, books, piano.

Grounds Woodland and lawns with croquet.

Nearest main road A272 from Midhurst to Petersfield.

A large woodland garden screens this comfortable brick house from the road, and beyond are fine downland views. Every bedroom is spacious, has large casement windows, and is pleasantly furnished – for instance, white bedpsreads and curtains contrasting with coral walls and chair-covers, flowers and bowls of pot-pourri on handsome mahogany or walnut furniture. In the green-and-grey sitting-room, there are pretty trifles around: ivory-framed miniatures, pots of velvety gloxinias or delicate streptocarpus, old china. Guests are welcome to play on the mellow and well-tuned Schiedmeyer, and to pass idle hours on the swing-seat in the garden, surrounded by varied firs, catalpa, magnolia and a fruitful fig-tree, chatting with Jon Aslett, who served with the Gurkhas. From the surrounding woods a deer occasionally wanders in, to be chased away by the tiny but ever-vigilant Licky, a Lancashire heeler.

Mrs Aslett is an excellent cook and produces imaginative meals – for instance, cucumber soup, Normandy chicken (with a creamy apple sauce) and chocolate-brandy mousse. Bread is home-baked; eggs and honey are home-produced, too. Breakfast options include home-made fishcakes.

Non-smokers preferred. Bicycle on loan.

Apart from the Georgian towns of Petersfield and Midhurst, both very near, Rogate is within a short drive of Chichester (cathedral, theatre, harbour, Roman palace); Petworth and Uppark, stately homes belonging to the National Trust; Broadlands (the Mountbatten home); Arundel (castle, river trips, antiques market, three museums, wildfowl trust); and even Portsmouth (for HMS *Victory* and Henry VIII's *Mary Rose*) and Brighton (the Regency Pavilion). There is polo to be watched at Midhurst; racing at Goodwood; a vineyard at Singleton. Among several gardens, West Dean is outstanding; there are antique shops in which to browse, and at least one good fruit farm in which to pick-your-own.

Readers' comments: Full of praise – maximum stars! Thoroughly enjoyed the welcome, and the cooking. Delightfully warm welcome, pretty rooms, delicious food, a great deal of trouble taken for our comfort. Excellent value. A charming and gracious hostess; house magnificent and peaceful. Very good home and grounds; excellent dinner, beautifully presented. Very comfortable, homely, lovely!

For explanation of code letters (**C, D, H, PT, S, S-C, X**) see page xxviii.

B & B FOR OXFAM

A few years ago, Rosemary Schlee (of Woodbridge in Suffolk) had an excellent idea to raise funds for Oxfam. She approached a number of houses in her area (and later in Norfolk and elsewhere too) and invited them to start taking guests at the usual rates but giving one-third of the proceeds to Oxfam.

The scheme has been a huge success and every year thousands of pounds are sent to Oxfam. The participants select which particular project to support: currently, it is a college in Kampuchea which trains young men in the vital engineering skills of irrigation.

Rosemary or colleagues inspect all houses in her scheme. They range from the cheap-and-cheerful to homes of very high standards indeed: in the next edition I shall be describing some which I have just visited (including Rosemary's own home). A few also serve excellent dinners.

Meantime, anyone interested in booking into an Oxfam 'b & b' in East Suffolk or around Diss can do so by telephoning Mrs Schlee (mentioning they are 'SOTBT' readers, and describing their requirements) who will then help them to book accommodation. (A list, but no brochure, describing the houses is available.) Her telephone number is 03943 2740 and her address is Deben Lodge, Melton Road, Woodbridge. When you pay your bill at each house, you get a special Oxfam receipt confirming the one-third that will go to Oxfam.

Rosemary is looking for organisers to start similar schemes in other counties, who will in turn find people willing to do b & b in aid of Oxfam. For details, telephone her.

Inclusive terms for dinner, bed-and-breakfast (particularly for a week) can be much lower than those quoted here for these items taken separately. For short-notice bookings you may be able to get a reduction.

No proprietor wants to have a room standing empty. This particularly applies to Sunday nights. Some hotels make a discount if you want only two courses from a three-course menu.

When to go? Seaside resorts or other places suitable for children will be at their busiest (and dearest) in July–August and during half-term holidays (especially, in late May, which is also a bank holiday period). Other peak periods are, of course, Easter, Christmas, New Year and the bank holiday in late August. (The bank holiday in early May is not usually a peak, because it comes rather soon after Easter, but much depends on the weather.) There are local peaks, too (the Gold Cup races at Cheltenham or the regatta at Henley, for instance, are apt to fill hotels for miles around), and local troughs (Brighton, a conference centre, is least busy in high summer). You won't get much personal attention when hotels are full to bursting.

DAIRY FARM

C S X

Cranford St Andrew, east of Kettering, Northamptonshire, NN14 4AQ
Tel: 053678 273

3 bedrooms (single, double or family) from £12.50. Less for 4 nights. Rooms have central heating or electric heaters; bathroom; armchairs; views of country or garden. TV on request.

Dinner £7.50 for 3 courses, at 7pm. Special diets if ordered. Lunches, packed lunches, snacks. Coffee, tea, for a charge. Non-residents not admitted. Drinks can be brought in.

Sitting-room with central heating, open fire, TV, books, record-player.

Garden with croquet.

Nearest main road A604 from Kettering to Cambridge.

This is not in fact a dairy farm but arable and sheep. Its name derives from the old dairy (now the dining-room) around which the manor house was built, in 1610. It is a fine building with mullioned lattice windows in limestone walls and a thatched roof. Its noble chimney-stacks, finials on the gables, dormer windows and dignified porch give it great character. In the grounds stands a circular stone dovecote (mediaeval) with unique rotating ladder inside, used for collecting the birds from the 400 pigeonholes that line it.

Audrey and John Clarke have hung old family portraits in the hall and sitting-room, and furnished the house with things like an oak dresser, chests and ladderback chairs that are in keeping with it.

Meals consist of straightforward home cooking – soups, roasts, fruit pies – using fruit and vegetables from the garden. Mrs Clarke also does a cordon bleu menu, which costs a little more and has to be ordered ahead.

Visitors enjoy local walks (beside a willow-fringed stream, across-country, or simply to the Woolpack Inn). This is good cycling country, too. Sightseeing possibilities include Burleigh House, Rockingham Castle, the mediaeval stone town of Stamford, Althorp (home of the Princess of Wales's father), Lamport and Kirby Halls, Peterborough Cathedral, Cambridge, Uppingham and Oundle; and at Kettering, Wicksteed Park is an ideal place to take children. Oundle is as attractive as many old Cotswold towns, for the local stone is the same, but much less frequented by tourists. The buildings of its famous public school are like an Oxford college. One can take boat trips on the River Nene, and visit watermills and a country park just on the outskirts, or the gardens at Coton Manor.

Readers' comments: Very special, will return. Delicious food; peaceful; attentive hosts.

When writing to me, if you want a reply please enclose a stamped addressed envelope.

If you want your hosts to post you things you have accidentally left behind, send them the cost of postage. (The trouble they take is free.)

DAMSELLS CROSS (AND DAMSELLS LODGE)   D H S PT
The Park, Painswick, south of Gloucester, Gloucestershire, GL6 6SR
Tel: 0452 813197 (Cross) and 0452 813777 (Lodge)

The following details refer to Damsells Cross:
3 bedrooms (double) from £15. Less for 2 nights. Rooms have central heating or gas heaters; TV, armchairs; views of country or garden; tea/coffee facilities. One en suite bathroom.
Sitting-room with central heating, open fire, books.
Large garden with tennis court and un-heated swimming-pool.
Nearest main road A46 from Stroud to Cheltenham.

Mrs Pointer and Mrs Cooke are sisters-in-law, living in houses next to one another. The first is a stone mansion in traditional Cotswold style (mullioned windows with leaded panes, solid oak doors that have iron fittings which were specially made by a local blacksmith, wide corridors and elegant arches indoors), and the second is a smaller but still very comfortable house, originally the lodge to the mansion. Both are in a peaceful rural lane and have truly spectacular views from every window. The Lodge has a small garden of lawns, stone terrace and flowering shrubs; Damsells Cross is surrounded by (at the front) a sunken garden with drystone walls and stone troughs of flowers and (at the back) terraces, tennis court and a swimming-pool, all against a backdrop of fine trees. At both only breakfast is provided – guests eat dinner at the nearby Royal William or in one of Painswick's restaurants: the Royal Oak or Country Elephant, for instance.

At the big house, Mrs Pointer has chosen very pretty fabrics for the large bedrooms – lacy bedspreads, or white flower-sprigged ones matching the wallpaper. The breakfast table of figured mahogany is in a bay window overlooking the garden, swimming-pool and leafy view beyond. (Sandwich suppers available.)

Mrs Cooke is a welcoming hostess who soon makes friends with her visitors. She has made the Lodge immaculate and very comfortable. The huge sitting-room has windows on three sides, and a big log stove. Everywhere there are thick carpets and good furniture (even the bathroom is pretty luxurious). In my view, the best bedroom is one separate from the house: it is in a one-floor garden cottage, with huge sliding windows through which to step straight onto the lawn or to view the distant hills while still in bed and ideal for anyone who finds stairs difficult. Peter is a landscape gardener; and some shrubs and conifers like those in his own fine garden are for sale.

Painswick church is famous for its 99 enormous yews, centuries-old, clipped into arches or other neat shapes, and for its fine peal of twelve bells. When the September yew-clipping takes place, children dance and sing round the church. The village has many antique shops. To the north lies the cathedral city of Gloucester, and to the south the wooded Cotswold hills, with particularly spectacular views from Minchinhampton and Rodborough commons (National Trust land). Go west for the Severn estuary with its throngs of seabirds and geese.

Readers' comments: Mrs Pointer is a delightful hostess – good breakfast, lovely garden. The Cross is the finest house we stayed at. Excellent accommodation at the Lodge; the place and the owners delightful.

DEDHAM HALL

H PT

Dedham, north of Colchester, Essex CO7 6AD   Tel: 0206 323027

12 bedrooms (single, double or family) from £15.50. Less for 7 nights. Rooms have central heating or electric heaters; shower or bathroom; armchairs; views of country, lake or garden; tea/coffee facilities.
Dinner £12 for 4 courses, at 7.30pm. Special diets if ordered. Non-residents not usually admitted. Drinks can be ordered. No dinner on Wednesdays.

2 sitting-rooms with central heating, open fire, TV, books, piano. Bar.
Large garden and paddock; with croquet.
Nearest main road A12 from Ipswich to Chelmsford.
Closed mid-December–February

Set back from the village, beyond a large green (where sheep graze) and a big duckpond, stands this lovely old house, with a wide-spreading magnolia tree in front of it and gardens all around. Wisteria and clematis clamber up its pink walls. Just beyond the barns and lawns is Dedham's fine mediaeval church.

When the Slingos moved here there was an immense amount to do. The house, which developed in stages from the 14th to 17th centuries, had once been the miller's house and a bakery (the watermill itself has been turned into flats). Now it is elegantly furnished with antiques, decorated in lovely colours and filled with flowers from the garden. Every room, from the beamed hall to the carpeted and wallpapered bathroom, is attractive. In the sitting-room, a log fire is lit on chilly evenings.

The food in the beamed dining-room is very good; home-grown vegetables are served and home-made bread. A typical dinner might consist of avocado and walnut mousse, outstandingly good roast beef with Yorkshire pudding, and meringues. Home-made jam, chutneys and honey are on sale.

Picturesque Dedham is, of course, celebrated for its Constable connection, and there are art holidays at Dedham Hall. A 15th-century barn is now a studio.

Readers' comments: Most enjoyable. Food and accommodation excellent.

For bed-and-breakfast only, **Upper Park** (tel: 0206 323197) at Dedham is excellent. It is full of family heirlooms, paintings and beautiful furnishings. (One can dine at Dedham Hall, by arrangement, or at the Marlborough Head in the middle of Dedham, for instance.) Miss Watson and her mother are attentive to visitors' every need.

Readers' comments: Friendly and accommodating; comfortable and well appointed house. Elegant. Thoroughly enjoyed ourselves. Charming Watsons, delightful home. Most comfortable and elegant.

95

DERWENT COTTAGE *New*

Portinscale, west of Keswick, Cumbria, CA12 5RF   Tel: 07687 74838

5 bedrooms (double) from £16. Some have own bath/shower; TV; tea/coffee facilities; central heating; views of garden.
Dinner £10 for 4 courses and coffee, at 7pm. Vegetarian or special diets if ordered. Packed lunches, snacks. Tea, coffee, free. Drinks can be ordered.
2 sitting-rooms with central heating, open fire, books; bar.
Large garden
Nearest main road A66 from Penrith to Cockermouth.
Closed from November–March

A previous owner, an Austrian, amassed a collection of paintings which sold for millions after his death some years ago. None of them remains in Derwent Cottage, nor does the statuary which he had in the garden, but this still contains the unusual trees he planted – stately conifers for the most part, around terraced lawns. The 1½ acres of grounds give a splendid view across to Skiddaw, the highest mountain in the northern Lake District.

The house is, despite its name, no mere cottage – for the original 17th-century dwelling was greatly extended in Victorian times in the picturesque but rather grand style favoured by those who built retreats in the Lake District in those days. The result is high-ceilinged and spacious rooms oriented to take advantage of the site, which is set back above the main street of a village.

The house is conventionally and comfortably furnished, with one sitting-room and a bar. In the colourful dining-room, with crisp linen and sparkling glassware, Sue Hoffmann and her partner Edward Compton serve a choice of soup or other first course (all home-made); a dish of the day, which might be a joint with a good sauce, beef Wellington or guinea-fowl; a pudding; and cheese.

Portinscale is a good base for those keen on sailing, boating and other water-sports, which can be pursued on Derwentwater (there are launch trips for the less active). On the lake shore are Lingholm Gardens, best known for rhododendrons and azaleas and for fine trees in the woodland area.

Readers' comments: One of the best value-for-money hotels we have stayed at.

Prices are the minimum *per person* in a double room at the beginning of the year.

Houses which do *not* take children tend to have vacancies in July and August.

Many houses have cards, chess, Scrabble etc. – just ask. And also such things as irons, hair-dryers, maps, gumboots and bridge-tables.

DRUMMOND ARMS

D PT

Albury, east of Guildford, Surrey, GU5 9AG   Tel: 048 641 2039

7 bedrooms (single or double) from £13. Rooms have central heating; bathroom; TV, armchairs; views of garden; tea/coffee facilities.

Dinner A la carte, from 7.30pm. Vegetarian or special diets if ordered. Lunches, packed lunches. Drinks can be ordered.

Nearest main road A25 from Dorking to Guildford.

The crowning jewel of this country inn is a fast-flowing stream (the Tillingbourne) which runs among the willows at the end of its secluded garden, enclosed by beech hedges and yews. It is surrounded by woods where pigeons coo.

The bedroom which has the best view of the garden is no. 7. All are spacious and well-carpeted, with armchairs, TV and pleasant colour schemes.

Downstairs, there is a formal dining-room (closed on Mondays), but I prefer to eat in the more convivial bar (traditionally furnished with tapestry seats, pewter and Toby jugs) where the Ransons' snacks are excellent and inexpensive: braised liver, for instance, and perfectly cooked fruit pies.

Albury is tucked away in one of the most scenic parts of the high Surrey Downs, with the famous viewpoint of Newlands Corner nearby, the brilliantly blue Silent Pool, picturesque Shere village and its stream, a celebrated blacksmith-automaton striking the hours at Abinger Hammer, National Trust woodlands, and – along the pretty little River Tillingbourne – trout farms and watercress beds.

Albury itself is an interesting village: many of its small cottages have immense, ornate chimneys copied from those at Hampton Court. Drummond is a family name of the Duke of Northumberland, local landowner. Parts of the local mansion, Albury Park (which he owns), are open to the public, and in its grounds – originally landscaped by John Evelyn – are two contrasting churches of historic interest. Near it are the RHS gardens at Wisley, Clandon Park and Hatchlands.

Surrey is full of contrasts – such as Guildford (castle, theatre and old byways), the coaching town of Dorking (good antique and craft shops here), Birdwold, Chessington World of Adventures, Winkworth Arboretum, garden centres, farm shops and much more. And all so very close to London!

Readers' comments: Pleasant, friendly; extremely comfortable (but front room gets traffic noise).

Don't complain if –
- because you booked at short notice, you do not get the best room
- because you did not order a meal in advance, you get something plucked from the freezer
- because you do not arrive on time, your room is let to someone else
- because you bring a dog without asking, it is refused entry
- because you don't express your wishes (for more heat, a second helping, or whatever), you don't get what you want!

EASTON HOUSE

Chidham, west of Chichester, West Sussex, PO18 8TF   Tel: 0243 572514

C D PT S

3 bedrooms (double or family) from £11. Rooms have central heating or electric heaters; washbasin, shower or bathroom; armchairs; views of sea, country or garden; tea/coffee facilities; laundering available. No smoking.
Sitting-room with central heating, open fire, TV, books, piano.
Garden
Nearest main road A27 from Chichester to Portsmouth.

Every corner of this Tudor house has been filled by Mary Hartley with unusual furniture and trifles. A modern white-and-red poppy wallpaper contrasts with old beams, oriental rugs with stone-flagged floor, scarlet folkweave curtains with antique chandeliers. Jim Hartley collects mirrors (Spanish, art deco, rococo – every conceivable kind) and pictures of cats; Mary makes patchwork; guests play on the Bechstein if so inclined. It's a free-and-easy atmosphere, a house full of character and cats. Even the bathrooms are pretty, with delicately sprigged wallpapers.

Although this is only a bed-and-breakfast house (one can dine well in Chichester, particularly at Thompson's, at the Old House at Home or in nearby waterfront inns), visitors are welcome to linger in the comfortable lime-green sitting-room with its log stove (where tea is served on arrival); or in the garden, under the shade of magnolia and walnut trees.

Peaceful Chidham looks across an inlet to ancient Bosham, one of the most picturesque sailing villages on the winding shores of Chichester's lovely natural harbour (with boat trips): very popular and therefore very crowded in high summer. Chichester itself is near. It has a mediaeval cathedral, Georgian houses and a festival theatre of considerable renown.

Wherever you drive or walk there is fine scenery; and plenty of interesting sights within a few miles – such as the Weald & Downland Open-Air Museum (acres of ancient buildings reconstructed), the huge Roman palace of Fishbourne, a brass-rubbing centre in Chichester and crafts complex in Bosham (which also has an open-air theatre), fine gardens at West Dean, a fascinating 'live' museum of mechanical music (organs, pianolas etc.), military aircraft at Tangmere, rose nursery at Apuldram, Kingley Vale nature reserve, Goodwood House, the gardens of Chidmere House and Chilsdown vineyard. Arundel, Petworth and Portsmouth are near.

Readers' comments: Peaceful house with great character, very reasonably priced. A marvellous place. Mrs Hartley anticipates her guests' every need. Excellent.

Further down the lane is the **Old Rectory** (tel: 0243 572088), built in 1830 and now well-furnished by Mrs Blencowe in traditional country-house style. The large garden has a swimming-pool (unheated) and the sitting-room a grand piano. Bed-and-breakfast only.

EBURY HOTEL   **C D H PT S-C**
65–67 New Dover Road, Canterbury, Kent, CT1 3DX   Tel: 0227 68433

15 **bedrooms** (single, double or family) from £17.85. Bargain breaks. **15% discount**

offered to readers of this book who stay for **2 nights or more** (other than bargain breaks). Rooms have central heating; shower or bathroom; remote-control TV, phone, armchairs; tea/coffee facilities.
Dinner £9.50 for 3 courses and coffee, at 7–8.30pm. Special diets if ordered. Packed lunches, snacks. Coffee, tea, for a charge. Drinks can be ordered. No dinner on Sundays.
Sitting-room with central heating, TV, books.
Large garden
Nearest main road A2 from London to Dover.

This is a very big Victorian mansion (run by Jane and Anthony Mason), set back from a main road out of Canterbury, with a large garden at the rear. The food and furnishings are conventional, with much emphasis on comfort and space. The sitting-room is huge and, like the other rooms, immaculately kept. An unusual feature is Anthony's collection of *oeil de boeuf* clocks. There is an undercover swimming-pool and spa bath in the garden.

As to dinner, there are eight choices at each course – mainly classic dishes like salmon mayonnaise, steak Bercy or roast duck.

The city centre is within walking distance. The Ebury Hotel, being on the road to Dover, is a useful place to stay before or after a ferry-crossing to the continent – or as a base from which to explore the historic south Kent coast, the Cinque Ports, Dover Castle and Dover's famous Roman 'Painted House' or the Kent country-side, the garden of England. Other attractions are Chilham Castle, Howlett's Zoo, the Romney miniature railway, and Sissinghurst's gardens.

There is a tremendous amount to do in this county – dozens of stately homes or castles to visit; craft workshops, wildlife parks, vineyards, a pinetum, old towns like Tunbridge Wells, Finchcocks (a 'live' museum of old musical instruments in a Queen Anne house) and the countryside itself. Many of the beaches of Kent are within motoring distance.

There is more about this scenic and historic part of Kent under other entries.

Readers' comments: Very friendly and helpful, good meals. Very good food, lovely room. Very comfortable, immaculate.

Two-thirds of the houses in this book have bargain breaks or other discounts on offer, some exclusive to readers. Only a third raise prices at the peak of summer.

It's best to stay at least 2–3 days: you cannot possibly appreciate an area if you only stay overnight (prices per night are often less, too, if you stay on). The vouchers on page ii are usable for 3-night stays.

EDENBRECK HOUSE

Sunnyside Lane, Lancaster, LA1 5ED   Tel: 0524 32464

C(3) **D PT S**

5 bedrooms (double) from £12.50. Rooms have central heating; TV, armchairs; views of country or garden; tea/coffee facilities; bathrooms.
Sitting-room with central heating and open fire, TV, books, record-player.
Large garden
Nearest main road M6.

To find this secluded house, with views of fields and hills, actually *in* the city of Lancaster is one surprise. Another is that, although it has all the detail and dignity of an 1860s mansion, it was built only a few years ago. Margaret Houghton and her husband wanted to recreate the style of a 'gentleman's residence' of that era – with all that implies in terms of quality, comfort and spaciousness – and the thought and care they put into it are impressive. They sought out furniture of the period too; but into old marble washstands modern basins have been fitted, and in the largest suite, running from front to back of the house and equally suitable for a honeymoon couple or for a family, is an outsize Jacuzzi bath and a bidet. The pink double bed is on a pink-carpeted dais. One room has a four-poster.

Only bed-and-breakfast is served but Lancaster has many eating places: the Taste of Scotland restaurant is very popular with visitors. Among popular local sights are Lancaster Castle and church, Hornsea pottery, old Glasson Dock, Blackpool and the Lake District. At Barton Grange is a good garden centre. Lancaster itself is a historic city, often overlooked by tourists. Even its name is historic, describing its role as a Roman fort (*castra*) on the River Lune. It is well worth visiting the quay, no longer busy and with its handsome Custom House (portico and pillars) now turned into a maritime museum. The wealth of trade conducted via the river in the 18th century accounts for the multitude of fine houses from that period which still make Lancaster an attractive city.

A leafy lane leads steeply up from the quay to the Norman castle looming overhead, and the 15th-century church which has finely carved choir stalls (and a café, where its silver is displayed). There are splendid views over the rooftops from here, towards great Morecambe Bay in one direction and in another to the hill where the enormous copper-domed Ashton Memorial dominates the skyline. Parts of the castle (including dungeons) are open to view; the rest is a prison. Celebrated trials have been held in its courtroom. It still has a portcullis.

There are cobbled byways to explore, interesting museums in historic houses, antique shops, a notable covered market, the canal (with boat trips), a lovely park on the hill around the Ashton Memorial, and in adjoining Morecambe an immensely long promenade overlooking sands which, when the tide is out, seem to stretch to infinity.

Readers' comments: Beautiful house and setting; luxurious; unsurpassed hospitality. Beautifully decorated, outstanding value.

EDGCOTT HOUSE *New*   C D S X

Edgcott, south-west of Minehead, Somerset, TA24 7QG   Tel: 064383 495

4 bedrooms (single, double or family) from £12. Less for 7 nights and bargain breaks. Some have own bath/shower; central heating; views of river, country or garden. (Washing-machine on request.)
Dinner £7.50 for 4 courses (with choices) and coffee, at 7.30pm. Vegetarian or special diets if ordered. Packed lunches, snacks. Tea, coffee, extra. Drinks can be brought in.
Sitting-room with central heating, open fire, TV, books, piano.
Large garden
Nearest main road A396 from Bampton to Minehead.

Trompe l'oeil murals, in 'Strawberry Hill gothick' style, cover the walls of the long dining/sitting-room. They were painted in the 1940s by George Oakes, who is now a director of the distinguished interior decorating firm of Colefax & Fowler. The tall bay windows of this room open onto a tiled terrace from which there is a fine hill view beyond the old, rambling garden where yellow Welsh poppies grow in profusion, and wisteria clambers over the pink walls of the house. In the long entrance hall (red quarry-tiled floor contrasting with whitewashed stone walls) are Persian rugs and unusual clocks. Bedrooms are homely; throughout there is a mix of antique and merely old furniture, with more *trompe l'oeil* alcoves or doors.

Gillian Lamble's style of cooking is traditionally English and she serves such meals as mackerel pâté, roast lamb, lemon meringue pie and cheeses.

Edgcott is right in the middle of Exmoor, a national park that was once, a thousand years ago, a royal hunting forest. It is a region of varied scenery – part of the moor is green and pastoral, part wild heath, and to the north it goes to the sea.

Readers' comments: Mrs Lamble is kindness itself. A house of character.

Outside nearby Luckwell Bridge is an 18th-century farm with apricot walls: **Cutthorne** (tel: 064383 255), where Ann Durbin – who once ran a restaurant – can produce anything from simple to gourmet candlelit dinners. Bedrooms in the house vary, some homely but one with a carved and tapestry-hung four-poster. In the sitting- and dining-rooms are antique rugs, log fires and brass-rubbings.

There is also a courtyard where chickens roam, a pond with exotic species of ducks and geese, and swings in a children's play area. (Very good value.)

101

EDGEHILL HOTEL

C D PT

Hadleigh, Suffolk, IP7 5AP   Tel: 0473 822458

6 bedrooms (single, double or family) from £15; less in new annexe. Less also for 2 nights or bargain breaks. Rooms have central heating, double glazing; shower or bathroom; TV, armchairs. Laundering available.
Dinner £9 for 3 courses (with limited choices) and coffee, at 7pm. Special diets if ordered. Packed lunches, snacks. Coffee, tea, for a charge (free on arrival, with cakes). Drinks can be ordered.
Sitting-room with central heating, open fire, TV, books.
Walled garden
Nearest main road A12 from London to Ipswich.

Hadleigh, once a rich wool town, went through bad times but is now prospering again. As a result, its very lengthy High Street is full of shops enjoying a new life as wine bars, antique shops and so forth. It is a street of colourful façades, gables, pargetting (decorative plasterwork), overhanging bay windows, carved wood details, ornamental porches and fanlights over the doors. Behind lie meadows and a river.

One of the High Street's many fine buildings to have been rejuvenated recently is a Tudor house with Georgian façade which is now this private hotel. Rodney Rolfe, formerly the manager of a motor dealer's, took over Edgehill Hotel in 1976 and began to convert it. The well-proportioned rooms have been furnished in good taste, and attractive wallpapers chosen for each one. In all the spacious bedrooms there are thick-pile carpets and good furniture. The large sitting-room has glass doors opening onto the walled garden.

Angela Rolfe, previously a teacher, and her mother do all the cooking and use home-grown raspberries, strawberries, vegetables and other produce from the kitchen garden. She serves home-made soup, roasts and 'good, old-fashioned puddings' like plum duff, rice or bread-and-butter pudding. She is not only a good cook, but makes and sells crafts.

This is a good base from which to explore the very pretty countryside and villages nearby, and such well-known beauty-spots as mediaeval Lavenham, Dedham, Woodbridge on the Deben estuary, Kersey, Long Melford and many others. There are stately homes to visit nearby and the castle at Colchester, Flatford Mill, gardens at East Bergholt and Kentwell Hall, two garden centres and any number of antique shops.

Readers' comments: Absolutely excellent. High standard.

Inclusive terms for dinner, bed-and-breakfast (particularly for a week) can be much lower than those quoted here for these items taken separately. For short-notice bookings you may be able to get a reduction.

No proprietor wants to have a room standing empty. This particularly applies to Sunday nights. Some hotels make a discount if you want only two courses from a three-course menu.

ELDOCHAN HALL *New*

Willimoteswyke, Bardon Mill, west of Hexham, Northumberland, NE47 7DB   Tel: 04984 465

C D H P T S

2 bedrooms (double or family) from £10.50. Less for 3 nights and bargain breaks. All have own toilet; tea/coffee facilities; central heating; views of river, country or garden. No smoking. (Washing-machine on request.)

Dinner £6 for 3 courses and coffee, by arrangement. Non-residents not admitted. Vegetarian or special diets if ordered. Packed lunches, snacks. Tea, coffee, free. Drinks can be brought in.

Sitting-room with central heating, open fire, TV, books, piano, cassette-player.

Large garden

Nearest main road A69 from Newcastle to Carlisle.

No stranger would guess that an extraordinary enclave lies just to one side of the busy Newcastle–Carlisle road, reached only by an inconspicuous turning or, from the east, by a network of narrow roads which lead to nowhere. It is where the rushing River Allen slows down to meet the South Tyne in its valley bottom. To reach Eldochan Hall, you will drive through old mixed woodland, pass a bastle house (an old fortified farmhouse – bastle is the same as *bastille*) and a miniature hamlet with a picture-postcard church and graveyard, and at the end of this winding road, probably having taken a wrong turning or two, you will see a half-ruined castle built into a farmstead. Eldochan Hall, which lies below the castle, is perhaps two centuries old, probably built on the site of another bastle.

The stone-slated porch leads into a dining-room with an old kitchen range, now with a wood stove incorporated. Here, teacher's wife Elaine MacDonald serves meals (such as melon, pork casserole, and chocolate pudding) when the house is full. When guests are few, they eat in what amounts to a private sitting-room, off which opens the best bedroom. This, like the upstairs rooms, has a pleasant mixture of antique and modern furniture. Much of the neat modernization of the house was the MacDonalds' own work. A stream rushes past the garden.

For walkers, there are footpaths and the wooded Allen Banks estate; for the carless, a railway station is only half a mile away over a footbridge. Photographers and naturalists will make the most of the nearby nature reserve, the tree-lined river banks, and the picturesque buildings at Beltingham and along little-used lanes.

A few miles eastward, and more accessible for a short stop, is **Geeswood House** (tel: 043484 220), an efficiently run guest-house on the outskirts of the town of Haydon Bridge, with a very large hillside garden containing a small waterfall. Doreen Easton's food is home-made, including the bread. It is a short walk from the station, with regular services to Carlisle, Newcastle, and points in between (connections for Scotland and west Cumbria).

ELM HOUSE *New*   **C D PT S**
Upper Holt Street, Earls Colne, west of Colchester, Essex, CO6 2PG
Tel: 07875 2197

4 bedrooms (double or family) from £12. Some have own bath/shower; tea/coffee facilities; central heating; views of garden. No smoking. (Washing-machine on request.)
Dinner From £9 for 4 courses (with choices) and coffee, at 7.45pm. Non-residents by arrangement. Vegetarian or special diets if ordered. Lunches, packed lunches, snacks. Tea, coffee, free. Drinks can be brought in.
2 sitting-rooms with central heating, open fire, TV, books.
Small garden
Nearest main road A604 from Colchester to Cambridge.
Closed in December and January

This gracious 18th-century house has been furnished with suitable elegance. The grass-green and pale pink sitting-room, where a log fire crackles behind a high brass fender is furnished with antiques (its high French doors open onto a large garden where meals are occasionally served). In the dining-room, which is sage-green, the mahogany table is laid with white-and-gold Spode and silver candelabra at dinner time; breakfast is eaten in the big L-shaped kitchen made cosy by a log stove. There is also a reading/writing-room for guests who want complete quiet.

Although on a main road, the house provides quiet bedrooms at the back, overlooking the walled garden (windows are double-glazed). I liked the coffee-and-white room with William Morris curtains; another is huge, with windows on three sides. There are pretty antique iron beds (painted white or black, with bright brass knobs) coupled with the modern comfort of pink duvets. Details like brass curtain-poles and decorative fanlights catch one's eye.

Lady Larcom so much enjoyed entertaining that she started to run a private catering service and to take guests in Elm House. Dinners here are therefore rather special. They may begin with bouillabaisse, for example, followed perhaps by stuffed peppers (baked in tomato and mushroom sauce, topped with sour cream, and served with wild rice and salad), then may come iced coffee soufflé and cheeses.

Earls Colne is in one of the best parts of Essex – the north-east. This is a region of peaceful water-meadows with willows, outstanding churches and great historic interest. Colchester is an exceptional Roman/Norman city, described elsewhere. All down the coast are winding creeks and wildernesses that attract migrant waterfowl. Where once the Vikings sailed in to plunder, boat enthusiasts now go yachting. There is very varied scenery to explore inland: heaths, woods and villages that once prospered from weaving wool and which still remain beautiful today.

If you have not arrived by, perhaps, 6pm your room may be let to someone else – unless you telephone to say you are on your way.

ENFORD HOUSE *New*   **C D PT S**
Enford, north of Salisbury, Wiltshire, SN9 6DJ   Tel: 0980 70414

3 bedrooms (double or family) from £12 with TV; tea/coffee facilities; central heating; views of river, country or garden. (Washing-machine on request.)
Dinner £9 for 4 courses and coffee, at 7–8pm (must be ordered by lunchtime). Packed lunches. Tea, coffee, free. Drinks can be brought in.
Sitting-room with central heating, open fire, TV, books.
Large garden
Nearest main road A345 from Marlborough to Salisbury.

The latest in telecommunications and 4000-year-old mysteries oddly combine in the telephone number of this house – Stonehenge* 70414: this world-famous monument is only a few miles away. In fact, Enford (being in Salisbury Plain) is surrounded by prehistoric remains of many kinds.

The 18th-century house (once a rectory) and its garden are enclosed by thatched-topped walls – a feature one often finds in those parts of Wiltshire where, stone being non-existent, a mix of earth and dung with horsehair or else chalk blocks were used to build walls (which then needed protection from rain). The house has pointed 'Gothick' windows on one side, glass doors to the garden on another. Antiques furnish the panelled sitting-room, which has a crackling fire on chilly nights. Bedrooms are conventionally furnished.

Sarah Campbell serves, on pretty Watteau china, soups that she makes from garden vegetables, roasts, puddings such as gooseberry fool or lemon soufflé, then cheeses. The Campbells sometimes dine with their guests, and tell them a great deal about the area – not just its historic sights but its considerable wildlife (Salisbury Plain has a tremendous variety of wildflowers as well as larks and lapwings), where to go for the finest views from the surrounding downs, the best walks (paths beside the historic Kennet & Avon Canal are level and the scene very pretty) and the best inns – which, incidentally, include the Swan, just across the river at Enford. This is the Avon which rises in the downs north of here, flows through an exceptionally lovely valley all the way into Salisbury and thence through Hampshire to the sea at historic Christchurch – it would be possible to follow its course by car, passing through many pretty villages along the way.

The vast green undulations of Salisbury Plain have changed little over the centuries; its grandeur is as imposing as ever, its fields of grain sweeping to the horizon like a prairie.

Near Enford is the lovely Vale of Pewsey: Pewsey itself (under an hour from London by train) is a small town of thatched cottages and 18th-century houses with a statue of Alfred the Great near the river. At the other end of the Vale is the market town of Devizes (its museum holds many of the prehistoric remains found in the Plain) and beyond it Trowbridge, the handsome stone buildings of which were built by rich cloth-merchants descended from Flemish weavers who fled here during periods of religious persecution. Another weavers' town is Westbury, near which is one of Wiltshire's many famous white horses, cut through the turf.

* The number 0980 quoted above is the dialling code for Stonehenge.

ESHTON GRANGE

Eshton, north-west of Skipton, North Yorkshire, BD23 3QE
Tel: 0756 749 383

C PT S S-C X

4 bedrooms (double or family) from £13. Rooms have central heating, electric heaters; shower, wc; TV, armchairs; views of country or garden; tea/coffee facilities. Clothes-washing facilities.
Dinner £6.50 for 3 courses and coffee, at 6.30–8pm. Vegetarian diets if ordered. Lunches, packed lunches. Drinks can be brought in.
Sitting-room with central heating, open fire, books.
Nearest main road A65 from Skipton to Settle.

Inquisitive brown eyes watched my arrival: two of the Eshton Grange stud of tiny Shetland ponies were in a paddock overlooking the courtyard.

Judy and Terry Shelmerdine have created a comfortable, informal atmosphere in their home even though it is furnished with fine antiques and good paintings. It has stone inglenooks, chintz or tapestry chairs and deep-set windows.

The beamed bedrooms are on two floors – at the top is a big attic room ideal for a family, for children shin up a ladder to their beds in the apex of the roof, tucked away above the king-post which supports it. It's a higgledy-piggledy room, with pretty trellis wallpaper, a circular window, and in one corner a cooker useful for preparing the children's supper.

Dinners are traditionally English – home-made soup, roast chicken with all the accompaniments, sherry trifle, and cheese, for example. You help yourself to as much as you want.

Eshton is surrounded by beautiful views. It is near Malham (in Airedale) famous for its massive crags, tarn (lake) belonging to the National Trust, and cove – a huge circular cliff. Go to Gordale Scar for the sight of twin waterfalls in a 300-foot gorge. There is a moorland road through wooded Littondale to Arncliffe and Litton, villages with quaint houses, ancient churches, swirling rivers – and few tourists.

Don't complain if –
- because you booked at short notice, you do not get the best room
- because you did not order a meal in advance, you get something plucked from the freezer
- because you do not arrive on time, your room is let to someone else
- because you bring a dog without asking, it is refused entry
- because you don't express your wishes (for more heat, a second helping, or whatever), you don't get what you want!

Single people may find more company in houses that have a shared dining-table, a bar, and no TV in the sitting-room. As my descriptions indicate, some owners mingle more with their guests than others do. Houses marked **S** charge singles little or no more than half a double.

ETCHILHAMPTON HOUSE

C D

Etchilhampton, south-east of Devizes, Wiltshire, SN10 3JH   Tel: 0380 2927

rear view

4 bedrooms (single, double or family) from £12.50. Rooms have electric heaters; TV, armchairs; views of country and garden; tea/coffee facilities.
2 sitting-rooms with open fire, TV, books, piano.

Large garden and paddock, with tennis, croquet and heated (75°) swimming-pool.
Nearest main road A342 from Devizes to Andover.

This gracious house (surrounded by lawns, fine trees and the herbaceous borders of a walled garden) was built by a local merchant in the 18th century. Now it is the home of Priscilla and Michael Maude, both widely travelled. Priscilla used to work in the British embassies of Rome and Paris, there developing a taste for the arts. She provides bed-and-breakfast only, but there is a plentiful choice of eating places in Devizes (five minutes away).

There is a yellow sitting-room with alcoves full of books; and from the big hall a fine staircase rises to spacious bedrooms – their large sash windows have garden views. Flowery wallpapers and simple furniture predominate.

Guests are welcome to use the garden, the croquet lawn, tennis court and heated, covered swimming-pool. The best view of the wisteria-covered house is from the back: to one side of the door, with pretty fanlight under its arch, is a great wall-sundial ('I only tell ye sunnie hours'). There is a sunken rose-garden.

Visitors staying here (only 2 hours from London) find the local scenery delightful, but can go further afield to visit Bath, Longleat and other stately homes, prehistoric Avebury and Stonehenge, Salisbury Cathedral. This is good cycling and walking country (with views of the famous white horses carved into the chalky downs), and one can go on the historic Kennet & Avon Canal. Other interesting places are Lacock Abbey, Devizes Museum and the gardens of Bowood.

Readers' comments: Could not have been made more welcome or comfortable. Delightful.

Take the trouble to get free booklets about the area before you set off. Every habitual traveller should keep a copy of the booklet of local Tourist Information Centres issued free by the English Tourist Board (Thames Tower, Blacks Road, London W6; tel: 01-846 9000) for this purpose.

FELDON HOUSE
Lower Brailes, west of Banbury, Oxfordshire, OX15 5HW   Tel: 060 885 580

3 bedrooms (double) from £17 with central heating; armchairs; views of garden or country. Bargain breaks.
Dinner £15.50 for 4 courses, served whenever required. Lunches, packed lunches. Special diets if ordered. Tea, coffee, free. Drinks can be ordered.
2 sitting-rooms with central heating, log fires, TV, books.
Garden
Nearest main road A34 from Oxford to Stratford-upon-Avon.

It is not only the outstanding cooking of Allan Witherick which brings visitors to this lovely and peaceful house by the village church. The leafy Cotswold views, a particularly pretty cottage-garden and the care with which Maggie has furnished every room all add up to something very special.

One approaches this mainly Victorian house up a long stone-flagged path, columbines and lupins brimming over the beds on either side and a huge lime tree shading the lawn. There is a south-facing terrace of herringbone bricks where guests often take their pre-dinner drinks (always served with crudités and a dip).

Inside are two dining-rooms (and two sitting-rooms) so that when there are separate parties of guests they can remain separate if they prefer. One dining-room (furnished, like all rooms, with well-chosen Victorian antiques) has redcurrant walls; and adjoins an older sitting-room, brick-walled and with views of the rear garden (it has an alcove with television). The other is in a former conservatory, now carpeted and with Aztec-patterned curtains; its adjoining sitting-room is decorated in sandalwood, against which the Withericks' collection of Victorian water-colours shows well.

Bedrooms (and bathrooms) are equally attractive; and all rooms are full of Maggie's personal touches – like her constantly growing collection of eggs (glass, alabaster or decorated), pot-plants or nosegays, masses of books, well-chosen pictures and, in winter, log fires. Later, there will be more rooms when plans to convert the adjoining coach-house are completed.

As to Allan's meals, not only is he an outstanding chef but the presentation of each dish is done with style. A typical dinner menu: lovage soup; salmon; chicken breast stuffed with pine kernels; peach with strawberry sauce. The vegetables are particularly imaginatively prepared – it's the only place where I've been served new potatoes with lavender leaves! The food is complemented by Chartreuse china, crystal glasses and candlelight; coffee is accompanied by a dish of petits fours. Breakfasts are both ample and varied.

This part of Oxfordshire is described under other entries.

Readers' comments: Our favourite. Food excellent. Congenial helpful hosts.

In holiday areas, travel on any day other than a summer Saturday if you can. Make ferry, Motorail or coach/train reservations well in advance if travelling at such periods.

FITZ MANOR *New*   **C D PT S S-C**

Fitz, Bomere Heath, north-west of Shrewsbury, Shropshire, SY4 3AS
Tel: 0743 850295

3 bedrooms (single, double or family) from £12.50. Less for 7 nights and bargain breaks. Rooms have TV; tea/coffee facilities; central heating; views of river, country or garden. (Washing-machine on request.)
Dinner A la carte or £10 for 4 courses (with choices) and coffee, at times to suit guests. Vegetarian or special diets if ordered. Lunches, packed lunches, snacks. Tea, coffee, free. Drinks can be brought in.
2 sitting-rooms with central heating, open fire, TV, books, piano, record-player.
Large garden
Nearest main road A5 from London to Holyhead.

This outstanding manor house was built about 1450 in traditional Shropshire style – black timbers and white walls. It is at the heart of a large farm where vegetables and grain are grown.

The interior is one of the most impressive in this book. A vast dining-room with parquet floor and Persian carpet overlooks rosebeds, pergolas and yew hedges. It is furnished with antiques, paintings by John Piper and a collection of Crown Derby. In the oak-panelled sitting-room there are damask and pink velvet armchairs around the log fire (or guests can use the glass sun-room). Between these two rooms are the arched hall and a winding oak staircase; one door here is carved with strapwork and vines, on the walls are ancestral portraits, and on the tiled floor Persian rugs and oak chests.

Bedrooms differ in size. For instance, adjoining one huge room with armchairs from which to enjoy views of the Severn valley and Welsh hills is a white cottage-style bedroom – a useful combination for a family (and Fitz Manor has a playroom with toys for children).

Dawn Baly's candlelit dinners often start with home-made pâté or soup; casseroled pheasant or wild duck sometimes appear as the main course, with home-grown vegetables; puddings may be fruit pies, meringues or chocolate mousse; and then there are cheeses – unless visitors want only a salad or shepherd's pie supper.

The garden is still much as it was when laid out in Tudor times, although now there is a heated swimming-pool and croquet lawn. Guests are encouraged to use the land – for barbecues, picnics, swimming or fishing in the river. Though Fitz Manor is a stately home in miniature, the atmosphere is very friendly and easygoing.

(Shrewsbury and north Shropshire are described elsewhere).

Inclusive terms for dinner, bed-and-breakfast (particularly for a week) can be much lower than those quoted here for these items taken separately. For short-notice bookings you may be able to get a reduction.

No proprietor wants to have a room standing empty. This particularly applies to Sunday nights. Some hotels make a discount if you want only two courses from a three-course menu.

FOLDGATE FARM

C PT S X

Corney, Bootle Village, near Millom, Cumbria, LA19 5TN   Tel: 06578 660

3 bedrooms (single, double or family) from £9. Less for 2 nights. Rooms have electric heaters, electric blankets; washbasin; armchairs; views of country or garden. Clothes-washing free.

Dinner £6 for 4 courses and coffee, at 6pm. Special diets if ordered. Lunches, packed lunches. Coffee, tea, free. Drinks can be brought in. Snack suppers available.

Sitting-room with open fire, TV, books.

Nearest main road A595 from Broughton to Whitehaven.

A real Cumbrian farm, and well outside the main tourist areas, it covers 100 acres on which are kept Swaledale and Herdwick sheep as well as some cattle. The approach to the farm is through a cobbled courtyard, with a great stone byre and stables at one side, Muscovy ducks perching on a dry-stone wall, and sundry old iron pots and kettles filled with stonecrop, London pride or primroses. A stream slips quietly by. Pat, the sheepdog, comes bounding out to greet visitors.

The rooms have old furniture. Guests sometimes eat with the family, by a dresser where mugs hang, the clothes airer suspended overhead and a grandfather clock ticking in one corner. There are bacon-hooks in the ceiling, old horn-handled shepherds' crooks stacked in the hall, and a bright coal fire in the evenings.

Mary Hogg does most of the talking as she serves guests a proper farmhouse meal, and her husband is glad to tell visitors about his sheep and all the local goings-on – guests are welcome to watch the life of the farm, and to join in at haymaking time in July or August.

You'll get real country fare here: Cumberland sausage, 'tatie pot', plum pudding with rum sauce, farm duckling, Herdwick lamb or mutton, rum butter on bread, currant cake with tea on arrival and at bedtime, and jams made from local bilberries, pears or marrow and ginger. There are free-range eggs for breakfast. This is a thoroughly unpretentious, homely and friendly place to stay – but not for those who want everything shiny as a new pin.

As to the countryside around, there are the moors of Corney Fell close by and roads winding up and down, with sea views. An unusual attraction is a smokery (for meats) where visitors are welcome.

Close to Corney are Wastwater, Eskdale, the 'Ratty' railway, Muncaster Castle and its gardens, Coniston and Ravenglass.

When writing to me, if you want a reply please enclose a stamped addressed envelope.

Unless otherwise agreed, send a 10% deposit when confirming your booking.

FORD FARMHOUSE *New* 　　　　　　　　　　　**C**(12) **D S X**
Harberton, south of Totnes, Devon, TQ9 7SJ　　Tel: 0803 863539

3 bedrooms (single or double) from £14.50. Less for 7 nights and bargain breaks. Some have own shower; central heating; views of garden. (Washing-machine on request.)
Dinner £8.50 for 3 courses and coffee, at 7pm. Non-residents not admitted. Vegetarian or special diets if ordered. Lunches, packed lunches, snacks. Tea, coffee, free. Drinks can be brought in.
Sitting-room with central heating, TV, books.
Small garden
Nearest main road A381 from Totnes to Kingsbridge.

In this little village are two houses of outstanding excellence. For years, Preston Farm has been one of the most popular places in this book (see elsewhere); now I am glad to include another, at the other end of the village, which will be of particular appeal to gourmets.

Within the white walls are a low-beamed dining-room with stone fireplace (furnished with country Chippendale chairs and a dresser with pretty plates), an upstairs sitting-room, and delightful little bedrooms, one with patchwork spread, some with flowery views of the small, wandering garden and its stream.

Mike Edwards (a Master Sommelier) and Sheila (who trained at the Cordon Bleu school in Paris) previously owned a restaurant and so the food here is rather special. She will produce French dishes if asked, or else her own specialities such as lamb prepared with a garlic-and-mustard marinade (which she may accompany with clove jelly, and cabbage in a creamy onion sauce) or gammon with sultana and cider sauce. She sometimes serves meringues with rum-and-chestnut purée or brandied peaches. Starters might include local mackerel with a lemon-and-horseradish sauce, or celery-and-cucumber soup.

Each day's breakfast is different, with options such as particularly tasty sausages, kidneys or liver, teacakes or croissants.

The dilemma is to choose which of Harberton's houses to stay at!

On the other side of the A38 and just within the Dartmoor National Park is an exceptionally pretty, 400-year-old cottage of white walls and thatch: **Corbyns Brimley**, Higher Brimley, near Bovey Tracey (tel: 0626 833332). It has been attractively furnished by Hazel White in a style that is in keeping with its age. B & b only as a rule – most visitors eat at the Cleave Inn, Lustleigh; the Rumbling Tum, Bovey Tracey; or the Rock Inn, Hayter Vale.

Readers' comments: Superb views, splendid accommodation, friendly and caring proprietors; shall return again and again.

For explanation of code letters (**C, D, H, PT, S, S-C, X**) **see page xxviii.**

FOREST GATE *New*   **D**
Denmead, north of Portsmouth, Hampshire, PO7 6EX   Tel: 0705 255901

2 bedrooms (double or family) from £11.50. Less for 7 nights. One has own bath; all have tea/coffee facilities; central heating; view of country or garden. No smoking. (Washing-machine on request.)
Dinner £6 for 3 courses and coffee, at 7.30pm. Non-residents not admitted. Vegetarian or special diets if ordered. Packed lunches. Tea, coffee, free. Drinks can be brought in.
Sitting-room with central heating, open fire, TV, books. No smoking.
Large garden
Nearest main road A3 from Portsmouth to London.

Many people use this country house as a stopover when heading for the continental ferries at Portsmouth, though it – and its lovely surroundings, especially the South Downs – are a good destination in themselves. The house is right on the Wayfarers' Way, a scenic 70-mile walk from Emsworth to Newbury.

The house was built about 1790, then extended; and although it is not smart it has graceful features from that period. A huge, antique-filled sitting-room runs from front to back with glass doors opening onto a paved terrace, lawns with fruit trees, hard tennis court and a pool fringed by weeping willows. There are handsome floors of polished mahogany throughout. A small room is set aside for television and for smokers. One spacious bedroom is comfortably furnished, with antiques; another is simpler in style. On one wall hangs the will of a 17th-century ancestor, cutting off with sixpence an unlucky son, 'a presumtious vainglorious person who has allwaies rejected my counseil' (father-son relationships never change!)

Torfrida Cox will do evening meals if these are ordered in advance, in which case you might perhaps get a home-made soup, Armenian lamb pilaff or moussaka, lemon mousse or meringue pie.

Hampshire, a county of many contrasts, is described elsewhere.

Don't complain if –
  – because you booked at short notice, you do not get the best room
  – because you did not order a meal in advance, you get something plucked from the freezer
  – because you do not arrive on time, your room is let to someone else
  – because you bring a dog without asking, it is refused entry
  – because you don't express your wishes (for more heat, a second helping, or whatever), you don't get what you want!

If you want absolute quiet, avoid any place that takes children or has a bar open to non-residents. Inns sometimes get extensions to their licensing hours for late private parties; and may lack quiet sitting-rooms.

FORTITUDE COTTAGE
C D H PT

51 Broad Street, Old Portsmouth, Hampshire, PO1 2JD   Tel: 0705 823748

3 bedrooms (single, double or family) from £12. Less for 4 nights. Rooms have central heating; shower or bathroom; TV; views of sea; tea/coffee facilities.
Nearest main road A3 to London.

Carol Harbeck's little cottage – one room piled on top of another – backs onto her mother's (also a guest-house), with a flowery little courtyard and fountain between the two. Hers is named for the Fortitude Inn, which was once here; itself named for HMS *Fortitude*, a ship-of-war which ended its days as a prison hulk in the harbour – overlooked by the big bay window of Carol's first-floor sitting-room. This is Portsmouth's most historic area. From here, Richard Lionheart embarked for the Crusades, Henry V for Agincourt, and the first settlers for Australia. It's a place of ramparts and bastions, quaint buildings and byways, much coming-and-going of ships and little boats. Now the waterbus leaves from the quay just outside the cottage.

All the rooms in the cottage are prettily furnished – even the bathroom; and Carol (who serves only bed-and-breakfast) can recommend a dozen good eating-places nearby. Handy as a stopover for people using Portsmouth's port, Fortitude Cottage deserves a longer stay. For Portsmouth (and its adjoining Regency resort, Southsea) have so much to offer: HMS *Victory*, the *Mary Rose*, HMS *Warrior*, the Royal Navy's museum and that of the Marines, cathedral and historic garrison church, Henry VIII's Southsea Castle, the sands of nearby Hayling Island and the wild places of Chichester Harbour, clifftop Victorian forts, Roman/Norman Portchester Castle, submarine museum at Gosport, a big new leisure centre, other museums (including Dickens's birthplace), the Searchlight Tattoo every September, trips to the Isle of Wight, and a fine downland countryside to explore inland. Southsea has outstanding seafront gardens. There are boat trips to Spitbank Fort and Southsea is an antique-hunter's paradise.

Readers' comments: Excellent accommodation, spotless. Absolutely excellent, high standard.

There is no point in turning up with a dog or child in tow if the description does not say these are accepted; nor in expecting a garden, or alcoholic drinks, if these are not indicated.

For explanation of code letters (**C, D, H, PT, S, S-C, X**) **see page xxviii.**

113

10 bedrooms (double or family) from £18. Much less for bargain breaks. All have own bath/shower; TV; tea/coffee facilities; central heating; views of country or garden. No smoking. (Washing-machine on request.)

Dinner A la carte or from £4.75 for 2 courses (with choices) and coffee, at 7–10pm. Non-residents admitted. Vegetarian or special diets if ordered. Lunches, packed lunches, snacks. Tea, coffee, extra. Drinks can be ordered.

Bars with central heating, open fire, piano, record-player.

Nearest main road A354 from Salisbury to Dorchester.

Although not particularly old (it started its flint-and-brick life as a Victorian home), the Fox is full of character and has a great reputation for food – from its cold carvery to its charcoal grill. Thirty salads; fourteen meats which include pheasants and ham on the bone; jacket potatoes with unusual fillings; pies, granary bread and home-made soups: this is exactly what authentic pub food should be but so rarely is. And, on top of this, the Fox is in one of the most rural parts of Dorset, surrounded by exceptionally fine scenery.

There is a succession of bars, used by locals at least as much as tourists. One has a huge collection of Toby jugs (800 at the last count), and another hundreds of plates. Among the inn's nooks and crannies are a children's games-room, a skittle alley, and even a heated swimming-pool (plus sauna).

Kathryn Witheyman has made the bedrooms very comfortable – some have sofas which is a thoughtful touch as there is no sitting-room, only bars. I particularly liked a large coral-and-white room which has an excellent view of the hills.

Ansty is well placed for visiting Dorchester and the Dorset County Museum, Athelhampton House, Chard and Forde Abbey, Corfe Castle, the swannery at Abbotsbury, the old market town of Blandford Forum, picturesque Milton Abbas and its great abbey church, the giant of Cerne Abbas, Shaftesbury and Sherborne – a particular jewel, often passed by. The Blackmoor Vale is undulating country threaded by streams, spreading northward into Wiltshire. Eastward is Cranborne Chase, less well known than some of Dorset's beauty-spots yet well worth exploring because there are exceptionally fine views from its hills with pretty valleys and villages in between. To the south lies Dorset's heritage coast, and the old-fashioned resorts of Weymouth and Swanage.

Some hotels and even farms offer special Christmas holidays; but, unless otherwise indicated (by the code letter X at top of entry), those in this book will then be closed.

FOXHILL

C(5) S

Kingsey, south-west of Aylesbury, Buckinghamshire, HP17 8LZ
Tel: 0844 291650

3 bedrooms (double) at £13. Rooms have central heating; shower (in two); armchairs; views of country or garden. No smoking.
Sitting-room with central heating, TV, books. No smoking.
Large garden and paddock, with heated (75°) swimming-pool.
Nearest main road A4129 from Princes Risborough to Thame.
Closed December and January

The first impression is delightful: a sparkling white house beyond green lawns where Muscovy ducks waddle with their young towards a pool crossed by an arching stone bridge. The gnarled remains of an immense 500-year-old elm tree stand beside the drive. At the back of the house is a large garden with swimming-pool, against a distant view of the Chiltern Hills.

The interior is just as attractive. The house having been the home of an architect, Nick Hooper, and his family for many years, it is not surprising that its modernization was done with imagination and with care to respect its 17th-century origins. In the hall, floored with polished red quarry-tiles, a wrought-iron staircase leads up to bedrooms with beamed ceilings, attractive wallpapers and rugs, and restful colour schemes. Board doors have the original iron latches. The breakfast-room (which also serves as a sitting-room) has brown gingham tablecloths and rush-seated chairs. Here Mary-Joyce – a warm, gentle hostess – serves only breakfast, recommending for other meals the Royal Oak at Moreton or restaurants in the ancient market town of Thame, only a few minutes away.

Thame is a lively place in autumn when the mile-long market place at its heart is filled with stalls for the annual fair, and is a mecca for gourmets; beyond lie all the attractions of Oxfordshire described elsewhere in this book. In west Buckinghamshire, too, there is plenty – from the wooded hills of the Chilterns down into the fertile Vale of Aylesbury. Early in the year there are bluebells and cherry blossom; in autumn the beech woods blaze with colour.

The centre of Aylesbury is picturesque, threaded with pathways and courtyards to explore on foot (one of the many inns, the King's Head, belongs to the National Trust). Of many villages worth visiting, go to Long Crendon not only for its lovely bridge, the river and rose-covered cottages but for two 15th-century houses (one belonged to Catherine of Aragon and is now owned by the National Trust). At Waddesdon is the Rothschild mansion, looking like a French château (also National Trust property); at Upper Wichendon, high up, a dramatic view of the Thames; Cuxham, in good walking country, has a stream through the middle. Hughenden Manor was Disraeli's house. Waterperry's gardens are outstanding.

All these are very near. Visitors staying for some time can also from here explore Oxford, West Wycombe, old Amersham, Henley and other Thames-side towns (even Windsor), and any number of castles, stately homes, museums, antique shops etc. London is only an hour away.

Readers' comments: Wonderfully kind hosts, lovely home, top of our list! Beautiful house, meticulously kept; charming, friendly and helpful. The Hoopers and their home are charming.

115

FRIAR HALL FARM

Caldbeck, south of Wigton, Cumbria, CA7 8DS Tel: 06998 633

3 bedrooms (single, double or family) from £10.50. Less for 5 nights. Rooms have central heating or electric heaters, electric blankets; washbasin, shaver-point; armchairs; views of country/farmland or garden.
Dinner £6.50 for 3 courses and coffee, at 6pm. Special diets if ordered. Coffee, tea, for a charge. Non-residents not admitted. Drinks can be brought in.
Sitting-room with open fire, TV, books.
Nearest main road A595 from Carlisle to Cockermouth.

As the name suggests, this farmhouse has a long history. The Prior of Carlisle built a hospital here, which was dissolved in the reign of King John. The 12th-century part of the house was once the monks' refectory (hence the name 'hall'), with the hospital proper next door.

Today it is the centre of a 140-acre sheep and dairy farm. Caldbeck Fells rise up above the village where John Peel was born and is buried (the little churchyard is right opposite Friar Hall, across a tiny humpback stone bridge spanning a tumbling stream with a weir). The Blencathra foot-hounds still roam these fells in winter, just as they once did with John Peel – but now hang-gliders go up there too.

Guests use a snug sitting/dining-room with big leather armchairs, crimson velvet curtains and, on wintry evenings, logs blazing in a fireplace made of greenish Buttermere slate, casting a flicker on the gleaming brass fire-irons. The ceiling is beamed, the walls are thick.

All the bedrooms look across the tiny garden and the stream to the far hills beyond, and to a sky of scudding clouds when the wind blows. Fresh paint and light colours make them attractive; carpets are good; colour schemes simple.

Dorothy Coulthard serves farm food, using plenty of home-grown vegetables and other produce for dishes such as egg mayonnaise, roast lamb and fruit pies with cream.

Caldbeck is one of the Lake District's prettiest villages, with a pond (used by Muscovy ducks), an old inn, and a Wesleyan chapel carved with the reminder, 'Remember NOW thy creator'. The approach from the north is particularly lovely, driving across a heath with gorse towards a view of a green valley, with bracken-coloured hills beyond.

Apart from all the obvious attractions of the area, visitors often enjoy going to the October auctions (in Wigton) of horses and Shetland ponies, although the spectacle of foals being separated from the mares can be distressing. Bassenthwaite Lake, Carlisle Castle and Cockermouth are other attractions.

Readers' comments: Beautiful view; comfortable bedroom. Good home cooking; made very welcome; pretty view of the beck. Thoroughly enjoyed our visit, well looked after. Food excellent, house delightful, shall return.

Prices are the minimum *per person* in a double room at the beginning of the year.

GAISGILL FARM

Gaisgill, south of Penrith, Cumbria, CA10 3UA   Tel: 05874 634

C(7) **D S X**

3 bedrooms (single, double or family) from £10.75. Rooms have central heating or electric heaters; armchairs; views of country or garden.
Dinner £5 for 3 courses and coffee, at 7.30pm. Packed lunches, snacks. Coffee, tea, free. Drinks can be brought in.
Sitting-room with central heating, open fire, TV, books, record-player.
Garden and farmland.
Nearest main roads M6 and the A685 from Kendal to Brough.

People who zip along the M6 to Scotland miss a lot that is just a little way off the highway – like the long stone village of Tebay with the River Lune's gorge to the south of it. Nearby is Gaisgill with the 18th-century farmhouse of a shepherd.

The huge living-room with low-beamed ceiling, odd nooks and windows set deep in thick stone walls, is welcoming even in winter – with comfortable armchairs and sofas grouped around a blazing fire at one end and two big dining-tables at the other, with patchwork place-mats and small bowls of flowers.

The patchwork is Joyce Leak's; during winter she keeps busy on this and other needlework, sold to summer visitors. The Afghan rugs and cushion-covers are hers too; and she was teaching herself to spin while I was there.

Among the antique furniture, the books and records, is a huge display of silver trophies and another of colourful rosettes – awards won by Alan and his dogs.

Although Alan has sheep on his own nine acres, he is largely occupied in training other farmers in the handling of their border collies. His father was a celebrated shepherd who went sheepdog trialling from his teens until he died at 82. And so was his grandfather, until his farm was sold to Beatrix Potter who lived at Troutbeck.

This is walking country, and Joyce cooks generous meals for appetites sharpened by the fells: home-made soups followed by a roast, for example, and then an array of help-yourself puddings (perfect pastry!) and cheeses.

After dinner, there are those fireside armchairs; while Alan, wearing a sweater his wife has spun and knitted, may reminisce about 'the worst spring in memory' when the force of the wind drove sheep before it and fifty were dug out of just one snowdrift, with hundreds more perishing; or he may explain the mysteries of 'gimmer hogs' and 'shearlings'.

The whole area around here is one of great beauty, from rugged crags and the ruins of Shap Abbey to valleys and fells full of wildlife.

Readers' comments: Charming house, lovely people – hospitality itself. Superb food. The best we have stayed at; a lovely position. Super atmosphere.

If you prefer a small 18th-century hotel to a farm, only a few miles away is the **White House** at Clifton (tel: 0768 55115), now run by the Broadbent sisters who use much garden produce. Light, pleasant rooms; and children particularly welcomed.

THE GRANARY   **S**
Fenny Compton Wharf, south-east of Leamington Spa, Warwickshire,
CV33 0XE   Tel: 029577 214

3 bedrooms (double) from £12. Rooms have central heating; shower and wc; armchairs; views of country or garden; tea/coffee facilities.
Sitting/dining-room with central heating, TV, books.
Large garden
Nearest main road A423 from Coventry to Banbury.

On the banks of the Oxford Canal, where colourful narrowboats pass by, the Cotterills – local farming people – recently inherited a derelict 18th-century warehouse, and completely modernized it to make a new home for themselves (upstairs) and rooms for guests (on the ground floor).

Everything indoors has been very neatly done, with pale colours predominating, while the garden outside is (though only a few years old) beautifully landscaped, rock plants and flowering shrubs grouped round a smooth lawn where one may sit to watch the boats glide by. All around are fields.

Dinner can be had at the waterside George & Dragon near the house, or at other restaurants (June Cotterill gives guests a list of eating places which she recommends).

The hamlet is close to where three counties meet, Warwickshire, Oxfordshire and Northamptonshire. Favourite day-trips for visitors include Coventry Cathedral, Northampton, the colleges of Oxford, Stratford-upon-Avon, Warwick Castle, the Cotswolds and the fruitful Vale of Evesham as well as the gardens of Hidcote and Kiftsgate.

Don't complain if –
– because you booked at short notice, you do not get the best room
– because you did not order a meal in advance, you get something plucked from the freezer
– because you do not arrive on time, your room is let to someone else
– because you bring a dog without asking, it is refused entry
– because you don't express your wishes (for more heat, a second helping, or whatever), you don't get what you want!

It's best to stay at least 2–3 days: you cannot possibly appreciate an area if you only stay overnight (prices per night are often less, too, if you stay on). The vouchers on page **ii** are usable for 3-night stays.

There is no point in turning up with a dog or child in tow if the description does not say these are accepted; nor in expecting a garden, or alcoholic drinks, if these are not indicated.

THE GRANGE *New* C(5) **D S X**

Sunderland Hill, Ravensden, north of Bedford, MK44 2SH
Tel: 0234 771771

rear view

3 bedrooms (single or double) from £14. Less for 7 nights and bargain breaks. Some have own bath or shower; TV; tea/coffee facilities; central heating; views of country or garden. No smoking. (Washing-machine on request.)

Dinner £10.50 for 3 courses (with choices) and coffee, at 6pm. Non-residents not admitted. Vegetarian or special diets if ordered. Lunches, packed lunches, snacks. Tea, coffee, free. Drinks can be ordered/brought in.

Sitting-room with central heating, open fire, TV, books. No smoking.

Large garden

Nearest main road A1 from London to Peterborough.

This large manor house has been divided into three dwellings, of which No. 1 is the handsome home of Patricia and Peter Mort, with views downhill of terraced lawns and great cedars, flowering shrubs and a copper beech. Patricia has furnished the rooms in keeping with the architectural style. Good paintings (some by her daughter) hang on silky coral walls; silver, big velvet armchairs and Chippendale furniture are in one room; in another the tulips and pinks of curtain and sofa fabric have inspired the colour scheme for the whole room. Even the bathrooms are carpeted and have flowery wallpaper. The snug little dining-room is in fact a book-lined alcove behind a blue satin curtain (sometimes another is brought into use when there are two families being accommodated).

Meals are very attractively presented. Salmon and pheasant often appear on the menu but guests can have whatever they like if it is ordered in advance. Beans, asparagus, strawberries and spinach are among the produce grown in the garden; honey comes from their own hives; and, because Peter runs a health-food shop in Bedford, vegetarian or other special diets are no problem.

Patricia has much information to share about sightseeing in Bedfordshire, and about the best places in which to hunt for antiques (Ampthill and Olney – even on Sundays, for instance).

It is still possible to identify, in and around Bedford, places which inspired passages in Bunyan's *Pilgrim's Progress*. Bedford has, in addition to its Bunyan Museum and a notable church, a good traffic-free shopping centre, twice-weekly market and fast trains to London. There are long garden walks beside the lovely River Ouse (boat trips, too). All around the town are pretty villages. At Cardington one can see ballooning and the giant sheds which once housed airships. Elstow (Bunyan's birthplace) has an old moot hall with museum, and half-timbered houses; Felmersham is a boating centre; Harrold has an ancient bridge and country park, Odell castle grounds, Podington old cottages and Hinwick Hall. A nature reserve in gravel-pits is at Sharnbrook, bird gardens at Stagsden, a windmill at Stevenington, an extraordinary Tudor dovecote (for 1500 birds) at Willington, and plenty of fine mediaeval churches throughout the area. A little further afield, Woburn Abbey (and safari park), Whipsnade Zoo, Dunstable Downs (to watch gliders), Wrest Park Gardens, Luton Hoo (art treasures), Castle Ashby and Chicheley Hall are other sights well worth half a day each. With so much of interest it is surprising that Bedfordshire is rarely thought of as a holiday destination – particularly by Londoners (only ¾ hour away).

GRATWICKE HOUSE *New* PT S
9 Gratwicke Road, Worthing, West Sussex, BN11 4BH Tel: 0203 213000

4 bedrooms (single or double) from £15. Less for 7 nights. All have TV and tea/coffee facilities; central heating. No smoking.
Sitting-room with central heating, open fire, TV, books, piano. No smoking.
Nearest main road A24 from Dorking to Worthing.
Closed from November–March

Royalty put Worthing on the map nearly 200 years ago, when Princess Amelia (youngest daughter of George III) visited what was then merely a fishing village. Amelia, 15, had TB and it was thought the sea would do her good. Her adored and adoring brother (Prince Regent) rode daily from his Brighton Pavilion to see her here – her mother would not allow her to go to Brighton. (She died when only 27.)

This patronage immediately made Worthing fashionable as a seaside resort, but not many buildings survive from that period, except in watercolours displayed in the town's museum. However, there is still an old quarter away from the modern razzmatazz; and it is here that Gratwicke House (1878) is found, in a sidestreet only a minute from the sea.

From the outside it looks just like many another. But Barbara and Rupert Webb, previously an actress and a county cricketer, have decorated the interior with great flair – Rupert did all the work himself. There is a shell-pink sitting-room with gilded mirrors, grand piano, Victoriana, leafy plants and open fire – rather as it may have looked when the house was first built. In total contrast is the pine dining-room where swags of dried flowers and a trellis ceiling give a country air to the room. Photos from Barbara's theatrical past and Rupert's cricketing high days hang on the walls here. The window, with festoon blinds, overlooks a tiny courtyard garden. Breakfast is served on Royal Worcester china (no dinners, but this part of Worthing is an enclave of restaurants, such as La Difference).

Every room is a pleasure to look at, with inspired combinations such as a pheasant wallpaper with a watermelon carpet; poppy pictures and poppy cushions contrasting with a cool colour scheme of moss green and white; pink and white lacy fabrics in a bedroom with stripped pine. One very charming single room has flowers and butterflies painted on the built-in cupboard and bedhead; in another, the patchwork bedspread is in glowing colours. All bedrooms have very good armchairs.

Some people come to Worthing because it is so sunny; or because it is a good centre from which to tour (there are many coach excursions); or because it is an international centre for bowls. The town itself has plenty to see and do: bathing beaches, pier, promenades, several theatres or concert halls, huge swimming-pools and other sports, day-trips to France, a costume museum.

West Sussex, described in more detail under other entries, has lush, rich countryside; hills and valleys give the scene great variety.

Readers' comments: Charm itself, warmly welcoming, and a sense of freedom.

GREY GABLES

CDS

Norwich Road, near Cawston, north-west of Norwich, Norfolk, NR10 4EY
Tel: 0603 871259

6 bedrooms (single, double or family) from £16. Less for 7 nights, full board or bargain breaks. Rooms have central heating; bathroom; TV, armchairs; views of country or garden; tea/coffee facilities; phone.

Dinner £12 for 3 courses (with choices) and coffee, from 7pm. Vegetarian or special diets if ordered. Lunches, packed lunches, snacks. Coffee, tea, for a charge. Drinks can be ordered.

Sitting-room with central heating, open fire, books.

Large garden Orchard and paddock. Lawn tennis.

Nearest main road B1149 from Norwich to Holt.

Every year James and Rosalind Snaith travel in Europe looking for interesting new wines and recipes to add to their repertoire, for this former rectory is no ordinary guest-house. There is a choice of a three-course dinner or five-course feast that may include, after an hors d'oeuvres, creamed salmon or Italian bean soup, chicken Wellington with apricots in puff pastry, or fillet steak with Marsala sauce, choux filled with lemon curd and cream, and then cheeses.

They have rung the changes on blue-and-beige colour schemes in nearly every room from the Victorian-style sitting-room and up the elegant mahogany staircase to the bedrooms. Dinner is eaten at mahogany tables with velvet-upholstered chairs; silver, rosy Royal Albert china and candles make it an elegant occasion. I was looking at a needlework sampler made by Rosalind's great-aunt in the 'twenties when her mother told me embroidery had been a family tradition through at least four generations of craftswomen ('We never buy anything if we can embroider it ourselves!'): Rosalind herself continues it.

My favourite bedroom is no. 1: pretty fireplace, big bay windows overlooking the semi-wild garden, blue-and-white flowery duvet on the king-size bed.

Readers' comments: Excellent; marvellous food. Very friendly, good food.

The big landscaped garden is the main attraction at **Glavenside**, Letheringsett (tel: 0263 713181), restored by John Cozens-Hardy. There are lawns and rosebeds, streams with ponds and waterfalls, a rock-garden and an area of heathers. He has got the old hydraulic ram to raise water; and the waterwheel (1802) of the mill turns again (you can buy stone-ground flour there). It is safe for children to paddle in the River Glaven, or to take out a boat on the mill-pond; visitors can also play croquet or deck tennis on the lawns, or walk by the river. The house is handsome; the furnishings homely; prices

moderate. (Bed-and-breakfast only.)
Readers' comments: Comfy beds, a relaxed holiday.

GROVE HOUSE

C D

Hamsterley Forest, west of Bishop Auckland, Co Durham, DL13 3NL
Tel: 0388 88203

3 bedrooms (single, double or family) from £15. Less for 7 nights. Rooms have central heating; armchairs; views of country or garden; tea/coffee facilities. Clothes-washing facilities.
Dinner £8.50 for 4 courses and coffee, at 7.30–8pm. Vegetarian or special diets if ordered. Lunches, packed lunches, snacks.

Coffee, tea, free. Drinks can be brought in. No smoking.
2 sitting-rooms with central heating, open fire, TV, books, record-player.
Large garden and woodland; croquet.
Nearest main road A68 from Darlington to Corbridge.

Hamsterley Forest is a 5000-acre Forestry Commission holding in the hills of County Durham. Much of it consists of commercial conifers, but down one side lie 1000 acres of old mixed woodland, which the Forestry Commission manages for recreational purposes, with drives, waymarked walks, two rivers, a visitor centre, and so on. A few houses are buried in this beautiful forest, among them Grove House, which was once an aristocrat's shooting box. (Another is the home of David Bellamy, the television naturalist.)

Grove House is now the home of businessman Russell Close, his wife Helene, and their three children. It is a peaceful place, surrounded by its own big gardens and reached only by a forest road (private but metalled). The windows of the prettily furnished guest rooms look across the lawn into the forest, where you can see woodpeckers at work. Birdsong is the loudest sound you will hear for much of the time.

The downstairs rooms have a touch of aristocratic grandeur, with the addition of some unusual fittings brought from Germany by Helene's grandparents, from whom she inherited them (notice the art deco doorhandles). Settees and armchairs in the enormous sitting-room are covered in William Morris fabrics, and the colour schemes everywhere are a pleasure. Television is confined to one room. Bicycles on loan.

Helene prepares all the food from fresh ingredients. Meals usually consist of a first course such as a fish gratin; home-made soup; followed by a main course which is often game from the forest; and then a cold sweet such as meringues with ice cream and hot chocolate sauce. She discusses guests' preferences beforehand.

Should you tire of walking, driving, or simply sitting in the forest, there is a huge expanse of deserted heather moorland a few miles away. The other attractions of this little-known county include High Force waterfall, Raby Castle, the magnificent Bowes Museum (château-style), Barnard Castle (which gives its name to the school on which Dickens is said to have based Dotheboys Hall), Beamish open-air museum and of course Durham Cathedral.

122

GUNNARSGILL HALL

CSX

Gunnerside, west of Richmond, North Yorkshire, DL11 6LA
Tel: 0748 86213

Much less for 2 nights or more. Rooms have central heating or electric heaters; views of country, farmland or garden; tea/coffee facilities; two have showers.
Dinner 4 courses (with choice of starters) and coffee, at 7pm. Special diets if ordered. Lunches and packed lunches. Coffee, tea, free. Non-residents not admitted. Drinks can be ordered.
2 sitting areas with central heating, open fire, TV, books, record-player, semi-grand piano.
Garden

3 bedrooms (single or double) from £27.50 with dinner; prices go up in high season.

Nearest main road A1 from London to Scotland.

The main room here, a huge beamed space like the nave of a church, with mullioned and latticed windows, was a schoolroom 130 years ago. One end is now a studio, for Ken and Lesley Jones are respectively an enameller and a painter. In the middle is the dining area, with an oak settle, elm tables, and farmhouse chairs. At the far end, under a gallery, the floor is covered with oriental rugs; and comfortable armchairs face a log fire.

Lesley, who loves cooking, prefers to use organically grown produce, and she has a network of local suppliers of fresh vegetables and eggs and a butcher who knows the quality of meat she insists on. You might perhaps choose soup made from local artichokes; chicken stuffed with pâté and mushrooms (served in a wine-and-garlic sauce); and pears in red wine (with chocolate-and-brandy sauce) – plus farm cheeses and coffee. Breakfasts are imaginative, and so are the vegetarian menus.

It is Ken's and Lesley's paintings that hang on the white-painted walls of the old schoolroom, where she and Ken can sometimes offer courses in painting. Enamelling as well as silverwork are done in a studio-workshop.

At one side of the building, in what was the schoolmaster's home, are the bedrooms, furnished mostly with stripped pine and cotton prints. All give views of Gunnerside Gill, in which tumbles a tributary of the River Swale that you can follow on foot to its source. Many of the plants and trees in the pretty garden (with stream) were gifts from guests.

The house is reached by a narrow lane alongside the gill from Gunnerside, one of the picturesque stone villages which are a feature of Swaledale. Waterfalls, woodlands, streams, fells and the ruins of old lead mines give the area its distinctive character. There is plenty more to see: ancient churches and abbeys, prehistoric remains, strange geological formations (including crags and caves).

Readers' comments: Genuine friendly service, outstanding cooking (including breakfast and imaginative packed lunches). Impossible to better it! Wonderful food, lovely people. Memorable experience. Fascinating building and location. Delicious meals. Remarkable personal attention. A warm and lovely home, food superb, the best place we have ever stayed. Absolutely marvellous; perfect hosts. Lovely house, beautiful location, excellent dinner. Outstanding hospitality. Gastronomic delight.

123

GUY WELLS   C
Whaplode, east of Spalding, Lincolnshire, PE12 6TZ   Tel: 0406 22239

3 bedrooms (single, double or family) from £12. Less for 3 nights or bargain breaks. Rooms have central heating; armchairs; views of country or garden; tea/coffee facilities.
Dinner £7 for 3 courses (with choices) and coffee, at 7pm. Special diets if ordered. Snacks. Coffee, tea, free. Drinks can be brought in.
Sitting-room with central heating, log stove, TV, books.
Large garden
Nearest main road A151 from Spalding to Holbeach.

Springs in the land around this Queen Anne house are what gave it its name. It is in a lovely and secluded position, surrounded by a traditional garden, trees, and beyond that the fens. The Thompsons have daffodil and tulip fields as well as glasshouses where they cultivate spring flowers and lilies. Boxes of flowers can be sent by courier, all the year round: prices on request.

The interior of the house is full of imaginative touches – like the addition of an alcove with domed top and scallop-edged shelves to one side of the brick hearth where a log stove stands. Raspberry velvet tub chairs contrast with homely stripped-pine doors. And there is no sound louder than a slow-ticking clock.

Hall and staircase are pretty (with sprigged wallpaper, prints and bouquets of flowerheads dried by Anne), leading to the bedrooms – one of which is huge, with antique bedhead and an old cedar chest. The best one of all has a spread with tucks and pink ribbons, chaise longue, and windows on two sides. One has a half-tester bed.

Visitors who choose Guy Wells do so in order to explore the superb churches of the county, to enjoy its bird life or the spring flowers, for the easy cycling (it's a level area) or just for the peace.

And for Anne's wholefood cooking (using their own vegetables and eggs). She makes all her own pâtés, soups, quiches or ratatouille for starters; a traditional roast or casserole may follow; and puddings like raspberry pavlova, cheesecake or (a speciality I found delectable) a crème brûlée in which yoghurt combines with cream as a topping to brandied grapes. (Non-smokers preferred.)

From Whaplode, one can easily explore most of Lincolnshire and much of Cambridgeshire, too – Peterborough, in particular, is worth a day for its cathedral, river trips, local museums and shopping centre, all described elsewhere. There is a butterfly park nearby. Great churches, Springfield bulb gardens, windmills, Burleigh House and many garden centres add to the interest of the area.

Readers' comments: Lovely people. Enjoyed the cooking so much. Delightful lady, friendly, excellent cook, very pleasant house. Lovely place, superb food, nice lady. Very warm welcome, happy atmosphere, glorious food. Interesting part of the country, have visited twice.

Prices are the minimum *per person* in a double room at the beginning of the year.

THE HALL   C(5) **D PT**

Great Hucklow, Tideswell, north-east of Buxton, Derbyshire, SK17 8RG
Tel: 0298 871175

2 bedrooms (double or family) from £13. Less for 3 nights or more. Rooms have electric heaters; armchairs; views of country or garden.
Dinner £7.50 for 3 courses and coffee, at 7pm. Vegetarian or special diets if ordered. Packed lunches. Coffee, tea, free. Non-residents not admitted. Drinks can be brought in.
Sitting-room with open fire and books.
Large garden and field.
Nearest main road A623 from Stockport to Chesterfield.
Closed December–February

This, like many Derbyshire villages, is famous for summer 'well-dressings': huge mosaics of flower-petals depicting religious themes, each ushered in by a blessing of the well. To enjoy this floral event, stay at The Hall, where you can also see the Whatleys' south-facing garden when it is at its most colourful (Angela grows the vegetables, her mother-in-law – who lives in the Hall's converted barn – the flowers).

The sandstone Hall was built – on mediaeval foundations – soon after Charles I became king. Like Highlow Hall (see elsewhere), it was one of several in similar style which a Derbyshire farmer (Bagshaw) provided for each of his sons. Rows of small, mullioned windows give it particular charm, and in the former kitchen (now a sitting-room) the original fireplace, which would have housed a great spit, has been exposed. Walls three feet thick, which keep the house warm in winter and cool in summer, have here been painted cream, a good foil to the handsome furniture and unusual mirrors (some for sale) which John makes in his spare time. When I visited, he was preparing to restore the unusual, very narrow, cellar-to-attic window (diamond-paned) which lights the staircase.

His craftsmanship is evident in the bedrooms too. For instance, in one of the very big family rooms there is a huge cockerel he carved, as well as stools and bedside tables made by him. The bathroom (cork, pine planks and unusual tiles) has more of his decorative mirrors. (No washbasins in bedrooms.)

Angela is a discriminating cook, using fresh garden produce, local game, and imaginative recipes. A typical dinner might comprise her own liver-and-bacon pâté (with watercress and toast); chicken pie accompanied by ratatouille, boulangère potatoes and other vegetables; then unusual water-ices (such as gooseberry and elderflower, or blackcurrant-leaf) accompanied by sponge fingers.

All around are the hills and lovely valleys of the Peak District and such sights as Chatsworth (and its garden centre), Haddon Hall, the micrarium at Buxton (also its operas) and Monsal Dale. There are Lea for rhododendrons, and Wellyarde – an exceptional private garden.

Readers' comments: More than satisfied. Dinner one of the most superb meals I have ever had, quite perfect. Most friendly welcome.

For explanation of code letters (**C, D, H, PT, S, S-C, X**) **see page xxviii.**

HALL BANK HOTEL   C(3) **H PT**
Beck Lane, Bingley, West Yorkshire, BD16 4DD   Tel: 0274 565296

10 bedrooms (single or double) from £15 with bath/shower (some); TV; tea/coffee facilities; phone; central heating; views of country or garden. (Washing-machine on request.)
Dinner £7.25 for 3 courses (with choices) and coffee, at 6.30–7.30pm. Non-residents not admitted. Vegetarian or special diets if ordered. Packed lunches, snacks. Tea, coffee, extra. Drinks can be brought in. No smoking.
Sitting-room with central heating, TV, books.
Garden
Nearest main road A650 from Bradford to Keighley.

The peaceful country surroundings come as a surprise to many. This Victorian house of brown stone ('millstone grit'), once the residence of an American consul, is perched high in its own grounds overlooking the Aire valley, woods and moors: from its sun-parlour or its paved terrace visitors often enjoy spectacular sunsets. The hotel is now run by Emmie and Jack Wright; with meals cooked by their son-in-law, a professional chef. All rooms have been refurnished to a high standard.

A typical dinner might (from several choices) comprise turnip soup, a roast or trout, and a gâteau.

There's plenty to see and do in this part of Yorkshire: moorland walks, a nature trail, the spectacular five-rise and three-rise locks on the canal which descends steeply near the hotel: hang-gliding, golf, riding, boating; Shipley Glen (ravine and stream); Saltaire model village – a very early little garden city (the woollen mill has a shop with sweaters and tweeds at half price, and canal cruises start here); stately homes like Harewood and the National Trusts's Jacobean mansion, East Riddlesden Hall; Haworth (the Brontës' home); the Worth Valley steam train; Skipton (castle); ruins like Bolton Abbey and Kirkstall; several museums. York, Harrogate and the Dales are within reach.

Some hotels and even farms offer special Christmas holidays; but, unless otherwise indicated (by the code letter X at top of entry), those in this book will then be closed.

If you want absolute quiet, avoid any place that takes children or has a bar open to non-residents. Inns sometimes get extensions to their licensing hours for late private parties; and may lack quiet sitting-rooms.

Two-thirds of the houses in this book have bargain breaks or other discounts on offer, some exclusive to readers. Only a third raise prices at the peak of summer.

126

HAMPSTEAD VILLAGE GUEST HOUSE *New*   C H PT S S-C X
2 Kemplay Road, Hampstead, London NW3 1SY   Tel: 01-435 8679

6 bedrooms (single, double or family) £17 or £14 without breakfast. All have own TV; tea/coffee facilities; central heating. No smoking. (Washing-machine on request.)
Small garden
Nearest main road A1 or A41 from London to the North.
(*Including a London house is an experiment: I may include more in the next edition if readers' response indicate this is wanted.*)

Both the house and the professional family who live there are very typical of Hampstead. Solidly Victorian, with many of the original features retained, the mansion is now furnished in a slightly bohemian style: homely, hospitable, totally unpretentious.

In the breakfast-room a big pine dresser is laden with jugs and pots, old English china rubbing shoulders with Mexican peasant crockery. The table overlooks a flowery paved patio (where breakfast is sometimes taken). Of the bedrooms, I particularly liked the blue room (even the television and anglepoise desk-lamp are blue, and on the mantelpiece are blue Delft pots), spacious and light, overlooking lime-trees. In another, family room, a ladder goes up to a child's bed on a gallery behind the parents'. Small drinks-refrigerators, many books, a cordless telephone, writing-tables and comfortable chairs are useful touches. In addition to these rooms, there is a basement one with its own door to the garden; and a self-contained suite in the garden.

Annemarie van der Meer does not do evening meals but Hampstead has a number of bistros and restaurants – along with boutiques, antique or craft shops, and bookshops. By Underground, central London is only 10 minutes.

Hampstead village is a conservation area, well worth walking round to see the 18th-century architecture, and houses where so many famous historic or literary people have lived – or still do. Local sights include Keats' House, Fenton House (old musical instruments), Kenwood (Adam mansion, famous paintings, grounds with lake), the elegant 18th-century parish church and Constable's grave, gardens with rose pergola at Inverforth House, Pavlova's house, and of course the famous Heath. Downhill is Camden Lock. Annemarie recommends the guided walks run by 'Footloose in London' (01-435 0259) and can send a leaflet describing these.

On the west side of London is Kew, Surrey, where there is a particularly elegant suite in **West Lodge**, 179 Mortlake Road (tel: 01-876 0584). Angela Butt has decorated the rooms in pale Wedgwood blue with festoon blinds at the windows. The suite has its own entrance; and the large kitchen where she serves guests' breakfasts can also be used by them for preparing snack meals. Within 10 minutes' walk are Kew Gardens and the Under-

ground direct to London's sights. Kew itself has a piano museum, steam engine-house and river trips.

127

HARE AND HOUNDS INN   C PT S-C
Talkin, east of Carlisle, Cumbria, CA8 1LE   Tel: 06977 3456/7

4 bedrooms (single, double or family) from £12.50. Less for 4 nights. Rooms have central heating or electric heaters; shower or bathroom in some; armchairs; views of country; tea/coffee facilities.
Dinner £6 for 3 courses and coffee, at 7–9pm. Lunches, packed lunches, snacks. Coffee, tea, free. Drinks can be ordered. Vegetarian diets.
4 sitting-rooms or bars with central heating, open fire, TV, books.
Beer garden
Nearest main road A69 from Carlisle to Brampton.

You could easily pass by this unassuming little inn in the middle of a quiet village – but there is more to it than meets the eye. Even the public bar is a bit different from the average, with wainy-edged yew tables made by the owner, logs in stone fireplaces at each end, and over the bar itself (where Theakston beer and draught cider are served) heraldic panels of stained glass.

Tucked away behind all this are peaceful, beamed bedrooms, and a farm-cottage annexe, quite attractively furnished and with pretty duvets on the beds. One has a four-poster.

The owner is Les Stewart, who was design and export director of Wetheralls until a takeover. He discovered the 200-year-old Hare and Hounds in a run-down state, and decided to give it a new life. Now it has a reputation for good, simple meals served in the bar at modest prices – fillet steaks and jacket potatoes with a variety of fillings, for instance. The breakfasts are interesting, with a selection that often includes black pudding and a variety of waffles to choose from.

There is a separate family room, still with the old black-leaded kitchen range and brass fender, where children's menus are served. When the inn is crowded service may be slow. Sometimes trout and salmon are available.

Talkin itself is situated in an interesting part of the country, surrounded by fells that are popular with walkers and near a large, unspoilt tarn with various water-sports. Hadrian's Wall is quite near: the most interesting parts at this end of it are the Banks Burn stretch and the fort at Birdoswald. The Scottish border-country and the Lake District are easily reached, too, and the beautiful Eden Valley lies to the south. Brampton is an old market town; Alston and the city of Carlisle are not far. Talkin used to be a stopping-place for monks making their way to Lanercost Priory: part of it is in ruins, but the very lovely nave is still used as a church and what was the guests' solar is a village hall. In the locality are a hand-loom weaver and a potter, a working watermill and fine gardens at Corby Castle; Naworth Castle; and a bird reserve.

Readers' comments: Much impressed by the welcome and hospitality. Have stayed repeatedly, and food is better than ever. Very friendly; good inexpensive food; delightful. One of the best pubs we've stayed in, for both food and room. Very good; caring hosts. Excellent breakfast and well cooked pub supper. Great fun like a house-party; 'esprit' was great. Warm welcome, good value, cosy atmosphere.

128

HARROW INN
Warren Street, near Lenham, south of Maidstone, Kent, ME17 2ED
Tel: 0622 858727

7 bedrooms (single, double or family) from £17. Less for 7 nights or bargain breaks, to which you can add a Sunday night for only £10. Rooms have central heating; shower or bathroom; views of country or garden; tea/coffee facilities.
Dinner £8.50 for 4 courses and coffee, at 7.30–9pm, Mon.–Sat. Special diets if ordered. Lunches, packed lunches, snacks. Coffee, tea, for a charge. Drinks can be ordered. Smoking discouraged.
Sitting-room with central heating, open fire, TV, books (no smoking.) Bar.
Large garden and paddock.
Nearest main road A20 from London to Dover.

Beyond the large, comfortable bar of this recently modernized inn is a spacious private sitting-room for residents – very pretty with flowery chintzes, pink curtains, white walls and a log stove. Bedrooms are equipped with Stag furniture, leafy curtains on wood poles and nice details like brass or wrought-iron fittings on the solid wood doors. Outside are rustic seats in a garden that has views of the quiet fields around.

Local produce (including game) and vegetarian dishes feature on menus which include such options as spinach and Stilton soup, pheasant stuffed with grapes, and hazelnut meringues. Mark Watson's bar food, too, is imaginative.

The countryside around here is very beautiful indeed, with small lanes twisting among the hills, ancient churches, and unspoilt inns. Apart from all the famous places (Canterbury, historic Faversham, Chilham Castle, Whitstable of oyster fame, etc.), one can soon reach Sittingbourne for its Dolphin sailing-barge centre and steam railway; the Isle of Sheppey with Sheerness port and ancient Minster.

Readers' comments: Most comfortable; excellent furnishings; well-cooked food with interesting choice. Beautiful room and surroundings. Delightful; made very welcome; tastefully decorated; food imaginative and well presented. Great food.

There is a particularly pretty little cottage at nearby Eastling, in the Faversham direction: **Plantation House** (tel: 079589 315), where Dany Fraser takes visitors for bed-and-breakfast only. Half-timbered and with low beams, brick hearth and French provincial furniture, it has an unusually large and wandering garden concealed behind it.

HATTON HALL *New*

Hatton Heath, south-east of Chester, Cheshire CH3 9AP   Tel: 0829 70601

4 bedrooms (double or family) from £14. Less for more nights by agreement. Some have own bath/shower; all have TV; tea/coffee facilities; central heating; views of moat, country or garden. (Washing-machine on request.)
Large garden
Nearest main road A41 from Chester to Whitchurch.

A moat dug by Normans surrounds this large 18th-century house, at the heart of a big dairy-farm. Once there was even a drawbridge.

The bedrooms are beautifully decorated and particularly well equipped (bathrooms quite luxurious). Australian-born Shirley Woolley likes, for instance, traditionally rosy cretonnes, countrified Chippendale chairs, antique bedspreads of white crochet. One room has a chair from the Prince of Wales' investiture at Caernarvon Castle at which Shirley's father-in-law (Lord Woolley, former president of the NFU) was a guest.

Visitors dine in Chester or at the Pheasant Inn, Burwardesley, as Shirley serves only breakfast (though for women travelling alone, she will do dinners), which includes unusual home-made jams (such as sloe-and-ginger or strawberry-and-loganberry) as well as honey 'which I steal from my bees at great risk to my person!' On the table will be flowers and fine china.

Beyond the garden and the rose-bordered moat are stables with a dozen horses (trained to compete at horse shows) as well as geese, guinea-fowl and free-ranging chickens ('I would use my own eggs if only I could find them!'). The Cheshire Hunt meets here every New Year.

Chester, described elsewhere, is only a few miles away as is (in the opposite direction) little Malpas where old houses overhang steep streets; in its mediaeval church of red sandstone are carvings, stained glass and a superb parish chest. Buy farmhouse Cheshire cheese here. The town is close to the Welsh border, and to Shropshire. The peaceful, pastoral countryside around is low and rolling (unlike east Cheshire with its ridges and crags), the weather often dry and sunny when other parts are wet. Centuries of prosperous farming means there are a number of substantial or even stately homes on large estates and some richly decorated churches; turbulent times have left their mark in castles that still stand.

Interesting places to visit include Tarporley with its gabled houses and notable church monuments, the Delamere Forest, the hilltop ruins of Beeston Castle, the pretty villages of Bunbury and Peckforton (the latter with an imposing Victorian 'castle') among the Peckforton Hills.

Single people may find more company in houses that have a shared dining-table, a bar, and no TV in the sitting-room. As my descriptions indicate, some owners mingle more with their guests than others do. Houses marked **S** charge singles little or no more than half a double.

HAWKS HILL

C(10) **D S X**

Great Witchingham, north-west of Norwich, Norfolk, NR9 5QS
Tel: 0603 872552

rear view

2 bedrooms (single and double) £12. Rooms have central heating and electric heaters; bathroom; armchairs; views of country and garden; tea/coffee facilities. Clothes-washing available.

Dinner £7.50 for 3 courses and coffee, served at any time. Vegetarian or special diets if ordered. Packed lunches, light suppers, snacks. Coffee, tea, for a charge. Non-residents not admitted.

Sitting-room with central heating, open fire, TV, books, record-player.

Large garden

Nearest main road A1067 from Norwich to Fakenham.

Being right next to the Norfolk Wildlife Park, guests at this elegant 17th-century house of mellow brick can glimpse herons and other birds flying free around one of the park's willow-fringed pools.

The house has its own lovely surroundings: at the front, a cobbled and paved forecourt with stone troughs of colourful busy-Lizzies, and at the back a very big rose garden and lawn with interesting features – circular paving around a sundial, honeysuckle climbing up old apple trees, flint walls incorporating here a tiled niche and there the head of a Roman warrior.

Inside is a large, beamed sitting/dining-room with a big log fire, handsome tomato-red curtains and an open-tread staircase leading up to a bedroom with pretty fabrics. There are interesting paintings, and small treasures collected from all over the world.

Patricia Wayre serves meals based on her own or local produce. For instance, a prawn-and-haddock savoury may be followed by pheasant or leg of Norfolk lamb with garden vegetables, and then perhaps lemon pudding or a meringue bombe with strawberries.

The adjoining wildlife park (40 acres) deserves repeated visits to see its huge collection of European species living in nearly natural conditions: otters, seals, waterfowl, owls and much else (more exotic species include apes and bison); with freedom to picnic or for children to run about. Norwich and its cathedral are only 14 miles away and there are plenty of stately homes, seaside beaches, mediaeval villages, museums or castles, bird reserves and boating centres to explore as well as Blickling and Holkham halls (with gardens), and the Broads.

Readers' comments: Very happy week. Delightful house and company. Happy and comfortable.

When writing to me, if you want a reply please enclose a stamped addressed envelope.

Many houses have cards, chess, Scrabble etc. – just ask. And also such things as irons, hair-dryers, maps, gumboots and bridge-tables.

HEAVERS

C D PT S

Ryarsh, West Malling, west of Maidstone, Kent, ME19 5JU
Tel: 0732 842074

3 bedrooms (double) from £14. Much less for 2 nights. Rooms have central heating; armchairs; views of country or garden.
Dinner £9 for 4 courses and coffee, at 7.30pm. Special diets if ordered. Packed lunches, snacks. Non-residents not admitted. Drinks can be brought in.
Sitting-room with central heating, open fire, TV, books, record-player.
Large garden and fields.
Nearest main road A20 from London to Maidstone. (M25 and M20 are near.)

Perched on a hilltop, this red brick farmhouse with dormer windows in the roof and clematis around the porch is at the heart of a smallholding which provides much of the produce that Jean Edwards (once a health visitor) enjoys cooking for her guests. Until a few decades ago, the old house was occupied by generations of the same farming family which built it in the 17th century. All around are country lanes, fields, woodlands and two long-distance footpaths.

The little sitting-room has very comfortable armchairs grouped around the brick hearth (stacked with logs), which still has the old bread oven alongside. It's a cosy room, with the soothing sound of clocks ticking, Gem (the Edwards' Jack Russell terrier) snoozing on the hearth, a collection of china pigs and good books.

Jean enjoys cooking a wide repertoire of dishes (whenever she and her husband travel in the wine regions of France, she always returns with new recipes). She bakes her own bread; honey, eggs, geese and lamb are home-produced.

Beamed bedrooms with white-boarded, latched doors are prettily furnished with Laura Ashley fabrics and attractive colour schemes (pink- or blue-and-white, or moss-green with red-and-white). The Edwards have collected stuffed birds and maps for the walls, and pot-plants for every window sill. Through the windows are views of the Downs or of the garden which, even in winter, is colourful with witch hazel, holly berries and winter-flowering cherry trees. There's an old pump in it, a swing-seat on the brick patio, and a children's swing.

Although only an hour from south London (Heathrow and Gatwick airports are even closer), this is a good centre from which to explore rural Kent, the mediaeval bridges of the upper Medway, and any number of castles – Allington, Leeds, Hever, Rochester – and historic buildings – Boughton Monchelsea house, the friary at Aylesford, Sissinghurst with its famous gardens, the Archbishop's Palace at Maidstone, Chartwell (Churchill's home) and Ightham Mote. There's county cricket, boating and sailing, and a famous collection of carriages at Maidstone. But the scenery is the main thing: hills, orchards, streams, hop-gardens with their conical oast houses (you can visit Whitbread's hop farm), half-timbered cottages, picturesque villages like Loose (a stream threads its way among the houses). West Malling itself is largely Georgian, with Norman remains; while Mereworth has an unusual classical church. Canterbury and Dover are under an hour away. Gardeners appreciate Great Comp, Sissinghurst, Bedgebury Pinetum and the herb gardens of Ightham and Staplehurst. Plenty of pick-your-own fruit farms.

Readers' comments: Very good indeed. As charming as could be; convivial hosts; mouth-watering and plentiful food. Charming house, food delicious.

132

HERMITAGE MANOR

C(12) S-C X

Canon Pyon, north-west of Hereford, HR4 8NR   Tel: 0432 760317

4 bedrooms (double) from £15. Rooms have central heating; bathroom or shower; armchairs; views of garden or hills; tea/coffee facilities.
3 sitting-rooms with central heating and electric or open fire; one with TV. Baby grand piano. No smoking in music room.
Large garden and orchard.
Nearest main road A4110 from Hereford to Knighton.
Closed in January and February

An *escalier d'honneur* sweeps grandly up to the front door which opens into a room of baronial splendour, its ceiling decorated with Tudor roses and strapwork, motifs which are repeated on the oak-panelled walls. Through stone-mullioned bay windows are some of the finest views from any house in this book. There is also a very lovely music room (damask walls and velvet chairs are in soft blue; the limewood fireplace has carved garlands). Throughout, carpets and other furnishings are of equal quality to the architecture.

The recently converted bedrooms, and their bathrooms, are of the highest standard and very large. No. 6 has a view of a hillside spring flowing through stepped pools of pinkish limestone (from a quarry in the area) which Shirley Hickling created when she was converting this exceptional house. She serves bed-and-breakfast only – but there are good inns nearby, and Hereford is only ten minutes away.

Walking and watching the deer or birds are main attractions in this scenic area – the Wye Valley (with Symonds Yat viewpoint), Malvern Hills, Welsh border, Offa's Dyke path, Brecon Beacons and Black Mountains are all accessible. This is a county of woods and streams. In addition there are historic houses such as Berrington Hall to visit, rural museums, Croft and other castles and abbeys. Hereford and Weobley, the 'golden valley' and Wyevale garden centre are also popular.

Travel northward for Worcestershire, which has a tremendous amount to see. Fine scenery, historic buildings (including churches), hill walks, waterside dairy-farms, a magnificent cathedral in Worcester itself, hop fields and orchards, woods, and sights which include Elgar's birthplace (Broadheath), an outdoor museum of salvaged ancient buildings (at Avoncroft), the Royal Worcester porcelain museum and factory (bargains to be had!) and a variety of stately homes. River trips, the Three Choirs festival and delightful villages or towns (like Abberley, Bewdley, Chaddesley Corbett, Feckenham, Ombersley, Stourport-on-Severn and Tenbury Wells) and, for garden-lovers, Treasures of Tenbury and Stone Manor make this a good centre.

Inclusive terms for dinner, bed-and-breakfast (particularly for a week) can be much lower than those quoted here for these items taken separately. For short-notice bookings you may be able to get a reduction.

No proprietor wants to have a room standing empty. This particularly applies to Sunday nights. Some hotels make a discount if you want only two courses from a three-course menu.

133

HIGH GREEN HOUSE

Nowton, south of Bury St Edmunds, Suffolk, IP29 2LZ   Tel: 0284 86293

C D H S X

6 bedrooms (single, double or family) from £12.50. Less for 7 nights or bargain breaks. Rooms have central heating or electric heaters; shower or bathroom (one); TV; views of country or garden; tea/coffee facilities. Laundering.

Dinner £7.50 for 4 courses and coffee, from 7.30pm. Special diets if ordered. Non-residents not admitted. Tea free. Drinks can be brought in. Packed lunches.

Sitting-room with central heating, open fire, TV, books.

Large garden

Nearest main road A134 from Bury St Edmunds to Sudbury.

Part Tudor and part Victorian, this delightful house is truly secluded – surrounded by brimming herbaceous borders, a paddock of geese and an old well, with wheat fields beyond. There are a lily-pool (it is all that remains of a moat), troughs of begonias and fuchsias, and, where only the great frame of a mediaeval barn survives, Rosemary Thew has created a suntrap in which to sit, training scented roses and wisteria over the timbers, and placing seats to face the view.

The interior of the house is full of nooks and crannies, cabinets of old china and glass, antique furniture and low beams. There are oriel and mullioned windows, a brick fireplace, and wrought-iron hinges on bedroom doors. Some bedrooms are small and simple; but one has a four-poster, windows on three sides, a carved chest and a cheval mirror with painted flowers. Rosemary (who worked with physically handicapped people until her retirement) has also provided a downstairs bedroom ideal for a disabled person.

She enjoys cooking (and grows fruit, asparagus etc. for the kitchen). The sort of dinner she serves can comprise a chicken vol-au-vent as a starter, then a roast joint, profiteroles and cheese. She is a genial, informal lady with whom one immediately feels at home; and, because she was formerly clerk to the local council, she is a mine of information about the area (and its people).

Bury and its environs are described elsewhere. Also within easy reach are Lavenham; the great houses of Ickworth, Kentwell and Melford; pretty villages like Clare and Cavendish; the gardens at Bressingham – and antique shops everywhere.

Readers' comments: Warm welcome and excellent food. Most tranquil house. Miss Thew is delightful. Charming building; a bargain; Miss Thew is a character. Peaceful and friendly, nothing too much trouble.

For explanation of code letters (**C, D, H, PT, S, S-C, X**) **see page xxviii.**

HIGH GREENRIGG HOUSE *New*   C(5) **D H S X**

Caldbeck, south-east of Wigton, Cumbria, CA7 8HD   Tel: 06998 430

8 bedrooms (single, double or family) from £18. Less for 7 nights. Some have own bath/shower. All have central heating and view of country or garden. No smoking. (Washing-machine on request.)
Dinner £10 for 4 courses (with choices) and coffee, at 7pm. Vegetarian or special diets if ordered. Packed lunches. Tea, coffee, free. Drinks can be ordered.

3 sitting-rooms with central heating, open fire, TV, books, piano, record-player; bar.
Small garden
Nearest main road A595 from Carlisle to Cockermouth.
Closed from November–February

This is a 17th-century house of great character, with low doorways and stone lintels, hidden in the moors above the village. Inside, modern furnishings have been well chosen to suit the beamed interior with no attempt at a 'ye-olde' effect. Pine and cane predominate in the dining-room; in the sitting-room, once a cow byre, ceilings and floor are cork-covered, and there is a self-service alcove where visitors can make unlimited tea and coffee. The bedrooms (which include some on the ground floor) have pine fittings and bedheads, and they give fine views of the surrounding fells. Good food is a speciality of Robin and Fran Jacobs (who used to be an engineer and a social worker respectively). They share the cooking and make their own bread and marmalade. A typical dinner might comprise marinated mushrooms, beef goulash, Lancaster lemon tart, and Stilton.

There is plenty of room for quiet relaxation in the evening; or one can go to a games room with a mezzanine bar, where plate glass has replaced the barn doors. This being an outstanding area for walkers, well away from the crowded part of the Lake District, the Jacobs, with the help of a National Park ranger, have prepared a well-produced booklet of recommended routes.

The Caldbeck area has attracted a number of celebrities to live (Chris Bonington, Margaret Forster, Sir Fred Hoyle, for example) and a lot of crafts people. A fairly recent addition to what was always a very pretty village is, in a converted watermill, a group of shops for books, antiques and various crafts, and a wholefood restaurant. The nearest places of any size are Carlisle (cathedral, castle, and shops of all kinds) and Wigton (home of Melvyn Bragg and subject of his book *Speak for England*).

Some readers tell me they have stayed at lots of places from *Staying Off the Beaten Track*. I wonder who has stayed at most? A free copy of the next edition awaits the reader who sends me his/her comments on the greatest number!

HIGHLOW HALL FARM   **C D S**

near Hathersage, west of Sheffield (Yorkshire), Derbyshire, S30 1AX

Tel: 0433 50393

6 bedrooms (single, double or family) from £13. Less for 7 nights. Rooms have electric heaters; armchairs; views of moors or garden; tea/coffee facilities.
Sitting-room with open fire, TV.
Garden and farmland.
Nearest main road A625 from Sheffield to Castleton and Manchester.
Closed in winter

At the heart of this huge farm (raising sheep and cattle) is a castellated stone manor-house of considerable historic interest – complete with not one but four ghost stories. It is one of several similar ones in the Peak District built by a 16th-century farmer for each of his sons: his name, Eyre, is now famous because Charlotte Brontë, who stayed at Hathersage vicarage, took it for her heroine Jane Eyre. (And in the locality was a house which had burned down with, reputedly, a mad woman in it – inspiration for Thornfield Hall.) In the square porch is a massive front door with old iron studs and hinges; the windows have stone mullions and small panes; and above the rugged walls of gritstone is a roof of dark stone slates. It is as if the house grew out of the land itself, for this is the northern (or 'dark') part of the Peak District, in contrast to 'white' limestone peaks further south.

The sitting-room was added in Georgian times, so it has large sash windows with views of the far moors, where the Wains' sheep graze, rising to slopes brilliant with heather in September and rusty bracken in October. The house is 800 feet above sea level (its name derives from 'high hlaw', meaning 'high hill'). Deep, velvety chairs are grouped round a blazing fire on cold days. Adjoining is the dining-room, with comfortably upholstered chairs around each table. Bed-and-breakfast only; most visitors dine at the Poacher's Arms or Hathersage Inn.

Bedrooms are roomy and comfortable, some with ancient stonework and all with fine views – not another building is in sight. One may wake in autumn to frost-sugared grass and grazing sheep; and, beyond, a line of graceful pines.

Margaret Wain will show you the most ancient part of the house (unused at present): the huge stone-flagged hall with great oak staircase. This was once the kitchen, and it still has an old stone sink, stone cheese-press, and ancient chest.

Many visitors come here simply for the scenery and the peace; but there are plenty of places worth visiting (and, of course, glorious walks – the Pennine Way starts in the Peak District). There are the Blue John caverns, stately homes such as Chatsworth and Haddon Hall, the summer 'well-dressing' ceremonies in the many historic villages, interesting old towns such as Buxton and Bakewell, and the city of Sheffield – a great deal more than just an industrial centre (its art gallery, cathedral and theatre are all good, and it has a working 'industrial hamlet'). In hilly Buxton are plenty of interesting places to visit. In its heyday as a spa it emulated Bath, so there are splendid Georgian crescents and squares, a superb Assembly Room (now housing the library) and flowery parks.

Readers' comments: Quite delightful; beautifully furnished; friendly and obliging; very impressed – made most welcome. Very hospitable; comfortable, quiet and in beautiful countryside. A wonderful experience; a beautiful setting.

HOLLY TREE
East Witton, south-east of Leyburn, Wensleydale, North Yorkshire, DL8 4LS   Tel: 0969 22383

4 bedrooms (single or double) from £12. Less for 7 nights. Rooms have central heating; bathroom; armchairs; views of country or garden. Clothes-washing facilities. No smoking.
Dinner £8 for 4 courses and coffee, at 7.30pm. Vegetarian or special diets if ordered. Coffee, tea, for a charge. Drinks can be ordered. No smoking.
2 sitting-rooms with central heating, open fire, TV, books.
Garden
Nearest main road A6108 from Ripon to Leyburn.

This is in one of Wensleydale's more peaceful villages, a pretty group of cottages around a green, where sometimes strings of racehorses trot by on their way to exercising on the moors. All around is some of England's most magnificent scenery – the Yorkshire Dales – and towns which are honeypots for antique collectors. In the 12th century, part of the house provided stabling for the horses of monks travelling between the great Cistercian abbeys which are a feature of this area: this part now serves as a curiously shaped breakfast-room, with built-in settle and window seat.

Beyond the sitting-room, which has a crackling fire and huge grandfather clock, are two small garden-rooms with glass doors opening onto terrace and lawn with seats from which to enjoy the far view. The formal dining-room has scarlet walls and curtains contrasting with white shutters, green alcoves filled with flowers, antique furniture. Everywhere there are steps and odd angles.

Bedrooms are particularly pretty. One, for instance, has a brass bed with white and apricot draperies; in its bathroom (green trellis wallpaper, cornflower curtains) are two basins and a bidet. Another has a rose-swagged frieze, pink-and-white beds, and a green chaise longue skilfully upholstered by Andrea Robson herself.

But Andrea Robson's greatest skill is cookery (she won the Gas Boards' 'Cook of the Year' award in 1981). Typically, one of her dinners (preceded by free sherry) might comprise salmon mousse and then her own recipe for chicken breast en croûte (it has a mushroom stuffing and a coat of pâté and ham, inside a flaky-pastry crust). The pudding might then be pears – stuffed with walnuts and cherries, coated with chocolate and brandy, and served with cream.

Altogether, this is a house that has everything – memorable food, attractive rooms, and very lovely surroundings.

Wensleydale is described more fully elsewhere. The nearest small town is Middleham: 18th-century houses cluster around the market place, there's a ruined castle, and racehorses can be seen exercising on the surrounding moors. Well worth a visit are Wensley's riverside church, Ushaw bridge, Jervaulx Abbey and an inn (at Carlton, in Coverdale) with a Saxon burial-mound in its yard. Richmond (with castle), Ripon (cathedral) and Newby Hall are all near – the last with fine gardens. A good area for antiques.

Readers' comments: More than comfortable. Food truly excellent. A lovely home. Very warm welcome.

137

HOLMHEAD
Greenhead, west of Haltwhistle, Northumberland, CA6 7HY
Tel: 06972 402

4 bedrooms (double or family) from £11. Less for 3 nights or bargain breaks (20% discount). Rooms have central heating; armchairs; views of river, country or garden;

tea/coffee facilities; laundering facilities. No smoking.

Dinner £8 for 3 courses and coffee, at 7.30pm. Special diets if ordered. Lunches, packed lunches, snacks. Coffee, tea, free. Non-residents not admitted. Drinks can be ordered. No smoking.

Sitting-room with central heating, TV, tape recorder, books, indoor games (including snooker and table tennis), piano, record-player.

Large garden with badminton, cricket, swingball, and swing. Helicopter flights over the Roman Wall start from the garden.

Nearest main road A69 from Newcastle to Carlisle.

Beside a salmon river, just where the walkers' Pennine Way crosses the Roman Wall, this remote house has the ruins of Thirlwall Castle looming overhead (Edward I once stayed there). Just outside are the remains of a Roman turret, somewhere under the lawn or sunken garden, awaiting excavation; and some Roman stones were re-used when the house was built. All this, with the distant moors, is within view through the windows of the guests' large and comfortable sitting-room upstairs – copiously equipped with games, toys and facilities to make unlimited hot drinks. Pauline Staff used to be a tour guide, and so is immensely helpful with advice on sightseeing. She occasionally gives visitors talks with slides, or may even show them around. Pre-Christmas party weekends are run; and discounts on tickets to local museums are available. Also Gretna Green weekends for honeymoons.

There are all kinds of unexpected 'extras' in this out-of-the-way house: a solarium; foot-massager for weary walkers; pure spring water; table tennis; snooker; snacks at any hour; the freedom of the kitchen – and the company of Rex, a Hungarian visla hound. Pauline likes to cook local dishes and has even experimented with Roman recipes cooked in the area around AD 300 (one favourite is honey-roast ham in pastry). She makes all the preserves, chutneys, cakes and scones. A typical dinner might comprise: melon with kiwi fruit; trout with Hollandaise sauce; almond meringue with wild raspberries in whipped cream.

Breakfast choices include haggis, black pudding, kedgeree, muffins, crumpets and occasionally a Scandinavian buffet. Pauline aims to offer the longest breakfast menu in the world, served at whatever time you choose.

This is a splendid area for walks (with or without a National Park guide). The Northumberland National Park starts here; there are associations with Walter Scott and Catherine Cookson. You can look at working shire horses, Roman forts or prehistoric remains (including rock carvings), four castles, Hexham Abbey, Lanercost Priory, Beamish and Hunday open-air museums, stately homes. Even Scotland, the spectacular Northumbrian coast and the Lake District are within reach, as well as the wild and beautiful moorland heights of the north Pennines. Some of the most popular sights include the Roman Army Museum, Naworth Castle and Talkin Tarn. But it is, of course, Hadrian's Wall that is the biggest attraction of all and at Holmhead you can get guided tours, and certain free tickets.

Readers' comments: Food very good, Mrs Staff a marvellous help. Enjoyable.

HOME FARM
Church Lane, Old Dalby, north-west of Melton Mowbray, Leicestershire, LE14 3LB Tel: 0664 822622

C

3 bedrooms (single, double or family) from £9. Less for 5 nights. Rooms have central heating, electric heaters; rural views; tea/coffee facilities.
Sitting-room with central heating, open fire, TV, books, piano.
Garden with swingball and swing.
Nearest main road A606 from Nottingham to Melton Mowbray.

Set in an idyllic garden and facing the church, this 18th-century house (extended in 1835) has great charm and an atmosphere of peace. Clematis and quinces grow up its walls. Beyond espaliered apples and herbaceous beds are lawns, a kitchen garden, and for children a separate play area with tree-swing. (It is no longer a farm.) Some plants are for sale.

Indoors, every room has old furniture, pot-plants and white walls. Country-style dining-chairs surround the long table where breakfast is served, a fire crackling on chilly mornings. Val Anderson's collection of 'twenties and 'thirties photographs of local hunting personalities hangs here (including one of the then Prince of Wales, who first met Mrs Simpson at nearby Burrough Court).

Normally, Val serves only breakfast as the snug little Crown Inn nearby is popular for other meals: 'the best food in the Vale of Belvoir', Val says.

Guests at Home Farm find plenty to do in the area (both Nottinghamshire and Lincolnshire are close), visiting Belton and Burghley houses, Belvoir Castle, Newstead Abbey (Byron's house), Wollaton Hall, Whatton Gardens and the Donington Motor Museum. The National Watersports Centre, Trent Bridge and Rutland Water are other attractions.

Don't complain if –
- because you booked at short notice, you do not get the best room
- because you did not order a meal in advance, you get something plucked from the freezer
- because you do not arrive on time, your room is let to someone else
- because you bring a dog without asking, it is refused entry
- because you don't express your wishes (for more heat, a second helping, or whatever), you don't get what you want!

Take the trouble to get free booklets about the area before you set off. Every habitual traveller should keep a copy of the booklet of local Tourist Information Centres issued free by the English Tourist Board (Thames Tower, Blacks Road, London W6; tel: 01-846 9000) for this purpose.

HOWE VILLA   C(5) **PT S S-C**
Whitcliffe Mill, Richmond, North Yorkshire, DL10 4TJ   Tel: 0748 850055

4 bedrooms (single, double or family) from £25 (with dinner). Less for 3 nights. Rooms have central heating; bathroom; TV, armchairs; views of garden; tea/coffee facilities.
Dinner 4 courses (with choices) and coffee, at 7pm. Special diets if ordered. Packed lunches. Non-residents not admitted. Drinks can be ordered or brought in.
Sitting-room with central heating, open fire, books.
Riverside garden
Nearest main road A6108 from Richmond to Reeth.
Closed November–March

Once past an unpromising approach, all you are aware of from the house is the large and beautiful garden and the River Swale rushing by it. (The river once powered the paper mill which went with Howe Villa.) The house is late Georgian, with large, light, rather grand rooms where house plants abound.

The bedrooms are spacious, each provided with fresh fruit, chocolates and flowers. All are on the ground floor – an advantage for those who do not like stairs.

The upstairs dining- and sitting-rooms have views across the river to a National Trust landscape. The plasterwork of the sitting-room ceiling is shown to advantage by an antique crystal chandelier, its drops reflecting the firelight.

Anita Berry is an enthusiastic cook who does a refresher cordon bleu course each winter. There is always a choice of first courses and of sweets, served by candlelight on tables spread with dark blue cloths, lace covered. A typical dinner: aperitif, seafood gratin, noisettes of lamb, lemon soufflé, local cheeses served with pickled mushrooms, celery and radishes. Breakfasts have a varied choice.

The house is within walking distance of the centre of Richmond. Best known for its Norman castle and hardly altered Georgian theatre, it is a good base for outings into the Yorkshire Dales and to Easby Abbey, Bowes Museum, Raby Castle and the Thorpe Perrow arboretum. This is a house of exceptionally high standards in every respect: quite outstanding.

Readers' comments: Lovingly renovated, relaxing, welcoming. Food delicious and plentiful. Very comfortable; cooking excellent. Our favourite, superb cooking, good-value wines. Delightful; excellent cook and hostess; beautiful and elegant room, superb view; enjoyed meals enormously.

Prices are the minimum *per person* in a double room at the beginning of the year.

Families which pick establishments with plenty of games, swimming-pool, animals, etc., or that are near free museums, parks and walks, can save a lot on keeping youngsters entertained.

HURDON FARM

south of Launceston, Cornwall, PL15 9LS   Tel: 0566 2955

C D H S

5 **bedrooms** (single, double or family) from £10. Less for 2 nights. Rooms have bathrooms (two); armchairs; views of country or garden.

Dinner £5 for 4 courses and coffee, at 6.30pm. Special diets if ordered. Snacks. Coffee, tea, for a charge. Non-residents not admitted. Drinks can be brought in. Free tea on arrival.

Sitting-room with open fire, TV, books.

Garden and farmland; pony for children.

Nearest main road A30 from Launceston to Bodmin.

Closed November – mid-April

This 18th-century stone house is in a picturesque area, not far from Dartmoor and Bodmin Moor (both the north and south coasts are within reach, too). It has large sash windows with the original panelled shutters and built-in dressers in the dining-room. The sitting-room has large and comfortable chairs and a great log stove. The most interesting room is, however, the big kitchen-scullery where an old slate sink and pump stand alongside the modern washing machine, and in the granite fireplace is an array of old jacks, trivets, and a built-in Dutch oven.

Upstairs, all is spick-and-span with fresh paintwork and light, bright colour schemes in the bedrooms. There is also a family suite (made pretty by an old-fashioned rosebud wallpaper) on the ground floor, where the dairy used to be.

Margaret Smith's meals are above average 'farmhouse fare', with imaginative starters, in particular. Her soups are accompanied by home-made rolls; lamb or coq au vin by such vegetables as courgettes au gratin, cabbage cooked with onion and bacon, potatoes Lyonnaise (with milk and cheese) or creamed turnips; her puddings include raspberry pavlovas, chocolate rouleau and home-made ice creams – always followed by cheeses. She uses the farm's own produce and clotted cream.

From Launceston you can visit the majestic and romantic north Cornish coast, described elsewhere in this book, or head inland to wild Bodmin Moor to discover hidden, unspoilt villages. The coast has stark cliffs, waterfalls and wide sands; the moor, high tors that can be reached only on foot or horseback. Don't miss the elaborately carved church (St Mary's) in Launceston itself, an old-world market town. The area is full of Arthurian legends; and Daphne du Maurier's Jamaica Inn is on the moor. An otter park, a steam railway, Lyford Gorge, Launceston Castle and a rare breeds park add to the varied interest of the region, together with garden centres and gardens open to visitors.

Readers' comments: Charming lady. Recommended for value, friendliness and atmosphere. Fantastic, very good value. Lovely room. Superb atmosphere. Idyllic – we were spoilt! Excellent meals, very comfortable, very reasonable. Enjoyable and relaxing. We return year after year. Well above average farm cooking.

If you want absolute quiet, avoid any place that takes children or has a bar open to non-residents. Inns sometimes get extensions to their licensing hours for late private parties; and may lack quiet sitting-rooms.

141

INVERLODDON *New*

Wargrave, west of Maidenhead, Berkshire, RG10 8ET   Tel: 073522 2230

2 bedrooms (single or double) from £12.50. Less for 6 nights. Both have own bath or shower; tea/coffee facilities; central heating; views of river, country, garden. (Washing-machine on request.)
Dinner £7.50 for 3 courses (with wine) and coffee, at 7.30 or 8pm. Non-residents not admitted. Snacks. Tea, coffee, free.
Sitting-room with central heating, open fire, TV, books, piano, record-player.
Large garden
Nearest main road A4 from Reading to London.

This 18th-century house is a combination of two flint cottages, one of which started life as a beer-house for passengers awaiting the ferry across the Thames. The ferry is no more, but the Hermons keep a dinghy which guests may use, and a century-old canoe, to explore this lovely reach of the river – frequented by herons as well as ducks and swans.

Past the hall with its array of Toby jugs on an inlaid dresser is a sitting-room with old-fashioned sofas (big and comfortable), oriental rugs on a wood block floor, mementoes of Eton (hatbands and the House rules of the 1920s), and an open fire. The dining-room has unusual chairs, each carved with an English monarch, around a large circular table. Other unusual antiques include a cockfighting chair in one bedroom that is attractively furnished with waterlily bedspread and curtains (the large, well-equipped bathroom has swan towels, and there are swans on doorknobs and fingerplates too). In a charming little single room even the cupboard doors are decoratively wallpapered. There are views of rosebeds, a summerhouse and the river. (The summerhouse is used for traditional teas: crumpets, scones, meringues – a feast!)

Pamela and her daughters are keen cooks and will prepare (if this is ordered in advance) a dinner such as pâté, steak-and-kidney pie, mousses and cheese, with wine. Alternatively the Bull Inn has a very good chef.

Wargrave is surrounded by the Chiltern Hills (famous for their beech woods), close to Windsor, Henley (for its regatta), Oxford and a great variety of pretty villages. The Royal County of Berkshire is a historic area, and one of great beauty. Windsor Castle is the largest inhabited castle in the world, with Eton just across the river and Tudor Dorney Court nearby. Walkers enjoy the Great Park and the Savill Garden, children Thorpe water park and the Windsor safari park.

Events of national importance include polo at Smith's Lawn, racing at Ascot, horse and rose shows, and carriage-driving championships. Go to Maidenhead for shopping, picturesque river locks, and the shire horse centre, Cliveden for landscape and the Astor mansion (now a hotel), picturesque Cookham (Stanley Spencer gallery). Marlow and Hurley are other riverside spots worth visiting. Plenty of entertainments, too – the Wilde Theatre is an outstanding arts centre, for instance. Stately homes are numerous, and scenic drives into the hills lead to some fine viewpoints. This is also an area of countless good restaurants, antique shops and crafts – with all the riches of Oxfordshire and Buckinghamshire only a few miles further. (Bicycles on loan.)

IVY COTTAGE *New*

CDS

Lanehead, Tarset, north-west of Hexham, Northumberland, NE48 1NT
Tel: 0660 40337

3 bedrooms (single, double or family) from £10.50. Less for 7 nights and bargain breaks. All have TV; tea/coffee facilities; central heating; views of river, country or garden. No smoking. (Washing-machine on request.)
Dinner £6 for 3 courses (with choices) and coffee, at 7pm. Non-residents not admitted. Vegetarian, vegan or special diets if ordered. Lunches, packed lunches, snacks. Tea, coffee, free. Drinks can be brought in.
Sitting-room with central heating, TV, books, record-player. No smoking.
Small garden
Nearest main road A68 from Darlington to Edinburgh.
Closed from November – February

This is a cottage of great charm, perched on a hillside, with clematis and roses growing up the walls. Jeanette Woods has furnished the dining-room in appropriate style, with frilled curtains and dark wood furniture, and here serves such meals as eggs with a Stilton stuffing, roast lamb with apricot sauce and home-made cheesecake topped with fruit and cream. Fruit and vegetables are home-grown. From this room one goes through the kitchen to a modern sitting-room extension, filled with pot-plants; there are picture windows on three sides through which to watch the sun go down in a blaze of glory. Outside is a stone terrace with pergola and chairs. Bedrooms are in typical Laura Ashley style (sprigged fabrics and wallpapers – one has a lacy half-tester) and bathrooms excellent.

Tarset is in the southern part of the Northumberland National Park – hills and moors that stretch from Hadrian's Wall to Scotland. Adjoining this is Kielder Forest with Kielder Water in the middle. The immense Forest of various conifers was first planted in the 1920s, there are scenic drives through it, and the lake is a great man-made reservoir – the biggest in Europe.

A few miles away is the Kershaws' **Pheasant Inn** at Stannersburn (tel: 0660 40382) which is everything one wants a country inn to be – nearly four centuries old, stone-walled and low-beamed and in particularly lovely countryside. The Kershaws are determined to keep it unspoilt. The bedrooms, however, are modern, in a former hemel (farm implements store) and barn; many of them are on the ground floor.

Food is freshly prepared – one interesting starter is avocado with grapefruit and Stilton; trout comes with a sauce of yogurt and herbs; venison appears often.

Alternatively, there is the **Cheviot Inn** (tel: 0660 20216), a 300-year-old coaching inn in the middle of the quiet little market town of Bellingham, an old range still providing glowing warmth in the dining-room, the sitting-room traditionally furnished with tapestry chairs (both are on the first floor, with bedrooms – modern, fresh and neat – on the second). Pat Dixon's game cookery is the speciality here.

JOHNSCLIFFE HOTEL   C D PT S
Newtown Linford, north-east of Leicester, LE6 0AF   Tel: 0530 242228

8 bedrooms (single, double or family) from £20 **with a 10% reduction to readers of this book**. Less for 2 nights or bargain breaks. Rooms have central heating, electric heaters; shower or bathroom; TV, phone, armchairs; views of country or garden; tea/coffee facilities. Clothes-washing facilities. No smoking.

Dinner £8.95 for 3 courses (with choices) and coffee, at 7.15pm. Vegetarian or special diets if ordered. Lunches, packed lunches, snacks. Coffee, tea, for a charge. Drinks can be ordered. No smoking preferred.

Sitting-room with central heating, open fire, TV, books, piano, record-player; bar. No smoking.

Large garden

Nearest main road A50 from Leicester to Derby.

Up on a cliff stands Old John (hence the name of this house), a curious memorial tower shaped like a huge mug. It dominates the hundreds of acres where deer roam in craggy Bradgate Park, bequeathed in 1928 to the people of Leicester city for their pleasure, along with the picturesque village of Newtown Linford. To cater for these visitors, many villagers put up tea-houses and chalets (still visible) in their gardens; and it was then that a baker built Johnscliffe as a café.

It has a reputation for exceptionally good food (cooked by Cadder Caravelli and two other chefs). This is served in a dining-room overlooking the landscaped garden; pink ceiling complemented by pink tablecloths.

Dinner includes such options as hot chicken mousse with a creamy cucumber sauce; then a crab and prawn salad; veal fillet in smoked ham, accompanied by a wine and cream sauce with slices of avocado; and well chilled fresh fruit salad if you cannot manage one of the many creamy desserts. On Fridays dinner-dances or musical entertainments are often arranged by David and Marion Smith.

Bedrooms vary greatly: I liked the cottagey room under the eaves where I slept but there are other more handsome bedrooms, some with four-posters (one has its own tiny sitting-room), and a particularly attractive one with a half-tester.

A little further west (in the flatter part of the county, but well placed for a visit to the excellent show at the Battle of Bosworth site) is Desford and **Old Manor Farm** (tel: 04557 2410) where Janet Allen provides inexpensive bed-and-breakfast in a particularly handsome stone house with mullion windows, dating from the 17th century.

KARSLAKE HOUSE HOTEL   C D S
Winsford, south of Minehead, Somerset, TA24 7JE   Tel: 064 385 242

9 bedrooms (double) from £15; bargain breaks. Rooms have electric heaters; armchairs; views of country or garden; some have bathrooms, and one a four-poster. TV and tea/coffee facilities.
Dinner £10 for 4 courses (with choices) and coffee, at 7.30pm. Vegetarian or special diets if ordered. Packed lunches. Coffee, tea, for a charge. Drinks can be ordered.
2 sitting-rooms with fire, TV, books. One is non-smoking.
Garden
Nearest main road A396 from Minehead to Exeter.

This one-time malthouse (parts of it date from the 15th century) is now run by Fred Alderton and Jane Young. Spring is an ideal time to visit, when it is surrounded by daffodils and azaleas in bloom.

Beyond the large, light dining-room is a small bar; and, for residents, two sitting-rooms – one still retaining an ancient bread-oven. Narrow, scarlet-carpeted passages twist and turn. Upstairs are pleasant bedrooms – two of the nicest have views of the garden lawn and herbaceous borders. The bathrooms are attractive. There's a snooker room and a solarium.

There are always choices on the 4-course menu, which features such things as baked crab followed by fillet steak cooked with port and peaches, strawberry pavlova and cheeses. (No dinners on Saturdays).

Winsford, an ancient village (and birthplace of Ernest Bevin), has eight bridges over the several streams which converge here, thatched cottages, a crafts centre in an 18th-century chapel, and the Royal Oak inn (12th century) which provided material for Blackmore's book *Lorna Doone*. It is a good centre from which to explore Exmoor: quite near are the Caractacus Stone, a 5th-century memorial to a nephew of Caradoc, one of the most valiant defenders of Britain against the Romans; prehistoric burial mounds; and Tarr Steps, a prehistoric bridge.

Readers' comments: High standards, we were delighted. Charming and hospitable, food excellent, rooms spotless and comfortable.

When to go? Seaside resorts or other places suitable for children will be at their busiest (and dearest) in July–August and during half-term holidays (especially, in late May, which is also a bank holiday period). Other peak periods are, of course, Easter, Christmas, New Year and the bank holiday in late August. (The bank holiday in early May is not usually a peak, because it comes rather soon after Easter, but much depends on the weather.) There are local peaks, too (the Gold Cup races at Cheltenham or the regatta at Henley, for instance, are apt to fill hotels for miles around), and local troughs (Brighton, a conference centre, is least busy in high summer). You won't get much personal attention when hotels are full to bursting.

KIMBERLEY HOME FARM

C(5) S

Wymondham, south-west of Norwich, Norfolk, NR18 0RW
Tel: 0953 603137

3 bedrooms (single, double or family) from £25 with dinner. Rooms have central heating or electric heaters; armchairs; views of country or garden. Laundering facilities.
Dinner 3 courses and coffee, at 7–9pm. Special dishes if ordered. Coffee, tea, free.
Sitting-room with central heating, open fire, TV, books.
Large garden with hard tennis and meadows.
Nearest main road A11 from Norwich to London.

This is a beautifully furnished farmhouse with stables at the front and a large garden at the back, onto which the glass doors of the large sitting-room open. There is a pond with ducks. Apart from the hundreds of acres of crops, the main activity at Kimberley is training and racing horses.

The bedrooms are particularly pretty, the bathroom excellent, and the dining-room has a long Regency table. Jenny Bloom is not only an excellent cook but a generous one, leaving pheasants, guinea-fowl or joints of meat on a hot-tray from which guests may help themselves, and apt to whisk away a half-demolished chicken merely in order to replace it with a fresh one. Starters are imaginative (avocado mousse, for instance), and puddings delicious. Most vegetables are home-grown.

You can have the exclusive use of rooms if you wish, or get more involved with the family and the activities of the farm. Jenny is a charming hostess.

Norwich is one of the most beautiful of mediaeval cities, complete with castle and cathedral, full of craft and antique shops in cobbled byways. The county has a great many stately homes and even statelier churches, wonderful landscapes and seascapes, and, of course, the Broads. The Sainsbury Art Centre outside Norwich is exceptional. The Norfolk coast, King's Lynn and Cambridge are all about one hour away.

This is an excellent spot from which to explore in all directions. Bressingham Hall has fine gardens and steam engines. Beyond Diss (market on Fridays) are the very colourful villages of Burston and Shelfanger. East Dereham has an unusual town sign (two legendary does), an interesting church, an archaeological museum in cottages with decorative plasterwork. Go to the Norfolk Wildlife Park to see bears and otters, to Harleston for spring blossom or summer roses and the River Waveney. Further afield, into Suffolk, there are historic Bungay and Earl Soham, riverside Debenham, Framlingham Castle, Heveningham Hall and a museum of rural life at Stowmarket. Yoxford village is famous for its cottage gardens. Farming is done on a prairie-size scale, but villages with their little greens, and occasional windmills, are a pretty sight.

Take the trouble to get free booklets about the area before you set off. Every habitual traveller should keep a copy of the booklet of local Tourist Information Centres issued free by the English Tourist Board (Thames Tower, Blacks Road, London W6; tel: 01-846 9000) for this purpose.

146

KING'S LODGE

C D PT S S-C(incl. **H**)

Long Marston, south of Stratford-upon-Avon, Warwickshire, CV37 8RL
Tel: 0789 720705

4 bedrooms (single or double) from £11.50. Less for 3 nights. Rooms have central heating; views of country or garden.
Dinner £7 for 3 courses and coffee, at 7pm. Special diets if ordered. Packed lunches, snacks. Coffee, tea, for a charge. Non-residents not admitted. Drinks can be ordered.
Sitting-room with central heating, open fire, TV, books.
Large garden and parkland, with croquet.
Nearest main road B4632 from Stratford-upon-Avon to Cheltenham or the A439 to Evesham.
Closed December and January

With his father beheaded and Cromwell ruling England, young Charles II (only twenty-one) made a desperate attempt in 1651 to regain the throne. Badly defeated at Worcester, however, he became a fugitive on the run – for weeks eluding escape by means of disguises and hiding-places, as he made his way to the coast to cross to France.

To get through Stratford-upon-Avon, swarming with Cromwellian troops, he dressed himself as the manservant of Miss Jane Lane (sister of one of his colonels), and together they rode to Long Marston and the house of her kinsman, John Tomes. This was on 10 September; and I stayed there on almost the same date, dining in the hall with great inglenook fireplace where he had a narrow escape: on being asked by the cook to wind up the jack that operated the roasting-spit, his ignorance of this homely task nearly gave the game away. Although other parts of the Tudor house have changed, this room is much as it was when he stayed here – and outside, too, the scene has altered very little. Probably, the willow-fringed duck pond and the trees laden with mulberries and pears are very like what he saw.

When the house came up for sale a dozen years ago, George and Angela Jenkins (who lived locally) could not resist buying it, even though it was very neglected and rather too large for their family. To pay for its restoration and upkeep, they decided to take paying guests.

After dinner (plain home cooking, often with produce from the garden) at a big refectory table by the famous fireplace, visitors can sit in a sitting-room or out in the large garden. Two of the bedrooms are small, but one has a four-poster made from elms felled in the grounds and a fine stone fireplace on which the Tomes children inscribed their initials over three centuries ago. The house is full of old pictures and trifles which the Jenkins have collected, many relating to Charles II or the Tomes family who sheltered him.

The house is ideally placed for visiting the beauty-spots, gardens and historic sights of three counties – Warwickshire, Gloucestershire (the Cotswolds), and Oxfordshire. Head for Evesham if you want pick-your-own fruit and to Stratford for its antiques centre and shops. Close to King's Lodge is an antiques warehouse.

Readers' comments: Delighted with situation, food and hospitality. Enjoyable and interesting. Very good value.

LAMB INN   **D PT**

Great Rissington, north-west of Burford (Oxfordshire), Gloucestershire, GL54 2LB   Tel: 0451 20388

7 bedrooms (single or double) from £16. (**Reduction to readers.**) Less for 7 nights, bargain breaks and winter discounts. Rooms have central heating; shower; armchairs; views of country or garden.
Dinner A la carte, at 7pm. Lunches, packed lunches. Coffee, tea, for a charge. Drinks can be ordered.
Sitting-room with fire, TV. Also bars.
Large garden with swimming-pool.
Nearest main road A40 from London to Wales.

This is exactly what one asks of a typical old Cotswold inn – the interior a place of little windows, zigzag corridors, quaint oak doors and thick stone walls; outside, magnificent views of the countryside, looking across to some of the highest points in Gloucestershire. Kate Cleverly has furnished the bedrooms with care – restful colours, everything neat, a pretty tulip wallpaper in one room, and in the dining-room pine chairs at lace-covered tables with candle-lamps lit at night. The menu is à la carte, with such dishes as Stilton-topped fillet steaks, veal-and-sweetcorn pies, salmon-and-prawn mousse, lamb with apricots. Outside is a landscaped garden from which to enjoy the summer view with a glass of local 'real ale' in hand; a covered swimming-pool (heated) and a summerhouse-cum-aviary. In cold weather, there is a log fire in the bar, and in the attractive residents' sitting-room. A recent addition is a restaurant extension created from an old barn and furnished with Laura Ashley fabrics.

Richard is an imaginative as well as skilled craftsman: the carving of a lamb over the sitting-room fire is his, and so are the conversions of old doors, pews and even school desks to new uses. When I last visited the Lamb, he was making a four-poster with carved decorations.

The Lamb is midway between two famous Cotswold villages (Bourton-on-the-Water and Burford, described elsewhere in this book). Most people come here simply for the scenery, but also in the vicinity are the Cotswold Wildlife Park, a rare breeds farm, and – only a little further – Oxford, Stratford-upon-Avon, Warwick and Woodstock (with Blenheim Palace). Stow-on-the-Wold and Broadway are picturesque villages. For gardens, go to Sezincote and Hidcote (and to Burford's garden centre) and nearly every village has antique shops. A good area, too, for pick-your-own fruit.

Readers' comments: Excellent.

Houses which do *not* take children tend to have vacancies in July and August.

LANGAR HALL

C D S S-C X

Langar, south-east of Nottingham, NG13 9HG   Tel: 0949 60559

5 bedrooms (single, double or family) from £16. Less for 7 nights. Rooms have central heating, electric heaters; shower or bathroom; TV, armchairs; views of country or garden; tea/coffee facilities. Clothes-washing facilities.

Dinner £15 for 4 courses (some choice) and coffee, at 7.45pm. Vegetarian or special diets if ordered. Lunches, packed lunches, snacks. Coffee, tea, free. Drinks can be ordered or brought in.

Sitting-room with central heating, open fire, TV, books; bar.

Garden and park with croquet.

Nearest main road A52 from Leicester to Newark.

For art-lovers, this must surely be the most interesting house in this book.

Imogen Skirving's great-grandmother bought the house thirty years after it was built in 1830, a fine country mansion of apricot stucco built on the site of an earlier one which had associations with many names famous in English history (particularly Admiral Lord Howe). When it came into Imogen's possession, she and her art-dealer husband had to refurnish it – which they have done with unusual antiques and well-chosen colours in each room. And every wall is hung with paintings of great interest (mainly 19th- and 20th-century pictures, some family heirlooms). Imogen is a picture restorer, and is willing to demonstrate to interested visitors. There are some paintings for sale.

The pillared yellow-and-white dining-room has a large circular table with a cloth of embroidered voile and tall, fluted, silver candlesticks. Across the stone-flagged hall (with a marble side-table from which visitors help themselves to pre-dinner drinks, recording what they take in a notebook) is the all-white sitting-room with alcoves of china and tall sash windows. Some of the paintings here were bought by Imogen in her teens – she used to save up all her pocket-money to buy pictures. A second sitting-room, book-lined, is for TV and smoking.

Some bedrooms are very grand (one has a four-poster with Nottingham lace), others are simple and cottagey (prices vary accordingly). One with a half-tester bed, lilac-and-roses fabrics, antique bamboo furniture and lemon walls has a dressing-room adjoining, containing sofa, desk and TV. The simpler rooms are in another wing of the house. Dinner, which Imogen and her chefs prepare, may include such dishes as marinated kipper fillets – the genuine thing, oak-smoked and delicate in flavour – as a starter; chicken breast with a stuffing that contains lobster and prawns; and orange ice cream with Cointreau and peaches.

I had a perfect meal with a perfect ending as I strolled into the large garden, dotted with urns and statues among the ancient trees, a path leading to the chain of fish-ponds, and lime trees lining the long drive.

Langar is in the best part of the famous Vale of Belvoir. Scenery is not the only attraction of this area, however. Next to the house is the village church, known as 'the cathedral of the Vale' (well worth a visit). There are many great houses: Belvoir Castle, Belton House, Holme Pierrepont Hall, Doddington Hall.

Readers' comments: One of the most delightful weeks I have ever had. Quite exceptional. Fascinating hostess, fine house.

149

LANGLEY WOOD *New*   D

Redlynch, south of Salisbury, Wiltshire, SP5 2PB   Tel: 0794 390348

3 bedrooms (double) at £13. All have views of garden.
Dinner A la carte. Sunday lunches. Tea, coffee, extra. Drinks can be ordered.
2 sitting-rooms with heating, open fire, books; bar.

Large garden
Nearest main road A36 from Southampton to Salisbury.

A restaurant of distinction is the principal *raison d'être* of Langley Wood, but it has comfortable bedrooms too – overlooking the surrounding lawns and woods. The house began life as three 17th-century cottages, but was transformed at the turn of the century. Panelling, Georgian doors and other handsome details were added. It still retains the sedate, old-fashioned style of that period, with dinners enjoyed by candlelight and, on chilly evenings, a log fire blazing.

David and Sylvia Rosen used to run a bistro near London's Camden Town, an area much populated by connoisseurs of good food; and many of the favourite dishes from those days are now enjoyed at Langley Wood – things like Brie en croûte as a starter (or egg mousse with devil sauce); prune-stuffed chicken with lemon cream sauce (or beef marchand du vin); orange fool (or hazelnut meringues filled with strawberries and cream) and vegetarian dishes.

Visitors who stay here can quickly reach Salisbury in one direction or the New Forest in the other: Redlynch is close to the border of Hampshire, and of Dorset too – for descriptions see other entries.

Wiltshire, despite its low population (which makes it a quiet and attractive place in which to travel), has a number of great houses such as Wilton and Stourhead, and great prehistoric remains too (Stonehenge and Avebury in particular). There is magnificent scenery on its chalk hills and by its many rivers and streams, where undisturbed villages are to be found.

When writing to me, if you want a reply please enclose a stamped addressed envelope.

It's best to stay at least 2–3 days: you cannot possibly appreciate an area if you only stay overnight (prices per night are often less, too, if you stay on). The vouchers on page **ii** are usable for 3-night stays.

150

LANSDOWNE HOUSE

C(5) PT S X

Clarendon Street, Leamington Spa, Warwickshire, CV32 4PF
Tel: 0926 21313 or 450505

10 bedrooms (single, double or family) from £17. Less for 2 nights or bargain breaks. **If included in a 3-night half-board stay, Sunday's accommodation is free to readers of this book except at peak periods.** Rooms have central heating; shower or bathroom; TV, armchairs; tea/coffee service. Laundry and cleaning service.

Dinner £11 for 3 courses (with choices) and coffee with home-made petits fours, from 6.30pm. Special diets if ordered. Lunches, packed lunches, snacks. Coffee, tea, free. Drinks can be ordered.

2 sitting-rooms with central heating, TV, books; bar.

Nearest main road A425 from Warwick to Banbury.

A pretty creeper-covered house built in the 18th century, this small hotel cannot be described as truly 'off the beaten track' for it stands at a crossroads not far from the centre of Leamington. But bedroom windows are double-glazed to reduce any sound from traffic – and the hotel is of such excellence that I wanted to include it.

David and Gillian Allen took it over only a few years ago and have furnished it to a very high standard and in keeping with its architecture. There is a particularly pretty sitting-room with sea-green and strawberry Victorian sofas, for example; in the small dining-room, meals are served on fluted Rosenthal china and wine in elegant glasses; the bar has cherry buttoned seats; and every bedroom is attractively decorated in soft colours with well chosen fabrics, stripped-pine furniture and thick, moss-green carpet. (No. 2 is the quietest, with roof-light not windows.)

The same care goes into the food. David, who trained as a chef in Switzerland, is a perfectionist. He sends to Scotland for his steaks, to the Cotswolds for his trout, has coffee specially blended to his taste, and damson and other sorbets made for him on a fruit farm nearby. Connoisseurs will appreciate some little-known wines among his very good selection, and the range of malt whiskies.

There are always several choices of good English dishes at dinner. Starters include particularly imaginative soups (such as celery-and-walnut or cream of parsnip), while main courses are likely to be such things as roast pork with freshly chopped rosemary or liver-and-bacon with fresh sage. Puddings might include walnut and chocolate fudge pudding or fruit cobbler.

Royal Leamington Spa is a health resort with a saline spring. It has fine Georgian terraces and lovely riverside gardens. A good base from which to visit not only Warwick and Kenilworth castles, described elsewhere, but also Coventry (modern cathedral, some historic buildings), Southam (old market town), Stoneleigh (mediaeval village and the great National Agricultural Centre) and fine country-side towards Stratford-upon-Avon. The Mill gardens in Warwick and Jephson gardens in Leamington are worth seeking out. For residents there are discounts at Warwick Castle and many other sights. Free guided local walks.

Readers' comments: Excellent.

LASKILL HOUSE FARM

Hawnby, north of Helmsley, North Yorkshire, YO6 5NB   Tel: 04396 268

C D S S-C

4 bedrooms (single, double or family) from £12.50, or £16.50 with dinner. Rooms have central heating or electric heaters; armchairs; views of country or garden.
Dinner £8 for 4 courses and coffee, at 6.30pm. Lunches, packed lunches, snacks. Coffee, tea, for a charge. Non-residents not admitted. Drinks available. Free tea on arrival.
Sitting-room with central heating, open fire, TV, books. Games room.
Garden and farmland.
Nearest main road B1257 from Stockesley to Helmsley.
Closed November–March

This stone farmhouse lies in a hilly, wooded area of great scenic splendour ('Herriot country'), and close to famous Rievaulx Abbey. Its courtyard is made pretty with stone troughs, flowers and rocks; and around lie 600 acres with cattle and sheep or wheat. There are white iron chairs for guests in the garden. Children are welcome to help feed the calves and to hold the lambs in spring.

In the sitting/dining-room is oak furniture hand-carved by local craftsmen, each of whom 'signs' his work with his own particular symbol – an acorn, a beaver or a stag's head. Here Sue Smith serves home-made soup or pâté before a main course which is likely to comprise meat and vegetables from the farm, followed by (for instance) lemon meringue pie or a fruit fool, and then an interesting selection of cheeses. Later she joins her guests for a cup of tea and tells them what is on in the neighbourhood and which places are most interesting to visit. Often there is a chance to see James Herriot himself, as he sometimes opens fêtes or gives talks.

The bedrooms vary in style: I particularly liked 'the blue room' with its sprigged wallpaper, thick carpet and cretonne fabrics. Sue aims eventually to make a patchwork quilt for every bed, and in each room puts flowers.

The North York Moors are one of England's finest national parks: whether you walk or drive, the views are spectacular, particularly when the heather is in bloom (late summer to autumn).

Readers' comments: Comfortable, welcoming, and good food. Excellent meals, complete relaxation. Charming and considerate hostess. Delightful; everything perfect. Mrs Smith was so welcoming and easy to get on with. Food excellent. Beautiful location. Comfort, good food and congenial company. Delightful room; huge and excellent meals. Perfect hostess, nothing too much trouble.

A little further south is **Newton Grange Farm** (tel: 04393 262) where Sue Ward's immaculate rooms have exceptionally fine views. Bed-and-breakfast only – but excellent pub meals nearby.

Readers' comments: Careful attention to detail, like clean towels daily and excellent breakfast.

LEIGH COURT

Leigh, west of Worcester, WR6 5LB   Tel: 0886 32275

C D S-C

3 bedrooms (twin, double or family) from £12. Less for 3 nights. Rooms have central heating and electric heaters; armchairs; views of country and garden; tea/coffee facilities.
Dinner £9 for 4 courses and coffee, at 7pm. Vegetarian or special diets if ordered. Non-residents not admitted. Drinks can be brought in.

2 sitting-rooms with central heating, open fire, TV, books, indoor games (including snooker, darts).
Large garden and farmland; coarse fishing in river.
Nearest main road A4103 from Worcester to Hereford.
Closed mid-October – mid-March

Passers-by often pause here, just to look – not only at the 16th-century manor house of mellow brick, with gables in both Dutch and Flemish style, but also at the 14th-century cruck barn, the biggest of its kind in the world.

Sally Stewart's ancestors were bailiffs here when, before Henry VIII dissolved the monasteries, the abbots of Pershore were lords of the manor.

She and her civil engineer husband modernized the comforts of the house when they inherited it in 1960, but have carefully preserved all the fine architectural detail. The entrance hall is particularly striking, a tiled floor and traditional acanthus-patterned wallpaper (blue-and-white) setting off the white staircase, handsome sash windows and fanlight over the door. The sitting-room has a pretty fireplace, all curlicues and swags, round which velvet or cretonne chairs are drawn up, while portraits of ancestral aunts adorn the walls. In the dining-room (in fact, in all rooms) there are family antiques; sprigged blue cloths cover the tables; and from the bay window there is a fine view of a weeping ash, the nearby 13th-century church and a huge copper-beech. Throughout the house, there are good wallpapers, homely old-fashioned furniture and (from room 3 in particular) fine views.

This is a good place for anyone who enjoys dogs and other animals for Sally breeds pedigree pugs, Cavalier King Charles spaniels and golden retrievers. (If you want to bring your own dog, it must have been vaccinated.) In the grounds, where hens range free, you will find a variety of rare farm breeds.

Sally serves such dishes as prawn vol-au-vents, chicken breasts in wine-and-mushroom sauce, peppermint ice-pudding.

In the grounds, a riverside walk appeals to many visitors (there is another good, level walk along the track where once a railway ran). In autumn, you can see the farm's cider mill in action, and taste the results. People touring by car use Leigh Court as a base to visit Malvern, Worcester (with china factory, cathedral etc.), Upton-on-Severn, Ledbury, Stourport-on-Severn and Evesham.

Readers' comments: Very comfortable; food delicious. Most enjoyable. A delightful week. Excellent food; peaceful. Enjoyed it so much I returned for a further eight days. Friendliness, hospitality and food delightful.

153

LEWORTHY FARM

Holsworthy, east of Bude (Cornwall), Devon, EX22 65S

C H PT S S-C X

Tel: 0409 253488

12 bedrooms (single, double or family) from £12. Less for 2 nights or bargain breaks. Rooms have central heating or electric heaters; shower, wc; armchairs; views of country or garden; tea/coffee facilities. Clothes-washing facilities.

Dinner £8 for 4 courses and coffee, at 7pm. Special diets if ordered. Lunches, packed lunches, snacks. Afternoon or bedtime coffee, tea etc. for a charge. Drinks can be ordered. No smoking.

3 sitting-rooms with central heating, open fire, TV, books, indoor games (including table skittles, snooker, table tennis, darts, badminton), piano, record-player. Video films. Bar.

Grounds Lawns, farmland and lake, with clay pigeon shooting, croquet, tennis, trout fishing, archery and pony riding.

Nearest main road A388 from Bideford to Plymouth.

Genial Eric Cornish deservedly won the AA's 'Farmhouse of the Year' award in 1981. His guests are greatly appreciated by him, and he goes to considerable lengths to give them a good time – young children in particular. Dozens of their drawings and letters to him are pinned up around the bar.

He has added to the rooms in the farmhouse to provide more accommodation in a bungalow close by, and sometimes has as many as forty people staying – laying on for this huge house-party all kinds of evening entertainments (games, dancing, conjuror, film) for which there is no extra charge. This is obviously appreciated by families tired of the spend-spend-spend involved in keeping the youngsters entertained in most resorts. Eric also takes visitors on tractor-drawn hay-rides (dogs following) to see his crops, sheep, beef-cattle, lake, river and woods, while explaining to them what work is going on. It's a place where parents can leave their older children to go their own way – they find plenty to do, like organizing table tennis, or badminton competitions. There are deer, herons and even otters to be spotted; abundant wildflowers; and lots of good picnic spots within the farm estate. Eric has produced a nature trail, with quiz. In low season, crafts including patchwork and farm activity courses are run; the latter include wine-making, clay pigeon shooting, fishing and pub skittle matches. And there is a wheelchair.

Something new is always afoot, so Eric and Marion keep in touch with past guests by means of a circular letter with news of what has been happening to the stock, the pets and the family. Cormorants steal the trout, son Paul moves to Australia, 'Just Country' gets booked for next season – it's all reported in these letters. Many guests become lifelong friends, and most get involved in Leworthy Farm in one way or another (the gumboot rack was made by a group of dads).

The bedrooms, like all the other rooms, are comfortable and unfussy: the best ones are in the converted farm building called Leeside. Marion produces typical farmhouse meals such as soup, roast beef, fruit pie and cream, cheese, coffee.

There is so much going on that many people hardly stir from the Leworthy lands. However, within a short drive are the beaches of Bude and superb clifftop views, Hartland's dramatic reefs and lighthouse and quaint little Clovelly.

Readers' comments: Very much enjoyed the Cornishes' company; they make you feel welcome. A delightful couple who spared nothing to see that everyone had a good time. We had a high time!

LINDISFARNE HOTEL *New*
Holy Island, south of Berwick-upon-Tweed, Northumberland, TD15 2SQ
Tel: 0289 89273

7 bedrooms (single, double or family) from £14.50. Less for 7 nights and bargain breaks. Some have own bath/shower; TV; tea/coffee facilities; central heating; views of garden. No smoking. (Washing-machine on request.)

Dinner £9.50 for 4 courses (with choices) and coffee, at 7–8pm. Vegetarian or special diets if ordered. Lunches, packed lunches, snacks. Tea, coffee, extra. Drinks can be ordered.

Sitting-room with central heating, books; bar.

Small garden

Nearest main road A1 from London to Scotland.

Closed from November–March

It is a great pity that this island, so beautiful and so full of history, is ill-provided with good accommodation.

One drives across a causeway (impassable at high tides). Sir Walter Scott described it:

> Dry shod, o'er sands, twice every day,
> The pilgrims to the shrine find way.
> Twice every day the waves efface
> Of staves and sandalled feet the trace.

It was at this holy place that monks illuminated the Lindisfarne Gospels over twelve centuries ago, made mead from honey (you can still buy this on the island) and built a priory the ruins of which to this day soar majestically. It is – except when coachloads of summer trippers ruin it – a place of beauty and mystery. Over all presides Lindisfarne Castle, topping a steep rock. This was built in Tudor times, a rather cosy little castle. Well modernized in 1903 by Sir Edwin Lutyens, it is filled with furniture and textiles chosen to harmonize with their surroundings. There is now an outstanding museum of Saxon history, too.

The Lindisfarne Hotel is unpretentious, well kept, and furnished in conventional style. From the choices on Susan Massey's 4-course dinner menu, one might perhaps choose, for instance, grapefruit with crème de menthe, seafood casserole, roast lamb or Holy Island crab, and a creamy dessert. Based here one could enjoy not only the tranquillity of the island and its wildlife after the coachloads have gone home, but also explore much of mainland Northumberland by day.

For instance, the border town of Berwick-upon-Tweed is only a little way further north. Its three bridges bestride the estuary, there are fine walks along the Tudor fortifications encircling it – some of Europe's best mediaeval walls and bastions, and the busy market is frequented by Scots as well as the English. Other attractions in the region are Norham Castle, Heatherslaw watermill, quaint little Ford – a model village of the Victorian era, still with smithy and a village hall lined with murals painted by the Marchioness of Waterford. Near Wooler, centre of good walking country, is the site of the Battle of Flodden; and round Chillingham Castle roam the famous white cattle, sole survivors of a wild breed once common in Britain. Along the coast to the south is a succession of spectacular castles, Craster (for kipper teas) and the little harbour of Seahouses – boats go from here to the Farne Islands where seals and puffins are to be seen at close quarters.

LINK HOUSE *New*   C(8) **PT S**

Bassenthwaite Lake, east of Cockermouth, Cumbria, CA13 9YD
Tel: 059681 291

have own bath/shower; TV; tea/coffee facilities; central heating; views of country or garden. (Washing-machine on request.)

Dinner £9 for 5 courses (with choices) and coffee, at 7–8pm. Vegetarian or special diets if ordered. Lunches, packed lunches, snacks. Tea, coffee, free. Drinks can be ordered.

2 sitting-rooms with central heating, open fire, books; bar.

Small garden

Nearest main road A66 from Keswick to Cockermouth.

Closed in December and January

8 bedrooms (single or double) from £16. Less for 7 nights and bargain breaks. All

Teacher May Smith so much enjoyed cookery as a hobby that eventually she gave up her career to start a new one, running a guest-house. That is why Link House, outwardly similar to many others in the Lake District, is in fact very different in the kind of meals that are served.

The small Victorian house stands in a garden near the north end of the lake. Everything inside is spick-and-span. One bay-windowed sitting-room has a log fire and comfortable chairs; the other, a conservatory bar, is attractively furnished, with cane seats and tiled floor. Beyond this is the dining-room where tables are laid with pink linen napkins, Wedgwood china, decorative silver and Cumbria crystal goblets; it is a light room with windows on two sides. The bedrooms are equally pleasant: pine woodwork and pale shades in one, modern furniture and cheerful colours in another, and so on. All around are fells and forests.

Dinner is a five-course meal with coffee. Prawn, celery and apple cocktail might be followed by a herby tomato soup (home-made), lamb roasted with rosemary, strawberry meringues, and then cheeses (with choices at most courses). Bread is home-made.

The lake is in a valley overlooked by the great peak of Skiddaw and by Thornthwaite Forest. Leafy Cockermouth has Wordsworth's birthplace and is, like most places in the northern Lake District, less crowded than the south. Loweswater and Ennerdale Water are particularly peaceful; go to Wastwater for wild grandeur. Ullswater, Buttermere and Borrowdale are particularly beautiful. Keswick is near: full of shops, craft studios, museums and theatre. All around are fells (with hunting on foot just as in John Peel's day).

Readers' comments: Could not have been more helpful; food ample and delicious.

When writing to me, if you want a reply please enclose a stamped addressed envelope.

No one in this book insists that you stay out all day. But do not necessarily expect heating to be on, drinks available, etc.

LITTLE HEMINGFOLD

Telham, Battle, north of Hastings, East Sussex, TN33 0TT
Tel: 04246 4338

13 bedrooms (single or double) from £32 with dinner. Less for 2 nights or bargain breaks. Rooms have central heating (some also have log stoves); bathroom; TV, phone, armchairs; views of country or garden; tea/coffee facilities. One four-poster.

Dinner 4 courses (some choice), wine and coffee, at 7.15pm. Special diets if ordered. Lunches, packed lunches, snacks. Coffee, tea, for a charge. Non-residents not admitted. Drinks can be ordered.

3 sitting-rooms with central heating, open fire, TV, books, piano, record-player; bar. No smoking in certain rooms.

Grounds Woods, fields and lake; with swingball, croquet, badminton, boules, trout fishing, grass tennis, archery, dinghy and swimming.

Nearest main road A2100 from Hastings to Battle.

Down a long woodland track one finds a group of buildings that have grown up over three centuries, in a very lovely setting with a trout lake.

The beamy interior has been most attractively furnished by Don and Ann Benton, daughter of sculptor William Reid Dick, with interesting pictures and objects everywhere, delightful fabrics and antique furniture. Guests are free to use the piano and the large collection of books (many about art), and may wander around the 38 acres of grounds, where there are pigs, cows and glasshouses.

Ann is a superb cook, rarely emerging from the kitchen. Guests are seated round three large candlelit tables and help themselves from abundant dishes: wine is included in the price.

Readers' comments: Wholly delightful. Excellent food, accommodation and company. A perfect week – nothing was too much trouble, food wonderful, setting perfect. Delighted! One of our best holidays in 25 years. Friendly, relaxed, excellent service, pleasant rooms, food out-of-this-world, delightful place, and so different. Really excellent, every comfort, marvellous food.

In the picturesque old town area of Hastings, Dorothea and Stanley Pelling (at **105 High Street**) take bed-and-breakfast guests in their attractive little Tudor house. At the back, a tiny garden (all steps and terraces, clinging to the steep hillside) is an afternoon sun-trap.

LONG CANDOVERS

Hartley Mauditt, south-east of Alton, Hampshire, GU34 3BP
Tel: 042 050293

rear view

3 bedrooms (single, double or family) from £12. Less for 3 nights. Rooms have electric heaters; armchairs; views of country or garden; tea/coffee facilities.
Dinner £7.50 for 3 courses and coffee, at 7pm. Vegetarian or special diets if ordered. Lunches, packed lunches, snacks. Coffee, tea, for a charge. Drinks can be brought in.

Sitting-room with open fire, TV, books.
Large garden and paddocks, with table tennis.
Nearest main road A31 from Alton to Winchester.
Closed January and February

There's a touch of Eden about this well-hidden retreat where, around the half-timbered 17th-century house, informal gardens and paddocks lead into one another – flowers in one, herbs in another; a wildlife haven with many species of birds and harmless grass-snakes (bats roost under the old tile cladding of the house itself); a barbecue corner; pasture for sheep; woods and a stream beyond. Garden produce of every kind supplies the kitchen. Even the name has an idyllic ring to it, for 'Candover' is a Saxon word meaning 'sweet water'.

In the great barn occasional folklore weekends are held. An authentic gypsy (who runs the local Romany museum) plays traditional music, there are clog or sword dances, and Morris men come for nurdling (a Hampshire pastime which tests skill and stamina).

Patricia and David Cooper have furnished their home very pleasantly (I particularly liked the blue bedroom, and its views); and delicious meals are served. The starter could be stuffed eggs or cheese soufflé, for instance; goulash or local venison or chicken provençale are typical main courses; and then might come orange mousse with walnut biscuits, or apple fritters. Rolls are home-baked.

The house is in an official 'area of outstanding natural beauty', close to Selborne where Gilbert White wrote his famous natural history of the area: his house and garden are open to the public and wildlife courses are run there. You can spot deer, natterjack toads and badgers locally. Jane Austen's house is one of many also open to the public. Other popular sights include Birdworld, the 'watercress line' steam train, and Hillier's garden centre. Winchester, Chichester, Portsmouth and the coast, the Royal Horticultural Gardens (Wisley) and the South Downs are all within an easy drive, as are numerous antique shops and farms with pick-your-own or other produce for sale.

For explanation of code letters (**C, D, H, PT, S, S-C, X**) see page xxviii.

LOW GREEN HOUSE
Thoralby, Bishopdale, east of Hawes, North Yorkshire, DL8 3SZ
Tel: 09693 623

C D S S-C

2 bedrooms (double and family) from £12. Less for 5 nights. Rooms have central heating; shower room; TV, armchairs; tea/coffee facilities; views of country or garden. No smoking.

Dinner £7 for 4 courses and coffee, at 6.45pm. Vegetarian or special diets if ordered. Packed lunches, snacks. Drinks can be brought in.

Sitting-room with central heating, open fire, books, record-player.

Small garden

Nearest main road A684 from Bedale to Kendal.

This stone house in a tiny hamlet is the home of Tony and Marilyn Philpott, who are founts of information on where to walk and what to see.

Within rugged walls are particularly comfortable and pretty rooms. I had a pink-and-white bedroom with deep brown carpet; the bathroom was excellent; and in the sitting/dining-room (which runs from front to back of the house, with a picture window looking towards Wensleydale) soft colours, deep armchairs around a log fire and plentiful books provide a relaxed atmosphere. For dinner Marilyn served – with decorative flourishes – local smoked trout, pork cooked with cream and mushrooms, blue Wensleydale cheese, and chocolate mousse. With the coffee came a dish of chocolates. (All carefully prepared, and remarkably good value.)

Wensleydale is only five minutes away. Bishopdale itself follows a stream south, the road rising high up at Kidstones Pass, to join Langstrothdale (see other entries) and, much more tourist-ridden, Wharfedale. Sights worth seeing include Aysgarth Falls, Malham Cove, Hardraw Falls, Jervaulx Abbey, Fountains (Abbey and gardens), the Settle-Carlisle scenic railway, Newby Hall gardens, Thorpe Perrow arboretum, Bolton Castle. (Bicycles for hire locally.)

Readers' comments: Comfort, hospitality and value cannot be bettered. Lovely hosts.

If you have not arrived by, perhaps, 6pm your room may be let to someone else – unless you telephone to say you are on your way.

Unless otherwise agreed, send a 10% deposit when confirming your booking.

Two-thirds of the houses in this book have bargain breaks or other discounts on offer, some exclusive to readers. Only a third raise prices at the peak of summer.

LOW GREENFIELD

C S S-C

Beckermonds, Langstrothdale, north of Skipton, North Yorkshire, BD23 5JN Tel: 075676 858

3 bedrooms (single, double or family) from £16. Less for 7 nights. Rooms have central heating; armchairs; views of country or garden. Clothes-washing facilities.
Dinner £10 for 4 courses and coffee, at 8pm. Vegetarian or special diets if ordered. Packed lunches. Coffee, tea, free. Non-residents not admitted. Drinks can be ordered. No smoking.
Sitting-room with central heating, open fire and books.
Garden with brown trout fishing.
Nearest main road B6160 from Skipton to Aysgarth.
Closed November–Easter

This secluded house – 1200 feet up, and about as far 'off the beaten track' as you can get – has had a varied history. The monks from Fountains Abbey farmed sheep here in the Middle Ages. The farm was rebuilt in the 17th century, then turned into a hunting-lodge late in the 19th century. You approach it along a 1½-mile track (well surfaced, but with four cattle-gates to be opened and closed) through fine scenery. Around it are sheep pastures, ungrazed moorland, stream and lake.

Part of the grounds is a nature reserve, rich in wildflowers during summer and with a hide from which to watch the waterfowl or other birds – some quite rare. (The house has a good collection of botany and bird books.) Nearby are stretches of three long-distance paths: the Pennine Way, the Dales Way and the Three Peaks Walk. Tired muscles appreciate the sauna.

Lindsay and Austin Sedgley have not attempted to smarten the house: all improvements and new comforts are in keeping with its turn-of-the-century country house style. They have retained mock-Jacobean effects put in by the Victorians, such as the pitch-pine ceiling and carved window frames in the white-walled dining-room (some of the woodwork came from Lowther Castle in Cumbria). Club-like velvet and leather armchairs face the fireplace in the sitting-room. The keynote is solid comfort – and that applies to the simple, old-fashioned furnishing of the bedrooms, too.

Lindsay's dinners use local produce with flair. Leek and cream cheese tartlets may be the starter, followed by pork stuffed with mushrooms, and apple crêpes served with cream (then local cheeses and unlimited coffee). On Sundays, only a snack supper is provided.

Altogether, this is a place for a stay-put holiday, utterly restful, and with no sound at night except the hoot of an owl. But there is a lot more to do, if you wish. This is an area of leaping streams, high peaks and ancient ruins, historic lead-mines and active craft workshops, many traditional inns and a few stately homes, museums of local life and spectacular natural formations (crags, caves, waterfalls): not an area you can savour fully if you hurry through it.

Secluded Langstrothdale is a tributary of more famous (and therefore more touristy) Wharfedale, with much-frequented villages like Grassington and, northward, Kettlewell – from the latter there is a spectacular road through Coverdale to Wensleydale. Well worth visiting are pretty Appletreewick, Bolton Abbey, Barden Tower and Linton (three unusual bridges) as well as innumerable gorges and waterfalls – some accessible only to walkers.

LOW HALL *New* C(10) **D S**

Brandlingill, south of Cockermouth, Cumbria, CA13 0RE Tel: 0900 826654

6 bedrooms (single or double) from £11. Less for 3 nights and bargain breaks. All have own bath/shower; tea/coffee facilities; central heating; views of river, country or garden.
Dinner £9 for 4 courses (with choices) and coffee, at 7–7.30pm. Non-residents not admitted. Vegetarian or special diets if ordered. Packed lunches. Tea, coffee, free. Drinks can be ordered.
2 sitting-rooms with central heating, open fire, TV, books, piano, bar. No smoking in one.
Large garden
Nearest main road A66 from Keswick to Cockermouth.
Closed from December–March

David and Dani Edwards gave up other careers to renovate this farmhouse, which is mostly of seventeenth-century origin. In carrying out this task, they uncovered a big fireplace and a blocked-up window just where they had planned to add one in what was the dairy and is now the dining-room. Because the house was enlarged to accommodate a big Victorian family, they have decorated it with a Victorian feel, using sprigged wallpapers and some attractive old furniture.

There is one big sitting-room for non-smokers, and a smaller one for smokers and television addicts – a problem for people with only one of these vices! In the larger, there is a help-yourself cupboard for drinks.

The bedrooms, most of which are spacious, give views of the Lorton fells on the north-western corner of the Lake District or of the grounds of the house, through which a stream runs. This is an area of great beauty, wooded rather than rugged, where the Cumbrian mountains start their descent to sea level. It is never overrun by tourists, yet the well known parts of the Lake District are only a short drive away. Cockermouth – birthplace of Wordsworth and among the most pleasant of Cumbrian towns – is three miles away. Buttermere and Ennerdale Water (the only lake with no road along it, and approachable only from the west) are near.

Dani's menus always include a vegetarian alternative to the meat course, and few meat-eaters have noticed that the other courses are vegetarian too. While enjoying the challenge of vegetarian cooking, the Edwards at times raise sheep, pigs or turkeys for the table. A typical menu: potted broccoli; soup; roast loin of pork with fig, apple and cheese stuffing, or sweet-and-sour almonds; and either cheese or a choice of puddings – one light, one richer, and one hot. Breakfasts are much more interesting than the usual egg-and-bacon routine.

Readers' comments: My favourite guest-house . . . fulfils all your criteria and more. Extremely comfortable.

A few miles away, on the edge of the village of High Lorton, Mrs Roberts provides bed-and-breakfast at **Owl Brook** (tel: 090085 333). This architect-designed bungalow of green lakeland slate with pine ceilings was built a few years ago, and all the airy bedrooms have fine views. It lies at the end of Whinlatter Pass, the least alarming of the Lake District passes. The accommodation is suitable for disabled visitors.

Readers' comments: Beautiful views and utter tranquillity. Breakfasts were superb. Very friendly family atmosphere.

161

LOXLEY FARMHOUSE

C D PT

Loxley, south of Stratford-upon-Avon, Warwickshire, CV35 9JN
Tel: 0789 840265

3 bedrooms (double or family) from £14. Less for 7 nights. Rooms have central heating; armchairs; tea/coffee facilities. Two with bathrooms and use of small kitchen.
Dinner £10 for 3 courses and coffee; time by arrangement. Special diets and packed lunches if ordered. Drinks can be brought in.

Sitting-room with central heating, open fire, TV, books.
Garden and paddock, with table tennis.
Nearest main road A422 from Stratford-upon-Avon to Banbury.

Loxley is a hilltop village with diminutive church. From a seat on its sloping green, where crab-apple trees are bright in autumn, there are far views across woodland and fields of red earth. Just downhill from here Loxley Farm is tucked away: a picture-postcard house of half-timbering and thatch, parts dating back to the 13th century. Perhaps Robin Hood ('Robin of Loxley') knew the house; there's a worn stone in the churchyard on which, tradition has it, he and his companions used to sharpen their arrow-tips. And certainly Charles I stayed here after the nearby Battle of Edgehill.

Inside, everything is in keeping with the style of the ancient house: low ceilings with pewter pots hanging from the beams, flagged floors, small-paned windows, log fires, oak doors. You can see the cruck construction of the house – at its heart, the unhewn trunks of two trees support the roof timbers. There is not a single straight wall or floor. The Hortons have furnished the rooms in appropriate style. In the dining-room, leather chairs surround a refectory table; in the sitting-room is a Knole settee, grandfather clock and wing armchairs, with Staffordshire figures and old silver on the shelves, lavender and dried flowers.

The bedrooms differ in size and style, the largest having a shaggy carpet, antiques and a sofa; the smallest, flowery frilled bed linen. Some are in a newly converted barn.

Evening meals are available, only if ordered beforehand. These may include their own lamb, or venison from the Charlcote estate, with local vegetables or field mushrooms. There is always a choice of starters and of puddings. At breakfast home-made buns and muesli are included.

It is very easy to visit Stratford-upon-Avon from here, and the rest of Warwickshire, the Cotswolds, and Oxford. Warwick Castle, Blenheim Palace, Charlecote, Hidcote (and many other great gardens) make this area a tourist honeypot.

Readers' comments: Idyllic surroundings. Much care and attention. Generous, flavoursome fare. Most welcoming and comfortable. Not a jarring note.

MAINS HALL C D PT X

Mains Lane, Little Singleton, east of Blackpool, Lancashire, FY6 7LE
Tel: 0253 885130

9 bedrooms (single, double or family) from £15. Less for 7 nights. Rooms have central heating; shower or bathroom; TV, phone, armchairs; views of river, country or garden; tea/coffee-facilities. One with four-poster, two have half-testers.
Dinner £10 for 3 courses and coffee, at 7pm. Special diets if ordered. Packed lunches, snacks. Coffee, tea, for a charge. Drinks can be ordered.
2 sitting-rooms with central heating, open fire, TV, books, indoor games (including table tennis); bar; garden room.
Large garden Meadow with riverside walk.
Nearest main road A585 from Fleetwood towards Preston.

A long drive through fields brings one to a vista of this historic house, white with leaded windows, at the end of its shrub-lined drive. Built in the time of Henry VII or VIII, it remained a manor house until the turn of the century.

Robert Owen knew and loved it as a boy. When the opportunity came he bought it; and his wife Beryl, who used to have a catering service, runs it as a country hotel. (He is a lecturer in mechanical engineering.) Its outstanding feature is the exuberant wood-carving: Jacobean garlands and nymphs abound, in the panelling of the hall and up the staircase.

It has a history of romance and plots, with secret hiding-places used by Cardinal Allen and Jesuit priests who were attempting the overthrow of Elizabeth I. The old barn, which carries the date 1686 in its brickwork, housed an illicit chapel. Jacobite rebels stayed here in 1745, and later the Prince Regent – wooing Catholic Mrs Fitzherbert, a connection of the family. All around are other ancient remains – an octagonal brick dovecote (from the time when pigeons were 'farmed' for their meat), a well, pool and fountain.

At the back is the River Wyre, and the grounds are full of wildlife – kestrels, woodpeckers, tawny and barn owls. There are two old walnut trees, and Beryl uses the nuts in the meals she cooks. A typical menu is Stilton soup, lamb in honey and orange, and syllabub. (No dinner on Sundays.) Popular breakfast options include stuffed croissants and creamed mushrooms.

My bedroom was spacious and comfortable, with a view right along the drive.

The house stands in an attractive area of countryside, and is within easy reach of plenty of other interesting places to visit such as Blackpool, Fleetwood (port and fishmarket), Beacon Fell, Salmesbury Hall (for antiques), Garstang's canal and farming museum and Barton Grange garden centre.

Readers' comments: Excellent. Will stay again.

Some readers tell me they have stayed at lots of places from *Staying Off the Beaten Track*. I wonder who has stayed at most? A free copy of the next edition awaits the reader who sends me his/her comments on the greatest number!

MALLYAN SPOUT HOTEL *New*   C D PT

Goathland, south-west of Whitby, North Yorkshire, YO22 5AN
Tel: 0947 86206

22 bedrooms (single, double or family) from £20 **with discount to SOTBT readers**. Much less for 2 nights and bargain breaks. Some have: own bath/shower; TV; central heating; views of country, garden.
Dinner £11.50 for 4 courses (with choices) and coffee, at 7–9pm. Vegetarian or special diets if ordered. Lunches, packed lunches, snacks. Tea, coffee, extra. Drinks can be ordered.
3 sitting-rooms with central heating, open fire, books; bar. No smoking in one.
Large garden
Nearest main road A169 from Whitby to Pickering.

The 'spout' of this ivy-covered hotel's name is a little waterfall nearby, one of many that sparkle in the scenic North Yorkshire Moors. This is a very traditional Yorkshire hotel, managed by Judith Heslop, in which much is still reminiscent of its beginnings as a Victorian hunting-lodge.

On one sitting-room floor is a tartan carpet, on its walls old prints and copper tankards; a coal fire crackles in the hearth. Among the green wing chairs are small oak tables made by 'the gnome man' and those in one of the bars were made by his apprentice 'the cat man': each identified his work by adding to every piece a small carved gnome or cat. There is a very big dining-room with blue velvet chairs; its stone-mullioned windows overlook lawns floodlit at night, and beyond these the hills. Of the many bedrooms, the best are mostly at the front.

The hotel has a reputation for excellent food. Even the bar snacks are very good. There are always many choices: one might choose between such things as a spinach roulade filled with mushrooms and Parmesan cheese; ham mousse; pork fillet with a sauce of mushrooms, Madeira and cream; wild moorland trout with almonds.

Goathland is a particularly pretty moorland village so peaceful that sheep sometimes roam down its greens, in a very lovely setting. The hotel stands on its own wide green, looking out across the moors and to the valley of the River Esk.

In Levisham near Pickering, is **Moorlands** (tel: 0751 60229), once a vicarage and now a comfortable guest-house run by John and Rita Bean. Room 3 has windows on two sides making the most of the fine views (the house is perched high up). Outside are terraced gardens, rhododendrons and a putting-green. Foxes and badgers can sometimes be spotted in the grounds. Traditional English cooking: soups, joints and pies.

rear view

MALTING FARM

C(2) X

Blo Norton Road, South Lopham, west of Diss, Norfolk, IP22 2HT
Tel: 037 988 201

3 bedrooms (twin or family) from £12. Less for 2 nights. Rooms have central heating; armchairs; views of farm or garden; tea/coffee-making facilities.
Dinner £7, at 6.30pm. Diabetic diets can be prepared. Lunches, packed lunches. Drinks can be brought in.
2 sitting-rooms with central heating, open fire, TV, books, indoor pursuits (including needlecrafts, spinning).
Nearest main road A1066 from Thetford to Diss.

When her daughters went off to university, Cynthia Huggins began to feel rather lonely. Her solution was to take paying guests in what (though the exterior gives no hint of it) is her very historic farmhouse. Over the years, she and her husband have transformed this – removing modern accretions to reveal the old timbers and a great brick fireplace, where a log stove now stands. Tapestry armchairs, a Berber carpet and folkweave curtains make a very attractive, big sitting/dining-room. In a smaller sitting-room, there are crimson damask chairs and glass doors opening on to a terrace with fields beyond, where the Huggins' cows graze.

One of the excellent bedrooms is in a modern extension at the back (which also has a bathroom with huge oval bath). Another – in the old part – had to have the legs of the pine half-tester bed adjusted to the slope of the ancient floor. The third has a four-poster.

Cynthia is a keen craftswoman (active in local societies of quilters, embroiderers, spinners and weavers); around the house are wall-hangings, bedspreads quilted with Laura Ashley fabrics, and draperies made by her. She has a large caravan outside as a studio where she teaches such crafts.

She uses traditional Norfolk recipes and much of her own produce (including ducks, chickens and pork) in preparing country-style meals. On cold days, her steamed puddings are particularly popular.

The farm is roughly half way between the two historic towns of Bury St Edmunds and Norwich (described elsewhere in this book), in one of the more scenic areas of Norfolk. Nearby Diss has old houses around a mere, and twisting narrow streets – good food at the Scole Inn. This is an excellent spot from which to explore in all directions. Bressingham is famous for the Hall gardens and steam museum. It is an area of colourful cottages, flint walls, elaborate and colourful village signs, two zoos and the lovely River Waveney. The Norfolk Wildlife Park (with otters) is well worth visiting; and there are lovely rides, with picnic spots, in Thetford Forest. Head for the Norfolk Broads to the north; or Beccles and the coast around Lowestoft further south.

Take the trouble to get free booklets about the area before you set off. Every habitual traveller should keep a copy of the booklet of local Tourist Information Centres issued free by the English Tourist Board (Thames Tower, Blacks Road, London W6; tel: 01-846 9000) for this purpose.

THE MALTINGS

C(10) **D S**

Aldwincle, east of Kettering, Northamptonshire, NN14 3EP   Tel: 08015 233

3 bedrooms (single or double) from £15.50. Less for 3 nights. Rooms have central heating; armchairs; views of country or garden. Clothes-washing facilities. No smoking. Coffee, tea, free.
Sitting-room with central heating, open fire, TV, books.
Large garden and paddock.
Nearest main road A605 from Thrapston to Oundle.

As soon as you enter the courtyard, you get an enticing glimpse through an old stone arch (framed in honeysuckle and jasmine) of a particularly lovely walled garden. Pebble and flagstone paths pass between stone troughs of flowers, and baskets of begonias hang overhead. Beyond is a paddock and wildflower reserve; and an alpine bed.

This is a long, low, 16th-century house with very thick stone walls. Its barn used to provide the warmth needed to make heaps of barley sprout – the malting process which is at the heart of brewing.

Its dining-room has a Persian carpet on the wood-block floor, and antique furniture, as does the sitting-room where, from a pale green sofa, you can enjoy logs blazing in the stone fireplace or a garden view through French doors. The walls of the house are lined with portraits or animal paintings which Margaret Faulkner collects (she used to work for an art dealer).

Upstairs, a long and wavering passage leads to bedrooms that have rose chintzes or pink patchwork, for instance, and to equally attractive bathrooms. Their 17th-century doors are of stripped pine; and, like all the rooms in the house, they are very light.

As only breakfast is served, most visitors go for other meals to the Falcon Inn at Fotheringhay; the Vane Arms at Sudborough; or into Oundle where there is very good food at Tyrrells – and at the Talbot.

In his childhood, the poet Dryden grew up in and around this village, a breezy spot but well placed for touring.

There are 14 stately homes in the vicinity including Burghley and Boughton (gardens too), as well as Rockingham Castle, historic Stamford, Huntingdon for its associations with Oliver Cromwell, bird reserves, Notcutt garden centre, and steam railways. London is less than an hour by train. (More about Northamptonshire under other entries.)

All prices are inclusive of any VAT or service charge. They are minimum prices: superior rooms or high-season bookings may cost more.

Single people may find more company in houses that have a shared dining-table, a bar, and no TV in the sitting-room. As my descriptions indicate, some owners mingle more with their guests than others do. Houses marked **S** charge singles little or no more than half a double.

MANOR FARM *New*   S
Crackington Haven, south-west of Bude, Cornwall, EX23 0JW
Tel: 084 03 304

3 bedrooms (single or double) from £16. Less for 2 nights and bargain breaks. All have own bath/shower; central heating; views of country or garden. No smoking. (Washing-machine on request.)
Dinner £7 for 4 courses and coffee, at 7pm. Non-residents not admitted. Tea, coffee, free. Drinks can be ordered.
2 sitting-rooms with central heating, open fire, TV, books, organ; bar. No smoking.
Large garden
Nearest main road A39 from Bude to Camelford.

Muriel Knight so much enjoys cooking and looking after guests that she gave up her job as a teacher in order to concentrate on this, in her outstandingly beautiful home near the sea (the garden of which provides fruit and vegetables).

It is a historic manor house (named in Domesday Book), much of the present building three centuries old, and furnished with taste. Past a stone-flagged hall is a beamed sitting-room with mullion windows, stone pillar, and wrought-iron screen concealing a log stove. Pinkish armchairs are grouped on a slate-grey carpet and there is a help-yourself bar. In the dining-room lyre-backed chairs with yellow seats surround the mahogany table which Muriel lays with silver, cut glass and starched napkins. There is also a room with TV and organ (with earphones!). Equal care has gone into bedrooms that have such things as 17th-century antiques, Berlin-work window seats, lattice windows, elegant bathrooms. (One has a Sitz bath which some elderly people appreciate.) I particularly liked the rose room.

In the grounds are a sloping lawn with herb border and, beside an old waterwheel, a games room with full-size billiards and table tennis.

Muriel's pleasure in cooking shows itself in the dinners she provides. Here is just one example. Choux-pastry swans with a filling of avocado and cream; Coronation chicken (that is, in an apricot and curry sauce) accompanied by jacket potatoes stuffed with cheese and basil, *and* cauliflower and date salad *and* rice; prawns and eggs in prawn sauce; a lemon and orange pavlova. It hardly needs saying that Manor Farm is a good choice for gourmets.

In such an idyllic spot, there is little temptation to go elsewhere. However, the resort of Bude is very near and the border of Devon. Bude is more sedate than many West Country resorts, in a setting of grassy downs and golden sandy beaches on which the Atlantic thunders in. There is a historic quarter by the port, where an old canal enters the sea via a lock. The area south of Bude has been described under other entries; to the north, the scenic coastline continues into Devon and to Hartland Point (the most exciting headland in the West Country; pretty waterfall; superb church), then Clovelly where there is no traffic in steep cobbled streets and the harbour is reached down precipitous steps; Bideford, an ancient port still with ships and 17th-century merchants' houses; and Appledore where pastel-coloured cottages slope down to the sea and you can look round the shipyard. The countryside differs from that of Cornwall. It becomes lusher, with valleys of oaks and wildflowers, rich farmland and red rocks.

Readers' comments: Gracious and warm, a beautiful ambience.

MANOR FARM   C S-C X
Kelmscott, north-west of Faringdon (Oxfordshire), Gloucestershire, GL7 3HJ   Tel: 0367 52620

2 bedrooms (double or family) from £11. Bargain breaks. Rooms have central heating; armchairs; views of country or garden; tea/coffee facilities. Clothes-washing facilities. No smoking.
Sitting-room with central heating, open fire, TV, books. No smoking.
Small garden and farmland.
Nearest main road A417 from Faringdon to Lechlade.

This Cotswold stone house (at the centre of a dairy farm belonging to the National Trust) stands on the outskirts of a carefully conserved village – utterly peaceful, for it is not on the route to anywhere else. Outside is a pigeon-house as old as the rest of the buildings; paddocks with a pony, pet lambs and calves; pollarded willows and cherry trees that flower prettily in spring.

The 17th-century windows, stone-mullioned and with panelled shutters, are a handsome feature of rooms which Anne Amor keeps immaculate as well as comfortable; with, in winter, a crackling fire framed by the Adam mantelpiece and, in summer, chairs on the lawn. Some people go to a riverside inn, the Trout, for dinner (or to the Tavern at Clanfield). Anne will, however, produce packed lunches.

Kelmscott's greatest claim to fame is William Morris's big manor house, still with tapestries and embroideries made by him and his wife; paintings by Rosetti; wallpapers, tiles and textiles which Morris designed. Occasionally, one-day embroidery courses are held here; and you can buy things made from William Morris fabrics. The house is rarely open, but Anne can usually arrange visits.

The Thames (merely a stream here) is 5 minutes' walk away. In addition to lovely countryside, visitors enjoy days spent at the Cotswold Wildlife Park, Cogges living farm 'museum', the steam railway centre at Didcot; touring Cotswold villages like Bourton-on-the-Water and Burford; and visiting Filkins (woollen weavers) or stately homes (Coleshill, Buscot, Pusey House and gardens, and Blenheim Palace). Oxford and Cheltenham are not far away.

Readers' comments: Very comfortable and welcoming. A lovely time; highly recommended.

Families which pick establishments with plenty of games, swimming-pool, animals, etc., or that are near free museums, parks and walks, can save a lot on keeping youngsters entertained.

It's best to stay at least 2–3 days: you cannot possibly appreciate an area if you only stay overnight (prices per night are often less, too, if you stay on). The vouchers on page **ii** are usable for 3-night stays.

MARINA HOTEL   **C D PT S**

The Esplanade, Fowey, Cornwall, PL23 1HY   Tel: 072683 3315

rear view

11 bedrooms (double) from £17 (**this price exclusive to SOTBT readers,** and for one room only). Much less for 2 nights. Rooms have central heating; shower or bathroom; TV, armchairs; views of sea or garden; balcony (some); phone.

Dinner About £11 for 4 courses (with choices) and coffee, at 7–8pm. Special diets if ordered. Lunches, packed lunches, snacks. Coffee, tea, for a charge. Drinks can be ordered. No smoking.

3 sitting-rooms with central heating, TV, books; bar.

Riverside lawn with sailing, fishing, windsurfing etc. Boat users can moor.

Nearest main road A390 from St Austell to Liskeard.

Closed November–March

Built in 1830 as a seaside retreat for the Bishop of Truro, this fine house has been furnished with the elegance it deserves. The handsome mouldings, arches and panelling of the hall and octagonal landing are now decorated in brown and cream; and each bedroom is different – a pale colour scheme in one; sprigged covers and pine in another (its rounded window overlooking the sea); four with covered verandahs of lacy ironwork facing the tiny walled garden and waterfront beyond it. The dining-room has Indian Tree china on peach tablecloths, with spectacular views from the big picture-window; the bar, rosy armchairs and a thick pale carpet. Recently, 8-foot marble pillars were uncovered in one bedroom!

David Johns gives equal attention to the standard of the food. Dinner is priced according to your choice of main dish, from a selection that includes (for instance) boned chicken in a sauce of mushrooms and cider, escallopes of veal with mushrooms and cream flamed in Madeira, and local fish in a variety of ways, cooked by Stephen Vincent.

Fowey (pronounced Foy) is on that mild stretch of the coast known as the Cornish Riviera. It is an old and picturesque harbour of steep, narrow byways (parking is difficult; a hotel car will take you to the town carpark), its waters busy with yachts and fishing boats. Some people arrive by car ferry. It is easy to find secluded coves and beaches nearby, or scenic walks along clifftops. The little town is full of antique, book and craft shops; historic buildings; restaurants and good food shops. Easily reached from here are Lanhydrock House and gardens, Restormel Castle, Charlestown, Wheal Martin China Clay Museum, Probus gardens. Cornwall has a spring gardens festival – ask the Marina for a leaflet about the 55 gardens that participate.

Readers' comments: Excellent; super room. Extremely helpful.

There is no point in turning up with a dog or child in tow if the description does not say these are accepted; nor in expecting a garden, or alcoholic drinks, if these are not indicated.

MARSHGATE COTTAGE *New* C D H PT X
Marshgate, west of Hungerford, Berkshire, RG17 0QX Tel: 0488 82307

10 bedrooms (single, double or family) from £13. Most have own bath/shower; TV; tea/coffee facilities; phone; central heating; views of canal, country or garden. (Washing-machine on request.)
Sitting-room with central heating, open fire, TV, books.
Small garden
Nearest main road A4 from Marlborough to Newbury.

The marshes which give this cottage its name stretch down to the 18th-century Kennet & Avon Canal, a haven for birds and wildflowers. The cottage (used as a pest-house during the plague of 1640) is even older than the canal, its thatched roof descending almost to ground level; and although it has been skilfully modernized and extended everything is in keeping with its original character. Most rooms overlook the marshes, which are a sheet of yellow in buttercup-time. Wild orchids grow there, frogs croak in spring, and among the network of little streams kingfishers can be spotted hunting, or redshanks on their nests.

Mike Walker, once a journalist, did most of the conversion himself, re-using old handmade bricks and wrought-iron locks; laying floors of beautiful chestnut boards. His Danish wife Elsebeth, a biochemist, has furnished the rooms with Scandinavian taste, hunting for finds such as mirrors or stained glass in the area's many antique shops. The breakfast-room is in white and pine; dried flowers are strung along the beams; hand-thrown pots contrast with curios such as an old mangle. From a quarry-tiled hall an open-tread staircase goes up to some bedrooms (others are on the ground floor), furnished with a pleasing simplicity.

In the grounds are goats and ducks – also a 'dipping hole' (that is, the point where an underground stream pops up – watercress grows in it). You can use the Walkers' canoe, or stroll along the canal path into old Hungerford.

Only breakfast is provided (a chance to sample fresh duck eggs and goat's milk if you wish) because Hungerford has excellent restaurants such as the Bear.

Around Hungerford there is scenic downland in every direction, and a great many stately homes or other sights described elsewhere in this book. Nearby Newbury's Watermill theatre is one of many interesting spots (the wheel is still to be seen). Thatcham Moors are relatively unknown even though they have an almost unique feature, a huge inland reed-bed. Walkers make for the high Ridgeway Path which is of prehistoric origin. Donnington has castle ruins.

Westward lies Marlborough and the **Ivy House Hotel** run by David Ball (tel: 0672 55333), its gourmet cooking well worth a detour and its bedrooms very well equipped, indeed. It has been in this book for many years; but continual upgrading has inevitably meant that its prices, too, have gone up. However, there are some **discounts for readers** of *Staying Off the Beaten Track*.

MEVAGISSEY HOUSE *New* C(7) PT S-C
Vicarage Hill, Mevagissey, south of St Austell, Cornwall, PL26 6SZ
Tel: 0726 842427

rear view

6 bedrooms (double or family) from £12. Less for 7 nights and bargain breaks. Some have own bath/shower; TV; tea/coffee facilities; central heating; views of sea, country, garden. No smoking preferred. (Washing-machine on request.)
Dinner £8.50 for 4 courses (with choices) and coffee, at 7.30pm. Non-residents not admitted. Vegetarian or special diets if ordered. Salad lunches, packed lunches, snacks. Tea, coffee, extra (free on arrival). Drinks can be ordered.
Sitting-room with central heating, open fire, TV, books, record-player; bar.
Large garden
Nearest main road B3273 from St Austell to Mevagissey.
Closed from November–February

Perched on a hillside above this very popular resort is a handsome 18th-century house (once a vicarage), looking south across garden and countryside towards the sea. A great picture-window in the large sitting-room makes the most of this view.

In the dining-room, dinner is served by candlelight, with Doulton daisy plates on green cloths that match the green carpet. Diana Owen's dinners are based on the best of traditional English cookery – mackerel pâté or chicken-and-leek soup might be followed by steak pie or sole stuffed with prawns. After a pudding such as chocolate fudge cake, petits fours will be served with the coffee.

I particularly liked the king-sized brass bed with crochet cover in one of the bedrooms, and the huge size of the carpeted bathroom: very good value.

At the end of June, the annual 'Mevagissey feast' week takes place here, with the Cornish floral dance through the streets. Mevagissey is still a fishing harbour though tourist shops predominate. There are a small museum of model railways, an aquarium, and shark-fishing trips. The nearest sandy beach is at Porthpean.

Readers' comments: Charming hosts who do everything possible to make your holiday a time to remember. Delighted; have booked again.

In Mevagissey itself, up a steep lane is **Anchor Cottage**, Cliff Street (tel: 0726 842089). A 200-year-old fisherman's cottage, it is only a minute from the harbour which tends to be packed with tourists on summer days and therefore best enjoyed in the evening (Cliff Street itself is peaceful). Virginia Dale-Stephenson has chosen William Morris fabrics to contrast with the slate walls and floor; the little dining-room overlooks a flowery courtyard.

Dinner may comprise fish soup, chicken with four vegetables, and apple pie with clotted cream (she also serves cream teas). Crafts, made by her

sister, are on sale. Accommodation here is very good value indeed.

Readers' comments: Very comfortable, well furnished and as good as any place we have found.

171

THE MILL
Millers Dale, east of Buxton, Derbyshire, SK17 85N   Tel: 0298 871832

5 bedrooms (single, double or family) from £9. Rooms have central heating, electric heaters; views of garden; tea/coffee facilities. One has a shower.
Dinner £6 for 3 courses and coffee, at 7pm. Vegetarian or special diets if ordered. Lunches, packed lunches. Drinks can be brought in. No smoking.
Sitting-room with central heating, open fire, TV, books.
Small garden
Nearest main road A6 from Bakewell to Buxton.

After the watermill ceased to function, young Nick and Fran Davidson moved in, converting it not only into a home for themselves but for their business also: from this out-of-the-way corner of England they run the world's largest supplier of specialist tools and materials for hand craftsmen in wood. Just across the little road is the pale stone house, clematis rambling up its walls, where the mill-owner once lived – now providing accommodation for visitors. (Some of these come to attend the 2-day courses in wood-turning run at the Mill for beginners – never more than five at a time – who go home with at least five small items completed in that period. There are other courses for experts.)

The visitors' rooms are white-walled and simply but pleasantly furnished. A family room is conveniently situated on the ground floor, and outside is a small paved terrace (racks of timber from all over the world behind it) on which to sit and enjoy the view of wooded hills opposite and the sound of water.

Provided at least three people are staying, Margaret Whitelaw comes in from the local farm to cook dinner (typically, this might consist of home-made soup, beef Bourguignonne and trifle). Otherwise, visitors go to a nearby inn.

They are welcome to go through the mill (its former wheelroom now displays woodware and woodworking supplies) to the very pretty garden beside the river, great crags rising up on the opposite bank.

Mid-Derbyshire is famous for its dales (river valleys) among wooded peaks: those of the rivers Dove, Wye and Derwent in particular. Wildlife, historic buildings, archaeological remains and old customs survive the years largely unchanged. This is a limestone area, dotted with springs around which small spas were built (Matlock and Buxton, for instance – the latter with some crescents like Bath) and caves (Matlock and Castleton). Places to visit include Ashbourne (markets, and a very fine 13th-century church with striking monuments); old Bakewell, of Bakewell pudding fame; Birchover village, surrounded by unusual rock formations; Chatsworth House, with the Duke of Devonshire's world-famous art treasures, and gardens designed by Paxton; Crich – a collection of vintage trams (you can ride in a horse-drawn one); the gorge known as 'little Switzerland', through which the Dove flows – Izaak Walton fished here; Matlock, with dramatic crags – a cable-car will take you to the Heights of Abraham; Haddon Hall and its nearby village of Rowsley, a moorland walking-centre; and other historic stone towns such as Wirksworth (of 'Adam Bede' fame) and hilly Youlgreave.

THE MILL

C D H

Mungrisdale, north-west of Penrith, Cumbria CA11 0XR   Tel: 059683 659

9 bedrooms (single, double or family) from £24 with dinner. Less for 5 nights. Rooms have central heating, electric heaters; shower or bathroom, wc; TV, armchairs; views of country or garden; tea/coffee facilities. Clothes-washing facilities.
Dinner 5 courses (with choices) and coffee, at 7pm. Vegetarian or special diets if ordered. Packed lunches, snacks. Coffee, tea, for a charge. Drinks can be ordered. No smoking.
2 sitting-rooms with central heating, open fire, TV, books; table tennis, snooker, darts.
Garden and woods.
Nearest main road A66 from Keswick to Penrith.
Closed November–February

It is little more than 20 years since the watermill in this Lake District valley stopped working. By the old stone building which used to house the saw which it powered is the sawyer's cottage, now a private hotel. It is a peaceful spot, with little more than the sound of the Glenderamackin River rushing down its rocky bed.

The Mill (which is next to, but not connected with, the Mill Inn) is a simple white house with moss on the slate roof and a small conservatory, facing a stone terrace and a lawn with seats by the water's edge. Eleanor and Richard Quinlan came here after years in big hotel management, having fallen for the place when they stayed as guests. Their aim is to give the polished attention to detail expected in a big establishment, combined with a less impersonal atmosphere. So Richard looks after the 'front-of-house' and the wines (on which he is an expert), while Eleanor exercises her talent for cooking. She has found sources of ingredients not usually associated with the Lake District, which explains the presence on the menu of such things as stuffed vine leaves, as well as excellent home-made soups accompanied by fresh soda bread (the last a fixture by popular demand). The main course might be chicken in ginger and lime sauce, or braised steak with green peppercorns, and there are four or five sweets on the trolley (cheese follows).

The main sitting-room is pretty (the stone surround to the log fire bears the date 1651), and there is a small TV room with well filled bookshelves. In the dining-room each small oak table has blue linen napkins, willow-pattern china, candles and a nosegay. Bedrooms are trim and simple, with restful colours.

Mungrisdale itself is a tiny village sheltered within a setting of blue-grey crags and slopes, and well placed for excursions to all parts of Cumbria. Close by are plenty of good walks (and even six-year-olds can take the fells in their stride for an hour or two, when not paddling in the stream). Birdwatchers and geologists often come here. There are historic buildings to visit and a wildlife park.

A great variety of places can be reached from here. Some people go trout-fishing, some watch the hang-gliders, some explore the strange rock formations. Popular sights include Wordsworth's Dove Cottage, Ullswater, Mirehouse.

Readers' comments: Beautiful, quiet, excellent food. Service attentive and friendly.

173

MILL HAY HOUSE

C PT X

Snowshill Road, Broadway, Worcestershire, WR12 7JS   Tel: 0386 852498

6 bedrooms (single, double or family) from £17.50. Less for 3 nights. Rooms have central heating or electric heaters; shower or bathroom; armchairs; views of country or garden; tea/coffee facilities.
Sitting-room with central heating, open fire, TV, books.

Large garden
Nearest main road A46 from Stratford-upon-Avon to Cheltenham.
Closed January and February

Picturesque Broadway, now world-famous, can get unpleasantly crowded with tourists – but Mill Hay House, in the oldest part, lies well away from all that, a very lovely house of Cotswold stone with a mossy roof and leaded windows. At the front is a formal garden of rosebeds and clipped yews; at the back, terraced lawns are surrounded by flowering shrubs, more roses and yew hedges, and a rock garden through which a tiny rivulet trickles down to where an old watermill still stands, its great wheel spotlit at night. From some of the yews a bower has been created, sheltering a seat.

Not only is the garden, with its millpond, quite exceptional but the building too is very special. To the stone part, brick additions were made in Queen Anne's reign; there are stone-mullioned windows, and curious carved heads built in here and there.

The furnishings are of the same high order – this is the only place I know where there is a *single* four-poster (18th-century) in one of the rooms, since singles often get the most meagre rooms. One bedroom (with king-size bed) has a view of the mill and garden. Others (one with four-poster and balcony) overlook the rose garden and pond. There is also a separate family suite with two rooms and its own bathroom.

Bed-and-breakfast only; for dinner, the Snowshill Arms is recommended.

The owner, Hans Will, also owns nearby Broadway Tower and its surrounding country park. From the top of this 18th-century folly there are fine views and inside is a museum, including displays about William Morris who once lived in the tower. In the park (famous for spring wildflowers and autumn colours) are a barbecue, with meat on sale, wildlife trails, and animals for the children as well as an imaginative play centre. It's worth a whole day for the family.

Not only is there the whole of the Cotswold area to explore, but three of England's most popular tourist cities or towns are equidistant – Stratford-upon-Avon, Oxford and Cheltenham, their environs all described elsewhere.

Readers' comments: Beautiful building, wonderful food, exquisite garden. A real find, most comfortable.

MILL HOUSE *New*

Berwick St James, north-west of Salisbury, Wiltshire, SP3 4TS
Tel: 0722 790331

7 bedrooms (single, double or family) from £17. Less for 3 nights and bargain breaks. Some have own bath; TV; tea/coffee facilities on request; central heating; views of river, country or garden. No smoking. (Washing-machine on request.)
Dinner (if ordered) £15 for 3 courses (with aperitif and wine) and coffee, at time to suit guests. Vegetarian or special diets if ordered. Tea, coffee, free.
Sitting-room with central heating, open fire, TV, books, record-player.
Large garden
Nearest main road A303 from London to West Country.

One crosses the little River Till by a footbridge in the garden to reach this 18th-century house, next to the old watermill itself (still in use for pumping water and generating electricity). Trout and grayling frequent its clear waters (dry fly fishing available), and a terrace has been built by Diana Gifford-Mead's son, a woodwork teacher, where visitors can sit at the waterside. In the garden, peaches grow – and an abundance of old-fashioned roses and hollyhocks. The best time for a waterside walk through the local nature reserve is in late June when, among many other wildflowers, the Southern Marsh orchid blooms.

From some of the bedroom windows, with leaded panes, there are views of the stream, lawn, tables made from old millstones and rambling herbaceous beds. In some rooms are patchwork bedspreads made by Diana's great-aunt. (One is on the ground floor.) Family photographs and pictures of horses line the walls of the comfortably furnished sitting-room (with log stove). The large breakfast-room, flint-walled, has blue Chatsworth pottery for the table and antique plates displayed.

Diana usually serves only breakfast. For other meals, visitors go to the noted Dove Inn at Corton or to one of the excellent nearby pubs. Diana has lived in the village all her life (her father owned it and the surrounding estate) and therefore is very knowledgeable about places to visit in the area.

Berwick St James lies between two lovely river valleys: the Avon (described elsewhere) and the Wylye, with the Nadder further south. All converge at Salisbury. Along the Wylye Valley are a number of interesting villages such as Great Wishford (look on the churchyard wall for a record of the price of bread since 1800, and wander in nearby Grovely Wood), Steeple Langford (some thatched cottages, some of chequered flint), streamside walks to Hanging Langford), and Wylye (more chequered stone and flint). One can also walk to Stonehenge. In the Nadder Valley lies pretty Tisbury with its huge thatched tithe-barn; Chilmark (17th-century houses and bridges of local stone – this stone was also used in the building of Salisbury Cathedral); Teffont Magna, where each cottage has its own little bridge over the stream; Dinton (three stately homes around it), and the great house of Wilton. (Wilton was the capital of Wessex a thousand years ago.)

A little nearer Salisbury is **Corner Elm**, Netton (tel: 072273 314), once a wool-collecting depot for the area; drovers going from the Marlborough Downs to Wilton used to pass the door. In 1854, it was converted into a rambling house and named for the great elm outside (now a colossal, hollow trunk prettily draped with flowery Russian vine): this was one of a series of 'mile elms' that used to mark the way. Diana Howard has furnished all rooms to very high standards. In the sitting-room, for instance, velvet chairs in pale or dark blue – toning with the carpet – look well against a marbled wallpaper; at deepset sash windows with white shutters are pretty blinds in a red and pink pattern, their colours echoing those of her huge, velvety gloxinias. There is a log fire. One of the bedrooms, blue and cream, has frilled curtains and a lace

bedspread. (All very good value.) In the low-beamed dining-room, Diana usually serves only breakfast, recommending for the other meals restaurants in Amesbury (the Coliseo), Salisbury (the Gondola) or the Wheatsheaf Inn at Lower Woodford. Typical of her own meals, served only on Mondays and Wednesdays: mackerel pâté, chicken Marengo with garden vegetables, raspberry bavarois, and cheeses.

When to go? Seaside resorts or other places suitable for children will be at their busiest (and dearest) in July–August and during half-term holidays (especially, in late May, which is also a bank holiday period). Other peak periods are, of course, Easter, Christmas, New Year and the bank holiday in late August. (The bank holiday in early May is not usually a peak, because it comes rather soon after Easter, but much depends on the weather.) There are local peaks, too (the Gold Cup races at Cheltenham or the regatta at Henley, for instance, are apt to fill hotels for miles around), and local troughs (Brighton, a conference centre, is least busy in high summer). You won't get much personal attention when hotels are full to bursting.

Don't complain if –
– because you booked at short notice, you do not get the best room
– because you did not order a meal in advance, you get something plucked from the freezer
– because you do not arrive on time, your room is let to someone else
– because you bring a dog without asking, it is refused entry
– because you don't express your wishes (for more heat, a second helping, or whatever), you don't get what you want!

Unless otherwise agreed, send a 10% deposit when confirming your booking.

MILTON FARM   C S
East Knoyle, north of Shaftesbury (Dorset), Wiltshire, SP3 6BG
Tel: 074783 247

4 bedrooms (single, double or family) at £15. Less for 2 nights. Rooms have central heating; shower or bathroom; TV, armchairs; views of country or garden; tea/coffee facilities.
Dinner £10 for 3 courses and coffee, at 7pm. Coffee, tea, free. Wine can be ordered. Vegetarian dishes if ordered.
Sitting-room with central heating, open fire, books.
Garden with heated (80°) swimming-pool.
Nearest main road A350 from Shaftesbury to Warminster.
Closed in winter

This is a truly picturebook farmhouse – a stone-flagged floor in the entrance hall, glimpse of a kitchen with pine table and a gun-case beside the gleaming Aga, narrow oak staircase. In the sitting-room, which has a boarded ceiling, logs hiss gently on the stone hearth. There are old oak furniture, deep chairs, silver and flowers everywhere (including the bedrooms).

The Hydes removed a lot of later accretions to reveal the original beams in this mainly Queen Anne house, and then added comfortable furniture and elegant fabrics (such as Sanderson's 'Country Trail'). Janice Hyde serves candlelit dinners – she is a superb cook – which consist of interesting dishes using local produce. One example: onion quiche, followed by a huge trout from the River Nadder (stuffed with almonds, mushrooms, lemon and I-know-not-what) and then the lightest of mousses. Clotted cream, milk and butter are from the farm's cows; pheasant, hare and rabbits are local. Her breakfasts are equally excellent.

Outside is a paved area with chairs facing a view of the hills, and total silence.

East Knoyle is a tiny old village with just one claim to fame: Christopher Wren was born there (his father was rector). So was Edward Strong, who became Wren's master mason and worked on St Paul's. In 1674, Strong built the cottage opposite, and possibly parts of Milton Farm too. Janice Hyde can sometimes show visitors a fascinating scrapbook of village history compiled by the local Women's Institute, including the memories of the local blacksmith and of the postman who used to deliver the letters on horseback. Every summer, there is a music festival in two local castles. Just wandering around here is a pleasure in itself, enjoying willows or magnolias or buttercups, and details like the old stone troughs or a well, and looking for the Victorian 'bun' penny set in the wall of Penny Cottage or the fire-bell on Bell Cottage. There are views over the Blackmoor Vale, a windmill, bluebell woods, and the Seymour Arms where Jane Seymour once lived.

Salisbury and Wilton House lie in one direction and in the other the ancient, cobbled, hilltop town of Shaftesbury, followed by Sherborne – one of England's jewels, and much underrated. It has two castles, a golden abbey, a quaint museum, and a nearby butterfly and silkworm centre in a historic house. Longleat and the Palladian mansion and gardens of Stourhead are within easy reach.

Readers' comments: Janice Hyde is a delight; countryside and house are beautiful. Very welcoming; delicious dinner; very comfortable. Welcoming and comfortable. Excellent service. Welcoming; superb cooking.

MOATENDEN PRIORY

Headcorn, south-east of Maidstone, Kent, TN27 9PT   Tel: 0622 890413

C D PT

4 bedrooms (single, double or family) from £12.50. Bargain breaks. Rooms have central heating; armchairs; views of country or garden. No smoking.
Dinner (weekends only) £10 for 3 courses, wine and coffee, at 7.30pm. Special diets if ordered. Coffee, tea, for a charge. Drinks can be brought in.
Sitting-room with central heating, open fire, books.
Large garden
Nearest main road A274 from Maidstone to Tenterden.

This is among the most ancient of the houses described in this book. It comprises the moated remains of a monastery founded in 1224, when Henry III was king: one of the monks' activities was the raising of money to ransom crusaders held prisoner by the infidels. The walls are of thick stone, the oak doors fit into arched doorways, pointed windows are deep-set.

After Henry VIII dissolved the monasteries, the Priory was owned by a succession of famous people – among them, Thomas Cromwell (Henry's chancellor) and the court poet Sedley, whose daughter became James II's mistress. Then for many years the building was used as a farmhouse.

It is not just the house (hidden at the end of a little lane) that is so outstanding, but the furnishings, too, which Jessie Barclay Deane has kept entirely in character. Guests eat at the big table in her huge dining-kitchen, under a ceiling of great oak timbers. The floor is of quarry tiles and wood, the seating consists of old wood benches and chairs. The big sink is the original stone one, which she retrieved from the garden. Even her Aga is something of an antique: its covers are not cream enamel but polished copper. The walls are whitewashed brick, the windows diamond-paned.

Here Mrs Barclay Deane serves weekend meals made largely with her own produce. A typical dinner might consist of egg mayonnaise, casseroled chicken, cheeses and fruit. Everything she prepares is fresh and simple, and she enjoys cooking for vegetarians.

The sitting-room has comfortable tapestry chairs and a Persian carpet; its walls are painted a soft terracotta and its paintwork white. The only sound is likely to be the slow ticking of the clock or the crackle of logs on the great hearth. There is a small conservatory and an outstandingly interesting garden with unusual plants, a pool and the moat.

Bedrooms are equally attractive and peaceful: beamed ceilings, antique furniture, warm colour schemes, pretty cast-iron fireplaces, and interesting furnishings (a fur spread from India and a woven wall-hanging from Peru, for instance). Jessie makes and sells distinctive knitwear.

Some visitors come for the peace, some for the many sightseeing possibilities in Kent, and many to visit Vita Sackville-West's famous garden at Sissinghurst (before she bought Sissinghurst she nearly decided to take Moatenden Priory, but it did not have enough land for her needs). The Priory's exceptional garden, surrounded by high beech hedges, has two ancient pillars over which honeysuckle clambers and an old orchard where mallards, moorhens and sometimes partridges wander.

Within easy reach are many of Kent's spectacular mansions and castles (Knole, Leeds and Hever, for example, or Scotney with its lovely gardens), and historic cities (such as Canterbury and Maidstone) and towns (Tenterden, Cranbrook). The country lanes are particularly beautiful in apple-blossom time (usually May) or even earlier, when the cherry trees are in flower. In September, the hops are gathered and taken to the oast houses for drying – a few allow visitors. There are several good garden centres.

Readers' comments: A delightful place. Beautiful, peaceful, hospitable: very good value. A gracious hostess. Very pleasant and welcoming. Friendliest and most cosy of all; charming building, warm welcome. Delightful, visited twice. Comfortable, food very good.

Northward, in Sutton Valence is **The Keep House**, Rectory Lane (tel: 0622 843305), so-named because it is built at the foot of the ruined Norman castle – one reaches it up 17 steep stone steps to a balustraded terrace. Below are views of red roofs and weather-boarded houses, and on clear days one can see right to the south coast. Terraced lawns and flowerbeds surround the 150-year-old house. A homely ambience, inexpensive accommodation, and good cooking: visitors particularly like Rhoda Wilson's casseroled rabbit with herby dumplings and her spiced pears with shortbread leaves, for instance. David takes people on guided walks through village or countryside.

Two-thirds of the houses in this book accept and provide for *children*; though nearly half of these stipulate a minimum age, often 4 (some, 10).

Over a third accept *dogs*, though not allowing them in all rooms.

Scores of houses are suitable for people in *wheelchairs* or otherwise handicapped.

Half can be reached without a car, by nearby *public transport*.

Half charge *singles* little or no more than people sharing a double room.

Several dozen of the houses or hotels also have some *self-catering* cottages or flats to let.

Over a quarter provide accommodation at *Christmas*.

About a third are licensed to sell *drinks*, while nearly a quarter allow visitors to bring their own in.

Travellers can book *meals*, without staying overnight, at over a third of the houses.

Packed lunches are provided by about half.

Two-thirds can produce, if notified in advance, vegetarian or other special *diets*.

Over half stay open throughout the *winter*.

An increasing number (several dozen) *ban smoking* in some rooms if not all.

In over a third, you can choose whether to have a *duvet or blankets*.

One-fifth provide either *extra-firm mattresses or bedboards* for back sufferers.

Over half have *TV* in the sitting-room; about a third, in bedrooms; the rest do not provide TV.

Nearly two-thirds provide *tea-making facilities* in bedrooms; the rest bring tea up on a tray. A few offer both alternatives. About a third are willing to provide *breakfast in bed*. About 100 give visitors a tray of tea on arrival, free.

Several dozen have *swimming-pools*, usually heated.

Several dozen provide *clothes-washing* facilities.

MODBURY PIPPIN *New*   **C PT**
35 Church Street, Modbury, east of Plymouth, Devon, PL21 0QR
Tel: 0548 830765

2 bedrooms (double) from £9. Less for 4 nights. Rooms have central heating. (Washing-machine on request.)
Dinner A la carte or £9.50 for 3 courses (with choices), at 7–9.30pm. Vegetarian or special diets if ordered. Lunches, snacks. Tea, coffee, extra. Drinks can be ordered.
Nearest main road A379 from Kingsbridge to Plymouth.
Closed in January

Modbury is a little market town in a hollow among the hills, on one of which perches its old church; it is a pleasant place in which to linger and perhaps to shop. In its main street is a small restaurant with a big reputation for its food: the Modbury Pippin. Here Frank and Muriel Mullery serve such specialities as fish mousses (into which sole or crab may go) with herby mayonnaise; pancakes stuffed with beansprouts and mushrooms; and navarin of lamb. The dining-room has a crisp colour scheme of green and white; Spanish rush chairs are placed at tables with lace over green cloths, candles are lit at dinner. There are bedrooms above – simply but agreeably furnished.

Dartmoor is only a few miles to the north, and outstandingly beautiful country scenery to the south, with unspoilt beaches. Plymouth is near, described elsewhere, and the Cornish border; together with a number of stately homes such as Saltram, Cotehele and Mount Edgcumbe. This part of Devon is called the South Hams ('ham' means sheltered) for it has almost the mildest climate in Britain and spring comes early. Four winding rivers have carved lovely valleys on their way to the sea, so every ride into the countryside goes up and down lanes. These lead to pretty thatched villages and picturesque inns. Views are of brown Devon cows grazing in fields sheltered by high hedges with oaks and pine trees. Westward lies picturesque Dartmouth, perched precariously on steep cliffs beside the estuary of the Dart – a place of coves and cobbles, old houses and subtropical gardens, a waterfront castle and river trips through spectacular scenery. Salcombe, Kingsbridge and Totnes are among other delightful little towns described elsewhere in this book.

Prices are the minimum *per person* in a double room at the beginning of the year.

No one in this book insists that you stay out all day. But do not necessarily expect heating to be on, drinks available, etc.

If you want your hosts to post you things you have accidentally left behind, send them the cost of postage. (The trouble they take is free.)

MON BIJOU HOTEL

Manor Road, Bournemouth, Dorset, BH1 3EU   Tel: 0202 21389

7 bedrooms (double) from £18, with a **10% discount to readers of this book**. Bargain breaks. Rooms have central heating; shower or bathroom; telephone, colour TV with video films, armchairs; views of garden; tea/coffee facilities.
Dinner £12.50 for 4 courses (with choices) and coffee. Coffee, tea, for a charge. Drinks can be ordered.
Sitting-room with central heating, TV, books; also a bar.
Nearest main road A35 from Dorchester to Lymington.

Once an early Victorian coach-house, this low white-shuttered building has more character than most of Bournemouth's innumerable small hotels: Judy and Trevor Foan have made many improvements. Bedrooms are very well furnished, and include some ground-floor rooms. Some beds have draperies of blue voile or are lacy four-posters. The Foans collect (and sell) Victoriana, much of which gives character to the rooms.

Dinners, cooked by a talented young chef comprise a fixed menu with several choices at the four courses, which may include mushrooms with a ginger, garlic and orange sauce as a starter; fillet steak with cream, mustard and tomato sauce; and oranges with mint and lime, caramelized then served chilled.

The hotel stands in the select East Cliff area of Bournemouth, where roads are wide and tree-lined (including many of the fragrant pines for which Bournemouth has always been famous); but it takes only a few minutes to get to the busy centre with its shops (famous department stores or speciality boutiques in the arcades), theatres, concert halls (the city has its own celebrated symphony orchestra), pier and museums. The sea and miles of golden sands are five minutes' walk away.

Although Bournemouth attracts a great number of older visitors, who like the absence of the razzmatazz which spoils some other resorts, it has an immense amount to keep children happy, too. The swimming is safe, and there are many entertainments for them, as well as outings which adults, too, enjoy. Here are just a few of the sights within easy reach: New Forest (ponies, wagon-rides, cycling paths), ancient Christchurch (historic priory, boat-hire on the river), Beaulieu (vintage motor museum in a delightful setting), Bucklers Hard waterfront (maritime museum), Lymington (sailing centre, trips to Isle of Wight), Salisbury and Winchester cathedrals, Poole harbour (trips to Brownsea Island, aquarium, maritime museum), Marwell Wildlife Sanctuary and Longleat Safari Park, the tank museum at Bovington, the gardens of Compton Acres, innumerable stately homes, and the breathtakingly beautiful coastline of Dorset at Lulworth Cove, Studland and Shell Bay, with equally lovely hill and valley scenery inland from here (Corfe Castle, picturesque thatched villages).

Readers' comments: Made most welcome. Excellent food, lovely room, very friendly and helpful owners. Excellent chef. All you said, plus!!

For explanation of code letters (**C, D, H, PT, S, S-C, X**) **see page xxviii.**

MORAR FARM

C(5) PT

Weald Street, Bampton, west of Witney, Oxfordshire, OX8 2HL
Tel: 0993 850162

3 bedrooms (double) from £11.50. Less for 2-nights. **Reductions to readers of this**

book staying 7 nights; and for winter bookings by over-60s. Rooms have central heating; views of country or garden; tea/coffee facilities. No smoking.
Dinner (winter only) £10.50 for 4 courses and coffee, at 6.30pm. Vegetarian or special diets if ordered. Lunches (in low season only) and packed lunches. Coffee, tea, free. Non-residents not admitted.
Sitting-room with central heating, open fire, TV, books, piano. No smoking.
Large garden and paddock.
Nearest main road A4095 from Woodstock to Faringdon.

This modern stone house, comfortable and trim, stands in an attractive garden; but what makes it a particularly nice place at which to stay is the personality of its owners. Janet and Terry Rouse are a lively couple, numbering among their accomplishments Morris-dancing, bell-ringing, barn-dancing and spinning (their pet sheep provide the fleece); and they gladly involve their guests too. One reader described Morar as the best place he had ever stayed at, because of the helpful hospitality and excellent food.

Janet takes quite exceptional care of her visitors, with much attention to detail – for instance, two fresh towels are provided every day; there are unlimited fruit juices at breakfast and a wide range of home-made preserves, as well as help-yourself strawberries and raspberries or figs, stewed fruits etc.; she does washing free for visitors who stay two weeks; and has plenty of maps on loan, fills vacuum flasks free, and gives refrigerator space to chill drinks visitors bring in.

For dinner Janet may, during winter, serve a menu such as soup made from home-grown vegetables; their own beef with Yorkshire pudding and six vegetables including red cabbage cooked with honey and juniper berries; Bakewell pudding and cream; a wide choice of cheeses and fruit. (In summer most visitors eat at the Clanfield Tavern.)

Bampton, a pretty village, is famous for its spring festival of Morris dancers when the village children all make wildflower garlands. It is well placed to visit Oxford, the Cotswold villages, Cheltenham, Blenheim Palace and gardens, Bladon (Churchill's grave), Cirencester (Roman museum), Avebury stone circle, and the Berkshire Downs. There's a wildlife park, rare farm breeds centre, arboretum, trout farm, restored watermill and farm museum all within easy reach. For garden-lovers, Puzey and Waterperry are of particular interest. Also, unfortunately, RAF Brize Norton is near too, so be prepared for some aircraft noise.

Readers' comments: Excellent!

Some readers tell me they have stayed at lots of places from *Staying Off the Beaten Track*. I wonder who has stayed at most? A free copy of the next edition awaits the reader who sends me his/her comments on the greatest number!

NEWBARN   *New*   C D S S-C X

Wards Lane, Wadhurst, south of Tunbridge Wells (Kent), East Sussex, TN5 6HP   Tel: 089288 2042

5 bedrooms (single or double) from £15. Less for 3 nights and bargain breaks. Some have own bath/shower; central heating; views of lake, country, garden. No smoking. (Washing-machine on request.) Packed lunches, Tea, coffee, free.

2 sitting-rooms with central heating, open fire, TV, books, piano, record-player. No smoking.

Large garden

Nearest main road B2099 from Tunbridge Wells to Ticehurst.

Sitting on the brick terrace with the blue lake view below and hills beyond, I could have imagined I was in the Lake District – but this was Sussex, and London only an hour away. There was a solitary angler in a boat, rabbits and wagtails on the lawn – perfect peace!

In the 18th century this was a farmhouse, lattice-paned and tile-hung in traditional Sussex style. Indoors, knotty pine floorboards gleam with polish, there are low beams, and the wood-latched doors were specially made by a local joiner for Christopher and Pauline Willis who took great care, when renovating the house, to ensure that every detail was in harmony.

Bedrooms are light and flowery, pale buffs and sandy colours predominating. The sitting-room, which has an inglenook, is decorated in cream and coffee. There is a games room in one barn, and one day they hope also to have a swimming-pool in another. Bicycles on loan.

Only breakfast is served (with Pauline's preserves to follow – marmalade made with treacle, gooseberry jam with elderflowers, for instance) because the area is well supplied with good restaurants.

The landscaped garden descends right to the edge of the lake, which is in fact man-made: Bewl Water reservoir. Around its perimeter and many inlets is a 15-mile footpath: there are boat cruises, a visitor centre, watersports, a wooden ark for children and picnic spots. Sometimes Morris dancing or crafts shows are to be seen. Birds from the nature reserve can be spotted.

Bewl Water is on the Kent/Sussex border and there is so much of interest in this historic area that one could happily spend a week or two without going far afield. Beyond the reservoir is a cluster of interesting mansions. At Finchcocks, a Queen Anne House, is a collection of early pianos and other instruments which visitors can hear played. Scotney is a decorative, turreted castle with particularly lovely waterside gardens. Bayham Abbey's ruins are beautifully sited by a river. Sissinghurst has not only the Court but also Vita Sackville-West's gardens around its castle. There's a pinetum at Bedgebury, a great windmill at Cranbrook. Crittenden House is a mansion with outstanding gardens – Great Dixter, too.

Tunbridge Wells is the nearest major town, with true spa elegance, tempting shops in the Pantiles and elsewhere, curious 'twittens' (footpaths) twisting behind the backs of elegant houses; and, on its large common, strange rock formations that challenge the skills of even experienced climbers. Antique shops abound.

Readers' comments: Views and peace superb. A pleasure to stay in. Warm, comfortable and excellent decoration. Friendly and helpful.

NEW CAPERNWRAY FARMHOUSE   C(10) **D X**
Capernwray, Carnforth, north of Lancaster, Lancashire, LA6 1AD
Tel: 052473 4284

3 bedrooms (single or double) from £16. Rooms have central heating; bathroom or shower; armchairs; views of country or garden; tea/coffee facilities; TV (some). **Dinner** £12.50 for 4 courses and coffee, at 7.30pm. Coffee, tea, free. Drinks can be brought in. **Sitting-room** with central heating, books. **Nearest main road** A6 from Lancaster to Kendal.

So close to the busy M6 motorway and yet so rural, this is a place of absolute peace. The oak beams and stone walls that are features of most rooms date from the 17th century when the house was built as a farm. Now, surrounded by lawns, it is simply the home of Peter and Sally Townend, who are both teachers. They moved north, to this house, when Peter got a deputy headship locally and they say frankly that it was only when the cost of central heating soared that they began, a little doubtfully, to take paying guests – and then found they really enjoyed the experience. Sally encourages people to treat the house as if it were their own home. After serving breakfast, she leaves for her work at the nearby primary school while her helpers get busy; she returns at 3.30 to cook an excellent dinner which could consist of avocado with prawns, roast turkey, a choice of two puddings (meringues, chocolate gâteau etc.), cheese, fresh fruit and coffee.

Meals are eaten in what was once the dairy, now furnished with Ercol elm chairs and table. In the sitting-room, velvet armchairs and sofa contrast with the rugged stone of fireplace and walls. Bedrooms have doors of dark wood with brass knobs, attractive colours and Edwardian-style pine furniture. There are cane armchairs.

Capernwray not only lies in attractive countryside but is midway between the Lake District and the Yorkshire Dales, neither much more than a half-hour in a car. Scenic walks, pretty villages, market towns and inns abound. Lakeland has its steamer trips, nature trails, theatres, arts and crafts.

Other areas 'of outstanding natural beauty' are the Lune Valley, Arnside and Silverdale, and the Trough of Bowland. Canal cruisers can be hired by the hour or day, there are bird reserves, stately homes, castles and a steam railway museum. Morecambe's beaches are near, so is historic Lancaster and its quaint little port at Glasson Dock with salmon smoke-house. Mediaeval Thurnham Hall has a permanent exhibition about the mysterious Turin Shroud. Other attractive places are Kirkby Lonsdale, Levens Hall (and gardens), Carnforth steam-town, Leighton Hall, Leighton Moss bird reserve, and Barton Grange.

Readers' comments: Every bit as comfortable as you describe it, if not more so! Food and friendliness first class. Four very happy nights. A real gem, superb food. Particularly enjoyable.

184

NEWLANDS FARMHOUSE

Aston Magna, north of Moreton-in-Marsh, Gloucestershire, GL56 9QQ
Tel: 0608 50964

rear view

3 bedrooms (double) from £10.50. Less for 7 nights. Rooms have central heating; armchairs; views of farmland or garden; Clothes-washing facilities. Coffee, tea, for a charge.

Sitting-room with central heating, TV, books.
Garden and farmland.
Nearest main road A429 from Warwick to Bath.

The spacious and well kept rooms inside this Tudor house do justice to its handsome stone exterior, a feature of which is the big archway through which high-laden wagons once entered the courtyard behind, where chickens and ducks wander. The large white hall has polished flagstones on the floor and a big dough-chest as old as the house; and off it is a very comfortable sitting-room (hung with Rugby photos – Jim Hessel was president of the local club). Beamed bedrooms are roomy and the bathroom is huge, with handsome basin units. From stone-mullioned windows one can see the village or hills beyond.

Pat Hessel serves only breakfast, but collects menus of local eating-places for dinner – from the popular Fox Inn, Broadwell, up to Lower Brook House, Blockley, run by a former chef of King Hussein, or the Lygon Arms.

Moreton-in-Marsh is one of the Cotswolds' show towns: a wide street of handsome and historic houses, with many antique shops. All around are gently rounded hills and wooded valleys with bright streams, quiet villages of the famous Cotswold stone (don't miss Bourton-on-the-Water, the two Slaughters, Broadway, Bibury, Chipping Campden and Stow-on-the-Wold), rich farms with sheep grazing, and superlative churches and manor houses built on wealth created by the mediaeval wool trade and richly embellished. Garden-lovers enjoy Batsford, Hidcote Manor and Kiftsgate in particular; pick-your-own fruit abounds in the Vale of Evesham, antique shops in the Cotswolds.

Readers' comments: Exceptionally friendly and welcoming. Very peaceful. Attractive and comfortable rooms.

Inclusive terms for dinner, bed-and-breakfast (particularly for a week) can be much lower than those quoted here for these items taken separately. For short-notice bookings you may be able to get a reduction.

No proprietor wants to have a room standing empty. This particularly applies to Sunday nights. Some hotels make a discount if you want only two courses from a three-course menu.

THE NODES

Alum Bay, Old Totland, west of Yarmouth, Isle of Wight, PO39 0HZ
Tel: 0983 752859

C D H PT S

11 bedrooms (single, double or family) from £13.50. Less for 7 nights or bargain breaks.

Rooms have central heating; shower or bathroom; TV, armchairs; views of sea, country or garden; tea/coffee facilities.

Dinner £6.50 for 5 courses (with choices) and coffee, at 6.30–7pm. Vegetarian or special diets if ordered. Lunches, packed lunches, snacks. Coffee, tea, for a charge. Drinks can be ordered.

2 sitting-rooms with central heating, open fire, TV, books, indoor games (including table tennis, darts), piano; bar.

Large garden with golf practice, putting-green and badminton.

Nearest main road From Yarmouth to Alum Bay.

Closed November–March

At the far west end of the island (with spectacular marine sunsets to enjoy after dinner) is a handsome mid-Victorian mansion standing in its own grounds: it is now a small hotel run by Kevin Harris, very suitable for family holidays.

Some of the bedrooms are in the original part of the house; while others (more modern and compact; each with its own front door) line a courtyard at the back. The one in the house that particularly appealed to me was the 'blue room', which has a magnificent sea-captain's bed and a view of the Solent. The dining-room is rustic in style: Italian pine and rush chairs, pink candles on chocolate or pink tablecloths; I thought the decor elsewhere less harmonious.

There are a number of choices at dinner – one might select, for example, fisherman's pie, roast beef and hazelnut meringue. There is a long wine list.

The foothills of Tennyson Downs extend into the grounds (which include lawns, a play area for children, a golf practice-net and a vegetable garden).

This end of the island and its superb coastline are unspoilt (much of it is controlled by the National Trust): an area of pretty little villages, lanes and country inns; with sandy beaches ideal for children. Visitors particularly enjoy the Tennyson trail, Alum Bay, the Needles, Blackgang Chine and (further east) Osborne House and Carisbrooke Castle.

Readers' comments: Thoroughly enjoyed our stay; staff always smiling; Kevin made us all feel like one big happy family. Peace and tranquillity. Thoroughly enjoyed it; food excellent; staff could not do enough for us.

Also at this end of the island, and within two minutes of sand and sea, is **Rockstone Cottage**, Colwell Bay, which Sheila Reason runs as an immaculate and comfortable guest-house with good home cooking. (Tel: 0983 753723.)
Readers' comments: Very good value.

NORTHLANDS FARMOUSE *New*
Ketches Lane, Sheffield Park, south of East Grinstead, East Sussex, TN22 3RX   Tel: 0825 790958

3 bedrooms (single, double or family) from £15. Less for 7 nights and bargain breaks. All have own bath/shower; tea/coffee facilities; central heating; views of country or garden. No smoking.
2 sitting-rooms with central heating, TV, books.
Large garden and paddocks.
Nearest main road A275 from Wych Cross to Lewes.

This is a low-beamed 16th-century house typically Sussex in style (tile-hung walls and roses round the door) surrounded by ancient barns, in an area of outstanding natural beauty.

Pat Frank has furnished it very attractively – for instance, oak chairs have rosy tapestry seats, there are violet-patterned curtains in one room, another has a blue and green colour scheme against which pine beds show well. Where breakfast is served depends on the weather: it may be on the terrace outside, in a sun-room with bamboo and glass tables, or cosily by an inglenook fireplace in the dining-room.

For dinner most visitors go to local inns. One, the Piltdown Man, gets its name from the famous hoax of 1912, the alleged discovery nearby of a 150,000-year-old skull: the fraud was not unmasked until forty years later. In this part of Sussex there are a great many gardens to visit, most notably Borde Hill, Leonardslee (best in spring), Nymans (NT) and Sheffield Park (NT), which has five big lakes linked by cascades – near this is the Bluebell Line steam railway which goes to the Tudor village of Horsted Keynes. There are castles and stately homes, too. The wooded ridge to the north is a remnant of the once huge Forest of Anderida, part of the Weald. It became denuded of oaks by the 17th century because these were felled to supply the furnaces of the Sussex iron-smelters. Many ponds were created at this time, the dammed waters being used to drive hammers in their forges. A number of rivers rise in these woods and then make their way south to the sea. The most extensive remnant of Anderida is Ashdown Forest where there is a mixture of woods, heath, moor and rocky outcrops: a varied area well worth exploring (a number of footpaths or drives start out from Wych Cross and Forest Row). In the other direction is West Hoathly, once populated by the iron-workers – and by smugglers. At Ardingly is a National Trust mansion, Wakehurst Place, with gardens under the control of Kew. Much of Cuckfield is still as it was in the 13th century, and one of the region's beautifully naturalized reservoirs is at Weir Wood, perfect setting for a picnic. The whole area is a good one for antique-hunting.

> If you want absolute quiet, avoid any place that takes children or has a bar open to non-residents. Inns sometimes get extensions to their licensing hours for late private parties; and may lack quiet sitting-rooms.

OLD BAKEHOUSE *New* **PT S**

33–35 High Street, Little Walsingham, north of Fakenham, Norfolk, NR22 6BZ Tel: 032872 454

3 bedrooms (double) from £13.50. Less for bargain breaks. All have tea/coffee facilities; central heating.
Dinner A la carte or £8.75 for 3 courses and coffee, at 7pm. Vegetarian or special diets if ordered. Drinks can be ordered.
Nearest main road A148 from Fakenham to King's Lynn.
Closed in January

Above a restaurant renowned for good food are excellent bedrooms, some very secluded at the back (with views of a paved garden and ancient cottages that have higgledy-piggledy pantiled roofs and flint walls).

From 1550 until recent times, part of this house was a bakery and the old ovens are still to be seen. Above an ancient cellar bar is a large, lofty dining-room – in the 18th century it was a corn exchange. There is a great brick fireplace at one end, and huge iron-hinged doors. When Chris and Helen Padley took over, they painted the walls pale pink and furnished the room with pine and rush furniture. Here they serve such delectable table d'hôte meals as fresh peaches baked with cheese and herbs (for a starter), banana-stuffed chicken with a mild curry-and-almond sauce, and ice-cream coffee-cake; with a wider à la carte choice too.

The bedrooms are very pleasantly furnished in pale colours such as mushroom and beige, with pine furniture, flowery or William Morris fabrics and wallpapers, pot-plants, bowls of pot-pourri and festoon blinds in some; excellent bathrooms.

Little Walsingham is full of mediaeval charm: few villages are so well preserved. It was a pilgrims' shrine before the Norman Conquest – and still is (both Catholics and Protestants come here). Really big pilgrimages fill the village three times a year, but at other times it is peaceful. Walsingham Abbey's riverside grounds are open at certain times, there is an ancient Franciscan friary, a museum of bygones, and a light railway which children enjoy. The sea shore is near, and also a great many stately homes and impressive churches for which Norfolk is famous.

Readers' comments: Gourmet food; friendly and efficient.

Two-thirds of the houses in this book have bargain breaks or other discounts on offer, some exclusive to readers. Only a third raise prices at the peak of summer.

No one in this book insists that you stay out all day. But do not necessarily expect heating to be on, drinks available, etc.

OLD BAKERY *New*   C(12) **D S**
Milton Abbas, south-west of Blandford Forum, Dorset, DT11 0BW
Tel: 0258 880327

5 bedrooms (single or double) from £10. Less for 7 nights and bargain breaks. Some have own bath/shower; tea/coffee facilities; central heating; views of country or garden.
2 sitting-rooms with central heating, open fire, TV, books, piano.
Large garden (also woods and fields).
Nearest main road A354 from Blandford to Dorchester.

Milton Abbas looks almost too good to be true, as if it had been created specially for a picture on a chocolate-box. Indeed, it is a special creation; for in the 18th century it was laid out as a 'model village' when the Earl of Dorchester razed a nearby mediaeval settlement to build himself a mansion (Milton Abbey) and resited its inhabitants here. The broad village street, grass-verged, slopes steeply down, lined all the way with trim white-and-thatch cottages.

One of these is the Old Bakery: the huge ovens are still there, in a vast sitting-room where breakfast is served. Margaret Penny has a decorative touch, so all the bedrooms (and even the toilet) are attractive. There are small but pretty single rooms – pink and lacy. She has found interesting wallpapers – poppies for one room, wildflowers in another, navy-and-white for a third – to complement twirly cane bedheads, board doors, neat pine cupboards within which basin and shower are concealed in one room, and the antiques that feature in every room. Behind the house are woods, pasture and stables for visitors who bring horses – this is a great area for riding and walking. There is an inn nearby for evening meals.

Some of Milton Abbey (now a school) can be visited, notably the huge chapel and its striking monuments: part of a 15th-century church of cathedral-like proportions which the Earl retained when he demolished most of the original monastery to make his great house. The Abbey is celebrated for its music weeks. The countryside all round is wholly unspoilt and tranquil, part of Hardy's Wessex: nearby Dorchester was his 'Casterbridge'. There are great contrasts, for in only a few miles one can find wild heaths, lonely hills stretching to the sea, the lush valley of the River Piddle (with the village of the Tolpuddle Martyrs).

Across the pretty Piddle Valley, is Cerne Abbas and, in Duck Street, **Sound o' Water** (tel: 030 03435), a former inn which Jean and Doug Simmonds have modernized to provide a comfortable guest-house. Some rooms are in an annexe opening onto a pretty garden that wanders down to the winding River Cerne. B & b only; all Cerne's inns do good food. Cerne is a lovely village with an ancient abbey.

OLD COURT

Newent, north of Gloucester, GL18 1AB Tel: 0531 820522

4 bedrooms (single, double or family) from £10. Less for 2 nights or bargain breaks. Rooms have central heating, electric heaters; shower or bathroom; TV, armchairs; views of garden; tea/coffee facilities.
Dinner £8 or à la carte, from 7pm. Vegetarian or special diets if ordered. Lunches, packed lunches, snacks. Coffee, tea, for a charge. Drinks can be ordered.
Sitting-room with central heating, open fire, books.
Large garden
Nearest main road M50.

A high wall and big garden give this handsome William-and-Mary house seclusion. One steps straight into a particularly fine hall – coral walls, white arches and a big chandelier, with the sun and moon revolving above the face of a grandfather clock which warns 'Time is Valuable'.

In the elegant dining-room, panelled in soft greens and with alcoves, a pretty skirted lamp hangs above the table laid with Copenhagen china, heavy silver and crystal. Margaret Reece serves interesting, very English food: things like artichoke soup, pheasant casserole (with four vegetables, which may include such unusual combinations as sprouts and mushrooms braised together with mustard seed), and a raspberry soufflé, followed by cheeses. Much produce comes from the garden.

Architecturally, the sitting-room is outstanding. One end is curved; there are fluted pillars, prettily arched windows, and the plaster garlands on the ceiling have been picked out in soft colours. Margaret chose an acanthus wallpaper and velvet-covered Victorian sofas to complement this; and in the carved pine fireplace logs crackle on chilly evenings.

I particularly admired one of the bedrooms, the lofty walls of which are covered in a butterfly wallpaper. It has windows on two sides, velvet bedheads, armchairs and tables with crochet covers and a big indigo bathroom which is luxuriously carpeted.

Old Newent (only 5 minutes from the M50) is at its best when spring brings out the thousands of daffodils. It is close to the Forest of Dean (20 million oak, beech and other trees) where sheep graze and ancient rights allow miners and quarrymen to take coal and stone free. Drives and walks take you into the heart of the forest. Newent has a world-famous falconry centre where you can see flying displays, the young in their nests and lovely gardens. Within easy reach are the Wye Valley, Cheltenham, Bath, Malvern, the Cotswolds and the many beauty-spots in South Wales.

Readers' comments: Excellent. Wonderful bedroom.

OLD FARMHOUSE

C D

Raskelf, north of York, YO6 3LF   Tel: 0347 21971

10 bedrooms (single or double) from £17. Less for 4 nights and bargain breaks. All have own bath or shower, and central heating.
Dinner £10 for 4 courses (with choices) and coffee, at 7–7.45pm. Vegetarian or special diets if ordered. Packed lunches. Tea, coffee, free on arrival. Drinks can be ordered.
2 sitting-rooms with central heating, open fire, TV, books.
Small garden
Nearest main road A19 from York to Thirsk.

Bill and Jenny Frost have established a reputation for very good food at their 18th-century guest-house, which has immaculate accommodation and decorative touches like a bouquet of silk flowers in the brick hearth whenever a log fire is not burning; a four-poster in one of the bedrooms; and, for sybarites, a particularly luxurious bathroom adjoining another.

But it is the outstanding dinners which bring most visitors here (for which reason advance bookings for bed-and-breakfast only are not usually accepted). At every course there are several choices, from which one might select (for example) deep-fried Camembert with cranberry compote as a starter; quail en croûte with gooseberry jelly; home-made coffee and Tia Maria ice cream; and finally the most interesting selection of a dozen English cheeses I have come across for some time, ranging from yarg (mild and low-fat, wrapped in edible nettle-leaves) to potted Stilton (buttery and port-laden); blue Wensleydale to snow-white Ribblesdale. Bread and preserves are home-made; local produce used wherever possible.

Nearby are the Hambleton Hills – splendid touring or walking country. It is a good base from which to explore both the North York Moors and the scenic coastline. York, Harrogate, the Dales, many stately homes and several spectacular abbey ruins (such as Rievaulx) are all within a comfortable drive, as are James Herriot's house, the Hambleton white horse, Newborough Priory, Beningborough Hall and the 'mouse-man' workshops for oak furniture. Easingwold is a good hunting-ground for antiques.

Readers' comments: Wholehearted recommendation. High standard.

Single people may find more company in houses that have a shared dining-table, a bar, and no TV in the sitting-room. As my descriptions indicate, some owners mingle more with their guests than others do. Houses marked **S** charge singles little or no more than half a double.

OLD FARMHOUSE HOTEL

C D H

Lower Swell, west of Stow-on-the-Wold, Gloucestershire, GL54 1LF
Tel: 0451 30232

13 bedrooms (double or family) from £17 or £25.75 with dinner. Less for 2 nights. Very good bargain breaks. Rooms have central heating; shower or bathroom; TV, armchairs; views of country or garden; tea/coffee facilities.
Dinner £10 for 3 courses (with choices), at 7–9pm. Vegetarian or special diets if ordered. Lunches, packed lunches. Drinks can be ordered. No smoking.
Sitting-room with central heating, open fire, books; bar.
Large garden
Nearest main road A429 from Cirencester to Stratford-upon-Avon.
Closed Christmas and January

A typical Cotswold stone house, dating from the 16th century, this small hotel lies in a pleasant valley right in the middle of England's most popular tourist sights – Stratford, Oxford and Cheltenham. Nearby runs the little River Dickler – its waters help to give the local Donnington ale its reputation, and they serve the Donnington Trout Farm too.

There is a series of pleasant downstairs rooms running into one another – from bar at one end to dining-room at the other, some with stone walls, one with old panelling. Here, as in the bedrooms, restful shades of pink, green or apricot predominate.

There is a particularly good pair of family rooms under the eaves, which children love; and two bedrooms with four-posters (in one apricot moiré silk, and in the other aquamarine clothe the bed). Most rooms are spacious and light, one of them with view of the stone-walled, sheltered garden – a lawn surrounded by roses. Some are in the former stables behind the house, together with a big sitting-room.

Rosemary Belsham sets high standards in the kitchen: vegetables are not only fresh but freshly cooked for each customer, to accompany such dishes as whole poussins served with a creamy pepper sauce; pork fillet with apricots, brandy and cream; or venison simmered in wine and juniper berries.

Walking or motoring in the Cotswolds is a pleasure in itself, but there are many other things to do too – the Roman villa at Chedworth, Sudeley Castle, the Cotswold Wildlife Park, horse-racing, shopping for antiques or country clothes, visiting gardens such as those at Hidcote, Kiftsgate or Batsford (it has a Japanese-style arboretum) or the many stately homes and even statelier churches for which this county is famous.

Stow itself merits exploration: it's a little town of antique and craft shops, restaurants and byways – one of many picturesque villages. And there are plenty of places at which to buy farm produce.

OLD GRANARY

D PT

The Quay, Wareham, Dorset, BH20 4LP Tel: 09295 2010

4 bedrooms (double) from £16. Rooms have electric heaters; bathroom; TV, phone, armchairs; views of river or country; tea/coffee facilities.

Dinner £11 or à la carte, from 6.30–9pm. Special diets if ordered. Lunches, packed lunches, snacks. Coffee, tea, for a charge. Drinks can be ordered.

Sitting-room with bar

Riverside terrace

Nearest main road A351 from Wareham to Swanage.

Standing right on the quay by the River Frome, this 18th-century brick building was once a warehouse for grain that went by barge to Poole, and it still has much of its old character.

Derek and Rose-Marie Sturton run a restaurant on two floors, with good food served on flowery china in two dining-rooms furnished with cane chairs and attractive colours. A typical meal might comprise haddock mornay, duckling and raspberry mousse. There is a riverside terrace with seats, for cream teas and drinks (the terrace is lit up at night), and a bar with open fire. Upstairs are two floors with pretty, beamed bedrooms, their windows giving a view of the river, swans and the Purbeck hills beyond. The local landscapes on their walls are for sale.

Wareham is a most interesting old town, encircled by great earth banks built by the Saxons to fortify their village against Viking raids. The roads within this were laid out, Roman-style, on a grid. St Martin's church is Saxon and contains, rather oddly, a memorial to Lawrence of Arabia (whose home at Clouds Hill is open to the public). Wareham is a great mixture of history and of architectural styles. One of its noblest buildings, the Priory, is now a particularly lovely hotel – too expensive for this book, alas, but people staying at the Old Granary could at least enjoy its lovely Tudor rooms and waterside garden for the price of a first-rate meal or even tea on the stone terrace, surrounded by roses.

All around this area are marvellous places to visit – the following is merely a selection. Poole Harbour, the second largest and loveliest natural harbour in the world, the Blue Pool, Corfe Castle, Lulworth Cove, the Purbeck hills; Arne – heathland nature reserve; Swanage, old-fashioned resort with sandy bay and architectural curiosities salvaged from London; Durlston Head – cliffs, birds, country park, lighthouse; Studland's beaches with Shell Bay beyond; Wool and Bere Regis (with Thomas Hardy associations); Bindon Abbey; the army Tank Museum at Bovington; Bournemouth, Compton Acres gardens, and any number of pretty villages down winding lanes.

Readers' comments: Superb in every respect; a real find; haven't words to describe food, room and attention to detail; absolutely professional but very personal; welcoming and friendly, spotlessly clean, excellent food. Lovely situation, a personal touch. Food superb. Pretty bedrooms, high quality food. Unique place, very comfortable. Wonderful!

For explanation of code letters (**C, D, H, PT, S, S-C, X**) **see page xxviii.**

OLD INN

C(7) **D**

Black Bourton, west of Oxford, Oxfordshire, OX8 2PF   Tel: 0993 841828

2 bedrooms (double) from £12. Rooms have central heating; bathroom; TV, armchairs; views of country or garden; tea/coffee facilities.

Dinner £8 for 4 courses and coffee. Special diets if ordered. Packed lunches, snacks. Coffee, tea, free. Non-residents not admitted. Drinks can be brought in.

Sitting-room with central heating, open fire, TV, books.

Garden with rough croquet.

Nearest main road A40 from London to Wales. M4 to south-west.

No longer an inn, this 17th-century house is now the elegant home of Pat and John Baxter, filled with fine antiques and old prints. It has 'Gothick' windows in its thick stone walls, low beams in the sitting/dining-room and outside are views of the village and old houses, with the mediaeval church close by.

The bedrooms are very attractive: one is all-white (a crisp and light effect); another is a beamy room with antiques. They have board doors with old iron latches. Even the bathroom has been furnished with style – soft green carpet and William Morris wallpaper. The breakfast-room has pine chairs, scarlet cloths and a garden view. Only one family (or group of friends) is taken at a time.

Mrs Baxter provides the best of typically English food, asking her guests beforehand what they would like. Melon with port might be followed by a joint or a steak-and-kidney pie, and then perhaps brandy-chocolate cake – all served on pretty Blue Baltic china with good silver. Afterwards, when guests relax on the flowery blue-and-white sofas and armchairs in front of the log stove, the Baxters may join them for coffee. And only a minute or two away is the very pretty village of Clanfield (a tiny stream runs alongside the road) where, as an alternative, the Tavern serves meals of gourmet standard.

Black Bourton is well placed to explore the Cotswolds, Oxford and Abingdon, the Berkshire Downs, Woodstock and Stratford-upon-Avon. Favourite outings include Burford, Bibury, the Roman villa at North Leigh, Minster Lovell, Fairford's church, Filkins woollen mill, the Cotswold Wildlife Park – and the gardens at Pusey, Buscot House and at the house of *The Countryman* magazine. Antique shops abound.

Readers' comments: Comfort and service superb. Excellent food served with zest and style. Extremely comfortable and pleasant; delicious dinner. Extremely good value, very hospitable.

Two-thirds of the houses in this book have bargain breaks or other discounts on offer, some exclusive to readers. Only a third raise prices at the peak of summer.

When writing to me, if you want a reply please enclose a stamped addressed envelope.

OLD JORDANS

CHX

Jordans, east of Beaconsfield, Buckinghamshire, HP9 2SW   Tel: 02407 4586

30 bedrooms (single, double or family) from £17.50. Less for 7 nights and bargain breaks. Rooms have central heating; armchairs; views of country or garden. Tea facilities. **Dinner** £6.50 for 3 courses and coffee, at 7pm. Special diets if ordered. Lunches, packed lunches, teas.

4 sitting-rooms with central heating, electric fire, TV, books.
Garden Orchards and fields.
Nearest main road A40 from London to Wales.

This is a place of beehives and belfry, granary and lily-pool, flagstoned paths bordered by lavender and honeysuckle clambering over old stone walls. It was a farm when Elizabeth I was on the throne, and a deed of purchase, 'signed' by thumbprints and dated 1618, hangs in one of the rooms. A brick-floored kitchen added in 1624 is now a dining-room, with Windsor chairs and elm tables, chintz curtains and a big inglenook with James I fireback and built-in bread oven.

The farm became a meeting-place for Quakers (including Fox and Penn), though many were arrested for gathering here; Penn's grave is at the 17th-century Quaker meeting-house just beyond the orchard. In 1910 the almost derelict farm was bought by the Quakers, repaired and turned into a guest-house.

Its Mayflower barn (built from the timbers of the historic *Mayflower* that carried the Pilgrim Fathers to America) is used for art exhibitions, concerts and so forth.

All told, this is a most unusual guest-house, open to all as a 'well from which to draw waters of peace'. Inside the house, winding corridors lead to simple but comfortable bedrooms and prettily decorated bathrooms. Board doors have wrought-iron latches and decorative hinges, each slightly different in design. Old furniture, pictures and other details in the sitting-rooms are all in character. Some carvings are from the *Mayflower*. It is run by a warden, Carole Hamer.

Meals are plain and wholesome: home-made soup, a roast or stew, gooseberry flan or pears in wine might be on the menu, followed by good coffee.

The neighbourhood is very interesting with beautiful scenery (typical of the chalk Chilterns, with beech woods on the hills, far views, and wooded valleys with tumbling streams). The village of Penn has a Norman church with the tomb of William Penn's grandchildren. Milton's cottage is at Chalfont St Giles, as is the Chiltern Open Air Museum, where ancient buildings (some 500 years old) have been saved from destruction and re-erected to provide a view of life in the Chilterns from past centuries. The area has innumerable antique and craft shops. Windsor is near and London and Heathrow are soon reached.

Readers' comments: Have stayed many times, very pleased with standards and friendly service. Quite wonderful.

195

OLD MANOR *New*   S-C
Dunster Beach, south-east of Minehead, Somerset, TA24 6PJ
Tel: 0643 821216

9 bedrooms (single, double or family) from £14. Some have own bath/shower; views of country or garden. (Washing-machine on request.)
Dinner From £9.50 for 4 courses (with choices) and coffee, at 7.30pm. Vegetarian diets if ordered. Lunches, packed lunches, snacks. Tea, coffee, extra. Drinks can be ordered.

2 sitting-rooms with open fire or wood burner, TV, books; bar.
Large garden
Nearest main road A39 from Taunton to Minehead.
Closed from November–February

This remarkable 15th-century building stands on the marshes that lead down to the sea and a bird reserve, away from Dunster itself (which claims to be Exmoor's most beautiful village). It once belonged to the Luttrells, owners of Dunster Castle. The most unusual feature is the chapel over the front porch, its barrel-vaulted roof decorated with carved bosses (today, this is used as a tiny, extra sitting-room).

Gillian Hill is a very good cook. Meals are served in a large dining/sitting-room with bar which has a great stone hearth for logs (there is also another sitting-room for residents). The furnishings here are homely, and the windowsill is crowded with pots of African violets. Here one can enjoy, for instance, tongue in a wine sauce en croûte, sorbets home-made from garden fruit and home-cooked ham in cheese-and-wine sauce. The garden's produce has inspired the fruit sauces which often appear: plum sauce with chicken, gooseberry with roast pork, apple-and-redcurrant with roast lamb. Freshly picked figs or other fruit may be served at breakfast. Gillian has a very light hand with pastry; she makes even the cheese-biscuits herself as well as cakes, jams, etc.

Bedrooms differ from one another, the most striking being a huge room with the wood pegging of the remarkable cruck-beamed roof open to view. There are shuttered windows with leaded panes and window seats from which to enjoy the view – cottage-garden flowers, orchard with sheep and Muscovy ducks, the untamed marshes beyond. Some other rooms (equipped also for self-catering) are in a Victorian addition at the back, built originally like a cricket pavilion.

Readers' comments: A most enjoyable two weeks. Delicious food.

196

At picturesque Allerford, on the other side of Minehead, is **Cross Lane House** (tel: 0643 862112), its restaurant well known to gourmets in the area (and, although on the A39, it has fairly quiet rooms, inexpensive and with country views). Lawrie Pluck's gourmet cooking began in a tent: he used to camp near here as a student. He and his Dutch-born wife Ida honeymooned here. Then he had a career in computers until, at 48, he at last realized his ambition to start a first-rate restaurant in the area.

Inside the old farmhouse, a small old-fashioned sitting-room is filled with African carvings among a host of other objects, and leather sofas. An old wig-cupboard has survived the centuries. The dining-room is furnished with spindleback chairs and check gingham cloths on the tables. Logs crackle in a stone fireplace. All rooms are simple and unpretentious.

As to the most important thing at Cross Lane, the food, the menu is extensive and contains some surprises. Some dishes are very English – such as watercress soup, salmon mousse, local venison (simmered in wine, cream and herbs) or the cider syllabub from a recipe of 1600. But, from travels overseas, Lawrie has also collected a number of exotic recipes. Loempia is a pancake with chicken and beanshoots in a spicy sauce. He does an Indonesian rijstaffel once a week in winter. Lamb saté comes with a peanut sauce. And, an indication of his attention to detail, when he cooks a Kenyan curry he offers Kenyan beer with it. All this in a setting of incomparable National Trust landscape, Exmoor on one side, the dramatic coastline on the other, and all around are woodland valleys where picturesque villages lie concealed.

There is no point in turning up with a dog or child in tow if the description does not say these are accepted; nor in expecting a garden, or alcoholic drinks, if these are not indicated.

If you want your hosts to post you things you have accidentally left behind, send them the cost of postage. (The trouble they take is free.)

If, when touring, you ask a host to book your next stop – at another *Staying Off the Beaten Track* house – remember to pay the cost of the telephone call.

OLD MANOR FARMHOUSE PT
Norton Fitzwarren, north-west of Taunton, Somerset, TA2 6RZ
Tel: 0823 289801

7 bedrooms (double) from £16. Less for 4 nights or bargain breaks. Rooms have central heating; shower, or bathroom; TV, phone; tea/coffee facilities.
Dinner 3 courses from £8, at 7pm. Special diets if ordered. Drinks can be ordered.
Sitting-room with central heating, books; bar.
Kitchen garden and orchard.
Nearest main road A361 from Taunton to Barnstaple.

This building is neither old nor a manor; and the farm lands passed into other hands long ago. Now it is a small hotel run by a hospitable couple, Eric and Vera Foley. I found a warm, spontaneous welcome there, a comfortable bedroom, well-prepared food, everything very spick-and-span.

Norton Fitzwarren is not in itself a very interesting village (although there is a cider factory which can be visited), but it is close to Taunton, a historic town of such interest (once you get away from the hustle of the main streets) that it is an excellent stopover on the way to the far West Country.

At breakfast as well as dinner there is much emphasis on wholefood, with a wide range of imaginative vegetarian dishes (as well as meat) – such as pear with tarragon cream, cashew paella and home-made damson ice cream; but steaks, lamb and venison are available too. There is an excellent selection of very good value wines.

The River Tone winds through Taunton and there are attractive riverside paths. The historic heart of the town lies around the castle remains (with excellent county museum inside). There are two notable churches and, after walking along pedestrianized shopping streets, one can wander through a particularly fine park which was where monks once had their fish-ponds.

The surrounding countryside is not only beautiful but varied: the Quantock Hills are gently rolling and well wooded, with small villages (Combe Florey, for instance, which is as pretty as its name suggests) and sparkling streams. Red sandstone is used for many buildings here. Eastward are the limestone Mendips – far more gaunt, with gorges and crags. The Vale of Taunton Deane is a fertile land, with apple orchards supplying the cider-makers. The sea is within easy motoring distance, and the little port of Watchet. There is fen country too; and Exmoor is quite close. As well as scenery, there are a number of stately homes in the area; numerous country shows and festivals; and excellent walks, easy or strenuous. Particularly attractive gardens surround Hestercombe House, Killerton, Barrington Court, and more are in Taunton's Vivary Park. Not only are there antique shops but a Monday antiques 'fair'.

Readers' comments: Pleasant, good food, good value. Very pleasant; very good food. Very comfortable, well looked after. Excellent fresh vegetables.

For explanation of code letters (**C, D, H, PT, S, S-C, X**) **see page xxviii.**

OLD MILL *New*
Little Petherick, south of Padstow, Cornwall, PL27 7QT   Tel: 0841 540388

7 bedrooms (double or family) from £12.50. Less for 7 nights and bargain breaks. Some have own bath/shower; tea/coffee facilities; central heating; views of river or country. (Washing-machine on request.)

Dinner £7.25 for 4 courses and coffee, at 7pm. Vegetarian or special diets if ordered. Lunches, packed lunches. Drinks can be ordered.

2 sitting-rooms with central heating, TV, books, record-player; bar.

Small garden

Nearest main road A39 from Wadebridge to Newquay.

This picturesque 16th-century watermill is beside a stream that winds its way into the Camel estuary, along a coastline celebrated for its many beautiful beaches (a number of them are protected by the National Trust).

Michael and Pat Walker have furnished the Mill very attractively. The beamy sitting-room has white stone walls, one with a mural of ploughing. William Morris sofas and Berber carpet contrast with the green slate of the floor. All around are unusual 'finds': an ancient typewriter and sewing-machines, clocks, and old tools such as planes and picks. The paved terrace by the stream is enclosed by suntrapping walls. Bedrooms are homely (very nice bathrooms).

For dinner, at tables covered with homespun cloths, you may be offered such choices as chicken in a Stilton-and-pineapple sauce or lamb with ginger and orange; or there is a more conventional table d'hôte available.

Little Petherick is a pretty village with (just across the road from the Mill) a beautiful church; close to Padstow which is still agreeably antiquated. Narrow, crooked lanes lead down to Padstow's harbour, a pretty group of houses encircles the quay, and there are several outstanding buildings including the Court House where Sir Walter Raleigh dealt out judgments when he was Warden of Cornwall. The world-famous Hobby Horse street dance takes place on May Day here. There are idyllic, golden beaches around here (go to Treyarnon to see surfing). Near St Columb Major (impressive church) is an Iron Age fort called Castle an Dinas; St Mawgan is a pretty village in a woodland valley while, by contrast, St Wenn is a wild and windy moorland spot; by the lighthouse on Trevose Head you can see the whole coast from St Ives to Lundy Island.

On the whole, north Cornwall is far less touristy than the south, its greatest attractions being scenery (not only coastal but inland too) with fewer commercial entertainments, sights, etc.

Prices are the minimum *per person* in a double room at the beginning of the year.

Book well ahead: many of these houses have few rooms. Do not expect dinner if you have not booked it.

OLD MILL HOTEL

Town Path, West Harnham, Salisbury, Wiltshire, SP2 8EU Tel: 0722 27517

C(5) PT S

7 bedrooms (single, double or family) from £15.50. Less for 7 nights. Rooms have electric heaters; views of river and garden; tea/coffee facilities. One has a shower.
Dinner A la carte, from 7–10pm. Lunches, teas and snacks in summer; special diets and packed lunches to order.

Bar and TV room.
Nearest main road A3094 from Salisbury to Wilton.
Closed December–March (except for restaurant).

It was by this ancient watermill that John Constable painted his famous view of Salisbury Cathedral seen across the water-meadows, and little has changed since then. The mill dates back to the 12th century, and was used to house the church records while the cathedral was being built. It is now a hotel run by Jerry Such. The bedrooms are simply furnished but some are pretty, with William Morris wallpaper and river views.

The meals served in the much better furnished restaurant (in the oldest part) are traditionally English: kidneys, pheasant, braised rabbit and so forth (cooked by Caroline Kerley and Steve Jackman). This is an unpretentious place to stay, in an idyllic setting and well placed for touring. The hotel can arrange day-permits for trout or coarse fishing, and squash.

In addition to Salisbury's ancient streets and cathedral, and the historic site of Old Sarum, there are such outstanding places of interest as Wilton House, Stonehenge, Salisbury Plain (wide open spaces, changing skies and mossy villages), Marlborough and its downs, innumerable prehistoric sites, old Amesbury (where Queen Guinevere is said to have been buried), Devizes with its noble market square and Norman church, Shaftesbury (abbey and cobble lanes) and, of course, the coast with Bournemouth and its sandy beaches. Weyhill Hawk Conservancy and Broadlands (Mountbatten's house) are very popular and there are at least eight fine gardens to visit. Breamore is a Tudor mansion; and picturesque villages, a Roman villa at Rockbourne and the New Forest are not far away.

Readers' comments: Our room was enormous and comfortable (but suffered noise from the bar below); very pretty surroundings; delicious meals. Accommodation and food excellent. Very welcoming – great service. Most obliging. Idyllic!

Houses which do *not* take children tend to have vacancies in July and August.

OLD RECTORY   C D H PT S S-C X
Belton, west of Uppingham, Leicestershire, LE15 9LE   Tel: 057286 279

rear view

7 bedrooms (single, double or family) from £11.50. Less for 5 nights or bargain breaks. Rooms have central heating or electric heaters; shower or bathroom; TV, portable phone on request, armchairs; views of country or garden; tea/coffee facilities. Clothes-washing facilities. No smoking.
Dinner £7.50 for 4 courses and coffee, from 7pm. Vegetarian or special diets if ordered.

Lunches, packed lunches, snacks. Coffee, tea, for a charge. Non-residents are not admitted to the dining-room. No smoking.
2 sitting-rooms with central heating, open fire (in one), TV, books, piano, record-player. No smoking preferred.
Large garden and pasture.
Nearest main road A47 from Great Yarmouth to Birmingham.

In the pretty stone village of Belton, Sue Renner and her husband David not only run a crafts centre and mini-farm of rare breeds but have accommodation, including converted stables. Guests use the Rectory's large sitting/dining-room furnished with antiques. One bedroom has a four-poster, with an original marble fireplace. At the other extreme are small, recent conversions – in some, you may find a fridge and sink for making your own snack meals if you wish.

The Victorian house has great character, and in its stone cellar is a huge display of locally made crafts which visitors can buy: sometimes, craftsmen demonstrate their skills or run courses. There are also old country bygones on display from the era of the big working horses, as well as rare miniature breeds of sheep, cattle, poultry, rabbits and ponies (with a children's play area). You can picnic by the lake or brook in the grounds. Bicycles on loan. (Sue also takes care of retired permanent residents in another wing of the house.)

As to dinner (by appointment), prawn cocktail, roast beef, apple pie and cheese are typical, but visitors are invited to say what they would like. Teas etc. served to the general public as well as guests. Old Rectory houses a multitude of enterprises!

Belton is in a superb part of England, the scenery and architecture standing comparison with the Cotswolds. There are a great many stately homes and castles (Belvoir and Rockingham, for instance), innumerable antique shops, the vast expanse of Rutland Water (for watersports, wildfowl etc.), Oundle, cathedrals at Ely and Peterborough, ancient villages, concerts and first-class theatre at Corby, Wildfowl Trust at Peakirk, and at Little Gidding a charming early 18th-century church associated with T. S. Eliot and with the influential religious community founded there by Nicholas Ferrar over three centuries ago. Stamford and Uppingham are historic towns. There are good garden centres at Thurmaston and Corby.

When writing to me, if you want a reply please enclose a stamped addressed envelope.

201

OLD RECTORY

Patrick Brompton, east of Leyburn, Wensleydale, North Yorkshire, DL8 1JN   Tel: 0677 50343

5 bedrooms (single or double) from £11.50. Less for 7 nights. Rooms have central heating; TV, armchairs; views of country or garden; tea/coffee facilities. One has a bathroom. Clothes-washing facilities. No smoking.

Dinner £8.50 for 4 courses and coffee, at 7.30pm. Vegetarian or special diets if ordered. Packed lunches, snacks. Non-residents not admitted. Drinks can be brought in. No smoking.

Sitting-room with central heating, open fire, books, record-player. No smoking.

Garden

Nearest main road A1 from London to the north.

Closed December and January

David and Felicity Thomas have furnished their home in keeping with its period (it was built early in the 18th century), complementing comfortable chintz sofas with a soft green colour scheme, the mahogany furniture of the dining-room with peach walls (the table is laid with Minton china and good silver). Bedrooms (on two floors, reached by a twisting staircase) are spacious and immaculate, some overlooking a walled garden with lawns beyond. There are alcoves, bay-windows and low doorways.

Felicity enjoys cooking. A typical dinner might comprise stuffed eggs, pork Dijonnaise with wine sauce, and blackberry mousse, followed by cheeses.

The village is surrounded by small market towns (there's at least one market on the go every weekday), great mediaeval abbeys such as Jervaulx, two cathedral cities and two spa towns, waterfalls (at Aysgarth in particular), famous crags and viewpoints, and the Dales – both Wensleydale and more rugged Swaledale are close by. Wensleydale (famous for cheese) is the broadest and most fertile of the Dales – heather-clad hills enclose fields marked by dry-stone walls, with stone cottages and prosperous 18th-century houses. Bolton, Richmond and Middleham have castles. The North York Moors and even the Lake District are accessible for a day's outing. Constable Burton Hall has a fine garden, Thorpe Perrow an arboretum. Antique sales and shops attract many visitors; and there is plenty of farm produce to buy or pick. In winter, there are activity weekends at the Old Rectory – painting, crafts, history, etc.

Readers' comments: Delicious meal, pretty rooms. The best yet! Beautifully furnished, genuine welcome, superb dinner, wonderful hosts. Outstanding. Very pleasant rooms. Delightful owners.

Inclusive terms for dinner, bed-and-breakfast (particularly for a week) can be much lower than those quoted here for these items taken separately. For short-notice bookings you may be able to get a reduction.

No proprietor wants to have a room standing empty. This particularly applies to Sunday nights. Some hotels make a discount if you want only two courses from a three-course menu.

8 bedrooms (double or family) from £17. Rooms have central heating, bathroom; TV; views of country or garden; tea/coffee facilities.
Dinner £10 for 5 courses (with choices) and coffee, at 7.30pm. Special diets if ordered. Packed lunches. Coffee, tea, for a charge. Drinks can be ordered. No smoking.

Sitting-room with central heating and open fire. Bar.
Large garden
Nearest main road A38 from Bodmin to Plymouth.

Throughout this house, there is an air of calm and dignity, with furnishings chosen to complement the early 19th-century architecture. Features like a fine fireplace of black marble, handsome staircase (with barley-sugar balusters and ruby glass in its windows) and panelled pine doors have fortunately survived the years intact.

There are handsome cushioned chairs around the tables in the dining-room (pale blue predominates in carpet and damask wallpaper) where, on fluted Wedgwood china, Doreen and Luis Sanz Diez serve such 5-course meals, impeccably prepared, as avocado and prawn salad, stuffed pancake, a roast and creamy desserts, plus cheese. Their fish comes straight from nearby Looe: Luis phones to a fishing-boat out at sea to place his orders.

In the sitting-room (which has glass doors to the garden) are capacious velvet sofas; and separated from it by a curtained archway is a turquoise and cherry bar. Bedrooms are equally distinctive. Two have lacy, four-posters; another, on the ground floor, would particularly appeal to anybody who finds stairs difficult.

St Keyne, being fairly high up, has panoramic views and is surrounded by varied scenery: moors, beaches, cliffs and woodland paths are all at hand. There are over forty places to visit, which include unusual museums and collections, steam rail, fishing villages, gardens, seal sanctuary, tin mines, tropical bird gardens, waterfall, Shire Horse Centre, watermills, river trips, craft centres and many National Trust houses.

Readers' comments: Excellent cooking with quality ingredients; warm and welcoming. Charming atmosphere of true repose and Victorian elegance. Food exceptional.

In holiday areas, travel on any day other than a summer Saturday if you can. Make ferry, Motorail or coach/train reservations well in advance if travelling at such periods.

OLD RECTORY *New*
Wetherden, north-west of Stowmarket, Suffolk, IP14 3RE   Tel: 0359 40144

2 bedrooms (single or double) from £15. Both have own bath or shower; TV; central heating; views of country or garden. (Washing-machine on request.)
Sitting-room with central heating, open fire, TV, books, piano.
Large garden
Nearest main road A45 from Stowmarket to Bury St Edmunds.
Closed from mid-December to mid-January

Readers who used the first edition of this book may have stayed with Pamela Bowden when she lived near Hadleigh. Now she has an equally elegant house here, into the decoration of which she has put the same tremendous amount of care.

The house, which dates from the 18th century, stands in extensive grounds. One steps into a hall with stone floor, a piano in one alcove and pot-plants all around. Up the deep pink and white staircase are elegant bedrooms – I particularly liked one decorated in apricot with an antique brass bed and comfortable armchairs. Fine paintings, graceful curtains and Persian carpets are features of the house, even in the television room. In the sitting-room is a wallpaper patterned with classical medallions; the raspberry dining-room has an Adam fireplace of pink marble and a most unusual table – immensely long, it was made in Renaissance Italy from a single piece of walnut. Pamela, a member of the Embroiders' Guild, has made many of the furnishings herself: cushions, curtains, bed-hanging and sheets with broderie anglaise, for example.

Bed-and-breakfast only. For other meals, Pamela recommends such local inns as the King's Arms at Haughley, Blue Boar at Walsham le Willows or Trowel & Hammer at Cotton.

Central Suffolk, once forested, is now an area of wide open fields with prairie-size farms. Villages cluster around greens, big mediaeval houses like that at Parham are often moated – less for defence than to drain the site and provide a water-supply for the inhabitants (rainfall being low in this part of England). The area has had a turbulent history, hence the presence of so many castles (the one at Framlingham is outstanding, and so are the monuments in the church). Nearby Stowmarket has an open-air museum of rural life.

The many attractive villages include Debenham, threaded by a pretty stream and with rush-weaving to be seen; Eye, for the fine roodscreen in its church and the Minstrels' Gallery at the White Lion; Hoxne, scene of St Edmund's martyrdom at the bridge. Earl Soham, unusually leafy for this largely treeless region, has a great variety of architectural styles from every period; Saxtead Green, a working windmill; Heveningham, a stately mansion in a park laid out by Capability Brown. Yoxford is called 'the garden of Suffolk' because of the abundance of spring flowers at every cottage.

From Wetherden, so centrally situated, it is easy to motor to the coast and Aldeburgh, celebrated for its music festivals, historic Bury St Edmunds, the mediaeval showpiece of Lavenham, Ipswich (and beyond it the seaside resort of Felixstowe) and even to Cambridge, Norwich and Colchester in adjacent counties.

204

OLD SCHOOL HOUSE

St James' Street, Castle Hedingham, east of Saffron Walden, Essex, CO9 3EW   Tel: 0787 61370

C(12) S

5 bedrooms (single or double) from £18.50. **For readers of this book substantial reductions for 2 nights or more.** Most rooms have central heating; shower or bathroom; armchairs; views of village. Clothes-washing facilities. No smoking.
Dinner £12.50 for 3 courses and coffee, served when requested. Coffee, tea, free. No smoking.
Sitting-room with central heating, open fire, TV, books. No smoking.
Garden
Nearest main road A604 from Colchester to Cambridge.

Garden-lovers in particular should go out of their way to stay here, for the Crawshaws have created – within a remarkably few years of taking over what was then a rough field – an elegant and lovely garden. Its several lawns are surrounded by shapely and brimming beds of shrubs and flowers, all grown from seed. Steps lead up to a lily-pool with koi carp, and at the end is hidden a neat vegetable garden which supplies the kitchen. And there's a population of little toads – hundreds of them – which come out at night.

Through the street door of the terracotta-and-white house, built in the 18th century, one steps straight into a quarry-tiled hall/dining-room. Between its ceiling beams is a trap-door, known as a coffin door – necessitated by the narrowness of the staircase – and a former inglenook is filled with flowers. There are Chippendale chairs around the dining table, and silver candlesticks on it. Here, Penny may serve, on Sundays and Mondays only (if ordered well in advance), such dinners as haddock soufflé in spinach leaves, rack of lamb and a choice of puddings – chocolate pots, lemon pie, etc. (she makes no charge for pre-dinner drinks). Some guests, however, dine at the many good restaurants in or near Castle Hedingham: the Moot House, the Trading Post and the White Hart, in particular. There is a second sitting-room (brick-walled and with a copper-hooded fire), opening onto a paved terrace made colourful by a dozen huge plant-pots.

The principal bedroom is attractively decorated, with colourful quilted bedhead and spread, while the other has roses on walls and bed. The view from either is of the public tennis court across the street which leads into the centre of the village (picturesque, and with interesting shops), over which the castle itself looms high. A cottage in the garden provides extra, pretty bedrooms and its own sitting-room.

Penny gets many overseas visitors, some of whom hire 18-speed bicycles with which to follow cycle tours in the area, and she also offers other services such as collection from airports and guided car tours.

This is a very scenic part of Essex, near the Suffolk border, with a great deal to enjoy, crisscrossed by footpaths and bridleways. Audley End and a large number of other stately homes are in the neighbourhood, as well as many very pretty half-timbered villages and towns: Saffron Walden and Thaxted in particular (the latter has music festivals). Mole Hall Wildlife Park is another attraction. Colchester and Dedham Vale deserve at least one whole day. Cambridge is little more than half an hour away (it, and Suffolk villages such as Lavenham and Long Melford, are described under other entries.)

205

3 bedrooms (double) from £13. Rooms have central heating and electric heaters; bathroom; TV, armchairs; views of country or garden; tea/coffee facilities on request.
Garden with croquet.
Nearest main road A35/31 from Dorchester to Poole.

Before Anthea and Michael Hipwell moved here, it was an ambassador's country home: a handsome Georgian house with fine doorways, windows and fireplaces – surrounded by smooth lawns and rosebeds within tall hedges of clipped yew, the old church alongside.

Anthea has a flair for interior decoration. Even the corridors are elegant, with portraits and flower-prints on walls of apple-blossom pink which contrast with the cherry carpet. In my bedroom, the curtains were of ivory moiré, the silky bedhead and bedspread patterned with rosebuds.

Breakfast is served in the prettiest dining-room in this book. Taking as the starting-point her collection of aquamarine glass (housed in two alcoves) and a series of modern lithographs in vivid turquoise, Anthea decorated the walls to match, and chose a dramatic turquoise curtain fabric reproduced from a Regency design in Brighton's Royal Pavilion. Against this all-blue colour scheme, the pale limed oak furniture shows to advantage. As no evening meal is provided, many visitors go to the Brace of Pheasants at Plush, the Fox at Ansty or the Frampton Arms at Moreton.

The Old Vicarage is well placed for a stopover on the long journey (by A35) to the West Country; when arriving or departing on the Weymouth-Cherbourg ferry; or while learning to fish for trout at the nearby angling school (tel: 0305 848450).

The Hipwells lend walkers Ordnance Survey maps, and will advise them on sightseeing possibilities, including less obvious ones – such as the huge bric-à-brac market held at Wimborne every Friday, or little-known beaches (one favourite is at Ringstead, surrounded by National Trust land). In addition, there are such favourites as Hardy's cottage and T. E. Lawrence's; Kingston Lacey House; Maiden Castle and Corfe Castle; Studland beach and the Purbeck hills; and several garden centres – one specializing in old roses. And, at the end of the day, you are welcome to relax in the Hipwells' garden chairs under sun umbrellas.

Readers' comments: Very pleasant. Excellent service.

It's best to stay at least 2–3 days: you cannot possibly appreciate an area if you only stay overnight (prices per night are often less, too, if you stay on). The vouchers on page **ii** are usable for 3-night stays.

OLD VICARAGE

C S S-C X

Blakesley, north-west of Towcester, Northamptonshire, NN12 8RA
Tel: 0327 860200

1 bedroom (double) from £12. It has central heating; shower-room; TV, armchairs; views of country and garden; tea/coffee facilities. Clothes-washing facilities. No smoking.
Sitting-room with central heating, open fire, TV. No smoking.
Large garden Pony paddocks and lake, with tennis, swimming, fishing and boating.
Nearest main road A5 from Birmingham to London.

Young George Gilbert Scott had yet to achieve fame as an architect – he would later create St Pancras Station and the Albert Memorial – when in 1838 he designed this vicarage (he had grown up in the vicarage of the next parish, Wappenham). Now it is the home of Rosemary and Philip Burt who have the adjoining pig farm, and every year they make more and more improvements to it: the large garden is particularly attractive with swimming-pool, rose pergola, a newly created lake (with boat and coarse fishing), tennis court and stone-built barbecue. There are huge antique urns and marble seats on the landscaped lawns.

The Burts collect antiques. In the panelled entrance hall, for instance, is a fine grandfather clock of 1720 with a case of Chinese lacquer, and a beautifully inlaid sewing-table. The elaborate marble fireplace of the dining-room is complemented by embossed wallpaper in an early Victorian pattern and handsome furniture on which silver candelabra stand. Adjoining the pink-and-green bedroom is an impressive shower-room with plum-coloured fitments (including bidet).

Rosemary does not do evening meals so most visitors go to the nearby Bartholomew Arms, French Partridge or, for more formal meals, to Peggotty's (3 miles away).

The most popular sights near here are Althorp, Castle Ashby, Canon Ashby, Silverstone racetrack, Towcester races and the shopping centre at Milton Keynes. There is a good garden centre. Bicycles on loan. There is more about this area under other entries.

Don't complain if –
  – because you booked at short notice, you do not get the best room
  – because you did not order a meal in advance, you get something plucked from the freezer
  – because you do not arrive on time, your room is let to someone else
  – because you bring a dog without asking, it is refused entry
  – because you don't express your wishes (for more heat, a second helping, or whatever), you don't get what you want!

Families which pick establishments with plenty of games, swimming-pool, animals, etc., or that are near free museums, parks and walks, can save a lot on keeping youngsters entertained.

OLD VICARAGE

C(12) PT

Church Square, Rye, East Sussex, TN31 7HF   Tel: 0797 222119

5 bedrooms (double or family) from £16. Bargain breaks. Rooms have central heating, electric heaters; shower; armchairs. Tea, and clothes-washing facilities (also packed lunches).
Sitting-room with central heating and books.
Nearest main road A259 from Folkestone to Hastings.

This pink-and-white, largely 18th-century house is virtually in the churchyard, a peaceful spot since it is traffic-free and the only sound is the melodious chime of the ancient church clock (its pendulum hangs right down into the nave of the church). One steps straight into a very pretty sitting-room, yellow sofas contrasting with grass-green walls. Curved windows, antiques and copious pot-plants complete the scene. Beyond is the breakfast-room.

The bedrooms are prettily decorated, mostly with pine furniture and flowery fabrics. Two have elegant four-posters. Those at the front have views of the church and its surrounding trees; others, of Rye's mediaeval roofscape. Henry James wrote *The Spoils of Poynton* while living here in 1896 with his fat dog, servants and a canary, before moving to nearby Lamb House. He said in a letter '. . . the pears grow yellow in the sun and the peace of the Lord – or at least of the parson – seems to abide here' (no pears now, but the rest is still true).

As only breakfast is served (and cream teas in the garden on sunny weekends), for dinner Julia Lampon recommends – out of Rye's many restaurants – the Landgate bistro, Flushing Inn or Old Forge.

Rye has a celebrated church at the heart of its narrow mediaeval streets, lined with antique and craft shops. There is a weekly sheep market and a general market. Romney Marsh (famous for its autumn sunsets and its spring lambs) attracts painters and birdwatchers. Rye itself was the setting for E. F. Benson's 'Mapp and Lucia' stories. Benson lived in Georgian Lamb House, formerly a home of Henry James (now a National Trust property).

The town deserves a lingering visit to explore its cobbled byways, antique and craft shops and historic fortifications, for there are few places where a mediaeval town plan and original houses have survived so little altered. In addition there are in the area twenty castles, historic houses such as Kipling's Batemans, Ellen Terry's Smallhythe and (with fine gardens) Great Dixter, Sissinghurst and Scotney. Battle Abbey and Camber's miles of sandy beaches are other attractions.

Readers' comments: Charming house, pretty rooms, friendly welcome.

Single people may find more company in houses that have a shared dining-table, a bar, and no TV in the sitting-room. As my descriptions indicate, some owners mingle more with their guests than others do. Houses marked **S** charge singles little or no more than half a double.

OLD VICARAGE

Higham, north of Colchester (Essex), Suffolk, CO7 6JY Tel: 020637 248

C D PT S-C X

4 bedrooms (single, double or family) from £16. Less for 3 nights. Rooms have central heating or electric heaters; shower or bathroom; TV, armchairs; views of river, country or garden; tea/coffee facilities. Packed lunches, snacks. Coffee, tea, free.
2 sitting-rooms with central heating, open fire, TV, books, record-player.
Large garden and fields, with tennis, swimming, boating and fishing.
Nearest main road A12 from London to Norwich.

One of the most elegant houses in this book, the Old Vicarage stands near a tranquil village and is surrounded by superb views, with the old church close by. Everything about it is exceptional, from the Tudor building itself (its walls colourwashed a warm apricot), and the lovely furnishings, to the pretty south-facing garden – which has unheated swimming-pool, tennis and safe river boats (it's surprising that few families with children have discovered it, particularly since the coast is near; Felixstowe and Frinton have sandy beaches).

Colonel and Mrs Parker have lived here for many years, and their taste is evident in every room. Lovely colours, pretty wallpapers and chintzes, antiques, flowers and log fires all combine to create a background of great style. In the breakfast-room, eight bamboo chairs surround a huge circular table (marble-topped), and the walls have a trellis wallpaper the colour of water-melon. Bedrooms are equally pretty: one green-and-white with rush flooring; another has mimosa on walls and ceiling (its tiny windows are lattice-paned); the family room is in lime and tangerine. There are lace bedspreads, Indian watercolours, baskets of begonias – individual touches everywhere.

Bed-and-breakfast only; most visitors dine at the Angel, Stoke-by-Nayland.

Lynne, from the village, comes in to help and (herself a lively source of information) is evidently as greatly impressed as the visitors themselves with all that the Parkers do to help people enjoy their stay – from information on sightseeing and eating-places or where to watch local wildlife, to offering a mother the use of their own washing-machine.

Higham is very well placed for a great variety of activities and outings. One could easily spend a fortnight doing something totally different each day. There are Roman Colchester (lovely gardens on the ramparts), Constable's Flatford Mill and Dedham, the seaside, racing at Newmarket, sailing, music festival at Aldeburgh, the mediaeval villages and great churches of central Suffolk, tide-mill at Woodbridge, market and Gainsborough's house at Sudbury, and lovely villages (like Lavenham). Beth Chatto's garden, Ickworth and East Bergholt Lodge attract garden-lovers. And everywhere superb scenery, with few people on the roads.

Readers' comments: Lovely house, very calm, beautifully appointed, charming staff. A firm favourite; superb and beautiful; hospitality outstanding. Perfect! Delightful weekend; privileged to be there. Excellent in every way. Most beautiful house. Very friendly.

OLD VICARAGE C(7)
Muker, west of Richmond, North Yorkshire, DL11 6QH   Tel: 0748 86498

4 bedrooms (double or family) from £29.75 with dinner (if you stay 2 nights). Rooms have central heating; bathroom; TV, phone, armchairs; views of country; tea/coffee facilities. No smoking.
Dinner 5 courses and coffee, at 7.30pm. Vegetarian or special diets if ordered. Packed lunches. Non-residents not admitted. Drinks can be ordered.
Sitting-room with central heating, open fire, books.
Large garden
Nearest main road A6108 from Ripon to Richmond.
Closed November–February

At the head of lovely Swaledale, this house (filmed in the TV series 'All Creatures Great and Small') provides accommodation that is furnished with comfort and in character with the age of the house. King-size beds, good carpets, fruit and flowers in the bedrooms, and open fires all contribute to its comfort; and from every room there are fine views – for close by is Great Shunner Fell (2400 feet), the famous Buttertubs Pass, and Kisdon Hill – good walking country.

Marjorie Bucknall's five-course meals are based on fresh produce; and all the bread (both white and brown) is home-baked. A typical menu might comprise home-made tomato soup, eggs mimosa, chicken casseroled in white wine with yogurt, pears in ginger syrup, local cheeses, and coffee with mints. If you want a daytime TV programme videoed for evening viewing, the Bucknalls will do it.

Muker is the largest of the villages of Swaledale. It houses a shop for woollens hand-knitted by a team of 40 farmers' wives and daughters, mostly from the wool of the breed of sheep to which the dale has given its name. From it, you can also visit the rest of the Yorkshire Dales, the Yorkshire Moors and the Lake District.

Readers' comments: Warm welcome, excellent value. Cannot praise too highly; rooms excellent, food superb, owners very attentive. Lovely people, went out of their way to make us feel at home; and the food . . . ! A delight; the Bucknalls are welcoming and perceptive; food excellent. Warm welcome, excellent food and value, we will visit again and again! Lovely house, superb views, quiet.

Inclusive terms for dinner, bed-and-breakfast (particularly for a week) can be much lower than those quoted here for these items taken separately. For short-notice bookings you may be able to get a reduction.

No proprietor wants to have a room standing empty. This particularly applies to Sunday nights. Some hotels make a discount if you want only two courses from a three-course menu.

Many houses have cards, chess, Scrabble etc. – just ask. And also such things as irons, hair-dryers, maps, gumboots and bridge-tables.

OLD VICARAGE
Parc-an-Creet, St Ives, Cornwall, TR26 2ET   Tel: 0736 79...

shower or bathroom; TV, ...
of country and garden; tea/c...
Dinner £8 for 4 courses (wit...
coffee, at 6.45pm (not in winte...
or special diets if ordered. Pac...
snacks. Coffee, tea, free. Non-r...
admitted. Drinks can be ordered...
2 sitting-rooms with central heating, open
fire, TV, books, indoor games (including bar
skittles, snooker), piano, record-player and
records; bar.
Garden with swing, putting, badminton and

10 bedrooms (single, double or family) from
£13. Less for 3 nights or bargain breaks.
Rooms have central heating; washbasin,

swing ball.
Nearest main road A30 from London to
Penzance.

Although part of the once extensive grounds (on the outskirts of this steep little
town) were sold off long ago to build modern houses all round, the trees in the
remaining garden shut these (and the church) from view.

The house itself, built of silvery granite in the 1850s, is entered via a small
conservatory and a great iron-hinged door of ecclesiastical shape, which opens into
a hall with red-and-black tiled floor. Mr and Mrs Sykes have done their best to
preserve this period ambience, furnishing the bar with crimson-and-gold flock
wallpaper and all kinds of Victoriana. There's a piano here, which occasionally
inspires visitors to join in singing some of the old songs of that period. In addition
there is a sitting-room, and blue-and-white dining-room. Big windows (some with
floor-length velvet curtains on poles) and handsome fireplaces feature throughout;
and the Sykeses have put in excellent carpets, along with good, solid furniture – a
'thirties walnut suite in one bedroom, and velvet-upholstered bedheads. There is a
refurbished Victorian loo, preserved in all its glory of blue lilies and rushes.

Jack Sykes, formerly an engineer, did all the modernization himself, even the
plumbing; while Irene, who used to be a confectioner and later took a hotel
management course, is responsible for the meals. At every course she provides
three choices which include such dishes as Stilton-and-walnut mousse, haddock
Wellington, and pineapple in kirsch with Cornish cream; then cheeses and coffee.

There are chairs and sun umbrellas in the garden; and a path leads down (in 10
minutes) to the sandy beach where there are beach chalets for visitors' use. A bus
will bring you uphill again. Another will take you out to the moors and rugged
cliffs that lie between St Ives and Land's End.

The colourful, one-time fishing village of St Ives, famous for its artists' colony,
is now a crowded tourist centre in summer. Beyond it lie (on the north coast) some
splendid scenery, outstanding prehistoric remains, tin mines and lighthouses. The
sheltered south coast has sandy coves like Porthcurno and Lamorna, the cliffside
Minack theatre, wildflowers in abundance and historic fishing harbours (Mouse-
hole and Newlyn in particular). The byways and curio shops of Penzance, as well
as its subtropical gardens, are well worth exploring on foot and from here there are
day-trips to the lovely Isles of Scilly and to the castle on the little islet of St
Michael's Mount. Much of the land around here belongs to the National Trust.

Readers' comments: Beautifully restored; excellent in all aspects. Pleasant, and
good value. Excellent in every way; superb home cooking.

...ley Gobion, south-east of Towcester, Northamptonshire, NN12 7UE
Tel: 0908 542454

3 bedrooms (single, double or family) £12. Much less for 7 nights. Rooms have central heating; views of canal and country. Clothes-washing facilities. No smoking.
Sitting-room with central heating, open fire, books, record-player.
Grounds Farmland.
Nearest main road A508 from Milton Keynes to Northampton.

'It's Arcadian!' and 'It's rather tatty': both comments are true, and both were made by the Bowens themselves who live here. The 18th-century house has had many lives – as farm, then inn, then wharfmaster's house and back to a small-holding before they took over. The Duke of Grafton helped to pioneer the canal system in this area and he used French prisoners-of-war to build the stables for horses to tow the boats along – now turned into a self-catering cottage next to the house.

The wharf alongside is still in use, servicing colourful canal narrow-boats (including originals run by John and friends to carry coal).

One enters through a tiled and beamed hall with an Orkney chair (made like the old straw beehives), interesting pictures and rugs. There's a deep green parlour for meals, with mahogany furniture, and a red-tiled sitting-room where old armchairs covered in William Morris fabrics are gathered round a log stove in the big inglenook. Board stairs lead to the bedrooms: one has a brass bed with ribbon-trimmed duvet and a grapevine peering through the window, while in a particu-larly pretty family room sugar-pink duvets match the walls. Lying casually about are such oddly assorted family treasures as the Bowens' own childhood teddy-bears and Bonzo, and the plush top-hat of showman C. B. Cochrane: John's father was a ballad singer in some of his variety entertainments. Other mementoes include a bust of John's father topped by the actual flying helmet he wore as an aviator in the First World War. Quadraphonic stereo is available for guests to use.

Outside there's a view of water-meadows, and a miscellany of animals ranging freely about, which children in particular enjoy: a donkey (which they can ride), goats, chickens, ducks, geese, pigs, a few sheep and two Jersey cows. A rowing boat can be borrowed, for fishing, exploring or picnicking. Old farm machines, the original Victorian weighbridge (for carts delivering coal, etc., to the barges), and a rope-ladder up into a spreading willow tree all contribute to the unique atmosphere of the Old Wharf – far from smart, but full of interest.

Only breakfast and snacks are provided by Susie: most visitors go for other meals to the Coffee Pot inn in the village (but there are several other choices of dining-places nearby). Tea and coffee are free – help yourself in the kitchen.

The southern part of Northamptonshire has agreeable countryside, easily reached from the M1 (use junction 15 for Yardley Gobion), with attractive stone villages among the folds of the hills. A special feature of the scene is water – rivers, canals, lakes and reservoirs abound (and on many of these watersports and boating are possible). The area was the scene of major battles in both the Wars of the Roses (15th century) and the Civil War (17th century). Sulgrave Manor is where George Washington's ancestors lived; other sights include the Waterways Museum at Stoke Bruerne, Turner's organ museum, Castle Ashby and its park, the huge

Northampton street market and shoe museum (two exceptional churches), Inigo Jones's pavilions at Stoke Park, and the gardens of Holdenby Hall. Among the many picturesque villages are Badby (thatched cottages and bluebell woods), Moreton Pinkney and Overstone. Towcester is a very ancient town; near it is Silverstone motor-racing circuit. London, Oxford, Cambridge and Stratford-upon-Avon are each about 1¼ hours away. Nearby towns are good for antique-hunting.

A large farm nearby at which guests can have dinner (or a 2-course supper tray) is 17th-century **Castlethorpe Lodge**, near Milton Keynes, Buckinghamshire. Mary Stacey has furnished the bedrooms very attractively, and there is a pretty garden. (Tel: 0908 510208).

An outstanding feature of this book is the high proportion of hotels and houses providing for the individual needs of their guests with a considerable degree of flexibility. The variety of amenities and services provided is impressive, as the following statistics show.

Two-thirds of the houses in this book accept and provide for *children*; though nearly half of these stipulate a minimum age, often 4 (some, 10).

Over a third accept *dogs*, though not allowing them in all rooms.

Scores of houses are suitable for people in *wheelchairs* or otherwise handicapped.

Half can be reached without a car, by nearby *public transport*.

Half charge *singles* little or no more than people sharing a double room.

Several dozen of the houses or hotels also have some *self-catering* cottages or flats to let.

Over a quarter provide accommodation at *Christmas*.

About a third are licensed to sell *drinks*, while nearly a quarter allow visitors to bring their own in.

Travellers can book *meals*, without staying overnight, at over a third of the houses.

Packed lunches are provided by about half.

Two-thirds can produce, if notified in advance, vegetarian or other special *diets*.

Over half stay open throughout the *winter*.

An increasing number (several dozen) ban *smoking* in some rooms if not all.

In over a third, you can choose whether to have a *duvet or blankets*.

One-fifth provide either *extra-firm mattresses or bedboards* for back sufferers.

Over half have *TV* in the sitting-room; about a third, in bedrooms; the rest do not provide TV.

Nearly two-thirds provide *tea-making facilities* in bedrooms; the rest bring tea up on a tray. A few offer both alternatives. About a third are willing to provide *breakfast in bed*. About 100 give visitors a tray of tea on arrival, free.

Several dozen have *swimming-pools*, usually heated.

Several dozen provide *clothes-washing* facilities.

Among a number of other little extras offered at some houses, mostly free, are the following: loan of cycles, gumboots and maps; car-washing facilities; hair-dryers and/or rollers; mending kits; sale of home-made preserves, crafts, travel books and maps; use of video recorder, video films, record-player and piano.

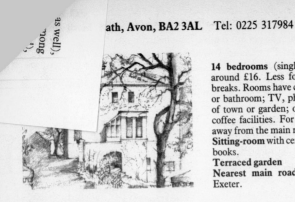

14 bedrooms (single, double or family) around £16. Less for 4 nights or bargain breaks. Rooms have central heating; shower or bathroom; TV, phone, armchairs; views of town or garden; one has a balcony; tea/coffee facilities. For quiet, ask for a room away from the main road.
Sitting-room with central heating, open fire, books.
Terraced garden
Nearest main road A367 from Bath to Exeter.

Although this late Victorian house (or, rather, two) of honey-coloured stone stands just off the steep main road out of Bath to Exeter, I spent a quiet night; and in a particularly attractive and spacious bedroom (pine-louvred doors to cupboards, a terracotta-and-cream colour scheme, sprigged Laura Ashley wallpaper, attractive modern pictures and lots of pot-plants). The big sitting-room is decorated in soft browns and mossy greens, with a marble fireplace (crackling fire in winter) and lace curtains from ceiling to floor at the high windows with their fine views of the city. But what I liked best about Oldfields were the owners, Anthony O'Flaherty and his wife Nicole, who are great fun. Breakfasts are generous (with herbal teas, if you like).

Apart from Bath itself (which deserves at least a week-long stay with Wednesday reserved for the influx of antique dealers and Saturday for the 'flea market'), you can visit the cathedral city of Wells, the Cheddar Gorge and the lovely Mendip hills, the sea at Weston-super-Mare, old market towns like Warminster, Chippenham and historic Bristol (a lively city, with plenty to interest tourists, theatre-goers etc.) And, of course, the beauties of Devon, the South Wales coast and hills, and the Cotswolds are not far away; also delectable villages like Lacock, Bradford-on-Avon, Biddestone and Castle Combe, as well as the gardens at Stourhead.

Readers' comments: Wonderful! Exceptionally nice people. Warmth and charm. Spacious comfort.

If you have not arrived by, perhaps, 6pm your room may be let to someone else – unless you telephone to say you are on your way.

Unless otherwise agreed, send a 10% deposit when confirming your booking.

Houses which do *not* take children tend to have vacancies in July and August.

ONE-EIGHT-FOUR
West Malvern Road, Malvern, Worcestershire, WR14 4AZ
Tel: 06845 66544

5 bedrooms (double) from £15. Rooms have central heating, electric heaters; shower or bathroom; armchairs; views of country. Clothes-washing facilities available. No smoking.

Dinner £12 for 4 courses and coffee, at about 7.30pm (not on Sundays). Coffee, tea for a charge. Drinks can be ordered.

Sitting-room with central heating, open fire, books; bar. No smoking.

Nearest main road A449 from Worcester to Great Malvern.

It's worth going to Malvern simply to stay, and eat, here. Only the name is unimaginative: everything else about this house is inspired, from the interior decoration to the food.

It is in an undistinguished road, but its steep site is superb: from the back windows, there is an uninterrupted rural view to the hills of Wales over thirty miles away, with glowing sunsets. The rooms are on five floors but, fortunately for the less agile, there are ground-floor bedrooms available.

Margaret Harvey was previously an interior designer, and her transformation of this ordinary house is a delight. Not only are the colour schemes sparkling but every detail – small trifles as well as the furniture – has been chosen with discrimination. Old prints and flowers are in each bedroom, and she has even found Victorian linen for some of the beds (*real* linen, with crochet). Very modern scarlet-and-white trellis fabric in one room contrasts with a curly cast-iron bedhead, its curves complementing the arched window of the room.

There's a huge sitting-room in which French chintzes contrast with pale velvets, and a collection of Gillray and Rowlandson cartoons line the walls. You can see through to the big brick and pine kitchen, with terracotta pots and innumerable baskets.

On a curving quarry-tiled worktop, Donald Tether produces mouth-watering meals – things like mussel soup or avocado mousse for a starter; then chicken roulades (breasts stuffed with Stilton and wrapped in bacon) or John Dory in mustard sauce; and such puddings as egg-nog pie or meringue surprise (finally, cheeses – and then chocolates with the coffee).

A footpath leads walkers to the Malvern hills. Malvern itself has been described elsewhere in this book, as well as the surrounding cathedral cities of Hereford, Worcester and Gloucester, each giving its name to counties that are amongst the loveliest in England. Elgar's birthplace, the Royal Worcester china factory, Malvern Priory and Little Malvern Court are popular sights.

Readers' comments: So welcoming and restful. Good value.

To the the south lies Welland and the Beetlestones' **Holdfast Cottage Hotel** (tel: 0684 310288), a historic house in a rural setting which has long been popular with many readers. Its prices are now higher.

215

THE ORCHARD

Bathford, near Bath, Avon, BA1 7TG   Tel: 0225 858765

4 bedrooms (double) from £16.75. Less for 7 nights. Rooms have central heating and electric heaters; bathroom; TV, armchairs; views of country or garden. No smoking.
Sitting-room with central heating, open fire, books.
Large garden with croquet.
Nearest main road A4 from London to Wales.
Closed in winter (except for house-parties of friends).

All the pleasures of Bath are within about ten minutes by car (or bus), yet this little village perched on a hillside seems deep in the countryside. There are stunning views over the River Avon to the far countryside and all around is peace.

The Orchard is a luxurious Georgian house standing in its own grounds. Sometimes one sees balloonists drifting by. The bedrooms are amongst the most elegant in this book, with private bathrooms and big windows overlooking the garden; and the other rooms are equally handsome with attractive colour schemes and antique furniture. Breakfasts include home-made muesli, free-range eggs and locally baked wholemeal bread. For dinner, the nearby Crown Inn is excellent.

Mr and Mrs London own a health club in Bath normally open only to members, but their own house-guests can (for one-third the usual fee) make use of it during their stay at the Orchard. It offers saunas, steam bath, cold plunge, jacuzzi whirlpool, solarium, exercise room and health bar.

Bath, described elsewhere, is full of interest as is the whole region – with innumerable stately homes and gardens, such as Stourbridge, the Westonbirt Arboretum and much else.

Readers' comments: House and appointments are a delight. Complete peace, beautiful surroundings, everything done perfectly. Went out of their way to make us feel welcome. Rooms fabulous. Delightfully furnished. Outstanding. A privilege to stay there.

It's best to stay at least 2–3 days: you cannot possibly appreciate an area if you only stay overnight (prices per night are often less, too, if you stay on). The vouchers on page **ii** are usable for 3-night stays.

Two-thirds of the houses in this book have bargain breaks or other discounts on offer, some exclusive to readers. Only a third raise prices at the peak of summer.

If you want your hosts to post you things you have accidentally left behind, send them the cost of postage. (The trouble they take is free.)

ORCHARD HOUSE
High Street, Rothbury, Northumberland, NE65 7TL   Tel: 0669 20684

C

6 bedrooms (double or family) from £13.25. Less for 7 nights. Rooms have central heating and electric heaters; TV; tea/coffee facilities; views of country or garden. Some have shower and toilet.

Dinner £8 for 3 courses and coffee, at 7pm. Special diets if ordered. Packed lunches. Coffee, tea, free. Non-residents not admitted. Drinks can be ordered.

Sitting-room with central heating, books; bar.

Garden

Nearest main road A697 from Morpeth to Coldstream.

Rothbury, a pleasant little market town with some interesting shops, stands in the very centre of Northumberland; so many of the pleasures of that large and underestimated county are within an easy drive: the Roman wall to the south, Holy Island to the north, and in between countryside which can change from open moorland to woods and arable fields within a few miles, with picturesque villages and historic monuments for punctuation. Castles and peel towers (fortified farmhouses) remind one of border raiders.

The Orchard is a Georgian house standing aside from Rothbury's bustling main street. Jeff and Sheila Jefferson took it over several years ago when Jeff left the RAF after years as an engineer (some of them spent in Malaysia) and have turned it into a comfortable and unpretentious place to stay. Like many people who provide good accommodation in relatively unknown spots, they have found that guests who stayed a night or two while passing through have returned for a longer holiday.

Sheila's three-course menus are out of the ordinary and varied, the only fixture being roast beef every Sunday. Otherwise you might get (for instance) French onion soup, pork scallopine with two vegetables (at least one of which is always fresh), and strawberry meringue. There is no choice except when fish is on the menu. Coffee is included, and there is free tea on arrival. In the lounge is a cabinet well stocked with miniatures of drinks for you to help yourself and enter in a book.

The sight closest to Rothbury is Cragside, the mansion which Norman Shaw (best known, perhaps, for his government buildings in London) designed for Lord Armstrong, the armaments king. It is one of the most complete late-Victorian houses there are and was opened to the public by the National Trust only a few years ago. Among the oddities it contains are a Turkish bath and a hydraulic lift, but its main distinction is that it was the first house in the world to be lit by electricity. The elaborately landscaped grounds are also notable. Brinkburn Priory, Alnwick Castle, Wallington Hall and gardens are all near. At Cambo is a garden centre specializing in cottage-garden and windy-site plants.

Readers' comments: Very impressed. A delightful couple, friendly and helpful. Outstanding food; rooms sparkling clean and spacious. Excellent food – first-rate value. Comfortable, spotless; we thoroughly endorse all you say. Excellent in every way. Exceptionally helpful, excellent food, very good value. Very good food, everything of the highest standard. Marvellous food and accommodation.

'PEYNT O' YALE OR SUMTHIN'

In common with owners of several SOTBT houses, the Jeffersons at Orchard House, Rothbury (see previous page) operate an 'honesty bar'. You help yourself to drinks and make a note in a book of what you have. One visitor wrote a poem about this trusting habit – in old Northumbrian dialect. Here it is (with translation into 'yon infeerior tungue, Inglish'!):

Gin ye shud stummle inti hior,	If you should stumble into here
Wairsh, cloffy, dowf, nat weel,	Weakly, bedraggled, downcast, unwell,
Wore oot bi speelin up wor fells,	Worn out by climbing up our hills,
Or corsed bi empty creel,	Or cursed by empty creel,
Faior soppin wet fra mizzlin rain,	Quite soaking wet from drizzling rain,
Or kizzind bi thi sun –	Or dried up/scorched by the sun –
Nee need is thior ti kick your heels,	No need is there to kick your heels,
Or forr i blunkit fyace;	Or for a sulky face;
Caz this, ye see, 'sa hyem fram hyem –	Because this, you see, is a home from home –
An oppen hoose, this plyace.	An open house, this place.
Ye need nat beyde thi maistor's teyme	You need not wait on the master's time (the bartender's arrival)
An' thootle on ees cummin;	And endure the delay;
Ye're welcum noo ti help yoursel'	You're welcome now to help yourself
Ti Peynt o' yale or sumthin'	To pint of ale or something (else);
Sa lang as ye meynd on ti wretyte	As long as you remember to write
Dyun i thi byuk wi caior	Down in the book with care
Your nyem an' hwaat ye've hed ti dreenk,	Your name and what you've had to drink,
Ti keep your recknin faior . . .	To keep your account right . . .
An' when ye gan fra Rathburry	And when you go from Rothbury
An' bonny Coquetdale,	And bonny Coquetdale,
Meynd on thit hior tha's trust an' faith,	Remember that here there's trust
An' gud will wi'oot fyail.	And good will without fail.

OTLEY HOUSE
Otley, north-west of Woodbridge, Suffolk, IP6 9NR   Tel: 047339 253

4 bedrooms (double) from £16. Rooms have central heating; shower or bathroom; armchairs; views of garden. Clothes-washing facilities. No smoking.
Dinner £12 for 4 courses (with choices) and coffee, at 7.30pm. Vegetarian or special diets if ordered. Lunches, packed lunches, snacks. Coffee, tea, for a charge. Non-residents not admitted. Drinks can be ordered. No smoking.

Sitting-room with central heating, open fire, TV, books, piano, record-player; bar. No smoking, except in billiard room.
Large garden with croquet.
Nearest main road A12 from London to Great Yarmouth.
Closed December–mid-February

It's a story frequently told about houses in this book: lovely old buildings, once occupied by a large family with many servants, prove too big and expensive for today's needs, and fall into sad neglect – until someone sees their potential for a new life sustained by paying guests who occupy rooms surplus to family needs.

When the Hiltons moved to mainly 18th-century Otley House, it was very run down and the grounds (once tended by seven gardeners) so overgrown with brambles that, when clearing them, they fell into a pool before realizing it was there. Within a few years all this was transformed. High French windows now open onto immaculate lawns and the two lakes that were part of a moat round the house. Wild ducks frequent these and a small island with marguerites and astilbes.

The sitting-room's wood block floor is scattered with oriental rugs, and on its off-pink walls hang some of the Hiltons' collection of watercolours. Many of these, like other objects around the house, come from Denmark – Lise's home country. The large hall (with handsome details such as arches and panelled doors) houses early Chinese porcelain which she has restored, and one of Michael's ship models.

Chippendale chairs surround the long mahogany dining-table with its crystal chandelier and family silver where Lise serves such meals as salmon mousse or a herby Danish pâté to start with; chicken in tarragon sauce; Danish lemon mousse or chocolate mousse with Grand Marnier; then Stilton. After dinner, a grand piano awaits – or the billiard room, with big leather armchairs around a coal fire.

Up the curving staircase with barleysugar banisters are very attractive bedrooms, from what Lise calls 'the cheapie' (rosebuds pattern the white quilted spreads, white wrought-iron bedheads are backed by the same plum-coloured velvet which covers the armchairs) to my favourite, which costs a few pounds more: this has windows in two of its aquamarine walls, and a pale pink carpet.

From Otley, beautiful stretches of the coast are only a few miles away and Aldeburgh (celebrated for its music festivals, started by Benjamin Britten).

Readers' comments: Delighted. Dinner excellent, room well above average; first-class.

219

OTTERBURN TOWER HOTEL   *New*   C D X

**Otterburn, north-west of Newcastle-upon-Tyne, Northumberland,
NE19 1NB**   Tel: 0830 20620

12 bedrooms (single, double or family) from £17.50. Less for 2 nights and bargain breaks. Some have own bath/shower; TV; tea/coffee facilities; central heating; views of country or garden.
Dinner A la carte or £9 for 3 courses (with choices) and coffee, at 7–9.30pm. Vegetarian or special diets if ordered. Lunches, packed lunches, snacks. Tea, coffee, extra. Drinks can be ordered.
2 sitting-rooms with central heating, open fire, TV, books, piano; bar.
Large garden
Nearest main road A696 from Newcastle to Jedburgh.

Though most of this battlemented 'castle' dates only from the last century, it has a much longer history. The first tower was built by one of William the Conqueror's cousins, given the estate 'to hold by the service of defending that part of the country forever from wolves and enemies'. It had a turbulent history, the most epic conflict in which it was involved being the Battle of Otterburn, 1388, when Percy ('Hotspur') led the English against the Scottish Earl of Douglas – as related in the 'Ballad of Chevy Chase'.

Just after the Hardings bought the lease in 1983, a great storm devastated the house but it has been handsomely restored since – a unique marriage of baronial splendour with relaxed family atmosphere. Well placed on one of the more picturesque routes to or from Scotland, it is also on the edge of the Northumberland National Park and stands in grounds that include over three miles of the River Rede (with fishing rights).

The interior lives up to the impressive exterior, with oak-panelled rooms, leaded windows carrying coats-of-arms of past owners, tapestry seats in the bar (a wide range of malt whiskies here), mock-noble decorations, and no less than five log fires. An upstairs sitting-room has murals of the Battle of Otterburn – occasionally re-enacted locally in August – and there is a library with buttoned leather armchairs. Bedrooms have been decorated with pretty wallpapers and matching curtains (some high-ceilinged and with four-posters, others more cottagey – prices vary accordingly).

Classic English dishes make up the dinner menu (cooked by Peter), the main courses of which usually include such things as sirloin of local Bellingham beef, haunch of venison, loin of pork and leg of Northumbrian lamb – served with interesting cream-based sauces freshly prepared for each person.

Among the immediate attractions of this area is the Otterburn mill, across the road, with bargains in tweeds. Other local villages include Elsdon (once the Norman capital of Redesdale), its historic houses – one of them a fortified parsonage – surrounding a huge village green; Harbottle, with the remains of a castle; and Alwinton, where hill farmers gather for agricultural shows.

220

OVERCOMBE HOTEL

C D H PT S X

Horrabridge, north-west of Yelverton, Devon, PL20 7RN   Tel: 0822 853501

rear view

11 bedrooms (single, double or family) from £16. Less for 7 nights or bargain breaks.

Rooms have central heating; shower or bathroom; TV, armchairs; views of country or garden; tea/coffee facilities.
Dinner £9 for 4 courses and coffee, at 7.30pm. Special diets if ordered. Lunches, packed lunches, snacks. Coffee, tea, for a charge. Drinks can be ordered.
2 sitting-rooms with central heating, open fire, TV, books; and a bar.
Large garden with swing-ball.
Nearest main road A386 from Plymouth to Tavistock.

Conveniently placed for one to explore Dartmoor and the coast, the Overcombe Hotel consists of two houses now joined in one to make a very comfortable small hotel. You can relax in any of three sitting-rooms, according to what you want – a bar in one, TV in another, log fires, pleasant views. From the bay window of the dining-room, one looks across to the moors. The walls are hung with local paintings, some of which are for sale.

Richard Kitchin used to be in the Army, stationed overseas. To raise the air fares to visit him, his wife Pam started with some hesitation to take visitors for bed-and-breakfast. Finding the experience enjoyable, the Kitchins expanded this modest enterprise until it gradually grew into today's hotel, open all year.

There is always a selection of dishes on the menu (my choice was: avocado with prawns, carbonnade of beef, grape pavlova and cheese).

Visitors come here for a variety of reasons (the least of which is that it's a good staging-post if you are on that long slog to furthest Cornwall). The Dartmoor National Park attracts people touring by car, anglers, riders, golfers and – above all – walkers (for them, Richard organizes special two- to seven-day bargain breaks, with experienced guides accompanying visitors on walks of eight miles or more, and illustrated after-dinner talks about the moors). Plymouth is near; and among visitors' favourite outings are Cotehele, Buckland Abbey and Saltram House (all National Trust), Morwellham Quay and the Shire Horse Centre.

Further east lie the delectable South Hams: flowery valleys, sands, mildest of climates. To the west is the Cornish coast: dramatic cliffs, sandy coves and some harbours so picturesque (Polperro, Looe, etc.) that popularity threatens to ruin them. But go inland, and you will still find undisturbed villages and market towns.

Plymouth was heavily bombed, which means that its shopping centre is very modern. But the old quarter, the Barbican, which Drake and the Pilgrim Fathers knew so well, survived, and it is to this that visitors throng. Here are the old warehouses and the harbours full of small boats, the narrow alleys with beguiling little shops and restaurants, the mediaeval houses now turned into museums, the fish market and, high above, the 17th-century citadel. Plymouth has an outstanding aquarium, Drake's Island out in the Sound (to be visited by boat), the naval dockyard and the famous clifftop – the Hoe – with its unique seascape, memorials and flowers.

Readers' comments: Excellent. Wonderful home cooking. Attentive hosts, very helpful. Food excellent and varied; most comfortable; lovely, informal, relaxed atmosphere. Happy, friendly owners and staff. Efficient, helpful, friendly. Good unpretentious cooking.

PARADISE HOUSE

88 Holloway, Bath, Avon, BA2 4PX   Tel: 0225 317723

C PT

9 bedrooms (single, double or family) from £17.50. Less for 5 nights. Rooms have central heating; shower or bathroom in seven; TV, armchairs; views of city, country or garden; tea/coffee facilities; phone.
Sitting-room with fire, central heating, books.
Garden with croquet and swing-ball.
Nearest main road A367 from Bath to Exeter.

It stands half way up a steep, curving road which was once indeed a 'hollow way': a lane worn low between high banks by centuries of weary feet or hooves entering Bath from the south: the last lap of the Romans' Fosse Way. It is now a quiet cul-de-sac in the lee of Beechen Cliff, with panoramic views over the city, the centre of which is only 7 minutes' walk away – downhill. (As to uphill – take a taxi! Or else a bus to the Bear Flat stop.) Look the opposite way and all is leafy woods.

The house itself was built about 1720, with all the elegance which that implies: a classical pediment above the front door and well-proportioned sash windows with rounded tops in a façade of honey-coloured Bath stone. But it had been sadly neglected in later times.

David and Janet Cutting took it over several years ago and have restored it impeccably throughout, stripping off polystyrene to reveal pretty plasterwork ceilings, for instance, and gaudy tiles to expose a lovely marble fireplace in which logs now blaze. They stripped dingy paint off the panelled pine doors and put on handles of brass or china. They have furnished to a very high standard indeed, with both antique and modern furniture, elegant fabrics, and well chosen colours, predominantly soft greens and browns. The sitting-room is especially pretty, with Liberty fabrics and wallpaper, pictures in maple frames and a collection of Coalport cottages. The bedrooms have been given as much care as the rest.

At the back, beyond a verandah with ivy-leaf ironwork, is quite a large walled garden (a suntrap in the afternoon), with lawns, fish-pool, a rose-covered pergola and marvellous views of the city and hills all around. This secluded setting extends behind the mediaeval Magdalen Chapel next door, which was once a hostel for lepers banned from the city. In 1982 David and Janet acquired the adjoining Georgian house, which has now also been completely restored. It provides two lovely suites comprising sitting-room, bedroom and private bathroom, furnished and decorated to the same elegant standards as the main house.

As to Bath itself – which attracts more visitors than any other place in England except London – the attractions are so varied that they can hardly be compressed into one paragraph. Just wandering among the Georgian perfection of its streets and squares, which spread from the historic centre right up the sides of the surrounding hills, and in its award-winning gardens, is a pleasure in itself, and it would take many days to explore them all (the best method is to take a bus to each hilltop in turn and walk back downhill, with far views succeeded by discoveries of lovely houses, streets, alleys or gardens all the way).

Readers' comments: Top-class! Truly excellent. Ideal, with excellent facilities. Superbly equipped, very attractive. Outstanding hotel.

222

PARKFIELD HOUSE

Hogben's Hill, Selling, south of Faversham, Kent, ME13 9QU
Tel: 0227 752898

5 bedrooms (single, double or family) from £12. Less for 2 nights. Rooms have central heating; armchairs; views of country or garden. Evening coffee, tea, free. No smoking.
Sitting-room with central heating, open fire, TV, books. No smoking.
Small garden
Nearest main road A251 from Faversham to Ashford.

There were Hogbens on this hill in 1086 (they are named in the Domesday Book) . . . and there still are!

It is Mr and Mrs Hogben who own Parkfield, a largely modern house with a pretty garden, as well as the small joinery works alongside – John Hogben's principal activity. It is worth staying at Parkfield House simply to listen to him talk about Kentish ways and history (especially his stories of past Hogbens, who were blacksmiths, farmers, wheelwrights and smugglers). Next door there used to be an inn, called Ye Olde Century in memory of a John Hogben who lived there until he was 101.

The house, built in 1820, had become run-down until about 30 years ago when Mr Hogben renovated and extended it. Now it is immaculate and very comfortable. Although only bed-and-breakfast guests are taken (they can dine, very well indeed, at the old village inn – the White Lion), there is a sitting-room for their use in the evening, with television and big, velvet armchairs in which to relax by a log fire. And if you want something special for breakfast (fish, fresh fruit, ham, cheese) Mrs Hogben will get it – and will do packed lunches.

Selling is in a very beautiful and tranquil part of Kent, well situated for touring, walking and sightseeing. It is, of course, the cathedral which brings most visitors to nearby Canterbury: one of Britain's finest and most colourful, with many historical associations, the site of Becket's martyrdom (commemorated in some of the finest stained glass in the world), the splendid tomb of the Black Prince, and much more.

The ancient walled city still has many surviving mediaeval and Tudor buildings, the beautiful River Stour, old churches and inns, Roman remains, a very good theatre, and lovely shops in its small lanes. It is in the middle of some of Kent's finest countryside, with a coast of great variety quite near (cliffs, sands or shingle; resorts, fishing harbours or historic ports) and ten golf courses. Howlett's Zoo and mediaeval Faversham are very popular, and the whole area is full of fine gardens and garden centres. It would be very easy to spend a fortnight here without discovering all there is to see in one of England's most beautiful and most historic counties, rich in towns with antique shops and fields of fruit where you can pick-your-own.

Readers' comments: Excellent in all respects, exceptional hospitality. Excellent service, well cared for. Warm welcome. Spotless. Attractive bedroom.

For explanation of code letters (**C, D, H, PT, S, S-C, X**) see page xxviii.

PEACOCK FARMHOUSE

C D H PT S S-C X

Redmile (east of Nottingham), Leicestershire, NG13 0GQ Tel: 0949 42475

9 bedrooms (single, double or family) from £11. Bargain breaks. Rooms have central heating; some have shower or bathroom; views of country or garden; tea/coffee facilities. Clothes-washing facilities.

Dinner £8 for 3 courses (with choices) and coffee, at 7.30pm. Vegetarian or special diets if ordered. Lunches, packed lunches, snacks. Coffee, tea, free. Drinks can be ordered.

Sitting-room with central heating, open fire, TV, books, snooker and table tennis, piano. Bar.

Garden

Nearest main road A52 from Nottingham to Grantham.

This guest-house with restaurant (built as a farm in the 18th century and later a canal bargees' inn) is ideal for a break when doing a long north-south journey on the nearby A1, particularly with children – or as a base from which to explore the many little-known attractions of Nottinghamshire and adjacent counties. It is on the edge of the outstandingly beautiful Vale of Belvoir, with the Duke of Rutland's Belvoir Castle (full of art treasures) rearing its battlemented walls high above a nearby hilltop: an unforgettable sight. The topiary yew peacock on the front lawn, started in 1812, was inspired by the peacock in the crest of the Duke.

The Needs have created a happy family atmosphere here. Bedrooms are simple but comfortable, and two are ideal for families: a self-contained pine cabin and a coach-house outside the main building. Children can safely play in the garden which has a large lawn, hammock, swings, small covered swimming-pool, play-room, pool-room, bicycles, barbecue, horses and dogs. All around are wheatfields.

Food (much of it cooked by daughter Nicki) is above average, with home-made bread and soups, herbs from the garden and much local produce. Starters may include stuffed tomatoes or pan-fried sardines; main courses, salmon or trout with sorrel sauce or game pie; puddings, chocolate and rum nut loaf.

There are many popular sights in this region: Belvoir Castle, Belton House, Stapleford Park, Rutland Water and Wollaton Hall in its park; also Holme Pierrepont Hall, Doddington Hall, and Newstead Abbey (Byron's home). Eastwood has D. H. Lawrence's birthplace. Lincoln (cathedral), Southwell (minster), Sherwood Forest (Robin Hood display) and Nottingham are also near – the last a much underrated city. I recommend the arts museum in the castle and others at its foot (the lace museum is fascinating), river trips and walks through the Georgian quarter. The historic market towns of Stamford (in particular) and Newark are of great interest. One can shop for local Stilton, crafts and Nottingham lace to take home – Melton Mowbray is famous for pies and other pork delicacies. Bicycles on loan.

Take the trouble to get free booklets about the area before you set off. Every habitual traveller should keep a copy of the booklet of local Tourist Information Centres issued free by the English Tourist Board (Thames Tower, Blacks Road, London W6; tel: 01-846 9000) for this purpose.

PEAT GATE HEAD

CHSX

Low Row, west of Richmond, North Yorkshire, DL11 6PP   Tel: 0748 86388

rear view

5 bedrooms (single, double or family) from £27.50 with dinner. Much less for 2 nights. Rooms have central heating; three have shower; armchairs; views of river and moor; tea/coffee facilities.
Dinner 4 courses and coffee, at 7pm. Special diets if ordered. Coffee, tea, for a charge. Drinks can be ordered. Packed lunches.

2 sitting-rooms with central heating, open fire, TV, books; bar. No smoking in some rooms.
Garden and meadows.
Nearest main road A6108 from Richmond to Leyburn.

It sometimes seems that anywhere north of Leeds now calls itself Herriot country, what with almost countless books, films, and television series. Though the author actually practices to the east of the county, much filming of his books was done in the Yorkshire Dales, and Peat Gate Head is just along the moor road (with watersplash) where the opening sequence of every television episode was recorded.

Alan Earl had long loved Peat Gate Head, a 300-year-old Swaledale farmhouse built of the local limestone, and when his job as a history lecturer ended with the closure of the training college where he worked he decided to buy it and to turn his enthusiasm for cooking to good use by opening it as a guest-house. From several choices at each course one might select, for instance, salmon mousse, chicken breasts in orange-and-tarragon sauce, and queen of puddings.

The beamed house is simply furnished. There is a vast stone chimneypiece in the dining-room, and in the sitting-room a wood-burning stove pleasantly scents the air. Two bedrooms are on the ground floor (one with own shower). The bathroom is on the ground floor (but with a toilet upstairs).

Outside the door, a summerhouse on the lawn looks across a sweep of Swaledale, a textbook illustration of a valley, from the river running along the flat bottom, through stone-walled fields, to open moorland. From the bedrooms on the opposite side of the house, you are at eye level with peewits and curlews. Richmond and other castles, especially Barnard Castle, are extra attractions, along with waterfalls and the Dales scenery.

Readers' comments: Made us so welcome and entertained us non-stop; delicious meals; peaceful atmosphere. Great charm, most acceptable dinner, massive breakfast. Very good value, most entertaining too. Three unforgettable days . . . the quality of everything. A fine man, a character! Took a great deal of trouble. Excellent cuisine. Food interesting, well cooked and presented. Delightful premises; high standard of comfort. Totally relaxed mood.

PENNINE LODGE

St John's Chapel, Weardale, west of Stanhope, Co Durham, DL13 1QX
Tel: 0388 537247

5 bedrooms (double or family) from £11. Reductions for 3 nights. Bargain breaks. Rooms have central heating; shower or bathroom; views of country; tea/coffee facilities. **Dinner** £6 for 3 courses and coffee, at 7pm. Vegetarian or special diets if ordered. Packed lunches, snacks. Drinks can be ordered. No smoking.
Sitting-room with central heating, TV, books.
Large garden
Nearest main road A689 from Stanhope to Alston.
Closed November–mid-March

Pennine Lodge was built in the 16th century, and it has the long and narrow shape typical of a Weardale farmhouse. Just below the windows of the corridor which connects the bedrooms is the upper River Wear, rushing over a small waterfall backed by trees, a beautiful spot. The rooms themselves are full of interest, with lots of timber and stone, antiques and bric-a-brac: in one a grandfather clock (silent!), in another a real Durham quilt.

Guests dine in a long, low-ceilinged room next to the garden, with a stone inglenook at one end. There are three courses: a starter (or else cheese), with a main course which is quite likely to be a casserole of pheasant or other game from the Raby estates, and, for example, rhubarb pie and cream. All is home-made by Yvonne Raine, including jams and bread; afternoon tea is available.

Raby Castle is one of the best of its kind, and High Force is England's highest waterfall. Killhope Wheel is a huge waterwheel which, with its associated buildings, has been very well restored to display the history of lead mining, the mainstay of the north Pennines for centuries. Over the highest road in England is the isolated town of Alston, and beyond that the lovely Eden valley and the Lake District. Hadrian's Wall, the Beamish open-air museum, Bowes Museum and Durham Cathedral are other outstanding day-trips.

Readers' comments: It's so good I've been back repeatedly. Lovely position, comfortable without being pretentious. Delightful old house, competent and delightful hostess, food excellent.

Families which pick establishments with plenty of games, swimming-pool, animals, etc., or that are near free museums, parks and walks, can save a lot on keeping youngsters entertained.

Some readers tell me they have stayed at lots of places from *Staying Off the Beaten Track*. I wonder who has stayed at most? A free copy of the next edition awaits the reader who sends me his/her comments on the greatest number!

PENSCOT FARMHOUSE HOTEL C(8) **D H**
Shipham, north of Cheddar, Somerset, BS25 1ZW Tel: 093 484 2659

18 bedrooms (single, double or family) from £14.50. Less for long stays. Discounts to people after a second visit. Rooms have central heating; shower and wc; armchairs; views of country or garden; tea/coffee facilities; TV for hire.
Dinner Wed.–Sat. £6 for 3 courses and coffee, at 7pm. Vegetarian meals if ordered. Lunches, packed lunches, snacks. Coffee, tea, for a charge. Non-residents not admitted to dining-room (but there is a restaurant too). Drinks can be ordered.
2 sitting-rooms with central heating, open fire, TV, books; bar.
Large garden and orchard.
Nearest main road A38 from Bristol to Taunton.
Closed December

Built in the 15th century as farm cottages, Penscot became an inn on the village green, and still retains much of that character. It is a long low building, white-walled and with low beams and log fires inside. The atmosphere is informal and comfortable. Bedrooms are simple, the sitting-room well provided with plenty of deep armchairs and doors to the garden where one can sit in the sun. There is a small conservatory with a flourishing vine and hanging baskets of flowers.

There are two dining-rooms. The one (non-smoking) for residents has pine alcoves and Scandinavian-style chairs. Here a set meal is served (such as home-made soup, chicken casserole with local vegetables, and cheesecake), while in a converted barn there is an à la carte menu, too: mainly conventional food such as trout, duck, steaks etc., with many vegetarian dishes.

Most of the bedrooms are quite simple but two (on the ground floor) have special features. One very attractive room has a four-poster, plus an extra bed; and the other would be ideal for a family as there is a children's room adjoining.

From peaceful Shipham there are far views to Bridgwater Bay and the Welsh hills. It lies on the edge of the beautiful Mendip hills (and half way along the walkers' Mendip Way which winds from the coast to Wells). In the neighbourhood are facilities for riding, golf, caving and painting. Plenty of sightseeing, too: castles, stately homes, gorges, woods, viewpoints, museums, wildlife, gardens, the Wookey Hole caves and innumerable churches of architectural interest. Plenty of gardens, too, including those at Longleat and Cricket St Thomas; and antique shops. The Tildens have produced a book of local walks.

Readers' comments: Delightful. Tasty home cooking. Every comfort, good service, happy atmosphere. Good food and welcoming atmosphere. Nice to see everyone smiling. Warm welcome, enjoyable atmosphere and food, very good value. Delightful rooms; food was great; personal attention. So friendly, so peaceful. Gracious hosts, food wonderful. Cheerful, willing staff made us feel so welcome.

227

PILLMEAD HOUSE *New*   C D H
North Lane, Buriton, south of Petersfield, Hampshire GU31 5RS
Tel: 0730 66795

2 bedrooms (double) from £17. All have own bath/shower; TV; tea/coffee facilities; central heating; views of country or garden. No smoking. (Washing-machine on request.)

Dinner £8 for 3 courses (with choices) and coffee, at 7.30pm. Non-residents not admitted. Vegetarian or special diets if ordered. Lunches, packed lunches, snacks. Tea, coffee, extra. Drinks can be brought in.

Sitting-room with central heating, open fire, TV, books, record-player. No smoking.

Large garden

Nearest main road A3 from London to Portsmouth.

Sarah Moss used to run a kitchenware shop of distinction, and so she is particularly well equipped with things to produce, for instance, home-made pasta or ice cream – and she sometimes demonstrates their use to interested visitors who end up in the big kitchen after they have enjoyed the gourmet results. She grows much of the produce that is used in the kitchen for such meals as carrot-and-orange soup followed by lamb chops with a gratin of courgettes and then French apple tart, for example. Dessert grapes come from John's greenhouse.

The house overlooks a valley, its lawn and rock-garden descending steeply among terraced beds of roses and lavender. To the side is a tree-swing for children. Sometimes breakfast is served out here so that visitors can enjoy a view of the Queen Elizabeth country park in the distance while eating eggs collected straight from the free-range hens.

The sitting-room's bow windows, too, make the most of the view. This is a pretty room, with pink wildflower curtains and sofas, Victorian tapestry chairs, cabinets of china and snuffboxes and an open fire.

Upstairs, white walls contrast with moss-green carpets. One bedroom, cottage-style, has pink fabrics and patchwork cushions; in another apricot predominates, there is a patchwork bedspread and bow window. Everywhere are good antiques.

Adjoining the house is a building that was once a schoolroom. John now uses it in connection with his work, which is renovating old buildings, a subject on which he is a mine of information. Pillmead House is itself of interest: its lozenge-paned windows and brick-and-flint walls are typical of many houses in this area, but the Tudor chimneys – very elaborate, and 8 feet high – are unusual, and came here after the demolition of a large mansion. The pale walls at one end, background to sweet peas, are of stone quarried locally.

From here, it is only a half-hour walk into historic Petersfield (described elsewhere), and the long South Downs Way passes near. The Way brings a number of serious walkers to stay at Pillmead House – on one occasion, a family of two adults, four children, three donkeys, two dogs and two bicycles.

This green valley amid the South Downs has churches that go back to Saxon times, flint-walled houses, and prehistoric burial mounds. To the south are woodlands, remnants of the once-great Forest of Bere, and then comes Portsmouth Harbour. Despite heavy traffic on roads into the port, this is well worth a visit – to see Nelson's *Victory*, Henry VIII's *Mary Rose* and his Southsea Castle, Victorian forts up on the hills and Norman Portchester Castle down by the waterfront. There are boat trips and ferries to the Isle of Wight.

228

PINE TREES HOTEL *New*   **D PT X**
Mead End Road, Sway, north-west of Lymington, Hampshire, SO41 6EE
Tel: 0590 682288

6 bedrooms (double) from £18. Less for 2 nights and bargain breaks. Some have own bath/shower; all have central heating. (Washing-machine on request.)
Dinner £19 for 5 courses (less for fewer courses) and coffee, at 8pm. Vegetarian or special diets if ordered. Packed lunches, snacks. Tea, coffee, extra. Drinks can be ordered.
Sitting-room with central heating, open fire, TV, books piano; bar.
Large garden
Nearest main road A337 from Cadnam to Lymington.

In 1876, Peterson, a judge from India, decided to use a novelty – concrete – to build a 'folly' tower nearby. This impressive demonstration inspired the building of this house – though one would not guess from its appearance that it is made of concrete. Exterior and rooms alike have all the handsome detailing of the 1870s. A large old-fashioned sitting-room is furnished with Victoriana and big cretonne-covered armchairs, its tall bay windows overlooking lawns that slope down to the pine trees that give the hotel its name – a view which obviously also inspired the pine-green colour scheme of the room. All around, rhododendrons grow wild, seen at their colourful best in May.

In the warm orange dining-room John David serves the meals which have given this hotel its reputation for good food. Dinner normally consists of five courses, such as lemon sole meunière, tomato and melon salad, roast beef béarnaise, cheeses, peach syllabub.

I thought the bedrooms, though comfortable, were not of the same standard as the other rooms, and prices a little high but there are good bargain breaks available.

Lymington, one of Hampshire's prettiest coastal towns, has sailing-boats thronging its old harbour and a Saturday market. Within a short car or bus ride are plenty of other interesting places to visit: particularly the whole of the New Forest, picturesque Beaulieu village and the world-famous motor museum of Lord Montagu, Bucklers Hard – an 18th-century boat-building village carefully conserved, the Hythe-Southampton ferry, Bournemouth, historic Christchurch and its ancient waterfront, an exceptional crafts centre, a new vivarium (reptiles), a deer sanctuary, the ferry to picturesque Yarmouth on the Isle of Wight, beaches, Tucktonia for the children (model village etc.), boat trips and much more.

The countryside around Lymington is a mixture of heaths and woods; the sea cliffs are sandy. It's a good area for bathing, walking or looking for rare wildflowers. There is Hurst Castle to explore, fossils to collect at Barton, the old village of Milford (good views from its beach) and quiet Keyhaven (wildfowl) to be visited.

> Prices are the minimum *per person* in a double room at the beginning of the year.

229

PIPPS FORD

Needham Market, north of Ipswich, Suffolk, IP6 8LJ   Tel: 044979 208

6 bedrooms (single or double) from £16. Winter discounts. Rooms have central heating or electric heaters; shower or bathroom; armchairs; views of country or farmland/garden; tea/coffee facilities; TV on request. **Dinner** £13 for 4 courses (with choices) and coffee, at 7.15pm. Drinks can be ordered. Vegetarian meals if ordered. Afternoon teas. No dinner on Sundays.

Sitting-room with central heating, open fire, books, record-player. TV room. Piano. **Garden** with unheated swimming-pool, croquet lawn; river, meadow and woodland, with coarse fishing; and a tennis court. **Nearest main roads** A45 from Ipswich to Bury St Edmunds and the A140 from Ipswich to Norwich.

On a stretch of the River Gipping that has been designated an 'area of outstanding natural beauty' stands a large Tudor farmhouse, its black-and-white half-timbered walls an ideal background to old-fashioned roses: everyone's idea of a rural idyll. (It is hard to find: ask for directions.)

When Anthony Hackett-Jones, a lawyer, bought the old farmhouse and eight acres of land, it was in poor shape; it is now not only comfortable but beautifully furnished with antiques, interesting paintings, good china, silver and pretty fabrics. Mrs Hackett-Jones has made patchwork quilts or cushion-covers for every room and searched out attractive fabrics (Laura Ashley, French ones and so on) for curtains or upholstery. She puts flowers in each bedroom. Many of the beds are collectors' pieces: a four-poster, a French provincial one and several ornamental brass beds. Oriental rugs cover floors of wood or stone. Even the bathrooms attached to each bedroom are attractive, with carpet and William Morris wallpapers. One is spectacular, with a huge oval bath. Some bedrooms are in newly converted stables, with sitting-room.

This is a house of inglenook fireplaces, sloping floors, low beams and historic associations, for it once belonged to Tudor chronicler Richard Hakluyt, and later to the wife of Sir William Harvey, discoverer of blood circulation. Visitors who use the sitting-room, with its deep armchairs and log fire, can enjoy the family's huge collection of classical records. Meals are served in a conservatory with bougainvillaea in profusion.

Breakfasts are exceptional. From an enormous choice, you could select exotic juices; home-made sausages or black pudding; home-made yogurt, croissants, jams, honey; eggs cooked in nine ways (coddled, baked etc. – from duck, goose or hen); French or cinnamon toast; waffles, crumpets, muffins; kidneys, mackerel, fishcakes, kedgeree; five kinds of tea . . .

Raewyn Hackett-Jones, a New Zealander, is an excellent cook. Her most popular dishes include kidneys in a sauce of mustard, sherry and cream; pears and Stilton in filo pastry; a roulade of salmon, turbot and spinach; pork with ginger and orange sauce; tropical fruits with *fromage frais* and blackcurrant sauce; honey and brandy ice cream. Fruit, vegetables, eggs and other produce, including chicken, veal and pork, are organically home-grown (in season) and bread is home-made.

The Hackett-Joneses keep a fluctuating population of calves, bees and pigs; and visitors, especially children, are welcome to get involved with feeding pigs, for example. The milk and cream are provided by Annabel, their Jersey cow. Occasionally there are courses on upholstery, art and other subjects.

Beyond the garden, there is coarse fishing in the river, where cricket-bat willows grow, and a Roman site. Interesting places to visit by car are Sandringham, Constable country, Lavenham, Aldeburgh, Southwold, Norwich, Ipswich and Bury St Edmunds. The area is full of pretty villages, ancient churches, antique shops, stately homes and a museum of East Anglian life at Stowmarket. There are an orchid nursery, Beth Chatto's garden, Notcutts, and the gardens at Bressingham, as well as a semi-wild garden of old roses, near here. Cycles for hire.

Readers' comments: Most impressed; made very welcome; food absolutely super; most hospitable place; relaxed and informal, thoroughly happy and comfortable; delightful house, beautifully furnished; food and service outstanding; one of the best holidays ever; friendly good humour. A fitting climax to our wonderful trip with 'SOTBT'. Charming and talented hostess, food beautifully garnished.

Two-thirds of the houses in this book accept and provide for *children*; though nearly half of these stipulate a minimum age, often 4 (some, 10).

Over a third accept *dogs*, though not allowing them in all rooms.

Scores of houses are suitable for people in *wheelchairs* or otherwise handicapped.

Half can be reached without a car, by nearby *public transport*.

Half charge *singles* little or no more than people sharing a double room.

Several dozen of the houses or hotels also have some *self-catering* cottages or flats to let.

Over a quarter provide accommodation at *Christmas*.

About a third are licensed to sell *drinks*, while nearly a quarter allow visitors to bring their own in.

Travellers can book *meals*, without staying overnight, at over a third of the houses.

Packed lunches are provided by about half.

Two-thirds can produce, if notified in advance, vegetarian or other special *diets*.

Over half stay open throughout the *winter*.

An increasing number (several dozen) *ban smoking* in some rooms if not all.

In over a third, you can choose whether to have a *duvet or blankets*.

One-fifth provide either *extra-firm mattresses or bedboards* for back sufferers.

Over half have *TV* in the sitting-room; about a third, in bedrooms; the rest do not provide TV.

Nearly two-thirds provide *tea-making facilities* in bedrooms; the rest bring tea up on a tray. A few offer both alternatives. About a third are willing to provide *breakfast in bed*. About 100 give visitors a tray of tea on arrival, free.

Several dozen have *swimming-pools*, usually heated.

Several dozen provide *clothes-washing* facilities.

Among a number of other little extras offered at some houses, mostly free, are the following: loan of cycles, gumboots and maps; car-washing facilities; hair-dryers and/or rollers; mending kits; sale of home-made preserves, crafts, travel books and maps; use of video recorder, video films, record-player and piano.

POLETREES FARM *New*
Brill, west of Aylesbury, Buckinghamshire, HP18 9TZ   Tel: 0844 238276

2 bedrooms (double or family) from £12. Tea/coffee facilities; central heating; views of country or garden. No smoking.
Dinner £10 for 4 courses and coffee. Drinks can be brought in.
Sitting-room with central heating, open fire, TV, books.
Large garden
Nearest main road A41 from Aylesbury to Bicester.

There is clematis round the porch, baskets brimming with begonias and lobelias hang on the walls, and all around are roses, apple trees and views of fields: a scene of total peace. But in the 16th century this was a coaching inn on the principal road (Roman in origin) from Oxford to Buckingham. Now that road is nothing but a grassy track, for the traffic goes another way.

Inside, stone walls, oak beams and an inglenook with a rare 15th-century window beside it – tiny oak mullions and wood-pegged shutters – have survived the centuries, though some features were plastered over or boarded up until the Coopers did careful restoration work. The water for the house still comes from a spring.

So ancient is the area that King Lud – that prehistoric (or mythical?) figure for whom London's Ludgate is named – is reputed to have hunted boar here when all was forest. Hence the name of a nearby village, Ludgershall; which is where Wycliffe started his great work of translating the Bible into English for the first time.

Anita has furnished her ancient home well. In the dining-room a thick blue carpet is complemented by chair and curtain fabric of flowery blue and bedrooms are pleasantly decorated too, with handsome walnut furniture. She caned the bedheads herself. On a wall of one room is a collection of keys – all from the old Brill railway, closed in 1926; and also what looks like a huge horseshoe but is in fact an ox shoe, from the time when oxen were used to draw carts.

For dinner you might be offered such dishes as stuffed tomatoes, roast beef, spotted dick and cheeses. Occasionally Anita cooks a local speciality, 'bacon clanger', which is a rolypoly made with bacon.

Apart from livestock (sheep, cattle, ducks, geese – and a donkey) the farm produces a rather unusual 'crop' – turf, sold to garden centres. And in the garden is another pleasant surprise, a swimming-pool.

Buckinghamshire is one of the loveliest counties around London: in the south are the Chiltern hills, with dense forests of beech – a handsome sight; and in the north the broad Vale of Aylesbury threaded by little streams – it is here that most of the stately homes and fine churches are to be found; great mansions include Ascott (outstanding furniture and paintings), Claydon (with Florence Nightingale museum), Hughenden (Disraeli's home), Stowe (by Vanbrugh) and Waddesdon (the Rothschild house of French Renaissance splendour).

The Thames runs along the southern edge of the county – with beauty-spots like Boulter's Lock, Bray (famous for punting), the spectacular reach by Cliveden (stately home, now an expensive hotel), Marlow, Medmenham and Hambleden.

Brill itself is of interest. It has a hilltop windmill, good buildings of the 15th to 17th centuries, and nearby is a mediaeval gatehouse, Boarstall Tower.

POLRAEN

Sandplace, north-west of Looe, Cornwall, PL13 1PJ   Tel: 05036 3956

C D PT S

rear view

5 bedrooms (single, double or family) from £17.85. Less for 7 nights or bargain breaks. Rooms have central heating; bathrooms; remote-control TV, armchairs; views of country or garden; tea/coffee facilities.
Dinner A la carte or £9.25 for 5 courses and coffee, at 7pm. Special diets if ordered. Lunches, packed lunches, snacks. Coffee, tea, for a charge. Drinks can be ordered.
Sitting-room with central heating, open fire, TV, books. Bar (open to non-residents).
Large garden
Nearest main road A38 from Plymouth to Liskeard.

In the 18th century this stone building was a coaching inn, but for a long time it has been a country house hotel, now run by Peter and Joyce Allcroft. They have created a large bar (using local slate blocks for the fireplace and the bar itself) and decorated the bedrooms in soft colours. The sitting-room opens onto an attractive south-facing garden with old apple trees, huge cedars and woodland rising up behind. At night, the fountain is lit up; and by day guests can sit at tables under sun umbrellas. Round the corner is the Allcrofts' vegetable garden.

The dining-room has a cottagey look, with the old cooking-range still in position and Windsor chairs around the tables. Here plain English meals are served – such as home-made soup, topside of beef with Yorkshire pudding and baked parsnips, and apple amber – or, if you're in luck, chocolate and whisky gâteau. Bread is locally baked.

The house is in a very lovely river valley with woodland walks, in an area full of interest: Cotehele and Lanhydrock (mansions and gardens), the Corin music centre, an 'Edwardian countryside' centre, Probus and Trewithin gardens, are all near. Both coast and moorland have good footpaths for walkers, there are sandy coves close by, river trips and an enormous variety of unusual museums or other tourist attractions.

Two-thirds of the houses in this book have bargain breaks or other discounts on offer, some exclusive to readers. Only a third raise prices at the peak of summer.

There is no point in turning up with a dog or child in tow if the description does not say these are accepted; nor in expecting a garden, or alcoholic drinks, if these are not indicated.

It's best to stay at least 2–3 days: you cannot possibly appreciate an area if you only stay overnight (prices per night are often less, too, if you stay on). The vouchers on page ii are usable for 3-night stays.

233

POND COTTAGE

Brandsby Road, Stillington, north of York, Y06 1NY Tel: 0347 810796

2 bedrooms (double or family) from £10. Rooms have central heating; views of country or garden. No smoking.
Sitting-room with central heating, open fire, TV, books. Tea, coffee, free. No smoking.
Garden with croquet, badminton and barbecue.
Nearest main road A19 from York to Thirsk.
Closed November–March

In a barn adjoining this primrose-yellow cottage is a treasure-trove of domestic bygones – from kitchen tools to antique bottles and cans, woodware to chamberpots. For the Thurstans are antique dealers, specializing in 'kitchenalia'.

The 18th-century house itself is furnished with antiques, and its shelves and nooks are filled with curios. There are collections of coronation mugs and Staffordshire dogs in the low-beamed sitting-room, where high-backed wing chairs are grouped around an inglenook fireplace. This is a house of twists and turns, unexpected steps and low windows. Its pleasant bedrooms overlook a terrace with stone troughs of flowers, a croquet lawn and a natural pond. The only drawback is the distance of the bath from the guests' bedrooms, a minor inconvenience considering the modest price charged.

Dianne serves only breakfast because (the citizens of nearby York being great diners-out) the area is very well supplied with eating-places.

Stillington is almost equidistant from the city of York, the coast, the North York Moors and the Dales – each described elsewhere in this book, and each offering totally different holiday experiences needing many days to explore. It is in the middle of the great Vale of York, a fertile area watered by the River Ure and its tributaries, unspoilt by industry. All around are traces of history, from prehistoric man and later the Romans to the Civil War, and onward. The nearest stately home is Sutton Park which has art treasures and furniture once in Buckingham House (precursor of Buckingham Palace) and gardens laid out by Capability Brown; the nearest market town is cobblestoned Easingwold; from nearby Crayke are superb views of York Minster. Byland Abbey, Nunnington Hall and Beningbrough Hall are well worth visits. Plenty of antique-hunting or pick-your-own fruit opportunities.

Readers' comments: Wonderful! Enjoyed very much. A warm welcome.

Some hotels and even farms offer special Christmas holidays; but, unless otherwise indicated (by the code letter X at top of entry), those in this book will then be closed.

Some readers tell me they have stayed at lots of places from *Staying Off the Beaten Track*. I wonder who has stayed at most? A free copy of the next edition awaits the reader who sends me his/her comments on the greatest number!

POND COTTAGE

The Green, Warmington, north-west of Banbury (Oxfordshire), OX17 1BU
Tel: 029589 682 (*evenings best*)

2 bedrooms (single and double) from £13.50. **10% less for readers of this book if they stay a week.** Rooms have central heating; views of village green or garden; double room has a shower.
Dinner £8.25 for 3 courses and coffee, at 7pm, or by arrangement. Coffee, tea free. Non-residents not admitted. Drinks can be ordered or brought in.
Sitting-room with central heating, open fire, TV.
Nearest main road A41 from London to Birmingham.
Closed November–March

This village, though near the A41, is so tucked away that, beauty-spot though it is, few tourists find it. Around a sloping village green with duck-pond and waterlilies, dominated at one end by a Tudor manor house, are ranged rows of charming cottages built from warm local stone, roses and honeysuckle climbing up their walls. Mrs Viljoen's home is one of these.

She has furnished its small rooms with great elegance. Gleaming antique furniture and silver contrast with the rugged stones of the sitting-room walls and hearth. She has chosen browns and lemon to harmonize with the colour of the stone. One pretty bedroom is all blue – from the silk spread and the cover of the armchair to the flowery Victorian wallpaper.

At the back is a tiny garden with a seat among roses and nasturtiums climbing up the walls.

Vi asks visitors to say what kind of food they like. A typical menu might include home-made soup, chicken with almond sauce, and a tart of her own fruit, or home-made ice cream.

Vi Viljoen is a Tourist Board guide – so is well qualified to advise visitors on sightseeing.

Pond Cottage has appeared on the cover of *Forever Ambridge* by Norman Painting (who plays Phil Archer in the radio series), a resident in the village. Within a few miles of it are: the castles of Broughton, Warwick and Kenilworth; Stratford-upon-Avon; Sulgrave Manor (home of George Washington's ancestors); sixteen stately homes belonging to the National Trust, a number of antique shops, and also fine gardens. The Cotswolds, Althorp and Oxford are not much further.

Readers' comments: A delightful stay. A pleasure to see so many lovely things in the house. Welcomed us like friends, and made our wedding anniversary dinner a feast. Delicious food, extremely good value. Most friendly and helpful; food memorable; pretty garden. Lovely little place. Delightful little cottage. Most enjoyable and relaxing. Charming house, warm welcome. Like staying with a friend, every need anticipated.

For explanation of code letters (**C, D, H, PT, S, S-C, X**) see page xxviii.

235

POOL HOUSE HOTEL

Hanley Road, Upton-on-Severn, south of Worcester, WR8 0PA
Tel: 06846 2151

C

rear view

9 bedrooms (single, double or family) from £14. Less for 7 nights or bargain breaks. Rooms have central heating or electric heaters; most have shower or bathroom; armchairs; views of country or garden.
Dinner £8.50 for 4 courses (with choices) and coffee, at 6.30pm. Vegetarian or special diets if ordered. Packed lunches, snacks. Coffee, tea, for a charge. Drinks can be ordered.
Sitting-room with central heating, open fire, books. Also a TV room; bar.
Large garden with fishing and croquet.
Nearest main road A38 from Worcester to Tewkesbury.

I have included this hotel for its superb river-bank setting, with gardens that make the most of this. Herbaceous borders wander among lawns with fruit trees, sloping down to the waterside. The 18th-century house is simply furnished. I thought bedroom 2 particularly attractive: it has a rose-and-white colour scheme and a good view of the river. Jill Webb's flower arrangements are a feature of the house.

Meals are traditional: home-made soup or a prawn cocktail might be followed by roast beef (with fresh local vegetables) and a rhubarb-and-raisin crumble, for instance. Beyond the peach dining-room is a hexagonal TV room with big armchairs and a door leading to the garden; and then a sitting-room with log fire.

From the house one enjoys views of the Malvern hills. Not far off is the River Avon, the Cotswolds, 'Shakespeare country' and the lovely Wye Valley. Other sightseeing possibilities include Tewkesbury Abbey, Cheltenham Spa, Worcester Cathedral (and the Royal Porcelain factory), Hereford and Gloucester (two more cathedrals). Upton itself is a delightful old market town, as is Ledbury. The Malverns have a spring garden show, Hidcote is near, and Pershore Agricultural College grounds are well worth visiting. Racing, fishing, cricket and birdwatching at the waterfowl sanctuary are other pursuits which bring visitors here.

In Upton-on-Severn itself (a small town that needs to be explored on foot and by boat), there are plaques dotted about on sites of historic events – the most photographed one describes how, on that spot, Cromwell was acclaimed in 1651 'with abundance of joy and shouting' after his victory at the Battle of Upton. The town's history, which goes back to Saxon times, is displayed in its heritage centre (in the old cupola-topped church tower). You can go as far as Tewkesbury on the pleasure-cruiser, or simply stay in Upton to make the most of its little shops, bistros and byways. The 'Three Counties' agricultural show takes place nearby.

Readers' comments: Most helpful. Food and accommodation excellent. Very enjoyable week's stay. The loveliest garden; friendly people. Beautiful setting.

Families which pick establishments with plenty of games, swimming-pool, animals, etc., or that are near free museums, parks and walks, can save a lot on keeping youngsters entertained.

236

PORTWELL HOUSE　　　　　　　　　　　　**C D H PT**
Market Place, Faringdon, Oxfordshire, SN7 7HU　Tel: 0367 20197

7 bedrooms (single, double or family) from £14.50. Less for 4 nights or bargain breaks. Rooms have central heating; own bathroom; TV, armchairs; tea/coffee facilities. Laundering facilities available.
Dinner £6–£7 for 3 courses (with choices), from 6.30–8pm. Special diets if ordered. Lunches, packed lunches, snacks. Non-residents not admitted. Drinks can be ordered.
Sitting area with central heating, books.
Nearest main road A420 from Oxford to Swindon.

David and Margo Manning run a small and friendly guest-house. The bedrooms are neat and fresh, each with its own bathroom, and the sitting/dining-room has hanging baskets of plants and an aquarium.

Margo used to be a hairdresser but enjoys this complete change of activity. She does a lot of the baking herself, and cooks such meals as: prawn cocktail or egg mayonnaise, followed by a roast or steak, with gâteau or cheese and coffee to follow. She enjoys doing special diets. David used to be a fruiterer, so there is often a good choice of fresh fruit and vegetables.

Faringdon is a pretty town – a place of mossy roofs, old inn signs, swinging lamps and clocks on brackets, with a colonnaded buttermarket. Brickwork, stone and colourful stucco give the streets variety, and there is an ancient church half-hidden behind great yews (one of many in this area). A good centre for public transport and for many sports, it is at the heart of an area full of interest with plenty to explore. In the spring, the grounds of nearby Faringdon House produce a wonderful display of flowers. This was the home of Lord Berners (the model for Lord Merlin in *The Pursuit of Love*), who also built the Folly Tower on the nearby hill. In his will, he asked to be stuffed and placed on top of it, but his executors thought otherwise.

In the surrounding Vale of the White Horse there are plenty of good canalside walks (with revitalizing little inns along the way); Uffington church, which has memories of Tom Brown (of *Tom Brown's Schooldays*); the prehistoric white horse itself, cut out of the turf on the chalk downs; and adjacent earthworks with far views. The old Ridgeway Path runs here, with Wayland's Smithy close by. Great Coxwell has a superb tithe barn; Coleshill and Buscot Park are two National Trust properties, and Ashdown and Littlecote are not much further. Then there are the wilder reaches of the Thames – Lechlade, the source, and Kelmscott (William Morris's lovely house). The theatres of Oxford, Swindon and Newbury are accessible. Pusey gardens, Blenheim, the Cotswold Wildlife Park, old Burford and the Lechlade garden centre (for fuchsias) are top attractions. In fact, from here you can easily reach a number of interesting areas described elsewhere: Hungerford, Cirencester, Marlborough and the Chilterns, for example.

Readers' comments: Kindness, attention and hospitality. Pleasant and comfortable; meals delicious; the best bargain for a long time. Excellent standards, friendliness, very happy atmosphere. Outstanding. Excellent in every way. Cannot praise too highly, warm welcome. Attractive, roomy bedrooms. Excellent food and atmosphere.

237

PRESTON FARM

Harberton, south of Totnes, Devon, TQ9 7SW   Tel: 0803 862235

C(4)

3 bedrooms (double or family) from £11. Rooms have central heating or electric heaters; shower; armchairs; views of country or garden; tea/coffee facilities. Washing-machine available.

Dinner £6 for 4 courses and coffee, at 6.45pm. Snacks. Coffee, tea, free. Non-residents not admitted. Drinks can be brought in.

Sitting-room with central heating, open fire, TV, video, books, record-player.

Garden and fields.

Nearest main road A381 from Totnes to Kingsbridge.

Closed to visitors in winter

It's unusual to find a working farm with its house right in a village (a very quiet one), but there used to be several such clustered together in Harberton. The Steers' house, built in 1680, has been in the same family for generations. All the rooms are comfortable, and there is good home cooking at dinner-time, with dishes as varied as pancakes stuffed with salmon au gratin, chicken marengo, roasts, pies, baked Alaska, treacle pudding. The ingredients are mostly home-grown or local. One bedroom is in 'Country Diary' fabrics; another has a matching pink-and-cream bathroom. Breakfast comes on 'help-yourself' platters – conventional bacon and eggs or more unusual things like hog's pudding or smoked haddock.

Harberton is a picturesque cluster of old cottages with colourful gardens, set in a valley. Its 13th-century church has a magnificent painted screen and stained glass windows. The local inn is of equal antiquity. Preston Farmhouse was once a manor house, which is why rooms are spacious.

Most visitors head for historic Totnes and its castle, or to Dartmouth and Salcombe, for example, via country lanes. Dartmoor lies to the north, the coast to the south, and neither is far off. Modbury is one of many picturesque towns near here, its Georgian or slate-hung houses clinging to a steep hill. Buckfastleigh (with abbey built in 1938; notable stained glass) is where the Dart Valley steam trains go, along a lovely route. Dartmeet, one of the most famous of beauty-spots, is where two rivers join – there is a pretty 'clapper' bridge of stone slabs nearby.

A little further is Widecombe-in-the-Moor with its huge old church, its September fair and 'Uncle Tom Cobleigh an' all'. Exeter, Plymouth and Torbay are easily accessible by car. River trips, Dartington Hall, the Shire Horse Centre, innumerable gardens and garden centres add to the interest of this area, as do its many antique shops, markets and fairs (e.g. every Tuesday in Totnes).

Readers' comments: Far more than we had hoped for; made most welcome; meals were excellent, good variety and generous helpings. Warm welcome, excellent accommodation, superb cooking. Absolutely marvellous. Everything perfect – especially the fish pie! Very comfortable; delicious meals; perfect company. Excellent accommodation, super meals, everything delightful. First-class in every way. Happy atmosphere. A delight to be there – visited twice.

PROSPECT HILL HOTEL   C
Kirkoswald, north of Penrith, Cumbria, CA10 1ER   Tel: 076883 500

rear view

10 bedrooms (single, double or family) from £16. Less for 3 nights. Special breaks include honeymoons (with champagne), group bookings, etc. Rooms have central heating; shower or bathroom; armchairs; views of country; tea/coffee facilities. TV available. Clothes-washing facilities.
Dinner A la carte, from 7.15–8.30pm. Special diets if ordered. Packed lunches, sandwich suppers. Coffee, tea, for a charge. Drinks can be ordered.
2 sitting-rooms with central heating, open fire, TV, books; bar.
Grounds Lawns and fields. Maps, gumboots and cycles for hire.
Nearest main road A6 from Penrith to Carlisle.

A group of 18th-century farm buildings close to a village that feels remote (though the M6 is only 9 miles away) has been turned into a hotel with great individuality by Isa and John Henderson (he was formerly a television designer). His style is visible in every detail: even the drawings in the brochure are his.

The one-time farm is in the beautiful Eden valley. It was virtually derelict when Isa and John started, in 1974, on the long process of conversion – at the same time building up his collection of old farm implements and domestic bygones. These are displayed on the sandstone walls in the bar (once a byre, with low-beamed ceiling and flagged floor) which has a wide choice of malt whiskies and vintage port.

During 1984 they reconstructed a fairly rare 19th-century farm building known as a gin case. This is a half-round room, dominated by a central pine beam 32 feet by over 1 foot square, within which yoked mules or ponies walked round and round powering wheels and belts to grind the grain. ('Gin' is an old word for engine.)

Every bedroom is individually decorated, and traditional materials have been used in many new features – even radiator shelves and curtain poles are of solid oak with brass screws, and old beams have been re-used as lintels. Though modern improvements are provided where they matter (bathroom fitments, for instance), many rooms still have walls of rugged stone, and a number have brass bedsteads with patchwork quilts. Homespun curtains, thick carpets and country colours like peat or moss are all in keeping with the character of the place. Even the corridors have well chosen touches such as woven hangings with a Celtic look, and the spiral staircase is of a cast iron. The former granary has been turned into an annexe that is ideal for a family.

There is a glassed-in porch with cane furniture and a terrace. The view, beyond a group of old ploughshares, is of fields, trees and hills.

In the beamed dining-room with wood-block floor, guests sit at Victorian tables. A typical dinner: leek-and-mushroom soup, lamb steak with honey and rosemary, strawberry shortcake and good, plentiful coffee. There is a vegetarian menu; and the good wine list includes plenty of half-bottles. For breakfast there is a huge choice including even such things as green figs and smoked haddock, followed by locally produced honey, marmalade and bread.

John and Isa do a great deal to help visitors enjoy the neighbourhood. They have lots of guidebooks, and John produced his own leaflets of walks from evening strolls to half-day hikes with notes about where deer can be seen, a spectacular waterfall in a gorge, riverside paths, a forest nature reserve with hide for watching badgers and hares or wildfowl, caves, old quarries and castle ruins. The neighbourhood is full of ancient villages; there's a working watermill, the prehistoric stones of 'Long Meg' and a traditional pottery still using a Victorian steam engine. Outings in an estate car are arranged. Kirkoswald is a good choice for a winter break. (There is a weather chart on display, covering several years, demonstrating how rare snow is in this sheltered spot.)

One nice touch: a wrought-iron screen dated 1974–80, which incorporates the initials of everybody who had a hand in the conversion.

Within easy motoring distance along scenic roads are the interesting old towns of Penrith and Alston, the city of Carlisle, the Lake District and Hadrian's Wall. John can give you an 'antiques trail' (Penrith and Carlisle).

Readers' comments: Comfortable and well organized; good cuisine; excellent amenities; nothing was too much trouble; very good in all respects; well decorated rooms; good and thoughtful service; value for money. Attractively converted and with good food.

Two-thirds of the houses in this book accept and provide for *children*; though nearly half of these stipulate a minimum age, often 4 (some, 10).

Over a third accept *dogs*, though not allowing them in all rooms.

Scores of houses are suitable for people in *wheelchairs* or otherwise handicapped.

Half can be reached without a car, by nearby *public transport*.

Half charge *singles* little or no more than people sharing a double room.

Several dozen of the houses or hotels also have some *self-catering* cottages or flats to let.

Over a quarter provide accommodation at *Christmas*.

About a third are licensed to sell *drinks*, while nearly a quarter allow visitors to bring their own in.

Travellers can book *meals*, without staying overnight, at over a third of the houses.

Packed lunches are provided by about half.

Two-thirds can produce, if notified in advance, vegetarian or other special *diets*.

Over half stay open throughout the *winter*.

An increasing number (several dozen) *ban smoking* in some rooms if not all.

In over a third, you can choose whether to have a *duvet or blankets*.

One-fifth provide either *extra-firm mattresses or bedboards* for back sufferers.

Over half have *TV* in the sitting-room; about a third, in bedrooms; the rest do not provide TV.

Nearly two-thirds provide *tea-making facilities* in bedrooms; the rest bring tea up on a tray. A few offer both alternatives. About a third are willing to provide *breakfast in bed*. About 100 give visitors a tray of tea on arrival, free.

Several dozen have *swimming-pools*, usually heated.

Several dozen provide *clothes-washing* facilities.

PYKARDS HALL FARM *New*
Rede, south of Bury St Edmunds, Suffolk, IP29 4AU Tel: 028489 229

2 bedrooms (single or double) from £14.50. One or both have own bath/shower; TV; tea/coffee facilities; central heating; views of country or garden. No smoking. (Washing-machine on request.)

Sitting-room with central heating, open fire, books, piano.
Large garden
Nearest main road A45 from Cambridge to Bury St Edmunds.

One of William the Conqueror's followers was rewarded with the gift of this land on which he built a hall with moat (now filled in). The present building dates from 1500: a terracotta house with white dormers, in a large garden with a willow-fringed duckpond.

Young Louise Drayton has decorated its rooms very attractively. In the low-beamed sitting-room, a pink-skirted table contrasts with the mulberry carpet, and armchairs are drawn up by the brick fireplace. The dining-room has Windsor chairs around a circular table and a dresser loaded with china. Outside there are seats on a paved terrace facing rosebeds.

An elegant welded staircase leads up to cottagey bedrooms with such pretty touches as a lace bedspread on a brass bed, a modern basin fitted into an old pine washstand, Laura Ashley fabrics used for festoon blinds.

Louise, being rather busy with her children, does not serve full dinners but is happy to provide simple family dishes like chicken pie or lasagne with salad. Otherwise, most visitors go to the Beehive at Horringer to dine.

Rede is very close to the historic abbey town of Bury, a place of mediaeval ruins and churches, fine gardens, Georgian byways, and some good shops for antiques or crafts. It has a Regency theatre (belonging to the National Trust) and some unusual museums. Newmarket and its races are near, too.

The famous mediaeval wool villages of Suffolk are within a short distance (see descriptions on other pages of Clare, Cavendish, Lavenham etc.), all with half-timbered houses and richly decorated churches. Georgian Ickworth Hall stands in grounds landscaped by Capability Brown. Among the undulating hills are pretty streams, mills, country parks and inns.

Take the trouble to get free booklets about the area before you set off. Every habitual traveller should keep a copy of the booklet of local Tourist Information Centres issued free by the English Tourist Board (Thames Tower, Blacks Road, London W6; tel: 01-846 9000) for this purpose.

241

RED HOUSE

Sidmouth Road, Lyme Regis, Dorset, DT7 3ES   Tel: 02974 2055

3 bedrooms (double or family) from £13.50. Less for 7 nights. Rooms have central heating; bathroom; TV, armchairs; drinks refrigerator; views of sea or garden; tea/coffee facilities.
Garden
Nearest main road A3052 from Lyme Regis to Exeter.
Closed December–February

Delightful old Lyme has many claims to fame – the profusion of fossils (including dinosaur bones) found along its beaches; the landing of the rebel Monmouth in 1685 to start his abortive rebellion; Jane Austen's *Persuasion*; and most recently *The French Lieutenant's Woman*, the author of which, John Fowles, lives locally.

When Geoffrey Griffin retired, he and his wife Elizabeth, a journalist, decided to move here and (inspired by reading previous editions of *Staying Off the Beaten Track*) run a bed-and-breakfast house. It wasn't any olde worlde cottage that they fell in love with but this handsome 'twenties house that had been built for Aldis (inventor of the famous signal-lamps which bear his name) on a superb site with a 40-mile sea view south-east as far as Portland Bill. It is a house with handsome features – iron-studded oak doors, leaded casements and window-seats, for example. On sunny mornings (occasionally even in late autumn), you can take breakfast on the wide verandah and enjoy sea breezes while you eat – at your feet, sloping lawns with colourful rhododendrons, camellias, fuchsias and wisteria. On chilly mornings, breakfast is served in an attractive room with a fire.

The bedrooms are excellent. Mine was 20 feet long, very comfortably furnished in period with the house, with a thick carpet. By contrast, the even larger family room in scarlet-and-white has Habitat furniture. Each bedroom is equipped with armchairs, TV, a refrigerator, flowers and books – the aim being to provide individual bed-sitters for guests, as there is no communal sitting-room, only a large landing which has seats and a supply of leaflets, maps and local menus.

This is a perfect base from which to explore the locality. Sandy beaches with their shrimp-pools are ideal for children. There are excellent walks (in Marshwood Vale or along the coast) including nature trails; drives along lanes of primroses, bluebells and subtropical wildflowers in the downs; Hardy villages; National Trust houses. You can watch or take part in sea-sports and cider-making.

Readers' comments: Just perfect, equal to the best hotels, excellent value. Kindness itself, so caring. The best ever. Good value. Splendid views and pleasant gardens.

An 18th-century house recommended by the Griffins when the Red House is full is **Springfield**, Woodmead Road (tel: 02974 3409), where Mrs Culpan provides inexpensive bed-and-breakfast, no dinners. It, too, is surrounded by a garden and has sea views.

rear view

3 bedrooms (single, double or family) from £16. Rooms have central heating or electric heaters; shower or bathroom; armchairs; views of country or garden; tea/coffee facilities.
Dinner A la carte, at 7–9pm. Lunches, packed lunches, snacks. Coffee, tea, for a charge. Drinks can be ordered.
Sitting-room with central heating, open fire, books, piano. Bar.
Nearest main road A350 from Chippenham to Warminster.

The National Trust owns this historic stone building run by the Levis family. In the 17th century it was a major coaching inn. Its big bars have been kept unspoilt and are full of character. Against terracotta walls hang old farming gear and birdcages; tapestry benches or carved oak settles on Turkey rugs face the stone fireplaces.

Upstairs is a huge dining-room with leather chairs, as well as attractive bedrooms – one has an old half-tester bed. Here, stuffed owls and modern paintings contrast; and on some walls a local artist has painted flowery murals – it was she who chose the good colour schemes of the bedrooms.

Local produce and home-baked bread contribute to the Red Lion's reputation for good food. Some of the house specialities are duck liver and damson pâté, pork stuffed with almonds and apricots (served with cider sauce), and ginger snaffles – a confection of shortbread, honey, ice cream, cream and ginger.

Lacock is a showpiece village (not one of its stone or half-timbered buildings is later than the 18th century). Its winding streets lead to Lacock Abbey (National Trust) which dates from the 13th century but was turned into a mansion in Tudor times. The village is within an area of great beauty, its rural peace unspoilt still. In days of wealth (from wool) fine houses and churches were built in creamy Bath stone, still to be found among the wooded dells or fields.

Within a short distance are such beauty-spots as Bath, Bradford-on-Avon, Castle Combe, Biddestone, Holt, Corsham Court and Bowood House (with gardens). The market town of Calne has some fine buildings. There is a pigmy pinetum, and a good garden centre in Lacock itself.

Readers' comments: The best of all!

> If you want absolute quiet, avoid any place that takes children or has a bar open to non-residents. Inns sometimes get extensions to their licensing hours for late private parties; and may lack quiet sitting-rooms.

243

REGENCY HOUSE

C D PT X

Neatishead, north-east of Norwich, Norfolk, NR12 8AD   Tel: 0692 630233

5 bedrooms (double or family) from £12. Less for 3 nights or bargain breaks. Rooms have electric heaters; TV, armchairs; views of country or garden; tea/coffee facilities.
Meals Packed lunches or snacks. Coffee, tea, for a charge.
Garden
Nearest main road A1151 from Norwich to Yarmouth.

Former Manchester bank-manager Alan Wrigley was so touched by the friendliness of Neatishead people towards a newcomer that, after a few years here, he began planting wayside trees as a 'thank you': the total has already reached 2000. He and his wife Sue, previously a *Daily Express* reporter, run not only this 18th-century guest-house to an immaculate standard but also the village stores adjoining it, in the heart of the Norfolk Broads area.

The breakfasts are outstanding: standard issue is 2 sausages, 4 rashers of bacon, 6 mushrooms, 2 whole tomatoes, 2 slices of fried bread and as many eggs as you request! But if you prefer it, she will produce a vegetarian breakfast instead. This is served in a fresh, white room with stoneware crockery on tables that were specially made by a local craftsman. On the walls are photographs of bygone Neatishead. Bedrooms have Laura Ashley fabrics (the bed in no. 6 is king-size) and, in some cases, garden views. (As to dinner, there are two good places in the village to choose from, and others at popular Horning – such as the Swan.)

Pretty little Neatishead, at the centre of the Norfolk Broads, fortunately does not attract the crowds which sometimes ruin Horning, Wroxham and other villages. There is a staithe (mooring) here for fifteen boats – the Wrigleys have a 14-foot dinghy which visitors can use for fishing – and pleasant picnic-spots by the waterside at, for instance, Burton Turf. Some families choose to divide themselves between cabin cruisers (for the younger generation) and Regency House (for older members, who prefer to sleep on shore and boat with their family only by day). There is good cycling around here, too; wildlife and birdwatching; and plenty of sightseeing in mediaeval Norwich and elsewhere. The sandy beaches are easily accessible, too. Rose nurseries, and the gardens at Blickling, Horeton Hall and Burnt Fen interest flower-lovers; antiques-hunters head for Holt and Norwich.

Don't complain if –
- because you booked at short notice, you do not get the best room
- because you did not order a meal in advance, you get something plucked from the freezer
- because you do not arrive on time, your room is let to someone else
- because you bring a dog without asking, it is refused entry
- because you don't express your wishes (for more heat, a second helping, or whatever), you don't get what you want!

RHYDSPENCE INN

west of Whitney-on-Wye, Herefordshire, HR3 6EU   Tel: 04973 262

C

6 bedrooms (single or double) at £18. Bargain breaks. Rooms have central heating; shower and bathroom; TV, armchairs; views of country or garden; tea/coffee facilities.
Dinner A la carte, from 7pm. Special diets if ordered. Lunches, snacks. Drinks can be ordered.

2 bars with central heating, open fire, books, indoor games (including darts).
Grounds Lawns and a stream.
Nearest main road A438 from Hereford to Brecon.

This spectacular black-and-white building, typical of so many fine old Herefordshire houses, is perched slightly uphill with splendid views of the lovely Wye Valley and the hills beyond – even so far as Brecon Beacons and the Black Mountains (sometimes snow-capped, sometimes hidden in cloud). There is no other building for miles. A one-time ford ('rhyd') in the River Wye brought the inn into being in the 14th century (though most of the present building is Tudor), at the spot where the Welsh drovers took their sheep and cattle across for sale in English markets. The border between England and Wales runs through here.

The ground floor is everything you might expect of an ancient inn. Its snug bars have low beams, small windows, stuffed fish in glass cases, and handpumps drawing real ale or draught cider from the cellars below. There's draught barley-wine in winter. Here locals – farmworkers (who drop in after milking the cows) and local doctors or businessmen – meet to chat and play darts or dominoes. Through little windows are views of the valley and hills, and the stone terrace where Peter and Pam Glover put out tables and sunshades in summer.

The building is full of crooked twists and turns, with some walls at a tipsy angle. The bedrooms have been furnished with an elegance and comfort rare in inns.

The food is equally exceptional, whether you choose a four-course dinner or just a bar snack (such as game pie). Even the breakfasts are outstanding, with choices that include kidneys and breaded whiting, cooked to perfection (orange juice is freshly squeezed, marmalade and bread are locally made). Some of chef Ray Grosvenor's beautifully cooked specialities for dinner are Wye salmon, guineafowl, beef Stroganoff, smoked eel and asparagus with Hollandaise sauce. Not, I fancy, the kind of fare provided when Kilvert wrote about the inn in his diary: 'ablaze with light and noisy with the songs of revellers' (May Day, 1872). But he may well have seen in use the old cider-mill (horse-operated) which stands outside, or heard the Cwmrafwr brook rushing down its pebbly bed.

Readers' comments: Very nice room and good food. Extremely comfortable. A little expensive but worth every pound. Best place we've stayed at for years. Service and food excellent. Well planned, well furnished, good cooking, pleasant staff. Expensive but worth every penny! Excellent in every way (two visits).

RIVER PARK FARM　　　　　　　　　　　　　　　　　　　　　　　　　C S

Lodsworth, west of Petworth, West Sussex, GU23 9DS　Tel: 07985 362

5 **bedrooms** (single, double or family) from
£9. Less for 3 nights. Rooms have central

heating or electric heaters; armchairs; views
of country or garden; tea/coffee facilities.
Dinner £4.50 for 2 courses (with choices)
and coffee, at 7–8pm (not on Wednesdays).
Packed lunches. Non-residents not admit-
ted. Wine can be brought in.
Sitting-room with central heating, open fire,
TV, books.
Garden (mainly lawn) and farmland, with
coarse fishing, table tennis.
Nearest main road A272 from Petworth to
Midhurst.
Closed in winter

This farm with 340 acres of corn, bullocks, sheep and poultry is in a secluded
position among woods where, if you are up early enough, you may encounter deer.
There is a 4½-acre lake with plentiful carp and ducks, and in front a pretty garden.
The house itself, built in 1600, is old and beamy with comfortable bedrooms along
twisting passageways, and outside are golden roses and wisteria clambering
around the door. Altogether it is a pretty and tranquil spot, full of nooks and
crannies – amazing, visitors think, because it is so close to London.

Pat Moss does not do full-scale dinners (available elsewhere locally) but has a list
of homely dishes like shepherd's pie or macaroni cheese, and for puddings like
banana split she uses rich Jersey cream from the farm's own cow. Bread is
home-baked and eggs free-range. There are flowers in every room.

People come for the local walks and birdwatching (Pat has pinned up bird-
identification charts and gives visitors field notes on the crops and wildlife in each
season, with map, and her own daily nature notes); or to visit the many outstanding sights in this neighbourhood – beginning with one of England's greatest houses
at Petworth; or the polo or point-to-points at Cowdray; or to see the local game of
stoolball played at Midhurst. There are many small country towns around here,
streams running down into the River Rother, woodlands and picturesque villages
with greens and duckponds, old inns and ancient churches, Arundel Castle,
wildfowl reserve, Goodwood House and Roman remains. Turner knew and loved
this area, staying at Petworth House where many of his paintings can be seen. It's
a good area for antique shops, too. Garden-lovers head for West Dean and
Denmans; and there is the open-air Weald and Downland Museum.

Readers' comments: Warm hospitality, generous home cooking. Enjoyed ourselves
so much that we have twice visited for a week. Marvellous setting and house, kind
hosts, good food. Outstanding. Very relaxed atmosphere.

If you want your hosts to post you things you have accidentally left behind,
send them the cost of postage. (The trouble they take is free.)

When writing to me, if you want a reply please enclose a stamped addressed
envelope.

246

ROCK HOUSE X

Alport, south of Bakewell, Derbyshire, DE4 1LG Tel: 062986 636736

3 bedrooms (single, double or family) from £12. Rooms have central heating, electric heaters; shower; armchairs; views of country or garden; tea/coffee facilities. Clothes-washing facilities. No smoking.

Sitting-room with gas fire, TV, books.
Small garden
Nearest main road A6 from Bakewell to Matlock.

The rock for which the Stathams' house is named is a great crag of tufa (a type of volcanic stone, perforated like Gruyère cheese, which was formed 300 million years ago) rearing up alongside it.

Only a few yards from the 18th-century house two rivers join, splashing over weirs constructed long ago to contain trout downstream – you can watch these drifting in water so transparent that the locals call it 'gin-clear' (its purity is due to the limestone bed over which it runs). Lathkill Dale is a National Nature Reserve, Tony and Jan are first-rate sources of information about the wildlife and history of this most beautiful of valleys. They will lend maps, tell you the best riverside walks, and where to find river pools (created for washing sheep), or where to buy the best local cheeses, trout or Bakewell pudding.

The front door opens straight into the stone-flagged sitting-room, its walls now painted mushroom, with grey buttoned velvet armchairs, where you will be served tea on arrival. Glass doors lead through to the breakfast-room where, by pre-arrangement, Jan sometimes also serves supper platters, beautifully presented (but most visitors go to the nearby Druid Inn or other pubs). Breakfast possibilities include muffins, poached fruit, Staffordshire oatcakes, home-made jams and some vegetarian dishes. All bedrooms are well furnished.

Alport is well placed for touring either the wild and dramatic 'Dark Peak' (the stone there is millstone grit) or the more benign 'White Peak' (limestone), a fertile and verdant region. It is close to Chatsworth House and park with garden centre (the autumn colours there are glorious), Dove Dale, Haddon Hall and Hardwick Hall – a great Tudor mansion, the Norman splendours of Southwell Minster – famous for its botanical carvings, Castleton (remarkable caves), the market town of Bakewell where the original Bakewell puddings are still to be had, Haddon Hall (mediaeval), the spa of Buxton, Melbourne's stately home, the Crown Derby porcelain museum, historic trams at Crich, the canal at Cromford, a cable car to the heights outside Matlock, Kedleston Hall (designed by Adam), and Alton Towers for its gardens and leisure park. Many mansions have fine gardens and there are good garden centres at Tansley and Darley Dale.

Readers' comments: Very comfortable and a warm welcome. Breakfast excellent, rooms large and comfortable.

ROCK WINDMILL *New*   **C D**
The Hollow, Washington, north of Worthing, West Sussex, RH20 3DA
Tel: 0903 892941

3 bedrooms (double or family) from £12. Less for 7 nights. All have tea/coffee facilities; central heating; views of country or garden. (Washing-machine on request.) Packed lunches, snacks. Tea, coffee, free.
Sitting-room with central heating, TV, books, record-player.
Large garden with swimming-pool (heated).
Nearest main road A24 from London to Worthing.

The composer John Ireland lived here until his death in 1962: much of his music was inspired by the surrounding landscape (for instance, the *Downland Suite*, *Equinox* and *Amberley Wild Brooks*). It had ceased to function as a mill long before – and the sails have gone – but part of the original building (1820) remains, further modernized in recent years: the octagonal sitting-room, for instance, which is now decorated in a restful celadon green and has modern leather armchairs. This opens onto a garden with swimming-pool (heated to 80°F). Bedrooms are in a modern extension, neatly furnished with pine and cane fitments.

Janice Langley provides only breakfast but she or David give visitors lifts to the Frankland Arms (immortalized in Hilaire Belloc's 'West Sussex Drinking Song' which is sometimes sung at the pub), where there is very good food and from which it is a pleasant walk back to the mill. Or drive to Barn Owls, see below.

Chanctonbury Ring is within sight and accessible by steep footpath from the village: a striking landmark, it consists of beech woods within the earthworks of an Iron Age hill fort; superb views all round. In this part of the lovely South Downs are such attractive villages as Findon (flint-walled cottages and three racing-stables), Steyning (mediaeval gabled houses and an outstanding church), Bramber (castle ruins, and a museum of pipes) and Ashurst (well preserved and with far views). The River Adur runs through this area to the sea at the small port of Shoreham, and everywhere there are good walks to be found – the long-distance South Downs Way goes by Washington on its way from Hampshire to Beachy Head (80 miles), and this is one of its most scenic, hilltop stretches. The nearest coastal resort is Worthing, described elsewhere.

Sights which most visitors want to see are great Petworth House (Turner paintings, and a noble park), Tudor Parham and its gardens, West Burton's watermill for stone-ground flour, the unusual museum in Amberley chalkpits, Roman villa at Bignor, Arundel Castle and wildfowl reserve, Chichester Cathedral (and harbour trips), Fishbourne Roman palace, sailing-boats at Bosham, Goodwood House (and racecourse).

At another village near here, Coldwaltham outside Pulborough, is **Barn Owls** (tel: 07982 2498), basically a restaurant in a Victorian house but with some bedrooms. Not 'off the beaten track', for it is on a road to London, but popular for Pat Hellenberg's cooking. As well as a standard menu, there are often 8-course feasts available, a traditional Victorian dinner, regional specialities, vegetarian dishes and special events (Hawaiian, Moroccan, farmhouse etc.): send for brochure of all these. Cream teas are served in the rock garden.

248

ROSE-IN-VALE HOTEL

C D H S S-C X

Mithian, east of St Agnes, Cornwall, TR5 0QD Tel: 087255 2202

15 bedrooms (single, double or family) from £25 with dinner. Less for 2 nights or bargain breaks. Rooms have central heating or electric heaters; shower or bathroom; phone, TV, armchairs; views of country or garden; tea/coffee facilities.

Dinner 4 courses (with choices) and coffee, at 7–8pm. Special diets if ordered. Lunches, packed lunches, snacks. Coffee, tea, for a charge. Drinks can be ordered.

3 sitting-rooms with central heating, open fire, TV, books, indoor games (darts, table tennis, bar billiards in separate games room); bar. Solarium.

Large garden Woodland and pasture; with croquet lawn, badminton and swimming-pool.

Nearest main road A30 from London to Penzance.

This handsome 18th-century mansion was originally the home of a local mine captain. A regular visitor to the Nankivel family here was the portrait painter, John Opie, who grew up nearby and painted Joyce Nankivel, 'the belle of Mithian'.

The Arthurs, who honeymooned here several years ago, made many discoveries after they took over and began making improvements.

In what is now the bar at the back, they uncovered a most unusual stone fireplace with a fringle (bread oven) built into what had been an inglenook fireplace in an old cottage adjoining the 18th-century house. They have added fire-baskets welded by Tony himself: he says his past experience as an engineer has come in handy! He installed central heating himself, too.

There are two large sitting-rooms, now fully refurbished to a high standard, with fine details preserved, such as sash windows with folding shutters. The curving staircase has a decorative window. In a modern extension at the back is a third sitting-room and a very long dining-room with huge windows giving a view of the lawns and rosebeds, with a primrose-banked stream behind. There is a small, sheltered swimming-pool heated by solar panels which, in a good summer, keep the water temperature at 78°. Some smaller, modern bedrooms open onto this, but for one with outstanding views from its four windows choose no. 1 upstairs with a four-poster, in the main house. There is also a family suite. (Special activity weekends in winter.)

The Arthurs have a good chef – Philip Simms was once at the Imperial Hotel, Torquay, and now lectures part-time at Camborne Catering College. He prepares such à la carte specialities as fish mousse in crab sauce; game or local fish as a main course – or perhaps duck in a sauce of Grand Marnier served with little pancakes containing orange segments and zest; and delicious puddings like an iced soufflé of peaches, surrounded by a purée of raspberries and cream. Take your mother here for the mid-March weekend when he does a special Mothering Sunday luncheon.

Beyond the sheltered valley and quaint village of Mithian are the well-known surfing beaches of St Agnes and Perranporth (a quieter one is at Trevellas), seal sanctuary, country park, and six National Trust houses (with gardens).

Readers' comments: Hospitality beyond reproach; extremely high standard. Very pleasant; comfortable but not luxurious; friendly and helpful owners. Very pleasant – return visit planned.

249

RUTLAND COTTAGES

Cedar Street, Braunston, south-west of Oakham, Leicestershire, LE15 8QS
Tel: 0572 2049

6 bedrooms (single, double or family) from £12. Less for 2 nights or bargain breaks. Rooms have central heating, electric heaters; shower or bathroom; TV, armchairs; views of country or garden; tea/coffee facilities. No smoking in one.
Sitting-room with central heating, open fire, TV, books. No smoking.
Garden with swing.
Nearest main road A1 from London to Scotland.

A 17th-century bakehouse is the home of John and Connie Beadman (she teaches music), with one bedroom available for guests; and in addition they own nearby cottages let either for self-catering or on a bed-and-breakfast basis. All b & b guests take breakfast together in the beamed dining-room of the house. Those who do not want to cook their own dinner (in their cottage) can eat at either the Blue Ball or the Old Plough in this pretty conservation village of golden stone. (Packed lunches can be provided; tea and coffee are free.)

The bakehouse bedroom is very neat and well decorated with an excellent bathroom, and guests have the use of the Beadmans' huge and beautifully furnished sitting-room (it has a see-through stone fireplace in the middle, and a 'curfew window' through which the village watchman could check that the baker's fires had been properly extinguished for the night). Its windows open onto a rose garden with a view of stately cedars beyond.

Furnishings in the cottages are more homely, but guests have the advantage of self-contained accommodation including fully equipped kitchens: particularly suitable for families.

John and his sons are keen bell-ringers, willing to take visitors on guided tours up into the bell-towers of local churches. This is a good area for walks or cycling (maps on loan), and other country pursuits, and for sightseeing too: the historic public schools at Uppingham and Oundle, Rutland Water (Europe's largest man-made lake, with wildlife reserve), the mediaeval town of Stamford, castles at Rockingham and Belvoir as well as Oakham, the stately homes of Burghley and Belton – at the former, horse trials take place each September. The former county of Rutland (now absorbed into Leicestershire) still has its own rural museum and farm park.

Prices are the minimum *per person* in a double room at the beginning of the year.

Some readers tell me they have stayed at lots of places from *Staying Off the Beaten Track*. I wonder who has stayed at most? A free copy of the next edition awaits the reader who sends me his/her comments on the greatest number!

ST CHRISTOPHER'S

Boscastle, south of Bude, Cornwall, PL35 0BD   Tel: 08405 412

C(11) **D S**

8 bedrooms (single or double) from £12.50. Less for 7 nights or bargain breaks. Rooms have central heating; some have shower or bathroom; armchairs; views of country or garden; tea/coffee facilities.

Dinner £7 for 4 courses (limited choice) and coffee, at 7pm. Special diets if ordered. Packed lunches. Coffee, tea for a charge. Drinks can be ordered.

Sitting-room with central heating, open fire, TV, books.

Nearest main road A39 from Bude to Truro.

Closed January–March

This 18th-century house is in an unspoilt harbour village (a conservation area) and now belongs, after many changes of owner, to Brenda and Brian Thompson who used to run a local restaurant.

One enters it through a slate-floored hall with roughcast walls. There is a large sitting-room, well furnished with damask wallpaper and a big velvet sofa. It is heated by an open fire, while a log stove warms the cottage-style dining-room that adjoins it. Bedrooms have well-chosen colour schemes: no. 2, for instance, which is L-shaped, is decorated in celadon and white, with cane chairs; the family suite is in tangerine, chocolate and white with pretty cushions and pictures.

A typical dinner might comprise a mushroom-and-wine savoury, then tenderloin of pork in a cream sauce, syllabub and cheeses.

Boscastle lies on one of the most scenic parts of the rugged north Cornwall coast, with Tintagel and its King Arthur associations nearby. This is an area of great contrasts. Castles, sandy beaches, glens, traditional crafts, moorland or coastal footpaths, National Trust houses or gardens and quaint inns all abound. There are fine gardens to visit, slate quarries and St Juliot's church (Thomas Hardy).

Readers' comments: Very good. Pleasant welcome and good food.

For explanation of code letters (**C, D, H, PT, S, S-C, X**) **see page xxviii.**

When to go? Seaside resorts or other places suitable for children will be at their busiest (and dearest) in July–August and during half-term holidays (especially, in late May, which is also a bank holiday period). Other peak periods are, of course, Easter, Christmas, New Year and the bank holiday in late August. (The bank holiday in early May is not usually a peak, because it comes rather soon after Easter, but much depends on the weather.) There are local peaks, too (the Gold Cup races at Cheltenham or the regatta at Henley, for instance, are apt to fill hotels for miles around), and local troughs (Brighton, a conference centre, is least busy in high summer). You won't get much personal attention when hotels are full to bursting.

ST JAMES'S HOUSE

The Green, Thirsk, North Yorkshire, YO7 1AQ   Tel: 0845 22676

C(12) **PT**

4 bedrooms (double or family) from £13.50. Less for stays of 7 nights. Rooms have central heating; two have shower or bathroom; TV; tea/coffee facilities. No smoking.

Sitting-room with central heating and TV. **Nearest main road** A19 from Thirsk to York.
Closed November–March

Barry Ogleby being an antique dealer, it is not surprising that every part of his 18th-century house is well endowed with period pieces. You may sleep in a room with a bedstead of prettily turned spindles or in a genuine Victorian four-poster; and in corridors as well as rooms there are such interesting pieces as inlaid blanket-boxes or unusual chairs. On the ground floor is a particularly convenient family room, looking onto the flower beds, winding paths and lily-pool of the enclosed garden.

Only two minutes' walk from the quiet green, a conservation area, is Thirsk's busy market-place and many restaurants (only breakfast is served by Liz Ogleby, who recommends the Carpenters' Arms for other meals). This is where the world's most famous vet, writing under the name of James Herriot, has his surgery. There are local guides who will accompany you on car tours, pointing out sites associated with Herriot, his books or the films (much filming was done not here but in the Dales); one shows videos en route.

In the immediate vicinity are landscaped gardens and an arboretum, more market towns, the stupendous view from Sutton Bank, great ruined abbeys (the beautifully laid out terraces above Rievaulx Abbey provide a bird's-eye-view of it), Castle Howard (famous even before 'Brideshead Revisited'), thriving Ampleforth Abbey and its school, the pretty villages of Coxwold and Kilburn – the latter associated with 'the mouse-man' and his furniture, the former with Shandy Hall (home of Laurence Sterne). A few miles away is Northallerton, a town of fine houses, with characterful villages all around. Fountains Abbey, Newburgh Priory, the white horse of the Hambleton hills, Byland Abbey, Helmsley (old market town), arboretum at Bedale and Harlow Car gardens are other attractions.

Inclusive terms for dinner, bed-and-breakfast (particularly for a week) can be much lower than those quoted here for these items taken separately. For short-notice bookings you may be able to get a reduction.

No proprietor wants to have a room standing empty. This particularly applies to Sunday nights. Some hotels make a discount if you want only two courses from a three-course menu.

SAINT MARIE'S GRANGE *New* C PT S
Alderbury, south of Salisbury, Wiltshire, SP5 3DJ   Tel: 0722 710351

3 bedrooms (double or family) from £15. Less for 2 nights and bargain breaks. Rooms have tea/coffee facilities; central heating; views of river, country or garden. No smoking. (Washing-machine on request.)
Dinner £15 for 4 courses, wine and coffee, at 7 or 7.30pm. Vegetarian or special diets if ordered. Tea, coffee, free.
Sitting-room with central heating, open fire, TV, books, piano. No smoking.
Large garden
Nearest main road A36 from Salisbury to Southampton.

Pugin, whose most celebrated work was done as architect (with Barry) of the Houses of Parliament, was largely responsible for the Gothic revival of the early 19th century, a style that was to dominate the building not only of churches but even libraries and prisons for decades to come. Saint Marie's was the first house that he built for himself, in 1835 when he was only 23, and it has many typically Puginesque features: the iron-studded front door, stained glass (some with Pugin's initials and motto), open-joisted and coffered ceilings, pointed windows with stone mullions, and a great fireplace of chamfered stone in the former library. Originally there was even a drawbridge; and there is still a bell-tower (though it now houses a shower). It is said that Mr Pecksniff in *Martin Chuzzlewit* was based on Pugin – Dickens once stayed at the Green Dragon in Alderbury, and later as the guest of another owner of Saint Marie's.

Peter Higgins says he is still making new Pugin discoveries hidden under layers of paint and other accretions, some in bedrooms used by visitors – for instance, a little alcove with pointed window framing an attractive view of the River Avon. Below the house are terraced lawns and lovely trees descending towards the water-meadows; and in an outbuilding is Peter's collection of vintage Humber cars.

Gina Higgins is an accomplished artist (her pictures hang on many of the walls) and cook too, producing such imaginative meals as courgette and Brie soup or a grapefruit sorbet with mint and prawns by way of a starter; lamb cooked with garlic, marjoram and rosemary; a rum-and-ginger trifle – followed by cheeses. Aperitifs, wine and liqueurs accompany the meals (these include local Fonthill wines). There is much emphasis on wholefood; and vegetables are steamed not boiled. After dinner the Higgins join their guests in the blue sitting-room with its William Morris fabrics and grand piano, and its bay windows through which to enjoy the valley view as night falls.

Outside Alderbury is one of England's oldest follies: a hexagonal 'pepperbox' built in 1606, high on the downs. Britford has another Gothic revival house, with moat, and Longford Castle which contains fine paintings. Salisbury, described elsewhere, is very close and Alderbury is well placed for visiting other historic cities too (Winchester and Southampton, for instance) as well as the New Forest and resorts such as Bournemouth. Romsey and its abbey are soon reached, and Broadlands – the Mountbatten home. Mottisfont Abbey (part Norman, part 18th-century) has paintings by Rex Whistler; Broughton is a pretty village with flowers against half-timbered cottage walls. The three Wallops (Nether, Middle and Over) are picturesque thatched villages.

253

ST MARY'S HOUSE   *New*   C D H PT S-C X
Kintbury, west of Newbury, Berkshire, RG15 0TR   Tel: 0488 551

7 bedrooms (single, double or family) from £13. Less for 7 nights. Some have own bath/shower; TV; central heating; views of river, country or garden.
Dinner £7 for 4 courses (with some choice) and coffee, at 7–8.30pm. Vegetarian or special diets if ordered. Packed lunches, snacks. Tea, coffee, extra. Drinks can be ordered.

Sitting-room with central heating, open fire, books; bar.
Small garden
Nearest main road M4 from London to Wales.
Closed in January or February

Old-fashioned roses and a grapevine up the walls add to the picturesque look of this unusual house. Its pointed windows are lozenge-paned, and little dormers punctuate the roof. In Victorian times it was a school.

All bedrooms are on the ground floor, one of them opening onto a paved terrace with lavender hedge. The sitting-room is furnished with antiques, and the dining-room with a great refectory table surrounded by leather chairs.

Margaret Barr prepares (if given adequate notice) such meals as fish mousse, chicken in a variety of exotic sauces, and meringues or fruity desserts, followed by cheese. Alan has a well-stocked wine cellar to complement her cooking.

The lovely Kennet & Avon Canal is only a hundred yards away, for Kintbury lies midway between Hungerford and Newbury – towns described elsewhere in this book (along with the rest of Berkshire). Only a few miles south are the Hampshire Downs; and, westward, Wiltshire's Vale of Pewsey, both of which are also scenic areas which take days to explore. Northward is a region rich in prehistoric remains – hill forts, barrows, ancient tracks and so forth. The valley itself is quite different: woodland, commons and meadows as the backdrop to villages of flint, brick and thatch with narrow lanes and some richly decorated churches. Birdwatchers and walkers love the whole area (as do anglers). A good way to enjoy the waterways is on a horse-drawn barge, for which Kintbury is a starting-point. Favourite outings include Littlecote House, Avebury (prehistoric ring), Marlborough, Newbury (racecourse), Bowood House and Highclerc Castle.

Single people may find more company in houses that have a shared dining-table, a bar, and no TV in the sitting-room. As my descriptions indicate, some owners mingle more with their guests than others do. Houses marked **S** charge singles little or no more than half a double.

SAXELBYE MANOR HOUSE   C D
Saxelbye, Melton Mowbray, Leicestershire, LE14 3PA Tel: 0664 812269

3 bedrooms (double or family) from £11. Less for 4 nights. Rooms have central heating, electric heaters; armchairs; views of country or garden; tea/coffee facilities. Clothes-washing facilities.

Dinner £6.50 for 4 courses and coffee, at 7pm. Vegetarian or special diets if ordered. Packed lunches, snacks. Coffee, tea, free. Non-residents not admitted. Drinks can be brought in.

Sitting-room with central heating, open fire, TV, books, piano.

Large garden and farmland.

Nearest main road A6006 from Melton Mowbray to Loughborough.

Closed in winter

In this little hamlet is an especially attractive farmhouse, tucked within a garden where willows and fuchsias flourish. Parts of it are 800 years old. Margaret Morris has furnished it with a fascinating collection of Victoriana (even in the cloakroom): little velvet chairs and chaise longues, old prints and pot-plants in abundance. Narrow passages lead to a grand staircase constructed four centuries ago in the old stone stairwell. There's even a big Victorian bath in the huge bathroom. She provides traditional 4-course dinners as well as bed-and-breakfast, all at a very modest price. One might, for instance, eat prawn cocktail, the farm's own lamb with four vegetables, sherry trifle and a cheeseboard that includes local cheeses and Stilton.

Melton Mowbray is a pleasant market town (from which you can go home laden with its famous pork pies and other products of the pig), and is well placed for visiting other historic Leicestershire towns such as Loughborough and Oakham (as well as Grantham and Stamford in Lincolnshire, and Nottingham for its castle and other historic buildings). Belvoir Castle and Rutland Water are well worth a visit, and also the Tudor mansion of Stapleford Park. The tiny county of Rutland still keeps its identity even though it was incorporated into Leicestershire decades ago, a region in which sheep graze on green wolds and leafy coverts are deliberately preserved for the foxes, which several hunts then pursue to their death across the fields. Roads wind up and down past cottages of pinkish stone, many of which have fine views across the great Vale of Belvoir to its castle. Villages worth touring include Bottesford (for its church monuments), Burley (for views), Lyddington (old almshouses, etc.), Uppingham (famous 16th-century boys' school), Wing (a mediaeval maze). There is a steam railway.

Readers' comments: Have stayed repeatedly.

When writing to me, if you want a reply please enclose a stamped addressed envelope.

Book well ahead: many of these houses have few rooms. Do not expect dinner if you have not booked it.

SCOTT ARMS *New*

Kingston, south of Corfe Castle, Dorset, BH20 5LH   Tel: 0929 480270

7 bedrooms (double or family) from £15. Tea/coffee facilities and central heating.
Large garden
Nearest main road A351 from Swanage to Wareham.

This creeper-covered country inn is in one of the most beautiful parts of Dorset, on a hilltop with magnificent views of Corfe Castle. There is a stone-walled family bar, fire blazing in inglenook, leather-upholstered fender; and tables both inside and out – some on stone-walled, terraced lawns with superb views. Bedrooms are neat and homely (choose Room 8 for its view, Room 7 for a stair direct to the garden).

Mrs Stansfield cooks traditional bar food; Dorset crabs and apple-cake are two local specialities. There are farmhouse wines and ciders, and real ales. And, to make the most of those superlative views, a former milking-shed has been converted into a lounge bar with panoramic windows.

Kingston stands nearly 500 feet high, overlooking Corfe Castle, the lovely Isle (no longer literally an isle) of Purbeck, and Poole Harbour – described elsewhere in this book. It's only two miles from the sea; 10 miles west of sophisticated Bournemouth.

When to go? Seaside resorts or other places suitable for children will be at their busiest (and dearest) in July–August and during half-term holidays (especially, in late May, which is also a bank holiday period). Other peak periods are, of course, Easter, Christmas, New Year and the bank holiday in late August. (The bank holiday in early May is not usually a peak, because it comes rather soon after Easter, but much depends on the weather.) There are local peaks, too (the Gold Cup races at Cheltenham or the regatta at Henley, for instance, are apt to fill hotels for miles around), and local troughs (Brighton, a conference centre, is least busy in high summer). You won't get much personal attention when hotels are full to bursting.

Don't complain if –
   – because you booked at short notice, you do not get the best room
   – because you did not order a meal in advance, you get something plucked from the freezer
   – because you do not arrive on time, your room is let to someone else
   – because you bring a dog without asking, it is refused entry
   – because you don't express your wishes (for more heat, a second helping, or whatever), you don't get what you want!

SHEARINGS *New*   C(12) PT
Rockbourne, south of Salisbury (Wiltshire), Hampshire, SP6 3NA
Tel: 07253 256

3 bedrooms (single or double) from £16. Less for 7 nights. All have own bath/shower; tea/coffee facilities; central heating; views of stream or garden. (Washing-machine on request.)
Dinner £10–£15 for 2–3 courses (with aperitif and wine) and coffee, at 8pm. Non-residents not admitted. Vegetarian or special diets if ordered. Packed lunches, snacks. Tea, coffee, free. Drinks can be ordered or brought in.
Sitting-room with central heating, open fire, TV, books. Piano.
Small garden
Nearest main road A354 from Salisbury to Blandford.
Closed from mid-December–January

This house may look familiar, for it has been photographed many times for calendars and greetings cards. Its thatched roof and porch overlook a clear stream (in hot summers this tends to dry up, alas); the cottage has its own footbridge. It was built in the 16th century (from oak beams that are even older), and when Colin and Rosemary Watts came here they took great care to decorate and furnish it appropriately. One pink-carpeted sitting-room has rosy cretonne sofas facing the inglenook fireplace; another, with chintz-covered chairs, is for television. The dining-room with ladderback chairs overlooks the twinkling stream; its table converts to billiards. Most meals are eaten, however, in the beamy kitchen/dining-room. (Bedrooms are, however, rather simply furnished.)

The garden at the back is particularly pretty: sloping lawn, brick summerhouse, a suntrapping brick patio. Here there is an annexe to the house that could be particularly suitable for youngsters, with upstairs bed-sitter; 'Portaloo' below.

Mr and Mrs Watts are interesting people to meet – she, musical and artistic; he, a retired brigadier. Rosemary is an excellent cook – of such meals as iced cucumber soup, beef, éclairs, cheeses; aperitifs and wine included.

The village itself is picturesque, and has a Roman villa. Within a very short distance are the New Forest, Breamore House (and carriage museum), and Salisbury.

Readers' comments: Excellent. Made very welcome. Truly beautiful and peaceful. Top marks.

Woodgreen is another village near here, where at **Cottage Crest** (tel: 0725 22009) the Cadmans provide bed-and-breakfast in a Victorian drover's cottage – no dinner. Bedrooms are of a very high standard (and moderately priced). A great brass bed with pink-and-white lacy linen is in one; it has an L-shaped room with windows on two sides from which to enjoy superb views of the River Avon in the valley below. One can sit on a paved terrace with a

little pool, or take a zigzag path down to a lower garden, to look for badgers.

6 bedrooms (single, double or family) from £14.50. Less for 2 nights and bargain breaks. All have own bath/shower; tea/coffee facilities; central heating; views of garden. (Washing-machine on request.)
Dinner £6.50 for 3 courses (with choices) and coffee, at 6.30pm. Non-residents not admitted. Vegetarian or special diets if ordered. Tea, coffee, free. Drinks can be brought in.
Sitting-room with central heating, open fire, TV, books.
Large garden
Nearest main road A696 from Newcastle to Edinburgh.
Closed from October–March

18th-century stone buildings enclose a courtyard where white fantails strut, the former barns to left and right providing very well-equipped ground-floor bedrooms for visitors – each with its own entrance. Meals are taken in a beamed dining-room in the centre, furnished with antiques and an inglenook fireplace (a typical dinner might be home-made soup, a roast or lasagne, and blackcurrant tart – with produce from the smallholding); and to one side is a sitting-room for visitors. From a patio with chairs one enjoys a serene view.

Stephen Robinson-Gay is an accomplished cabinet-maker, happy to show visitors the workshop where he makes or restores furniture. Many of the bedrooms have examples of his work. For example, beyond the arched doorway of the mahogany room is a colonial-style bed with very fine inlay, and in the oak room a four-poster with carved canopy, copied from a Flemish bed in Lindisfarne Castle (on Holy Island), complete with a secret cupboard to hold a shotgun – necessary bedside equipment in the troubled times of three centuries ago.

Celia is a fount of information on local history and what to see. Close by is one of the National Trust's biggest houses, Wallington Hall (very fine grounds), with others not far afield – Cragside, Belsay and a great number of castles. Capability Brown was born in the area, there are Pre-Raphaelite associations, and the whole region is one of impressive landscapes – from the hills and valleys of the Cheviots to the dramatic coastline more fully described elsewhere.

Flemish bed

SHOTTLE HALL FARM

C D H PT S-C

Shottle, west of Belper, Derbyshire, DE5 2EB   Tel: 077 389 276

9 bedrooms (single, double or family) from £15. Discount for over 65s or long stays. Rooms have central heating; armchairs; views of country or garden. Tea/coffee facilities available. No smoking.
Dinner £8.50 for 4 courses (limited choice) and coffee, at 7pm. Special diets if ordered. Packed lunches, snacks. Coffee, tea, free. Drinks can be ordered.
Sitting-room with central heating. Games room with snooker and TV; bar.
Garden and farmland.
Nearest main road A517 from Ashbourne to Belper.

The house is over a century old and has all the solid Victorian quality of that period: big rooms, fine ceilings and doors, dignity in every detail. Not only the bedrooms but even the bathrooms are large and close-carpeted, with paintwork and everything else in pristine condition. As well as a sizeable sitting-room, there are two dining-rooms – one is used for breakfasts because it gets the morning sun. From both, the huge windows have views of hills and of the fertile valley stretching below the house – much of it is the Matthews' land, on which 120 cows graze (and they also grow cereals). There are a rose garden and lawns – and not another house in sight.

Philip is a former county chairman of the National Farmers Union, a governor of the county agricultural college and an extremely interesting person with whom to discuss agricultural politics, Common Market affairs and so forth. Occasionally, vintage cars rally here. Her guests enjoy Phyllis's straightforward home cooking. A typical dinner menu might include: salmon mousse, chicken in apricot sauce, meringue with raspberries, English cheeses, and coffee with cream. Phyllis collects antique cheese dishes; and has other antiques for sale.

Shottle is in the middle of a rural area of fine landscapes. Close by are the Derbyshire Dales and the Peak District (described elsewhere). The Matlocks are a hilly area with pretty villages to be found. The old spa of Matlock Bath has interesting places to visit (stately gardens, wildlife park, model village, a museum of mining, and the tower, terraces and caverns of Abraham's Heights). Cromford is both attractive and historic, with Arkwright's first mill, old waterside buildings, a good bookshop etc. At Crich is a tramway museum. There are six stately homes (including Chatsworth), a museum of childhood and innumerable good walks in the Peak District, the famous Alton Towers gardens and leisure park, and a cable-car up the Heights of Abraham.

Readers' comments: Lovely room, excellent dinner: a winner. Good and friendly. Wonderful! Delightfully warm and friendly couple. Superb cook. Thoroughly enjoyed our stay, charming and friendly people. Very impressed; could not have been more helpful.

If, when touring, you ask a host to book your next stop – at another *Staying Off the Beaten Track* house – remember to pay the cost of the telephone call.

SHOULDER OF MUTTON INN
C(3) D

Kirby Hill, north of Richmond, North Yorkshire, DL4 7JH   Tel: 0748 2772

5 bedrooms (double) from £12.90, or £21.50 including dinner. Less for 3 nights or bargain breaks. Rooms have central heating; shower or bathroom; TV, armchairs; views of country; tea/coffee facilities.
Dinner 7.30–9pm. Special diets if ordered. Bar lunches and packed lunches. Drinks can be ordered.
Nearest main road A66 from Scotch Corner to Penrith.

The Shoulder of Mutton is the sort of ivy-covered village inn to stay in if you like talking to the locals in a beamy, stone-walled bar in the evening – in fact, holiday-makers have been known to flee here from the formal atmosphere of a nearby hotel of the grander kind. There is no sitting room, however, but a pool room. Now run by Hylton and Shirley Pyner, the inn has been extended to create a restaurant where you can order such dishes as steaks, guinea-fowl (in a sauce of asparagus, mushroom and cream), or plaice stuffed with smoked salmon and prawns.

Kirby Hill is a small village, complete with green and old church. As the name suggests, it stands on a hill giving impressive views of the valley, which extends as far as the North York Moors. It is in a quiet spot close to the A1 and also to the historic town of Richmond, with its Georgian theatre and Norman castle, Barnard Castle and the Bowes Museum. The Shoulder of Mutton is popular with race-goers, for Catterick is also within a few miles. You can do day-trips to Hadrian's Wall, Durham Cathedral, York and the superb coastline of Northumberland and North Yorkshire.

Readers' comments: Super position, nice people. Idyllic; view from our corner room was magic; good food and attentive owners.

Prices are the minimum *per person* in a double room at the beginning of the year.

In holiday areas, travel on any day other than a summer Saturday if you can. Make ferry, Motorail or coach/train reservations well in advance if travelling at such periods.

It's best to stay at least 2–3 days: you cannot possibly appreciate an area if you only stay overnight (prices per night are often less, too, if you stay on). The vouchers on page **ii** are usable for 3-night stays.

SINGLETON LODGE

C D PT X

Lodge Lane, Singleton, east of Blackpool, Lancashire, FY6 8LT
Tel: 0253 883854

10 bedrooms (single, double or family) from £15. Less for 7 nights. Rooms have central heating; shower or bathroom; TV; views of country or garden; tea/coffee facilities.
Dinner from £8 for 5 courses (with choices) and coffee, or à la carte, from 7pm. Special diets if ordered. Snacks. Coffee, tea, for a charge. Drinks can be ordered.

4 sitting-rooms with central heating, open fire, TV, books; bar.
Large garden with croquet and swing, and pastures.
Nearest main road A585 from Preston to Fleetwood.

This early 18th-century house has played many roles – a vicarage, a school, the home of Fleetwood admirals, a farmhouse (as it was when I first included it in this book) and now – though Alan Smith still owns and farms from it – a hotel.

Beyond the handsome panelled doorway of the mellow brick front is now an elegant sitting-room with silvery-blue armchairs of buttoned velvet, cream walls hung with Victorian watercolours and big sash windows overlooking a lawn with rustic seats. There is a pink-and-pine bar with log fire; and in the dining-room are lace-clothed tables with peach velvet chairs.

Bedrooms are now of a similar standard – specially made frilled and flowery bedlinen features in most of them, colour schemes are restful (cream-and-pink or cream-and-blue, for instance), one has fine inlaid furniture and another a romantic, canopied bed. Upstairs is a second, small sitting-room for quiet reading.

Ann's chef now produces meals with such classic dishes as veal in a sherry and cream sauce, duckling with Madeira and cherries, scallops Mornay or salmon in cucumber sauce.

It's a tranquil place, yet Blackpool is easily accessible for its sands and entertainments, or the quieter resort of Lytham St Anne's. There are plenty of stately homes to visit, the port of Fleetwood, Lancaster's historic streets, old Glasson Dock, the great sandy bay of Morecambe, Garstang (market town) and the magnificent, wild Trough of Bowland. The Lake District is within easy motoring distance. Shooting and fishing can be arranged.

In the immediate neighbourhood are plenty of good walks. Nearby Poulton-le-Fylde has an ancient church, stocks and fish stones. For garden-lovers: Stanley Park, Jubilee Gardens at Fleetwood and Barton Grange at Preston.

Readers' comments: Very welcoming. Remarkable value.

> **Book well ahead:** many of these houses have few rooms. Do not expect dinner if you have not booked it.

THE SKAKES

C D PT

Glewstone, south-west of Ross-on-Wye, Herefordshire, HR9 6AZ
Tel: 098 984 456

8 bedrooms (double or family) from £9.65. Less for 3 nights or bargain breaks. Rooms have central heating; views of country or garden.

Dinner £5.50 for 3 courses and coffee, at 6.30pm. Vegetarian or special diets if ordered. Packed lunches. Morning tea and late drink, free. Non-residents not admitted. Drinks can be ordered. No smoking.

2 sitting-rooms with central heating, open fire, TV, books.

Grounds Grassland.

Nearest main road A4137 from Monmouth to Hereford.

An expressive Norse word, skakes means 'a place of twisting tracks' – which well describes this part of the Herefordshire countryside. The 18th-century house is now the home of Raymond Vivian and his wife Beris whose love of cooking was a prime reason why they decided to run a guest-house.

A typical meal might comprise mushroom soup and rolls (both home-made), followed by spatchcock – a Tudor recipe for baking chicken with a crisp coating of crumbs – with peas and potatoes in a mustard-and-cream sauce, then Austrian coffee-cake. Meals are served in a former barn, overlooking a herb garden. Like other rooms, it has chunky stone walls. Interesting objects give the house character – an heirloom grandfather clock 8 feet tall, horse harness and pitchforks found on the land, a collection of old bottles and jars (to which visitors contribute); outside, a working pump and an old stone cider-press. Bedrooms are pleasantly decorated, with louvred cupboards. There is a well-planned family room on the ground floor, the children's end curtained off from the rest.

Most visitors come to enjoy walking and birdwatching, but there is plenty of sightseeing too. Hereford and its cathedral are near, also Chepstow (castle) and Bath (elegant spa town). Some of England's most scenic areas are round here: Symonds Yat, the Wye Valley, Brecon Beacons and the Black Mountains.

For explanation of code letters (**C, D, H, PT, S, S-C, X**) **see page xxviii.**

Inclusive terms for dinner, bed-and-breakfast (particularly for a week) can be much lower than those quoted here for these items taken separately. For short-notice bookings you may be able to get a reduction.

No proprietor wants to have a room standing empty. This particularly applies to Sunday nights. Some hotels make a discount if you want only two courses from a three-course menu.

There is no point in turning up with a dog or child in tow if the description does not say these are accepted; nor in expecting a garden, or alcoholic drinks, if these are not indicated.

SLIPWAY HOTEL *New*
Port Isaac, north-east of Padstow, Cornwall, PL29 3RH   Tel: 0208 880264

11 bedrooms (single, double or family) from £17. Some have own shower; phone; central heating; views of harbour; balcony. (Washing-machine on request.)
Dinner A la carte or £10.95 for 3 courses (with choices) and coffee, at 7.30pm. Vegetarian or special diets if ordered. Lunches, packed lunches, snacks. Tea, coffee, extra. Drinks can be ordered.
2 sitting-rooms with central heating, TV, books; bar.
Nearest main road A39 from Bude to Wadebridge.
Closed from early November–mid-March

Slate pillars and great beams give character to the dining-room – the most important room in this small harbourside hotel, for the food is its particular attraction. The room is on two levels with a gallery, and there are tapestries on the white stone walls.

Once, this was a ships' chandlery shop and, in converting it to a restaurant-cum-hotel, Graham and Ruth Carpenter have preserved most of the old features (some of which date from 1527).

Dinners here offer such choices as seafood pancakes or (an almost forgotten recipe now) mulligatawny soup; chicken Marengo or salmon from the Tamar River; apple pie with clotted cream. Afterwards, a comfortable sitting-room awaits upstairs.

The bedrooms here vary – some have harbour views; some, stone walls and beamed-ceilings. Children love the ones that are tucked under the eaves.

Port Isaac, at the foot of a steep lane, is still a fishing village of slate-hung cottages (it supplies crabs, for instance, to the hotel), and from it run footpaths along the coastline, which is spectacular hereabouts and frequented by a great variety of seabirds.

Resorts like Newquay and Bude are soon reached, as well as tourist honeypots such as Tintagel (castle ruins and Merlin's cave) and Polperro. But in the immediate vicinity there is plenty to see, and with fewer people about: Tregeare Rounds (an Iron Age fort), for instance; Rock, with ferry to ancient Padstow and Prideaux Place (a Tudor house with carvings by Grinling Gibbons); inland, Bodmin Moor – some of it really wild and little-visited, with peaks rearing up dramatically, and at other places green and flowery; Bodmin, market town; Lanhydrock, a 17th-century NT house; attractive villages like Blisland and Bolventor, the latter with Daphne du Maurier's Jamaica Inn, or Altarnum which has 'the Cathedral of the Moor'. Everywhere there are legends connected with King Arthur (Dozmary Pond is said to be where the sword Excalibur was thrown in, and Camelot was reputedly at Camelford).

Many of the houses in this area incorporate local slate as well as Cornwall's ever-present granite, from which the hundreds of Celtic crosses that dot the countryside also are made, many of them from the era when Irish saints sailed here in such numbers to convert the Cornish to Christianity. Centuries later, Wesley was to come on a similar mission, leaving a trail of small Methodist chapels in his wake.

SLOOP INN *New*   **C D S-C**

Bantham, south-east of Plymouth, Devon, TQ7 3AJ   Tel: 0548 560489

5 bedrooms (single, double or family) from
£16. Less for 2 nights and bargain breaks.
Some have own bath/shower; TV; tea/coffee
facilities; central heating; views of sea, river
or country. (Washing-machine on request.)
Dinner A la carte, at 7–10pm. Vegetarian or
special diets if ordered. Lunches, packed
lunches, snacks. Tea, coffee, extra. Drinks
can be ordered.
Nearest main road A379 from Kingsbridge
to Plymouth.
Closed from mid-December–mid-January

It goes without saying that this 400-year-old inn by the sea has a history of
smuggling. One owner was in fact a notorious wrecker, luring ships (by means of
false lights) onto rocks in order to plunder them. Since the law was that 'if any man
escape to shore alive, the ship is no wreck – and so plundering it would be theft',
wreckers were murderous wretches too. Neil Girling can tell you many stories of
the smugglers and point out places in the village where they hid their kegs of
French brandy. Once, the Sloop minted its own coins (some are now in the
interesting museum at Kingsbridge) with which to pay for goods and services – the
coins were usable only to buy drinks at the Sloop: good business!

The inn is unspoilt: everything one hopes that a lively waterfront inn will be but
rarely is, low-beamed, stone-flagged and snug. Some walls are of stone and some
panelled. One of its several bars is made from old boat-timbers. You can take on
the locals at a game of darts or table-skittles after enjoying an excellent bar meal or
stroll down to the sandy dunes to watch the sun set over the sea. Bathing, building
sandcastles and exploring rock-pools delight children; and there is surfing. Many
of the unpretentiously furnished bedrooms have a view of the sea or River Avon.
There is a yard and well at the back with seats.

Soups are home-made and ham home-cured; smoked salmon, crabs and steaks
are all local produce; granary bread is served. Fish is, of course, particularly good
and fresh. All portions are generous.

Bantham is one of Devon's most ancient villages (the remains of prehistoric
dwellings were laid bare in an 18th-century storm, and there was a Roman camp
here later). Once, its main livelihood was pilchard-fishing but there are no more
pilchards now.

The whole area is remote, peaceful and unspoilt with good walks through
particularly beautiful countryside or along the coastal footpath; and yet the
historic cities of Plymouth and Exeter are within reach, and the great resort of
Torquay. In early spring, wildflowers are everywhere and the blue waves are
already beginning to be dotted with boating enthusiasts. This is a rich farming area
('the fruitfullest part of Devonshire'), with villages full of well-kept colourwashed
cottages thickly thatched.

On the other side of the Avon is Bigbury where a strange, long-legged 'tram'
takes people across the sea to Burgh Island and further still is Newton Ferrers on
the Yealm estuary, a medley of gabled houses and thatched cottages in steep lanes.
On May Day, Noss Mayo still has a traditional procession.

SNOWFORD HALL FARM C

Hunningham, east of Leamington Spa, Warwickshire, CV33 9ES
Tel: 0926 632297

3 bedrooms (double or family) from £11. Rooms have central heating; two have shower; armchairs; views of country or garden. No smoking.

Dinner £9 for 4 courses and coffee, at 6.30pm. Coffee, tea, free. Non-residents not admitted. Drinks can be brought in. No smoking.

Sitting-room with central heating, TV, books, piano.

Garden and farmland.

Nearest main road A423 from Coventry to Banbury.

A very long drive through fields leads to this spacious 18th-century house at the heart of a 300-acre farm (cattle and crops) with fine views around it. One enters through an interesting hall with old china on a big dresser and polished wood floor. The huge sitting-room is very attractively furnished. Here and there around the house are many things made by Rudi Hancock herself, a skilled craftswoman – samplers, for example, and corn dollies; and furniture which she has restored.

Dutch-born, she was previously a cookery teacher and so (except at harvests, when she has no time to cook evening meals) you can expect a good dinner, if booked in advance. She uses many home-grown vegetables and fruit, and makes her own jam.

The most interesting of the bedrooms has a very unusual and decorative Dutch bed of solid mahogany, handsomely carved.

Snowford Hall is near Leamington Spa and its environs, described elsewhere, and such sights as Warwick and Kenilworth castles, Stratford-upon-Avon, Coventry Cathedral and Draycote water country park. Packwood House has an exceptional garden, and the National Centre for Organic Gardening is near. Southam is an old market town; Stoneleigh a mediaeval village (with the great National Agricultural Centre outside it). And all around are some of England's finest landscapes.

Readers' comments: Lovely rooms; gorgeous, silent countryside. Wonderful reception, beautiful house, plenty of very good food, wholly pleasurable.

Houses which do *not* take children tend to have vacancies in July and August.

All prices are inclusive of any VAT or service charge. They are minimum prices: superior rooms or high-season bookings may cost more.

Unless otherwise agreed, send a 10% deposit when confirming your booking.

SOMERSET HOUSE

C(9) **D H PT S X**

35 Bathwick Hill, Bath, Avon, BA2 6LD   Tel: 0225 66451

9 bedrooms (single, double or family) from £28.50 with dinner. Less for 5 nights. Rooms have central heating; bathroom; phone, armchairs; views of city or garden; tea-making facilities; No smoking.
Dinner 4 courses and coffee, at 7pm (not on Sundays). Vegetarian and special diets if ordered. Lunches on Sundays. Drinks can be ordered. No smoking.
2 sitting-rooms with central heating, open fire, TV, books, piano. No smoking.
Large garden
Nearest main road A36 from Bath to Southampton.

The Seymours moved to this handsome Georgian mansion from a smaller house down the steep hill. Above the Doric-columned portico is a decorative iron verandah; wisteria and roses climb up the walls of honey-coloured stone.

The entrance hall (marble-tiled and with a Greek key border round the ceiling) leads to a sitting-room, with conservatory opening onto lawn, grand piano, fire and abundant books and records. There is one bedroom on the ground floor. The dining-room is below stairs (it, too, has an open fire), furnished with pine dresser.

On the first floor is another sitting-room with a particularly pretty plasterwork ceiling and very old Venetian glass chandelier. The original panelled shutters flank the hugh sash windows; outside is the long verandah, with fine city views.

Bedrooms are large and pleasantly furnished, many with antique fireplaces (one has an antique loo) and attractive views. Some have Laura Ashley fabrics.

Malcolm (once director of a regional tourist board) is a mine of information on what to see in the neighbourhood. Throughout the year he arranges weekends with special themes: Georgian Bath, exploring the Mendip and Cotswold hills, Brunel, or opera whenever the Welsh National Opera Company visits nearby Bristol. Jean, formerly a teacher, enjoys finding recipes appropriate to each of these occasions (even Czech ones on the night when a Janacek opera was being performed).

At breakfast, few people opt for the full cooked version because there is such an array of home-baked breads (nutty, spicy or fruity), preserves, muesli, freshly squeezed fruit juice and so forth; often haddock, kidneys, Cumberland sausage or muffins are offered. As to dinner, when nothing more exotic is afoot, Jean may produce something like (for example) game soup, her own 'rolypoly, gammon and spinach' recipe with home-grown vegetables, and apples in cider served with home-made ice cream. She precedes meals with a 'lecturette' on the recipes.

Perhaps the greatest glory is the garden. Every tree flowers at a different season, and the centrepiece is a great 300-year-old Judas tree – at its purple best in May. All around, between beds of paeonies and columbines, is a 7¼-inch rail track installed by a former owner. Adjoining is a herb and fruit garden.

Readers' comments: The best establishment I've stayed at, where people count; the cooking reinvigorates the taste-buds. Superb comfort and food. Excellent accommodation; the most interesting and nicest food we have ever experienced. Particularly delighted. A favourite. The Seymours make guests welcome; one meets interesting people there. We stay regularly. Comfortable; very good food.

266

SPIDERS BARN

C(4) **D PT S**

Cross Keys, Pickwick, north of Corsham, Wiltshire, SN13 0DT
Tel: 0249 712012

4 bedrooms (single, double or family) from £12. Much less for 2 nights or bargain breaks. Rooms have central heating; armchairs; views of countryside or garden. Breakfast in bed is available.
Sitting-room with central heating, open fire, TV, books.
Garden
Nearest main road A4 from Chippenham to Bath.

The Pickwick Papers got its name from this hamlet on the way to Bath, for it was here – at the Cross Keys Inn – that Dickens reputedly stayed while writing his book. The old coaching stables, adjoining the Cross Keys (which provides good bar meals; or you can eat at the Biddestone Arms), are now the very well converted home of Anne Norris who takes guests for bed-and-breakfast. (There is a kitchen in which to prepare your own snacks, too.)

In the stone-walled sitting-room with parquet floor are a huge chesterfield and pieces of antique furniture. Every bedroom is attractive, with the emphasis on well chosen fabrics, stripped pine for the latched doors and the staircase, good carpets, cane chairs and pleasant colour schemes such as coffee and cream.

Wiltshire is, I feel, an undervalued county, for in addition to its rolling countryside there is so much to see – outstandingly, its 4500 prehistoric sites (of which Stonehenge may be the most famous but is less impressive than Avebury). South of Spiders Barn are Wilton, Stourhead, Mompesson House (within the precincts of Salisbury Cathedral); even nearer, Bowood, Lacock Abbey and Longleat. In fact, the county has more listed buildings than any other, and many of its villages are little beauties.

Readers' comments: Very comfortable. Made most welcome.

Two-thirds of the houses in this book have bargain breaks or other discounts on offer, some exclusive to readers. Only a third raise prices at the peak of summer.

Some hotels and even farms offer special Christmas holidays; but, unless otherwise indicated (by the code letter X at top of entry), those in this book will then be closed.

If you want absolute quiet, avoid any place that takes children or has a bar open to non-residents. Inns sometimes get extensions to their licensing hours for late private parties; and may lack quiet sitting-rooms.

SPORTSMAN'S ARMS

C D PT

Wath-in-Nidderdale, Pateley Bridge, west of Harrogate, North Yorkshire, HG3 5PP   Tel: 0423 711306

6 bedrooms (single, double or family) from £17.50. Less in winter and for bargain breaks. Rooms have electric heaters; shower, wc; TV, armchairs; views of country or garden; tea/coffee facilities. No smoking.
Dinner £8.50 for 3 courses and coffee, from 7.30–9.45pm. Special diets or vegetarian dishes if ordered. Lunches, packed lunches, snacks. Coffee, tea, for a charge. Drinks can be ordered.
2 sitting-rooms with open fire, TV, books; bar.
Garden with badminton.

A delightful place, in a delightful setting: Wath is a hamlet tucked away beside the River Nidd.

A pine-panelled bar leads to the dining-room (and, beyond this, two sitting-rooms) which has palms, pink-and-grey colour scheme and bentwood chairs, reflected by the light of cut-crystal candle-lamps in the big mirror of a carved Victorian sideboard. Jane Carter has chosen blue/green/beige colour schemes for bedrooms in which curtains and bedspreads match. Huge Victorian baths have been retained. Ray, who used to be a catering lecturer, cooks all the meals, assisted by a team of enthusiastic young people. A typical summer dinner: salad with scallops and sweetbreads; salmon filled with prawns, and Hollandaise sauce; and summer pudding with cream. The cooking is exceptional, and most produce is local. Wines are outstanding and reasonably priced.

Lovely Nidderdale, being outside the National Park area, is less frequented than some other dales. It has some very old reservoirs created by damming the River Nidd, now well naturalized and full of ducks, geese, herons and other birds (200 species have been recorded, including some rare migrants). The effect is reminiscent of the Lake District. How Stean is a romantic gorge with a stream cascading into a rocky cleft 70 feet deep (good home-made cakes at the modest café nearby). From the churchyard at Middlemoor, high up at the head of the dale, there are spectacular views down the length of it.

From here one can easily motor to York, Ripon spa (with gardens and cathedral), and a great array of spectacular abbeys – Fountains, Bolton, Jervaulx, Rievaulx and Byland. Also Harewood Hall, Newby Hall and garden, and half a dozen castles; as well as the strange natural formations of Brimham Rocks and Stump Cross caves. Pateley Bridge is a regular Britain in Bloom winner.

Readers' comments: Food fabulous, staff well trained and friendly. Food very good, and staff appeared to be one largish happy family. Delightful; good food, excellent value. Could not be faulted; food, rooms and surroundings all outstanding in every detail.

268

SPRING END   **C D S X**
Low Row, west of Richmond, North Yorkshire, DL11 6NL   Tel: 0748 86341

11 bedrooms (single, double or family) from £22 with dinner. Less for 7 nights and bargain breaks. Rooms have central heating or electric heaters; shower or bathroom; TV, armchairs; views of country; tea/coffee facilities.
Dinner 4 courses (with choices) and coffee, at 6.30pm. Vegetarian dishes if ordered.

Packed lunches, snacks. Coffee, tea, free. Drinks can be ordered.
3 sitting-rooms with central heating, open fire, books; bar.
Small garden
Nearest main road A6108 from Leyburn to Scotch Corner.
Closed January and February

Swaledale is a place for active holidays: the roads are too narrow, steep and twisting for relaxed motoring, and there are few contrived 'attractions' for the passive holiday-maker. So the Thompsons have organized their guest-house with walkers in mind.

After a day on the fells, you can have a drink at the bar, eat a meal of generous and fairly simple food (such as leek soup, chicken casserole and chocolate gâteau), and then collapse in a comfortable sitting-room, where there are shelves of books – guides, local history, and fiction – but no television to kill conversation. On sale is a huge selection of books of local interest as well as some well chosen souvenirs.

Spring End is a long and rambling house, with bedrooms in a modern annexe. The house is furnished for comfort rather than effect, and Marion and David Thompson radiate unpretentious hospitality.

Spring End takes a little finding – it is perched on the fell side with spectacular views, with a village far below – but, once there, visitors tend mainly to abandon the car until it is time to go home again. They enjoy visiting various waterfalls, Kisdon Hill, and art galleries at Reeth. There is more about Swaledale under other entries.

Readers' comments: Very comfortable, marvellous food, good company. Homely and casual, ideal for walkers.

Families which pick establishments with plenty of games, swimming-pool, animals, etc., or that are near free museums, parks and walks, can save a lot on keeping youngsters entertained.

Prices are the minimum *per person* in a double room at the beginning of the year.

THE STABLES

Bootle village, near Millom, Cumbria, LA19 5TD   Tel: 06578 644

C PT S

2 bedrooms (single, double or family) for £19.50 with dinner. Less for 2 nights. Rooms have central heating; own bathroom and wc; armchairs; views of country or garden.

Dinner 4 courses and coffee, served by arrangement. Special diets if ordered.

Drinks can be brought in. Free tea on arrival.

2 sitting-rooms with central heating, open fire, TV, books.

Garden

Nearest main road A595 from Barrow to Whitehaven.

Where four horse-drawn coaches were once parked is now a huge sitting-room, with picture windows on three sides. This was the carriage-room of stables which used to serve the great house of a family that grew rich from the manufacture of candles (their tallow was made from sheep fat). The original beams and doors have been kept and the fireplace is simply an opening in the old brick wall, so the room retains something of the character of the original building. Similarly, when the tack-room was converted into a dining-room the hooks on which harness used to hang were kept.

All this transformation was the work of Pete and Mary Walker, who now run the old stables as a guest-house. They used to come to this part of Cumbria for their holidays, and fell in love with it.

The deep-carpeted bedrooms are attractive. One, decorated in a coffee-and-cream colour scheme, has a huge circular window opposite the bed. There are always flowers in the bedrooms (and on the candle-lit dining-tables too). Both have private bathrooms.

The same menu is never repeated within a fortnight and, as far as possible, Mary cooks whatever dishes her guests like best. A typical menu might be: eggs with home-made mayonnaise; a joint or chicken which guests carve themselves, or perhaps local trout with almonds; lemon meringue pie, cheese and coffee. As an alternative to traditional breakfasts, Mary offers kedgeree, smoked mackerel or haddock and other choices.

The two are a particularly warm, genial couple who make their guests feel at home – for instance, encouraging them to wander off with a tray of tea to where, at the end of the little bluebell copse, their bubbling stream joins the River Annas. They grow vegetables and fruit, have an array of wild daffodils that now brings viewers from miles, and forget-me-nots; and laid a terrace of great slabs from St Bees, the red sandstone headland along the coast. There are marvellous views over lawn and fields to the hills, and you can smell the sea in the air.

Readers' comments: Memorable holiday. Warm and friendly welcome, excellent accommodation, beautiful situation, superb meals – a jewel of a place.

270

STAPLEFORD HALL *New*
Tarvin, east of Chester, Cheshire, CH3 8HH   Tel: 0829 40202

2 bedrooms (single, double or family) from £18. Less for 3 nights and bargain breaks. Both have own bath/shower; TV; tea/coffee facilities; central heating; views of country or garden. No smoking.
Sitting-room with central heating, open fire, TV, books. No smoking.
Large garden
Nearest main road A51 from Chester to Nantwich.

'His table was bountiful . . . he made provision for the multitude'. This was said of John Bruen, squire of the original Hall (the present building dates from 1789). He used to hunt in nearby Delamere Forest with a dozen 'great-mouthed dogs' until converted to Puritanism, when he maintained his own preacher and chapel instead. On his estate were warrens of conies (rabbits), fishponds and a flight of pigeons kept for the table.

These days, Margaret Winward's table provides only breakfast for visitors: most dine in Chester, only a quarter-hour away, or at the Rising Sun in Tarporley, returning to the modern comforts of conventionally furnished and spacious bedrooms, and to enjoy either log fires indoors or else the peace of the large garden (with immense beech trees, tennis and croquet), surrounded by acres of dairy-farm. There are views of two castles (ruined Beeston is particularly romantic, perched on a steep hill with terraced woods and overhanging rocks below it) and of the hills of Wales.

The nearest small town, Tarporley, is surrounded by woods and rich farmland, its ancient churchyard filled with roses in summer. North of it is Delamere Forest, 4000 acres of dense woodland concealing bright-gleaming meres.

Still further, in the direction of the Mersey estuary, are Daresbury (in the church of which Alice and the Mad Hatter are depicted in stained glass, for this was the birthplace of Lewis Carroll), and Helsby hill from which there are fine views across marshes to the estuary – and of climbers practising on its rocks. Liverpool is soon reached from here, via the Mersey tunnel – well deserving of a visit to see its waterside maritime museum, two modern cathedrals, outstanding art gallery and concert hall among much else.

Also near Tarporley is 18th-century **Duddon Lodge** (tel: 082 924 372), where Mrs Joynson was still in the throes of upgrading the accommodation when I visited. This house would appeal to anyone interested in the arts, not only for its contents (antiques, grand pianos, artistic wallpapers, paintings, porcelain figures) but because Mrs Joynson is well informed about arts festivals, opera and similar events in the region. One four-poster. B & b only, which costs much less than

at Stapleford Hall. (There is a covered swimming-pool and sauna, croquet and lawn tennis.)

THE STEPPES

C(12) **D H X**

Ullingswick, north-east of Hereford, HR1 3JG   Tel: 0432 820424

3 bedrooms (double or family) from £16.50. Less for 3 nights or bargain breaks. Rooms have central heating; shower and wc; TV, telephone, armchairs; views of country or garden. Tea and coffee facilities available. Laundry room (for a charge).

Dinner £12.50 for 4 courses and coffee. Choices if ordered. Vegetarian or special diets if ordered. At 7pm or later on request. Lunches, packed lunches, snacks. Coffee, tea for a charge. Non-residents not admitted. Drinks can be ordered. No smoking.

Sitting-room with central heating, log stove, TV, books.

Large garden

Nearest main road A417 from Gloucester to Leominster.

This is one of the prettiest old houses in this book, very attractively furnished by its owners Henry and Tricia Howland. Part of the house is mediaeval, most of it 17th century. Originally, the ground floor was one great hall (the old flagstoned floor is still intact).

The dining-room has a great inglenook fireplace with its original log-irons, and there is a bread oven adjoining its chimney. In the thick walls are original built-in cupboards, and between some rooms 'borrowed lights' (that is, internal windows) with their original glass. The red-and-black tiles of the dining-room are also old.

The beamed dining-room, with a patterned rug on the tiled floor and some dried hop-vines draped across the fireplace, has great character. There are corn dollies on the white walls, flowers on each table, interesting prints, and a melodiously chiming clock.

There is a small bar which includes half a dozen kinds of local cider, from clear-and-sparkling to rough-and-heavy. In the sitting-room, flowery chairs and pale velvet curtains contrast with the rugged stone fireplace. Quaint pastry dolls hang on some walls – made by Tricia (a few for sale).

Each bedroom has a different and colourful style – raspberry-pink wall and rosebud fabrics in one, crisp blue-and-white in another; built-in pine storage fitments, pretty lace curtains or deep-pile carpets contribute to the individual character of each one. Each has its own shower. Views are of rounded hills, sheep or cows, hop kilns and the old garden where collared doves perch in cherry trees or lilac spreads its fragrance in early summer. The old pump still draws water to fill a stone trough.

Tricia cooks a wide range of very imaginative dishes and ensures that not one is repeated during a guest's stay. One local speciality which she serves is cheese-and-cider soup (chilled and creamy); another unusual starter is grapefruit with mint ice. The main course might be boned duck with a stuffing of beef, onions, bacon and herbs, or turkey saté (served with peanut sauce and cucumber relish – a Thai recipe). A pudding such as zabaglione, or raspberry meringue gâteau may follow.

Readers' comments: Thoroughly enjoyed it. Superb. 5-star food! Attentive and comfortable. Local food specials and the puddings were excellent. A wonderful few days; delicious and individual cooking served on lovely china; cannot praise it enough. Imaginative dishes. One of the prettiest houses, wonderful garden. First-rate, quiet, cordon bleu cooking. Enchanting house, superb food.

272

STOKE FARM   C PT S S-C

Broad Chalke, west of Salisbury, Wiltshire, SP5 5EF   Tel: 0722 780209

2 bedrooms (double) from £16. Rooms have central heating or electric heaters; shower or bathroom; TV, armchairs; views of farm or garden; tea/coffee facilities.
Dinner £9 for 3 courses and coffee, at 7pm. Special diets if ordered. Coffee, tea, for a charge. Non-residents not admitted. Drinks can be ordered or brought in.
Sitting-room with central heating, open fire, TV, books, indoor games (including billiards, darts), piano, record-player.
Garden with tennis and croquet.
Nearest main road A354 from Salisbury to Blandford.
Closed November–February

This is a gracious house at the heart of a 1000-acre farm overlooking the Ebble Valley. It is very typical of many other such farms set among the rolling downs of Wiltshire: a mixture of arable fields and of pastures for beef-cattle and dairy-cows.

One approaches the house past mossy rickstones, old cattle-troughs now filled with flowers, and tree-strumps overgrown by periwinkles. A lovely magnolia covers the front wall. Inside, the early Victorian features have been retained – panelled doors, arches and window shutters. My bedroom had windows on three sides with pretty 'cottage garden' curtains and views across fields of cows to the hills. Late in the year, the pens immediately below are full of calves. Throughout the house, soft colours predominate, with carefully arranged flowers, baskets of trailing plants and interesting paintings well lighted (one is by Cecil Beaton, who used to live in the village). There are good carpets and attractive wallpapers everywhere, even in the bathroom. In the big sitting-room, deep armchairs are grouped around a log fire, a record-player and well stocked bookshelves. Last but far from least, Mrs Pickford is an excellent cook. Meals are served in a dining-room that still has the old built-in bread oven, with local trout and pheasant often on the menu.

Many guests go walking. The Pickfords have produced their own map of local footpaths, all well waymarked in this region, which lead down to watercress beds in the valley or up to the Ridgeway which was once a drove road for oxen being taken to market.

I first stayed here in order to visit nearby Salisbury and its cathedral. In addition there is plenty to see in the area – Elizabethan Breamore House, attractive villages (like Downton, Fordingbridge or Tilshead), the Celtic fort on top of Figsbury Hill, Old Sarum with the ruins of its Norman castle on another hilltop, the Roman villa at Rockbourne, Wilton's historic carpet factory and Wilton House, for example. Other leading sights: Stonehenge, the New Forest, two shire horse centres, and plenty of gardens (garden centres too).

Readers' comments: The best b & b in England! Everything about Stoke Farm would be difficult to fault. Very pleasant and helpful. Wonderful! Most comfortable; huge towels, wonderful bathroom. Great kindness.

For explanation of code letters (**C, D, H, PT, S, S-C, X**) **see page xxviii.**

273

STONE HOUSE FARM

C D PT X

Tillington, north-west of Hereford, HR4 8LP   Tel: 0432 760631

3 bedrooms (single, double or family) from £14. Much less for 2 nights or bargain breaks. Rooms have central heating or electric heaters; armchairs; views of country and farmland; tea/coffee facilities on request. Laundry facilities.

Dinner £6 for 4 courses and coffee, served at any time. Special diets if ordered. Lunches, packed lunches, snacks. Coffee, tea, for a charge. Drinks can be ordered. Free tea on arrival.

Sitting-room with central heating, open fire, TV, books, piano, record-player; but sometimes visitors are allotted the 'den'. No smoking.

Grounds Farmland.

Nearest main road A480 from Hereford.

This is a good, solid stone farmhouse typical of many in the rich agricultural lands of Herefordshire. Well away from any town or road, it is completely peaceful, and with fine views at both front (distant Aconbury Hill beyond a small orchard) and back (field of grazing horses and then woodlands). At the front, a small garden (with a seat on the stone terrace) still has the old pump.

In the sitting-room, big velvet armchairs surround the fireplace, but in winter guests use a cosy 'den' with wood stove. The dining-room, too, has an open fire, and a large oak table laid with Royal Worcester bone china. Straightforward dinners are cooked by Judy Seaborne: typically, soup followed by a stew or roast (the farm's own beef, lamb or pork), and then perhaps a pavlova or fruit pie. Milk, butter and cream are usually from Stone House cows, and Mrs Seaborne makes all the cakes, pickles and marmalade, and will cook fish for breakfast if you prefer it. Bedrooms are comfortable; the carpeted bathroom is huge (but shared by all).

Children particularly enjoy this small farm in spring when lambs, calves and foals are to be seen. Graham Seaborne, whose family has farmed here for generations, will tell visitors where to go to watch the big cattle and horse auctions every week in Hereford, or to see cider being made and ploughing matches.

From Tillington, there are plenty of sightseeing options. The picturesque black-and-white village of Eardisland is close, as is Weobley. There are a dozen bookshops (most belonging to Richard Booth) in Hay-on-Wye, now nicknamed 'Book City'. Brecon, Offa's Dyke and numerous stately homes provide other destinations for a day out; and, as this is an area of orchards and nursery gardens, many people return home laden with pot-plants and pick-your-own soft fruits. The Malvern hills and the Black Mountains are within sight, and several market towns are nearby. Hereford Cathedral is within view. Add to these the Brecon Beacons, Radnor Forest, the 'Golden Valley', Welsh and Shropshire market towns, a motor museum, a lovely drive along Wenlock Edge, Ironbridge Industrial Museum, the Wye Valley and innumerable garden centres.

Readers' comments: Very comfortable; well fed and received with great friendliness; no book could describe the warmth and friendliness and the trouble to ensure our stay was enjoyable; accommodation and food of very high quality . . . ample. Mrs Seaborne is most welcoming. The best farmhouse we've found in 25 years. Warm and friendly home, the most enjoyable we have visited. Mrs Seaborne is an excellent cook and hostess.

274

STONE HOUSE HOTEL

Sedbusk, north of Hawes, Wensleydale, North Yorkshire, DL8 3PT
Tel: 09697 571

CDHSX

13 bedrooms (single, double or family) from £17. Less for 3 nights or bargain breaks. Rooms have central heating, electric heaters; shower or bathroom; TV, armchairs; views of country or garden; tea/coffee facilities. Clothes-washing facilities.
Dinner £10 for 4 courses (with choices) and coffee, at 7.30–8pm. Vegetarian or special diets if ordered. Lunches, packed lunches, snacks. Coffee, tea, for a charge. Drinks can be ordered.
3 sitting-rooms with central heating, open fire, TV, books, billiards, piano, record-player; bar.
Large garden with tennis lawn.
Nearest main road A684 from Hawes to Sedbergh.
Closed in mid-winter

P. G. Wodehouse, with a new novel near completion, was still searching for a good name to give his principal character. On holiday here, he sat watching village cricket – and in to bat went the Stone House gardener, *Jeeves*. Problem solved!

To this day, Stone House looks exactly right for a house-party with Bertie Wooster and Jeeves drawing up in a sports car at the front door. It was built in Edward VII's reign as a country gentleman's retreat, and some of the oak-panelled rooms, the leather club chairs, 'Spy' cartoons and racehorse shoes on the wall, the billiard table, and the library with books from floor to ceiling, have changed very little.

The present owner, Peter Taplin, is an incurable collector, and on show are his many vintage slot-machines (with a supply of pre-metric pennies with which to operate them), hundreds of old 'Dinky' cars, and antique thimbles. He and Jane have furnished the house well: red chinoiserie fabric on the bar's armchairs; comfortable cushioned seats in the dining-room (which has an aquarium built into one wall); and light, immaculate bedrooms with sprigged fabrics (four are on the ground floor), their stone-mullioned windows overlooking paved terraces, neat box borders and far views. Some bedrooms have their own conservatory/sitting area, opening onto the garden.

Peter used to be a butcher, so it is not surprising that Stone House has a good reputation for straightforward English food – roast beef and Yorkshire pudding naturally being pre-eminent, perhaps preceded by crofter's soup and followed by old-fashioned trifle.

Jeeves would have approved!

For details of the Wensleydale area, see other entries. There are waterfalls (Hardraw and Aysgarth), folk museum and market at Hawes, the Settle railway and the Buttertubs Pass – both very scenic. It is easy to reach Swaledale from here – totally different scenery from Wensleydale.

STOURCASTLE LODGE *New*   C

Gough's Close, Sturminster Newton, south-west of Shaftesbury, Dorset, DT10 1BU Tel: 0258 72320

4 bedrooms (single or double) from £15. Less for 7 nights and bargain breaks. Some have own shower; central heating; views of country or garden. (Washing-machine on request.)

Dinner £9 for 3 courses (with choices) and coffee, at 7pm. Non-residents not admitted. Vegetarian or special diets if ordered. Lunches, packed lunches, snacks. Tea, coffee, free. Drinks can be brought in.

Sitting-room with central heating, open fire, TV, books.

Small garden

Nearest main road A357 from Blandford to Wincanton.

Although just off the market-place of this little town, Gough's Close is traffic-free and peaceful: a narrow lane opening out into a green and pleasant place, with the River Stour beyond. The Lodge, which was built in 1739, has been agreeably furnished by Jill Hookham-Bassett, with soft greens and pinks predominating. Everything is very spick-and-span, the bedrooms cottagey in style, and many rooms have views of the secluded garden where one can take tea.

Jill and Ken, who achieved a gold star for cooking when he trained at Ealing Technical College, also run a catering service, so food here is well above average. A typical dinner might be: kedgeree, chicken cooked in a tarragon and mushroom sauce, and charlotte Malakoff (made with cream and almonds). An unassuming house with a lot to offer in the way of hospitality.

From the Lodge, it is easily possible to explore not only Dorset but parts of Wiltshire and even Somerset too. These are described under other entries.

Readers' comments: Friendly; eager to help and please.

When to go? Seaside resorts or other places suitable for children will be at their busiest (and dearest) in July–August and during half-term holidays (especially, in late May, which is also a bank holiday period). Other peak periods are, of course, Easter, Christmas, New Year and the bank holiday in late August. (The bank holiday in early May is not usually a peak, because it comes rather soon after Easter, but much depends on the weather.) There are local peaks, too (the Gold Cup races at Cheltenham or the regatta at Henley, for instance, are apt to fill hotels for miles around), and local troughs (Brighton, a conference centre, is least busy in high summer). You won't get much personal attention when hotels are full to bursting.

All prices are inclusive of any VAT or service charge. They are minimum prices: superior rooms or high-season bookings may cost more.

STRATFORD LODGE *New*   C(8) **PT**
4 Park Lane, Castle Road, Salisbury, Wiltshire, SP1 3NP   Tel: 0722 25177

4 bedrooms (double or family) at £16. Less for 2 nights and bargain breaks. All have own bath/shower; TV; tea/coffee facilities; central heating; views of park or garden. Non-smokers preferred. (Washing-machine on request.)
Dinner £9 for 4 courses and coffee, at 7pm. Non-residents not admitted. Vegetarian or special diets if ordered. Tea, coffee, free. Drinks can be brought in.
Sitting-room with central heating, open fire, TV, books. Non-smokers preferred.
Garden
Nearest main road A345 from Salisbury to Amesbury.

In a quiet byway overlooking a park stands a fine Victorian house, now a handsomely furnished guest-house. Jill Bayly has taken a lot of trouble to find good furniture in keeping with the style of the house. The sitting-room has much Victoriana and a large array of African violets; the pale green dining-room, a big mahogany table laid with pretty rosy china (napkins to match) and wildflower curtains at the windows. Bedrooms are attractive, particularly one with a cane and carved bedhead on a bed with a rosebud cover to complement the shell-pink walls. In another room, pale blue, a brass bed has a lace spread. After dark one can go on sitting in the garden which is enclosed by flowering shrubs, because Jill brings out candle-lamps. Beyond it is the vegetable plot which provides fresh produce.

Jill has a varied repertoire of dishes for dinner (not served on Sundays), and she cooks to a high standard. A typical menu: pears baked with Roquefort cheese; duckling with a sauce of port and black cherries; syllabub made with Tia Maria or apple strudel with clotted cream; then cheeses. Breakfasts, too, are generous, with options such as kedgeree and marmalade which she makes herself.

Salisbury is also known as New Sarum (new in 1220!) because the first town was elsewhere, on the hill now known as Old Sarum which began as an Iron Age fort – you can still see traces of a Norman cathedral up there. When it was decided to rebuild on a better site, two miles away from the water meadows, the new cathedral, with the tallest spire in England, was surrounded by grass and big walls to keep the township that followed at a respectful distance. Thus the cathedral can be well viewed all round, unlike some which have buildings crowding right up to them. Inside are fine tombs, the oldest working clock in the country, some fan vaulting, and immense cloisters. Historic houses surround the precincts, some open to the public. There is a big market in the town's central square.

Farthings, at 9 Swaynes Close (tel: 0722 330749), is quite central (there's a view of the cathedral spire over roof-tops) yet very quiet, and it has a garden with brimming flowerbeds. All rooms are immaculate, and pleasantly furnished. Gill Rodwell serves breakfast only (choices include fishcakes, crois-sants and much else). Very good value.

7 bedrooms (single or double) from £14. Less for 7 nights and bargain breaks. All have central heating; some have views of garden. No smoking.

Dinner £10 for 3 courses (with choices) and coffee, at 7–9pm. Vegetarian or special diets if ordered. Packed lunches, snacks. Tea, coffee, free. Drinks can be ordered.

Sitting-room with central heating, TV, books. No smoking.

Small garden

Nearest main road A4 from Bath to Bristol.

Closed in January

It is difficult to locate a good but inexpensive hotel in the centre of Bath, so the Strathavon is quite a find. It is in a terrace of 18th-century houses, with a very small garden at the back and a road at the front (bedrooms at back are quiet). Rooms are conventionally furnished, and immaculate.

What makes the Strathavon special, however, are Tom Waugh's outstanding gifts as a chef. I have eaten at many of Bath's innumerable restaurants but – price-for-price – never better than at the Strathavon. Small though this little hotel is, he is able to offer many choices at each course by the sensible expedient of asking visitors to make their selection by midday (he will post the menu to you). That way he can shop for and prepare every dish freshly for each person – things like a particularly good seafood mornay, as a starter, chicken breast stuffed with spinach, and delicious fresh fruit desserts. Not only does he cook well, but the food is beautifully presented.

Many of Bath's major attractions are within a short stroll. In the city centre there is much to see: the abbey, the Roman temple and baths, the botanical gardens, the shopping arcades and much else. Wells is near, as are Stourhead and Corsham Court.

Only a little further out is **Parkside**, an Edwardian villa (11 Marlborough Lane, tel: 0225 29444). The bay window of the comfortable sitting-room (with simulated coal fire) overlooks, currently, an archaeological dig in progress, with the Royal Victoria Park nearby, as well as the beautiful Botanic Gardens. The dining-room opens onto a garden with paved terrace (presided over by a teak lady from Thailand), lawn and pergola. I particularly liked bedrooms 2 and 3, on the second floor, because they are so big and airy.

Katy Putler produces not only such dinners as melon, lamb chops, blackberry parfait, and West Country cheeses but specializes in vegetarian dishes – using organic produce from one of the allotments opposite the house. Breakfast options include wholefood cereals with fruit salad, and a raw mix of celery, carrots, cucumber and onions as a refreshing change from the bacon-and-egg routine.

STREET FARMHOUSE *New*   C D X
South Warnborough, south-east of Basingstoke, Hampshire, RG25 1RS
Tel: 0256 862225

3 bedrooms (double or family) from £14. Some have own shower; all have TV; tea/coffee facilities; central heating; views of country or garden. (Washing-machine on request.) Packed lunches and snacks.
Sitting-room with central heating, open fire, TV, books.
Large garden
Nearest main road A32 from Odiham to Alton.

Two 16th-century cottages were combined into one to make this attractive house, beamed and with inglenook fireplace, in an ancient village through which a stream runs. Wendy Turner's choice of furnishings admirably complements the old house. There are prettily carved chairs in the pale green dining-room; pine doors have been stripped and brick walls exposed; buttoned chairs in rust-colour covers are gathered around a log stove in the sitting-room. Bedrooms are very pleasant – for instance, furnished with chest-of-drawers of woven cane, with very good armchairs and colour schemes. One bathroom has an oval bath in peach, and a bidet. Standards throughout are high. Bed-and-breakfast only; for other meals Wendy recommends the Poacher in South Warnborough or the Hoddington Arms in Upton Grey.

North Hampshire (quickly accessible along the M3) is an area often overlooked by people hurrying on to Winchester, Southampton or the New Forest. But anyone who lingers here will find plenty of interest, not least because this is Jane Austen country (her house is at Chawton, and scenes from the area feature in her books). Farnham still has streets much as she knew them, and a hilltop castle. Not far away is Selborne where White wrote his natural history (1789) and here, too, one can still see countryside that he saw. Both his and Jane Austen's homes are open to the public – his has a museum about Captain Oates and Scott's Antarctic expedition and is surrounded by National Trust woodlands. Nearby Odiham, too, retains the appearance of an 18th-century market town, with ruined castle nearby; and there are pretty villages – Greywell, Upton Grey (houses encircling a pond), Sherborne St John (with a Tudor mansion, The Vyne – NT, and moated Beaurepaire), Basing (castle ruins). Silchester was once a great Roman fort with a road running to Salisbury – now this is a mere track in a region of woods, streams and fields. The several fast roads in the area mean that most traffic has been siphoned off to leave the lanes peaceful. South of Basingstoke are the North Downs (running into Surrey) with splendid viewpoints.

Westward lie Litchfield, a flowery village in an area of prehistoric remains; Wherwell, a real showpiece – all timber and thatch, with fine views of the famous River Test; streamside Hurstbourne Tarrant; and Highclere – castle and hilltop grave of Lord Carnarvon (who discovered Tutankhamen's tomb in 1922); Burghclere (Stanley Spencer paintings in a chapel); the two beautiful Clatford villages with pretty river bridges.

In marked contrast to all these quiet pleasures are Farnborough's air show and Aldershot's military tattoo. And if you want to go further afield there are a number of famous tourist spots within easy reach – Windsor, for instance, and of course London itself.

279

SUGARSWELL FARM

C(2) **X**

Shenington, south of Stratford-upon-Avon, Warwickshire, OX15 6HW
Tel: 029 588 512

3 bedrooms (single, double or family) from £16. Less for 2 nights or bargain breaks. Rooms have central heating or electric heaters; shower or bathroom; TV, armchairs; views of country or garden; tea/coffee facilities.
Dinner £12 for 3 courses and coffee, at 7pm. Special diets if ordered. Lunches, packed lunches, snacks. Coffee, tea, for a charge. Drinks can be brought in.
2 sitting-rooms with central heating, open fire, TV, video, books.
Grounds Farm and woodland.
Nearest main road A442 from Stratford-upon-Avon to Banbury.

Rosemary Nunnely is a cook of cordon bleu calibre – her greatest delight is preparing meals. Visitors who stay with her are likely to get something very different from ordinary 'farmhouse fare': on the day of my first visit, she had prepared seafood gratin followed by fillet steak (home-produced) in a sauce of port, cream and garlic, with home-made lemon sorbet to finish. Rosemary uses wine and cream in many of her dishes, rum in such specialities as Jamaican torte.

The house is modern but made from old stones taken from a demolished cottage. It has big picture-windows, and a striking staircase with 18th-century portraits. Sofas are grouped round a huge stone fireplace in the sitting-room which, like the dining-room, has lime green walls. Guests sit on Chippendale chairs to dine; there is good silver on the table, and one side of the dining-room consists of a see-through glass wall filled with Rosemary's collection of Crown Derby.

Upstairs are elegant bedrooms, one with a sofa from which to enjoy woodland views beyond the fields where cows graze, and a very large bathroom decorated in bright mulberry.

Included in the price is the gift of a touring map of the region, showing how to get to (for instance) Warwick, Stratford, the Cotswold towns, Woodstock (Blenheim Palace), Oxford, Silverstone (car races) and Sulgrave (the Washington ancestral home) or such stately homes as Upton House, Compton Wynyates and Farnborough Hall. In Shenington itself is an outstanding garden, at Brook Cottage.

As to the curious name Sugarswell, Rosemary explained its origin: shuggers (mediaeval slang for robbers) made a settlement here, which their more respectable neighbours destroyed. Vestiges can still be seen from the air.

Readers' comments: Lovely home, superb cooking. A marvellous place. Time-capsule of the good life! Food well above average. Charming hostess, comfortable and delightful accommodation, delicious food. Very pleasant rooms and good views; lovely welcome; spacious room. Comfortable accommodation, superb cooking. A lovely place to stay. *And from the former manager of a 5-star hotel:* We have been back seven times.

280

SWALCLIFFE MANOR

C(8) **D S**

Swalcliffe, west of Banbury, Oxfordshire, OX15 5EH   Tel: 029578 348

4 bedrooms (single or double) from £15. Rooms have central heating or electric heaters; shower or bathroom; TV, armchairs; views of country and garden; tea/coffee facilities. One four-poster.
Dinner £12 for 4 courses and coffee, at 8pm. Vegetarian or special diets if ordered. Lunches, packed lunches. Non-residents not admitted. Drinks can be brought in.

2 sitting-rooms with central heating, open fire, TV, books, piano, record-player. Table tennis in games room.
Large garden Orchard and fields, with unheated swimming-pool.
Nearest main road A423 from Oxford to Banbury.
Closed mid-December–March

Certainly the most striking entrance of any in this book is here: one passes through a 13th-century undercroft, the vaulted stone ceiling supported on massive circular pillars. Beyond is the former great hall of the house with a vast fireplace. Judith and Francis Hitching (he is the author of several books on prehistoric mysteries) have furnished this with antiques and oriental rugs, a grand piano, and a carved mediaeval chest which contrasts well with pink walls. Traces of ancient wall-paintings can be seen, Tudor roses much in evidence.

The drawing-room is completely different, for in the 18th century an extension was added in Georgian style. This classical room, decorated in pale green, has Corinthian pilasters and a very pretty fireplace of green marble in a pine surround carved with acanthus leaves. Through high sash windows, set in deep panelled embrasures, is a view of the croquet lawn and a former studio now used as a games room for children. This is part of a large garden which includes a suntrapping stone terrace, a Saxon font planted with daisies, swimming-pool (unheated) and a sunken garden with a parterre of flowers grown in Tudor times: Judith put much research as well as hard effort into re-creating this. The big arrangements of dried flowers throughout the house are hers.

A gifted cook (once nominated 'Gourmet of the Year' by a London newspaper), she will cook whatever her visitors prefer, or devise the menu herself – in which case you might be served scallops cooked with ginger and leeks; very good roast meat or game, in which this area excels (accompanied by vegetables from the garden, and herby sauces); then her own Swalcliffe Pudding – a sponge with gooseberries, sultanas and honey. Food is served on flowery Portmeirion pottery.

Upstairs, bedrooms open off a broad gallery, full of pictures and antique toys. The one Georgian bedroom overlooks thatched roofs in the pretty village; while older ones have small stone-mullioned windows with church views. Pointed stone arches of the 13th-century frame baths or bathroom entrances.

Readers' comments: Charming. Nice people, interesting house, good food. Lovely welcome, splendid dinner.

THORNLEY HOUSE *New*   C D X
Allendale, south of Hexham, Northumberland, NE47 9NH   Tel: 043483 255

4 bedrooms (single or double) from £14. Less for 7 nights and bargain breaks. All have tea/coffee facilities; central heating; views of country or garden. (Washing-machine on request.)
Dinner £7.50 for 3 courses and coffee, at 7pm. Vegetarian or special diets if ordered. Lunches, packed lunches, snacks. Tea, coffee, free. Drinks can be brought in.
2 sitting-rooms with central heating, TV, books, piano, record-player.
Large garden
Nearest main road B6305 from Hexham to Allendale.

Allendale town is a large village in a sheltered valley amid some of the most open scenery in England – deserted grouse moors and breezy sheep pastures which stretch for uninterrupted miles, punctuated only by isolated farmhouses and the occasional relic of the lead mining which once made this area important. On the outskirts of the village is Thornley House, a large and solid inter-war house in a big garden. Eileen Finn runs a small language school here, so visitors may mix with a few (adult) students from Denmark or other countries. Rooms are spacious and light, with views of the wooded roads into the village and of the Pennines.

Mrs Finn is a keen cook, and though guests are offered conventional fare (vichyssoise soup, breaded chicken, salad, and chocolate mousse, for example), she needs only a little encouragement to cook a dish from Mexico, where she lived for eight years, or from another of the many countries to which she has paid long visits. As well as being a linguist and passionate world traveller, she is an able pianist, and there is a Steinway grand in one of the two sitting-rooms. Visitors may be taken on guided walks.

A few miles away, Isabel and John Wentzel offer b & b plus imaginative cooking (for vegetarians especially) at **Crowberry Hall** (tel: 043483 392), a one-time farmhouse set in a very remote spot overlooking the valley of the East Allen.

A little further south, specialities of Terry McMullon's **Allenheads Inn** (tel: 043485 200) are fish and game from the surrounding estate. This is a friendly, family-run place in a village which has recently started to make more of its historic heritage. Accommodation includes a small suite. There is more about the Allendale area on another page.

Two-thirds of the houses in this book have bargain breaks or other discounts on offer, some exclusive to readers. Only a third raise prices at the peak of summer.

TIGHE FARM

Stone-in-Oxney, north of Rye, Kent, TN30 7JU   Tel: 023383 251

3 bedrooms (double or family) from £12. Much less for 2 nights or bargain breaks. Rooms have central heating or electric heaters; armchairs; views of country or garden. Coffee, tea, free.
Sitting-room with central heating, open fire, TV, books, piano.

Garden and farmland, with coarse fishing.
Nearest main road A259 from Hastings to Folkestone.
Closed Christmas–February

This 17th-century house is full of works of art and unusual antiques (collected by Jimmy Hodson's father, a sculptor before he took to sheep-farming here) and also oriental pieces (Elise's family lived in India for many years). The blue bedroom, for instance, has not only a carved mediaeval table but geisha-girl prints and Numdah rugs; a Jacobean chest has Indian paintings above it; in the oldest room, with mullioned windows, are carved marquise chairs from Paris and a Kashmir chainstitch rug. The Hodsons have retained a curious feature – a concealed iron winch above the staircase, which they think was used when hiding contraband (Romney Marsh was notorious for smuggling).

One breakfasts at a polished refectory table with rush chairs in a particularly interesting room – hop-bines are strung across the inglenook, with a copy of a statue of the Virgin Mary in Notre-Dame; there's a carved oak sideboard and brass rubbings from the local church. In the beautiful sitting-room are unusual chests and other antiques; the old iron fireback carries the royal coat-of-arms.

The garden is equally attractive, especially a paved terrace, brimming with fuchsias and roses.

As dinner is not served, Elise provides visitors with menus gathered from good local inns (such as the Crown) and restaurants – and with a series of postcards on which she has detailed routes recommended for sightseeing tours.

Being midway between Rye and Tenterden (each described elsewhere), Tighe Farm is ideally placed for exploring historic and beautiful parts of both Sussex and Kent. Guests usually visit Smallhythe (Ellen Terry's Tudor house), Sissinghurst and Great Dixter gardens, Bodiam Castle, Tenterden and its steam railway, Camber sands and the Romney Marsh churches.

Readers' comments: Very welcoming and helpful. Excellent room, peaceful. Have stayed three times: so welcome; peaceful; a stately home in miniature. Made very welcome. Mrs Hodson very helpful. Very good value for money. Wish we had stayed longer.

TOR HAVEN HOTEL

PT S X

King Street, Brixham, south of Torquay, Devon, TQ5 9TH
Tel: 0803 882281

10 bedrooms (single or double) from £16. Much less for 7 nights and bargain breaks. Rooms have electric heaters; shower, wc; TV, video films (extra), armchairs; views of sea; tea/coffee facilities.

Dinner £7 for 3 courses (with choices) and coffee, at 7pm. Vegetarian or special diets if ordered. Lunches, packed lunches, snacks. Coffee, tea, for a charge. Drinks can be ordered.

2 sitting-rooms with TV, books, indoor games (including darts); bar.

Nearest main road A3022 from Torquay to Brixham. (Car park is distant.)

Built about 1800, this small hotel is run by Pat and Stephen Nicholls (he is a radio 'ham'). Though bedrooms are small, nearly every window has a panoramic view (across the road) of the busy fishing port, and of distant lights twinkling at night. Everywhere there are pictures of birds or landscapes, and patchwork wall-hangings by Pat (she gives weekly lessons in this craft, and runs some weekend courses too). Some rooms have exposed stone walls; the little bar is actually cut into the rock face. Steep steps lead up to the house; and at the back others rise to a small sun terrace at rooftop level. (Ask where to park nearby.)

Two readers said they did not like the proximity to the road (I myself slept undisturbed); more enthuse about the harbour views and the Nicholls' friendliness.

At dinner, one of Pat's specialities is Brixham plaice; and her puddings are delicious gâteaux, meringues, summer pudding, etc. (Non-smokers preferred.)

The hotel is about five minutes' stroll from the town and harbour (with replica of Drake's *Golden Hind*), or the beach. There are many good coastal walks to the innumerable bays and beauty-spots of the area. To the north is the West Country's leading resort, Torquay (which has a slightly continental air, with sophisticated entertainments and shops), at the centre of golden sands and luxuriant gardens, yachts filling its bay with colour. Behind are lush countryside, flower-farms, and the distinctive red soil of Devon. Steep little Brixham is quite different from all this, a still-busy fishing port that has hardly changed in the last hundred years. On Berry Head are Victorian forts, you can take a ferry to Dartmouth, and the miniature gardens of the model village at Torquay are well worth seeing, as is Coleton Fishacre garden (NT).

Readers' comments: Wonderful hosts, beautiful vista. Food excellent and good value.

When writing to me, if you want a reply please enclose a stamped addressed envelope.

Book well ahead: many of these houses have few rooms. Do not expect dinner if you have not booked it.

TREGONY HOUSE

Tregony, east of Truro, Cornwall, TR2 5RN   Tel: 087 253 671

rear view

6 bedrooms (single or double). Dinner, bed-and-breakfast costs from £21.50 a night (for 2-night stays). Rooms have electric heaters; two with shower or bathroom; armchairs; views of garden.
Dinner 4 courses (with choices) and coffee, at 7pm. Special diets if ordered. Coffee, tea, for a charge. Drinks can be ordered.
Sitting-room with central heating, open fire, TV, books, record-player. Also a bar.
Garden
Nearest main road A390 from St Austell to Truro.
Closed November–February

Years ago, some owner had the bad idea of coating the façade of this house with rendering: from the street it looks quite undistinguished (the drawing shows the back). But inside is a very different story. Part dates from the 17th century; later, additions were made – so the dining-room, for instance, is low-beamed and thick-walled while the hall and sitting-room have 18th-century elegance, particularly since the addition of well chosen fabrics, a pomegranate wallpaper in the hall, rounded alcoves crammed with books, and interesting antiques.

One green-and-white bedroom has a quilted bedspread and particularly pretty antique chairs; a pink room at the back, with tiny windows, has velvet bedheads and a patchwork table-cover. Two double rooms with bathroom between make a good family suite.

In the dining-room (furnished with oriental rugs, oak tables and Windsor chairs) Mario and Verna Marin serve such imaginative meals as avocado and orange salad, boned and stuffed chicken with mushroom sauce, and pears cooked with brown sugar and lemon (plus cheeses). Herbs, raspberries etc. come from the cottage garden at the back, where you can have tea; a greenhouse provides vegetables.

Because Tregony, although interesting, is not one of Cornwall's show villages, it remains uncrowded even in high summer. From it you can quickly reach the warm south coast of Cornwall, with all its coves, beaches, harbours and scenic drives in the Roseland peninsula, an area of outstanding natural beauty, with numerous stately homes and gardens to visit too. Truro and St Mawes are interesting towns, and a feature of the region are the old beam engines (for mines).

Readers' comments: Food marvellous: imaginative and beautifully cooked. The Marins are very relaxed, friendly and efficient. Meals excellent, rooms comfortable; warm and friendly. Interesting food; comfortable, friendly. Outstanding; excellent, imaginative meals attractively presented. A very happy week; accommodation excellent, comfortable, tastefully decorated; delicious food; friendly and hospitable.

Families which pick establishments with plenty of games, swimming-pool, animals, etc., or that are near free museums, parks and walks, can save a lot on keeping youngsters entertained.

TRENT VALE FARMHOUSE

Hyde, north-west of Wareham, Dorset, BH20 7NX   Tel: 0929 471642

C(10) **PT S**

rear view

4 bedrooms (single or double) from £12. Less for 3 nights. Rooms have central heating; bathroom; armchairs; views of country or garden.
Sitting-room with central heating, TV, books.

Grounds Woodland, fields, tennis court.
Nearest main road A35 from Bournemouth to Dorchester.

A mile-long, rough-surfaced rhododendron drive leads deep into the heart of Wareham Forest. Suddenly the scene changes: sunny meadows open out, and there springs into view a spacious modern house with wide picture-windows.

This became the secluded home of Ken Durran when he retired from business. On his grounds there is much wildlife to see – not only birds but also badgers, glow-worms, rare sand-lizards, and deer from the forest.

There's a pale-carpeted breakfast-room of distinction, with lightly patterned hessian walls, concealed lighting, and rosewood sideboard. Beyond is a sun-room with sliding glass doors, an acacia and a vine growing overhead. Bedrooms, too, are attractive (and bathroom luxurious): for instance, one has white carpet, powder-blue colour scheme and rounded bedhead of cane. Bed-and-breakfast only (one can dine at the Royal Oak, Bere Regis, or at several Wareham restaurants including the Old Granary, see earlier entry).

You are welcome to wander round the grounds, which include river, lake with swans, paddocks with Ken's horses (show-jumpers, hunting or racing horses and a Shetland pony), tennis court, birch woods. Ken will pilot you in a light aircraft for a day-trip to Cherbourg or the Channel Islands, for a share of the cost.

And, of course, all the other pleasures of east Dorset are within reach – Poole Harbour and Brownsea Island, Lulworth Cove and Durdle Door, Corfe Castle and old Wareham itself – described elsewhere in this book. Gardens: Compton Acres, Kingston Lacey. An excellent area for birdwatching.

Readers' comments: Perfect host; food and service excellent. High standards. We were pampered and spoilt. Have visited six times; hospitality second to none, nothing was too much trouble. Thoroughly recommend it.

Single people may find more company in houses that have a shared dining-table, a bar, and no TV in the sitting-room. As my descriptions indicate, some owners mingle more with their guests than others do. Houses marked **S** charge singles little or no more than half a double.

TREVENA HOUSE HOTEL

Alton Road, Farnham, Surrey, GU10 5ER   Tel: 0252 716908

C PT S

19 bedrooms (single, double or family) at £17.75, weekends. 2-day breaks all through the week. Rooms have central heating; shower or bathroom; TV, phone, armchairs; views of country or garden; tea/coffee facilities.

Dinner £9 or à la carte, from 7pm. Special diets if ordered. Lunches, packed lunches, snacks. Coffee, tea, for a charge. Drinks can be ordered.

3 sitting-rooms with central heating, open fire, TV, books; and a bar.

Large garden and orchard, tennis and swimming-pool (70°).

Nearest main road A31 from Farnham to Winchester.

Mr Trimmer, a millionaire brewer, bought himself rolling acres of Surrey parkland in the 1890s on which to build an appropriate home. But Trevena House had fallen into a sorry state when Norman Levitt, formerly managing director of a flooring company, later took it over, to restore to its former handsome style. He even found great club-like oak chairs, deep-upholstered, to go with the oak panelling of the bar-lounge. This has a window-seat overlooking the lawns and stately trees such as weeping ash, cedar, mulberry and chestnut, with the lovely Surrey hills beyond. On wintry nights, guests gather round the inglenook fireplace. This is a place of thick carpets, hefty beams and solid brass fittings on the doors. In the summer, drinks can be taken out to the swimming-pool which is illuminated after dark by strings of coloured lights.

The dining-room, too, overlooks the lawn. Here are served, on tables with nosegays and candle-lamps, such dishes as prawns mornay followed by beef Wellington and unusual ice creams.

The bedrooms are comfortable, furnished in conservative taste. Throughout, the accent is on spaciousness and ease. Being so close to London, the hotel tends to be used by executives on weekdays, but is less full at weekends.

Nearby Farnham is a lovely Georgian town (with castle), parts of it still very much as Jane Austen knew them (her house, near Alton, can be visited). It is full of antique and craft shops, wine bars and boutiques. It has a good repertory theatre, a new sports centre, a monthly country market, fortnightly auctions, weekly street market.

Close by are: Alice Holt woodlands for walks, the great lakes of Frensham Ponds (at one end, there is a sandy beach for swimming), Guildford and its cathedral, tropical bird gardens, country inns, National Trust woods and heaths. Riding, golf and Britain's largest car auction attract some guests; Winchester Cathedral and the music festivals of picturesque Haslemere (harpsichord centre) bring others. The north Surrey hills make very varied scenery – oaks and holly alternating with pine and birch. Roads go up and down, streams meander. There are bulrushes and water-lilies in summer, coppery bracken and blackberries in autumn. A steam railway and the RHS garden at Wisley are other attractions.

For explanation of code letters (**C, D, H, PT, S, S-C, X**) see page **xxviii**.

6 bedrooms (single, double or family) from £9.50 with central heating and views of country or garden. No smoking. (Washing-machine on request.)
Dinner £3 for 3 courses (with choices) and coffee, at 6.30pm. Non-residents not admitted. Vegetarian or special diets if ordered. Lunches, packed lunches, snacks. Tea, coffee, extra. Drinks can be ordered.

2 sitting-rooms with central heating, open fire, TV, books, record-player; bar. No smoking in one.
Large garden
Nearest main road A30 from Okehampton to Penzance.
Closed from November–Easter

Trerice, owned by the National Trust, is an Elizabethan manor house of stone, with lattice-paned windows (one has 576 panes) and elaborate plaster ceilings. The watermill was built in 1639 to provide flour for the household; now it is a guest-house, the wheel stilled but a stream still flowing by. Ponds attract wildfowl, dragonflies and frogs; a donkey called Crumpet is a family pet.

One passes through a stone-flagged hall to two sitting-rooms, the first overlooking a lawn with millstone tables where home-made cakes are served at teatime, and the second with big leather armchairs around a log fire and a window through which there is an inside view of the waterwheel. Bedrooms are small and neat (there is one large family room), the dining-room simply furnished with gingham tablecloths and Windsor chairs. Here Ethel Grateley serves, for instance, turkey soup with home-baked rolls, local plaice in cheese sauce with home-grown vegetables and fruit crumbles with custard – all for a very modest price indeed.

Newquay has Cornwall's best sandy beaches, vast and much frequented by surfers. Its high cliffs have caves to explore, and the harbour is picturesque (the centre is fairly characterless), there are headlands with notable views, and at Trenance Gardens is a zoo. Nearby villages worth exploring include St Columb Minor (a particularly fine church tower) and Crantock (smugglers' haunt, splendid sand dunes).

To the south of the Mill lies Truro, a market town with a cathedral and with 18th-century terraces that would not disgrace Bath itself (Lemon Street and Walsingham Place in particular) and Cornwall's best museum (history, art, geology). Day-long river trips to Falmouth and back are very pleasant. Beyond Truro are the gardens of Trelissick with subtropical flowers. (The Padstow and St Agnes areas are described elsewhere in this book.)

Readers' comments: Food plain but well cooked, bedrooms very comfortable, garden a delight. A lovely, restful weekend.

A few miles south, at Trispen (near Truro), is something completely different, **Trevispen** (tel: 0872 41371): the modern home of Rita Heggie, a mecca for gourmets. Not only do her house-guests enjoy her professional skills as a home economist and cook but she runs 2 to 3-day courses when she demonstrates cookery. Rita says she has a love affair with food, the result of which is that visitors are treated to such meals as avocado and kiwi fruit cocktail, salmon trout coulibiac (in puff pastry) and rumptoff fruits with cream. Her husband, Brian, who is secretary of Truro Golf Club, keeps a good cellar. (Immaculate bedrooms, all on ground floor.) Non-smokers preferred.

Two-thirds of the houses in this book accept and provide for *children*; though nearly half of these stipulate a minimum age, often 4 (some, 10).

Over a third accept *dogs*, though not allowing them in all rooms.

Scores of houses are suitable for people in *wheelchairs* or otherwise handicapped.

Half can be reached without a car, by nearby *public transport*.

Half charge *singles* little or no more than people sharing a double room.

Several dozen of the houses or hotels also have some *self-catering* cottages or flats to let.

Over a quarter provide accommodation at *Christmas*.

About a third are licensed to sell *drinks*, while nearly a quarter allow visitors to bring their own in.

Travellers can book *meals*, without staying overnight, at over a third of the houses.

Packed lunches are provided by about half.

Two-thirds can produce, if notified in advance, vegetarian or other special *diets*.

Over half stay open throughout the *winter*.

An increasing number (several dozen) *ban smoking* in some rooms if not all.

In over a third, you can choose whether to have a *duvet or blankets*.

One-fifth provide either *extra-firm mattresses or bedboards* for back sufferers.

Over half have *TV* in the sitting-room; about a third, in bedrooms; the rest do not provide TV.

Nearly two-thirds provide *tea-making facilities* in bedrooms; the rest bring tea up on a tray. A few offer both alternatives. About a third are willing to provide *breakfast in bed*. About 100 give visitors a tray of tea on arrival, free.

Several dozen have *swimming-pools*, usually heated.

Several dozen provide *clothes-washing* facilities.

Among a number of other little extras offered at some houses, mostly free, are the following: loan of cycles, gumboots and maps; car-washing facilities; hair-dryers and/or rollers; mending kits; sale of home-made preserves, crafts, travel books and maps; use of video recorder, video films, record-player and piano.

TUDOR FARMHOUSE

C D H PT X

Clearwell, Coleford, south-west of Gloucester, GL16 8JS   Tel: 0594 33046

8 bedrooms (single, double or family) from £16. Less for 7 nights or bargain breaks. Rooms have central heating, electric heaters; shower or own bathroom; views of country or garden; tea/coffee facilities. Clothes-washing facilities.

Dinner £9.25 for 3 courses (with choices) and coffee, at 7pm. Vegetarian or special diets if ordered. Coffee, tea, for a charge. Drinks can be ordered.

Sitting-room with central heating, open fire, books; bar. Conservatory.

Grounds Hillside.

Nearest main road B4228 from Chepstow to Coleford.

Parts of this house date back to the 13th century, and panelled walls are almost as old. Oliver Cromwell stayed here while hunting in the Forest of Dean – Clearwell is one of the prettiest villages on the edge of the forest – and may well have warmed his toes at the same inglenook fireplace round which big, flowery sofas are now grouped. In the dining-room, rugged stone walls contrast with tables attractively laid with delicately sprigged china.

The house, still surrounded by fields of sheep, now belongs to a young and lively professional couple (Sheila and James Reid) who produce their own vegetables, fruit and eggs for the table. Dinner may start with a home-made soup, pâté or quiche; perhaps followed by beef cooked with Guinness and orange, or pork with cider and apples. Puddings are traditional favourites (crumbles, mousses, pine-apple upside-down cake, etc.); and then there is a choice of cheeses.

To reach the pleasantly decorated bedrooms you ascend either a spiral stair or a wide oak one; or go to a converted barn just outside, past an ancient stone cider-press now planted with flowers. There are low, iron-studded doors, leaded window-panes, stone mullions. A spacious family room in the stone barn is particularly attractive (rather like a little self-contained cottage).

Clearwell has Roman iron mines and a network of caves you can visit; a neo-Gothic castle; and mysterious Puzzle Wood – extraordinary and huge boulders from which trees sprout. Newland's impressive church is known as 'the cathedral of the forest'. Not only is there the beautiful forest to explore (in autumn, the colours are at their best) but also the nearby Wye Valley and the gorge at Symonds Yat, South Wales' beauty-spots (including Tintern Abbey's spectacular 12th-century ruins), and the market town of Ross-on-Wye. Newent's falconry centre, England's oldest house (part-Saxon), the forest's heritage exhibition and its steam railway, Lydney Park gardens and deer park, tours of the Stuart crystal glass factory, bird gardens, a model farm, a great maze, and a tropical butterfly garden are just some of the other sights which make it worth staying here for at least a week if you can.

Readers' comments: First-class accommodation, food superb, made us very welcome.

For explanation of code letters (**C, D, H, PT, S, S-C, X**) **see page xxviii.**

UNDER ROCK

C(10) **H PT S**

Shore Road, Bonchurch, east of Ventnor, Isle of Wight, PO38 1RF
Tel: 0983 852714

7 bedrooms (single or double) from £16. Less for 3 nights. Rooms have central heating; TV, armchairs; views of sea and garden. **Dinner** £7 for 3 courses and coffee, at 6.30pm. Vegetarian or special diets if ordered. Packed lunches, snacks. Coffee, tea, for a charge. Drinks can be ordered.
2 sitting-rooms with central heating, open fire, books.
Large garden
Nearest main road A3055 from Shanklin to Ventnor.
Closed November–February

Garden-lovers will appreciate the grounds of this small hotel, which clings to a cliff-side. It was built about 1790 for a nephew of Sir Robert Peel (founder of the police force), and the owners have created a small paradise around it: from every cleft spring flowers such as New Zealand flax or Californian tree poppies; palms, hydrangeas or Japanese anemones. It is a quite exceptional garden.

Fresh flowers are in every room, too, now that the house is run as a small, award-winning hotel by Mollie and Dennis Kelleway. One steps from the garden into a sitting-room where rosy armchairs contrast with a thick, pale carpet. In the dining-room, curtains are of quilted patchwork and place-mats of crochet (over pink cloths): there's a view of the rock garden, 20 feet high, brimming with tobacco-plants and fuchsias. A curving stair leads to the bedrooms – the prettiest has pink moiré paper and a frieze of roses matching the curtain fabric.

Mollie's meals often include fresh fruit starters (such as minneola and orange segments) before, perhaps, a traditional roast and then puddings such as meringues with blackcurrants or grapes. All her soups, bread, preserves and fruit juices are freshly made at home.

Bonchurch is probably the prettiest village in the Isle of Wight and, facing south, gets sunshine even in winter. It adjoins Ventnor, a resort with an old-fashioned air, botanical gardens (bananas fruit outdoors there), a smuggling museum well worth visiting, and a scenic undercliff drive among myrtles, palms and cork trees. It is well placed for visiting the innumerable sights in the lively east half of the island; or the wild and peaceful scenery in the west half.

Readers' comments: Very good, most hospitable.

If you want absolute quiet, avoid any place that takes children or has a bar open to non-residents. Inns sometimes get extensions to their licensing hours for late private parties; and may lack quiet sitting-rooms.

Two-thirds of the houses in this book have bargain breaks or other discounts on offer, some exclusive to readers. Only a third raise prices at the peak of summer.

UNICORN HOTEL
Keighley Road, Skipton, North Yorkshire, BD23 22P   Tel: 0756 4146

10 bedrooms (single, double or family) from £17.50 **to readers of this book**, with own bath; TV; tea/coffee facilities; phone; central heating. No smoking. (Laundering on request.)

Dinner A la carte at 7–8.30pm. Non-residents not admitted. Vegetarian or special diets if ordered. Lunches, packed lunches, snacks. Drinks can be ordered.

Sitting-room with central heating; bar. No smoking.

Nearest main road A59 from Preston to Harrogate.

You might not notice the Unicorn, hidden in a modest row of shops on a nondescript street leading into the town. You enter through a small door and go upstairs to a receptionist who takes you to your room and brings you a tray of tea or coffee with biscuits when you arrive.

What makes the Unicorn special is the quality and size of the rooms. Ours had an attractive brown-and-cream colour scheme and was more like a sitting-room than a bedroom, with comfortable armchairs and sofa (convertible into a third bed if required) grouped round the large colour TV. There were good paintings by local artists on the walls, prettily arranged flowers on a table, a pile of magazines, a folder of information (about local events and sights) and well-placed lights.

Since Paul and Jean Dolan took over, they have added an attractive pink and green dining-room with upholstered chairs. Here are served 4-course dinners that are very good value, and with a wide choice at each course: for instance, main dishes often include veal Milanaise, sauté chicken with mustard sauce, pheasant Normande, a roast, steaks and a vegetarian option.

The emphasis is on quality and comfort – each room has a heated, carpeted bathroom, for instance. And, although my first visit was in July, the receptionist offered to turn on the central heating because the weather was unseasonably cool.

Skipton is an old town of great character, its wide main street thronged with market stalls leading up to the castle and church at the end. Down by the bridge are interesting craft and antique shops, and historic riverside buildings. It is a good centre from which to explore Ribblesdale, Wharfedale, Wensleydale and Airedale and all the famous beauty-spots – the crags, caves, waterfalls, villages and ruined abbeys with which the region abounds.

Ilkley Moor is within reach, as are the stylish spa town of Harrogate (for shopping), and an officially designated 'area of outstanding natural beauty', the Forest of Bowland. This is largely moorland (the heather is superb in September), with parts comparable with the crags and valleys of the Lake District. Some of the finest countryside of the north-west is here. In addition there are charming villages like Bolton-by-Bowland, winding rivers, stately homes and abbeys and castles, a Roman museum, inns and markets. Boats can be hired on the canal.

Readers' comments: Delighted. A charming couple. Cooking, presentation and service are faultless. Blissfully quiet though in town centre. Meals well presented.

292

UPPER GREEN FARM

S

Manor Road, Towersey, east of Thame, Oxfordshire, OX9 3QR
Tel: 084421 2496

3 bedrooms (single or double) from £13. Rooms have central heating; shower in one; TV; views of country or garden; No smoking. Packed lunches; coffee, tea etc.
Sitting-room with central heating, TV, books. No smoking.

Large garden Orchard, pond and farmland.
Nearest main road A4129 from Thame to Princes Risborough.

A building of whitewash and thatch with a pretty duckpond at the front, this house was a near-ruin when Marjorie and Euan Aitken took it over not long ago. They uncovered 15th-century beams with the original carpenters' identification marks; came across Elizabethan coins; restored the wood shutters which (window-glass having yet to be invented) were all that kept out wintry blasts five centuries ago; found a secret priest-hole where, in the days of religious persecution, a Catholic priest might have to hide for days when the search was on. In one huge chimney, there were still the iron rungs up which small boys were forced to clamber to clear the soot. In what is now the quarry-tiled breakfast-room, an old kitchen-range and adjoining copper boiler have been preserved, together with the rack on which spits for roasting whole sheep were kept, and the special hooks used for drying the farmer's smocks by the fire. In the hall is a pump (still working).

Marjorie, who used to be an antique dealer, has filled every room with fascinating trifles – Victorian jugs and jam-pots on the sprigged brown tablecloth at breakfast, shelves of old bottles (found discarded in the garden), beadwork pincushions and watch-cases, a huge marble washstand in the downstairs cloak-room, naive Staffordshire figures, old brass scales (which she uses) and tin toys.

The Aitkens not only tell visitors about well known sights nearby (Claydon House, Waddesdon Manor, Ryecote Chapel, West Wycombe's 'hellfire' caves, the horses' home of rest, etc.) but introduce them to other sides of local life. For instance, you may go and see the sorting and grading of sheep fleeces, join in bell-ringing, pick up bargains at local markets or auctions, chat up balloonists as they glide by only a few yards above the farm – silently, unlike the wild swans in clattering flight. They will tell you where to find a true country butcher for game, faggots, deep brown eggs and other treats hard to come by.

And, of course, their sheep, ducks, chickens and geese are an entertainment in themselves. (Bed-and-breakfast only; but with plenty of options for dinner in Thame.)

Readers' comments: Charming home, warm hospitality: we arrived as guests and left as friends. Much impressed by warm welcome, delightful house and excellent breakfast. Wonderful couple – it always feels like going home!

293

UPPER ORCHARD

C D PT S S-C

Hoarwithy, east of Ross-on-Wye, Herefordshire, HR2 6QR
Tel: 043 270 649

6 bedrooms (double) from £10. Bargain breaks. Rooms have central heating; views of country or garden.
Sitting-room with central heating, open fire, books, piano.
Garden
Nearest main road A49 from Ross-on-Wye to Hereford.
Closed December and January

Both walkers and wine-lovers come to Upper Orchard.

In summer, Heather – who writes books and articles on walking – provides visitors with carefully worked out routes through the lovely countryside of the Wye Valley, varying in distance from a mere 2½ to 14 miles (with wellies, maps and walking-sticks on loan); and as a voluntary warden of the Wye Valley, she also gives talks and conducts walks, in between running the guest-house. It is her husband Jon Hurley, an award-winning writer on wine for several quality newspapers, who runs the wine-tasting weekends at other seasons. These are of three kinds: for beginners; sampling fine wines; and tasting great classics, some of them collectors' items half a century old. (You can send for a leaflet with full details.)

The house itself is unpretentious – in the 18th century it was an inn (its cellars now house Jon's wines). The sitting-room furniture is homely, even old-fashioned – armchairs are grouped round a log fire in winter, while in summer the focal point is a large bay window with a view of grazing cows. In the bedrooms soft pinks and greens contrast with pine furniture.

The beamed dining-room is very pleasant, the colour of the mulberry walls repeated in china with old scenes of country life. On wine weekends only, Heather cooks such 4-course meals as home-made pâté or soup; roast meat with garden vegetables; apple crunch and thick cream; followed by English and Welsh cheeses.

Hoarwithy is a pretty village on the banks of the River Wye and near it are such popular sights as Goodrich Castle, Symonds Yat rock, Skenfrith Castle, Ross (market town with garden centre), Hereford (cathedral city) and Hill Court gardens.

When to go? Seaside resorts or other places suitable for children will be at their busiest (and dearest) in July–August and during half-term holidays (especially, in late May, which is also a bank holiday period). Other peak periods are, of course, Easter, Christmas, New Year and the bank holiday in late August. (The bank holiday in early May is not usually a peak, because it comes rather soon after Easter, but much depends on the weather.) There are local peaks, too (the Gold Cup races at Cheltenham or the regatta at Henley, for instance, are apt to fill hotels for miles around), and local troughs (Brighton, a conference centre, is least busy in high summer). You won't get much personal attention when hotels are full to bursting.

294

UPTON HOUSE   C D S
Upton Snodsbury, east of Worcester, WR7 4NR   Tel: 090560 226

3 bedrooms (single or double) from £18.50 but with **10% reduction to readers of this book**. Less for 3 nights. Rooms have central heating and electric heaters; bathroom; armchairs; views of country or garden; tea/coffee facilities.
Dinner From £13 for 4 courses and coffee, at 7.30–8pm. Vegetarian or special diets if ordered. Drinks can be brought in. Sandwich suppers.
Sitting-room with central heating, open fire, TV, books.
Large garden and orchard, with croquet.
Nearest main road A422 from Stratford to Worcester.

Part 14th-century, part Tudor and part 18th-century, this building is full of individuality. It has been furnished in character, with antiques collected by Hugh and Angela Jefferson over the years. They decided to take guests to help with the cost of educating four young children, then found how much they enjoyed entertaining them.

Their colour schemes are fresh and imaginative. In the dining-room, chairs covered in watermelon satin contrast with primrose walls (this room has a vast fireplace); in the sitting-room, sofas covered in pink or blue brocade are grouped round another log fire. A feature of this room is the pretty little bay window with wide sill, through which one looks across the lawn (surrounded by trees and rosebeds) to half-timbered cottages and the Norman church, the clock of which chimes every quarter-hour.

The pink bedroom, low-beamed, has sweet peas on curtains and duvet (and in its bathroom, a plethora of things like bath essence, talc, etc.), a moss-green carpet and violets on the Royal Albert bone china for early-morning tea. The peach room has an elegant Victorian bathroom. The blue room is almost as attractive.

Some visitors eat at the Wheelbarrow and Castle Inn (Radford) or award-winning Brown's (Worcester), but menus at Upton House are good – a typical meal might comprise seafood vol-au-vent, stuffed lamb, chocolate truffle cake and cheeses.

It is hoped to get the old cider-mill at the back restored in due course. Meantime, if you want to see cider being made in the traditional way (in October) there is another mill nearby which you can visit. Children enjoy exploring the orchard, and meeting the ducks. From Upton House one can readily visit the Bredon and Malvern hills (Hereford and the Wye Valley beyond them); such Cotswold beauty-spots as Broadway or Chipping Campden; and, in the other direction, Stratford-upon-Avon in Warwickshire. Worcester (cathedral and china factory), Spetchley gardens and several garden centres are other options.

Readers' comments: Excellent. Comfort and friendliness.

VILLAGE FARM

Sturton-by-Stow, north-west of Lincoln, LN1 2AE   Tel: 0427 788309

4 bedrooms (single, double or family) from £10. Less for 2 nights or bargain breaks. Rooms have central heating or electric heaters; armchairs; views of garden; tea/coffee facilities. No smoking.
Dinner £7 for 4 courses with coffee. No smoking. Drinks can be brought in.
Sitting-room with central heating, open fire, TV, books, record-player.
Garden and farmland, with hard tennis court, coarse fishing, rough shooting.
Nearest main road A15 from Lincoln to Humber Bridge.
Closed to visitors November–February, (except for house-parties of 6.)

In the middle of this usually quiet village stands an early Victorian house, now pleasantly furnished by Sheila Bradshaw – at the heart of a 350-acre farm where pedigree cattle and sheep are raised. For the sitting-room she chose a pale green carpet, pink velvet curtains held back in tasselled loops, and flowery chintzes; among many Victorian heirlooms are things of her own making – canvaswork or patchwork cushions, for instance. She is a keen Women's Institute member, a handbell-ringer, loves flower-arranging and, when I visited, had just completed a big sampler depicting the house itself. Her husband's family farmed in Sturton for many generations back: among his enthusiasms is driving a gig, with a high-stepping Hackney horse bred for the purpose.

Guests have the use of two small dining-rooms. A typical menu: crème de menthe grapefruit, chicken casserole, chocolate mousse. Upstairs are very attractive bedrooms: one, with matching Sanderson wallpaper and fabrics, has a sloping ceiling and odd windows; in the peach-and-cream one is a rocking-chair; one of the prettiest has blue Laura Ashley sprigged linen and a Philippine cane chair. In the garden is a vast walnut tree; to one side are pantiled barns.

The Wolds, the coast and the great Humber Bridge are easily reached. Nearby sights include Doddington Hall, a country park, Gainsborough Old Hall, Tattershall Castle, Pennell's nursery gardens and Stow's cathedral-like church. The Red Arrows aerobatic team is based near here. Lincoln is described on other pages. It is full of antique shops and at Helmswell is a massive antiques centre.

Readers' comments: Very helpful, a lovely week. Sheer magic! Comfort, views and value – all very good.

A modern alternative in Lincoln itself (5 minutes' walk from the centre) is **Carline Guest House** (tel: 0522 30422) which is kept in immaculate and comfortable style by Gill and John Pritchard. Bed-and-breakfast only but unusually well-equipped; and very moderate prices for rooms with TV, own bathroom, etc. – and eggs from their own hens.

WALDON COTTAGE

The Square, Sheepwash, Beaworthy, north of Okehampton,
Devon, EX21 5NE   Tel: 040923 382

CDS

4 bedrooms (single, double or family) from £12. Less for 7 nights. Rooms have electric heaters; bathroom; armchairs; views of country. Tea in bed available.
Dinner £7.50 for 4 courses and coffee, at 8pm. Coffee, tea, for a charge. Drinks can be brought in.

Sitting-room with open fire, TV, books, piano.
Nearest main road A3072 from Hatherleigh to Holsworthy.
Closed November–Easter

This pair of pink cottages with clematis on the walls are the prettiest of all the thatched houses surrounding the village square. Here Josh Behenna (previously an electronics engineer) and his wife Constance have a tea-room and guest-house. Josh is the author of a book on West Country shipwrecks, photos of which fill the walls of the low-ceilinged dining-room, while pot-plants cram the deep window-sills; and, on chilly evenings, a fire crackles on the stone hearth. The sitting-room fireplace has a great beam possibly a thousand years old, from a demolished chapel mentioned in Domesday Book, and a bread oven alongside. The green velvet armchairs are particularly comfortable, and there is an upholstered rocking-chair too. Bedrooms have antiques, rosy fabrics and latched board doors.

Constance cooks traditional meals such as home-made soup with hot wholemeal rolls; roast beef; fresh fruit salad with clotted cream; followed by cheese and freshly ground coffee.

Sheepwash, a conservation village, is near both Dartmoor and Exmoor; and the coast, too, is within reach to the north. Popular sights include Okehampton Castle, Meldon Dam, Alscott Farm Museum, the gardens of Crosspark and Rosemoor, Hartland Quay and quaint little Clovelly.

Readers' comments: A gem. Exceptionally nice people. Marvellous in every way.

> Prices are the minimum *per person* in a double room at the beginning of the year.

> It's best to stay at least 2–3 days: you cannot possibly appreciate an area if you only stay overnight (prices per night are often less, too, if you stay on). The vouchers on page **ii** are usable for 3-night stays.

WALLACE FARM *New*   **C PT S-C**
Dinton, south-west of Aylesbury, Buckinghamshire, HP17 8UF
Tel: 0296 748660

3 bedrooms (double or family) from £12. Some have own bath; tea/coffee facilities; central heating; views of country or garden. (Washing-machine on request.)
Sitting-room with central heating, open fire, TV, books.

Large garden
Nearest main road A418 from Aylesbury to Oxford.

The same family had farmed here since the 16th century until very recently when the Cooks took over, bringing with them some unusual furniture collected when they lived abroad – a Chinese wedding-chest of scarlet leather, for instance, and one from the Philippines with mother-of-pearl inlay. An Indonesian dowry chest has carvings of bride, groom and dragons. Jackie has an eye for what is decorative and unusual, whether old or new – such as the hand-painted bathroom tiles which feature rare breeds of British animals.

Bedrooms differ in style – a small room in crisp white, for instance, and a very large one in pale green and pink with old pine furniture including a dresser loaded with books. There is a tiled breakfast-room with sturdy oak table and log stove (for dinner, visitors usually go to local inns: the Bugle Horn, Stone; the Bottle and Glass, Gibraltar; the Seven Stars, Dinton); by one stone hearth, an original bread oven has survived the centuries; and the guests' sitting-room has shuttered casement doors on two sides, opening onto a terrace with seats, croquet lawn, orchard, and cows seen grazing across a haha. Also in the grounds are ponds (with coarse fishing), Jacob sheep, ducks and geese. Bicycles on loan.

This peaceful spot is roughly equidistant to Heathrow Airport and London. There is a 'Capital Card' available for a few pounds which covers the cost of rail to London (1¼ hours) and unlimited bussing about on arrival, so that visiting London can alternate with tranquil country days.

The nearest town, Aylesbury, has a lively market, a 15th-century inn belonging to the National Trust, and historic houses in its byways. Other towns well worth visiting include Old Amersham – a particularly charming main street, very wide and flanked by historic buildings; Georgian Beaconsfield; Buckingham (a splendid beech avenue leads from it to Stowe, the Vanbrugh mansion that is now a famous school, grounds open to the public); High Wycombe (centre of furniture-making, with Disraeli's home – Hughenden – nearby); riverside Marlow; and Eton.

Dinton itself is a pleasant old village with stocks and whipping-post on its green, a Tudor manor house and mock ruins (look for fossils in its stones). Another attractive village is Bradenham, preserved by the National Trust.

298

WALLETT'S COURT *New*   **C H PT**
West Cliffe, north-east of Dover, Kent, CT15 6EW   Tel: 0304 852424

7 bedrooms (single, double or family) from £17. All have own bath/shower; TV; tea/coffee facilities; central heating; views of sea, country or garden. (Washing-machine on request.)
Dinner A la carte or £12 for 3 courses (with choices) and coffee, at 7–8pm. Vegetarian or special diets if ordered. Snacks. Tea, coffee, extra. Drinks can be ordered.
Sitting-room with central heating, open fire, books, piano. No smoking.
Large garden
Nearest main road A258 from Dover to Deal.

Built on cellars that date back to Norman times is a magnificent 17th-century manor house. But it is not just the building, or even the surrounding scenery (protected by the National Trust), which bring visitors here: Chris Oakley is an exceptional chef who has worked with the Roux brothers, at La Gavroche.

The huge sitting-room with carved oak beams and two fireplaces, one of stone and one of brick, has deep-set, pine-shuttered sash windows with window-seats; buttoned velvet chairs and antiques furnish the room. In the elegant dining-room, tables are laid with bronze cutlery and Royal Worcester china decorated with game birds. Dining chairs are upholstered in pink, there is a log fire, brass-rubbings decorate the walls and on elaborately carved woodwork are the date 1627 and the initials of the Gibbon family (its most celebrated member was the author of *The Rise and Fall of the Roman Empire*). Bedrooms in the house are excellent (some with large, buttoned, velvet armchairs; all with antiques), bathrooms elegant. Other bedrooms, in modern pine style, are in a converted barn. (The patchwork spreads were made by Lea.) There are murals on some walls; handsome newel-posts on the stairs; mellow brickwork exposed here and there. The Norman cellars are used for snooker and table tennis.

As to the meals, these are very special and people come from far afield to dine at Wallett's Court (non-residents admitted on Saturday; no meals on Sundays). The Saturday dinners often include such choices as game terrine with citrus salad followed by turbot with lobster sauce, a sorbet, haunch of venison in claret, and a wide choice of puddings. With the coffee come petits fours. Weekday dinners, though less extensive, are of similar quality.

The peaceful countryside along this coast, facing the Dover Straits, is only three miles from Dover, its castle and its harbour (for day-trips to France). One can walk along the famous white cliffs here, and there is a fine garden (The Pines) with waterfall and Nemons' statue of Churchill. St Margaret's Bay is where cross-Channel swimmers start from, and further along are Walmer and Deal – both with castles, a string of which (Norman through to Victorian) dot this coastline as it faces Europe. The white cliffs are in fact the end of the South Downs, one of the region's most beautiful features, with many good drives or walks among the hills and historic villages (Canterbury is quite near).

For explanation of code letters (**C, D, H, PT, S, S-C, X**) **see page xxviii.**

WALNUT COTTAGE   C(14) **H PT**
Old Romsey Road, Cadnam, west of Southampton, Hampshire, SO4 2NP
Tel: 0703 812275

3 bedrooms (single or double) from £13. Much less for 2 nights or bargain breaks. Rooms have central heating; shower or bathroom; TV, armchairs; views of country or garden; tea/coffee facilities.
2 sitting-rooms with central heating, open fire, TV, video, books.
Garden
Nearest main road M27 from London to Bournemouth.

The road no longer leads anywhere (its days ended when a nearby motorway replaced it). The little white cottage, with brimming window-boxes and a red rambler-rose by the door, stands in a pretty garden (with an old well) which traps the sun. One bedroom opens onto this.

All the rooms have been attractively furnished by Charlotte and Eric Osgood, who did much of the work themselves (even the tiling of the showers, and the flowery china door-knobs on each bedroom door). There are two sitting-rooms with pale carpets, cretonne armchairs, flowers on the window-sills and interesting objects on the shelves. One has windows on all three sides. In the dining-room are Regency chairs, cupboard and mirror; a diminutive iron grate, as old as the cottage, has been preserved (though the only fireplace still in use is in the larger sitting-room). Here Mrs Osgood serves breakfast on Royal Doulton vineleaf china, but for other meals, she recommends a thatched and whitewashed inn a few yards down the lane (the 12th-century Sir John Barleycorn).

The cottage is on the edge of the New Forest (it was originally occupied by foresters). Romsey and Broadlands are very near; Beaulieu, Breamore House, Bucklers Hard (historic waterside village), Salisbury, Winchester and Bournemouth only a little further. From Southampton (with Spitfire and maritime museums – and sometimes the *QE2*) there are trips to the Isle of Wight, and London is under a two-hour journey. The nearby motorway, its hum just within earshot, makes many distant sights easy to reach.

The Osgoods not only lend maps and cycles free, but have photocopied useful hints for a selection of car outings in the area, describing the route for each, listing sights, and also recommending the best inns for lunches, good bookshops etc. They have also mapped out a 'Howards' Way' tour; and can tell you where to buy trout, venison, local fruit etc.

This is a good choice for an October break, when the forest colours are superb; but book well ahead if you want to go in September when Southampton's boat show and Beaulieu's 'auto jumble' sale are on. May is a good month for the many superb gardens such as Exbury, Furzey, Spinners, Compton Acres and various garden centres.

Readers' comments: Beautifully located . . . most helpful people. Delightful couple, charming rooms, comfortable; superb breakfasts. Excellent: a charming couple. Very impressed by their care and attention. A spacious and comfortable bedroom; helpful hosts. Their interest in the comfort and pleasure of their guests has to be experienced to be believed. Faultless accommodation and welcome. Welcome, care, attention, food – all generous.

WARDEN'S HOUSE C(5) D
Lode Lane, Wicken, south of Ely, Cambridgeshire, CB7 5XP
Tel: 0353 720274

rear view

1 bedroom (double) from £8. Less for some stays of 7 nights. Room has central heating or electric heater; views of country and garden; tea/coffee facilities. No smoking.
Sitting/dining-room with central heating, gas fire, books. No smoking.
Garden and orchard.
Nearest main road A1123 from Stretham to Soham.

Many who visit historic Ely and its superb cathedral prefer somewhere quieter to stay overnight. This comfortable house with garden, tucked away behind high beech hedges on the edge of Wicken Fen (Britain's very first wildlife reserve), provides the answer. It is the home of naturalist Tim Bennett – head warden of the Fen – and his wife Cindy (an amateur botanist), an interesting couple with whom to stay before spending a day exploring this fen, one of the few areas of true wilderness that are still left. (Bed-and-breakfast only; pub meals in the village at the Maid's Head.)

The fens' history is well explained in the National Trust's interpretation centre at Wicken. This is a marvellous place for anyone who enjoys watching waterfowl and strolling by the waterways. Cambridge itself is within easy reach, and Anglesey Abbey (with gardens); also Saffron Walden (Essex) and Bury St Edmunds (Suffolk), both historic towns in very pretty landscapes. This is also an area for boating – for example, you can go on the Great Ouse to Huntingdon, and watch or join in watersports on Grafham Water. Ely and Peterborough have particularly fine cathedrals; March, a church with 200 flying angels; Newmarket, its heath where you can see racehorses exercising. The dykes and Roman ways throughout the county provide good footpaths for walkers.

Inclusive terms for dinner, bed-and-breakfast (particularly for a week) can be much lower than those quoted here for these items taken separately. For short-notice bookings you may be able to get a reduction.

No proprietor wants to have a room standing empty. This particularly applies to Sunday nights. Some hotels make a discount if you want only two courses from a three-course menu.

All prices are inclusive of any VAT or service charge. They are minimum prices: superior rooms or high-season bookings may cost more.

In holiday areas, travel on any day other than a summer Saturday if you can. Make ferry, Motorail or coach/train reservations well in advance if travelling at such periods.

THE WATERMILL
near Hildersham, south of Cambridge, CB1 6BS   Tel: 0223 891520

C PT S(off-peak)

1 bedroom (double or family) at £13.25. Less for 7 nights or bargain breaks. Discounts for repeat bookings. Central heating, electric heater; bathroom; armchairs; views of country and garden. Clothes-washing facilities. No smoking.
Dinner £4.50 to £6.75 for 2 or 4 courses (with choices) and coffee, about 7pm. Vegetarian or special diets if ordered.

Lunches, packed lunches, snacks. Coffee, tea, free. Drinks can be brought in. No smoking.
Large garden with birdwatching, trout fishing (extra) and boating.
Nearest main road A604 from Cambridge to Colchester.

A track through fields, past the stump of a windmill and by a narrow stretch of the River Granta, suddenly comes to this very large watermill – last used (for grinding wheat or sawing wood) in 1904. Its present owner, engineer David Hartland, is engaged in the long task of restoring the 7-ton waterwheel. One day he hopes it will generate enough power to run a heat-pump for the house. He has amassed a collection of old photographs and drawings illustrating the history of the mill, which dates from the 11th century (the present buildings are early 19th century).

Guests are accommodated in one-time stables (converted in the '30s, when a door from Cambridge Castle was salvaged and installed here). Meals are brought to their roomy bedroom (or served on the lawn by the river when the weather is sunny). The unusual bedroom (white plank walls, sloping ceiling) is furnished in cottage style: sprigged fabrics, and rugs on the floorboards. The oak bedstead dates from the 18th century. The room has views of lawn, weeping willows and the mill-stream, the sound of which lulls one to sleep.

The Hartlands' bees, chickens and sheep (and trout from the stream) contribute to the meals which Lynne cooks superbly – home-made game soup might be followed by lamb with fennel and scalloped potatoes; then caramelized oranges with home-made florentines; and cheeses.

Cambridge is only a few miles away. If your time is limited, the best selection of colleges to visit is perhaps King's, Corpus Christi, Queen's and Trinity – and there are also the Botanic Gardens, the great art treasures of the Fitzwilliam Museum, the lawns and gardens of 'the Backs' and an unusual house, Kettle's Yard, with beautifully arranged modern art and artefacts just as the owner left them. A boat or punt on the River Cam is a particularly enjoyable way of seeing the Backs (of colleges). Other sightseeing options include Saffron Walden, Newmarket, Ely, a number of stately homes such as Audley End, Wimpole Hall and Chilford Hall.

Readers' comments: Superb – a lovely weekend. Enjoyed very much. Warm welcome.

302

WELLPRITTON FARM

C D S

Holne, Ashburton, west of Newton Abbot, Devon, TQ13 7RX
Tel: 03643 273

4 bedrooms (double or family), £11. Less for 7 nights. Rooms have central heating or electric heaters; shower; views of country or garden; tea/coffee facilities. Laundering facilities.
Dinner £6 for 4 courses and coffee, at any time to suit guests. Special diets if ordered. Packed lunches, snacks. Non-residents not admitted. Drinks can be brought in.

Sitting-room with central heating, TV, books. Games room with snooker and table tennis.
Garden and open fields, with unheated swimming-pool.
Nearest main road B3357 from Ashburton to Tavistock.

Tucked away in a fold of the gentle hills south of Dartmoor is this small farm where sheep and pigs are kept; donkeys, goats and rabbits too.

Sue Townsend has furnished the bedrooms very prettily, and she equips them with supplies of fruit-squash and biscuits as well as tea. There is a 'family unit' of two rooms and a shower, and a ground-floor suite. A comfortable sitting-room is available to guests.

Four-course dinners are served in the dining-room. After a starter such as melon or pâté, the main course will probably be a roast, poultry or steak-and-kidney pudding, perhaps followed by fruit pie or flan, always accompanied by Devonshire cream, then cheese and coffee. Sue tries to cater for every guest individually. There is no charge for washing and ironing facilities, mealtimes are flexible, the welcome warm, and many extra services provided (loan of maps, hair-dryer, free tea on arrival, dog kennel etc.).

From the farm, which has a small swimming-pool, there are views of the moors, and within a short drive one can reach Exeter, all the resorts and beaches of Torbay, Plymouth and innumerable beauty-spots in the countryside and along the coast. Dartmoor has a wild beauty all its own – a vast expanse of open country (one of the National Parks) with market towns and villages here and there, streams in the valleys and rocks high on the hills where sometimes mist or rain are dense. Nature trails, prehistoric remains, minibus tours, Buckfast and Buckland abbeys, steam railway, butterfly farm, Shire Horse Centre, Dartington Hall, great gardens, six garden centres, museums and historic buildings are among the possibilities for sightseeing.

Readers' comments: We were pampered, the situation is an absolute dream. Loud praises of all aspects, especially the food. The very best: nothing is too much trouble. One of our favourites; Sue is one of the best cooks; food beautifully presented. Very enjoyable; warm welcome, good food, comfortable. Excellent accommodation; extra touches meant so much.

WEST CROSS HOUSE

High Street, Tenterden, Kent, TN30 6JL   Tel: 05806 2224

C PT S

7 bedrooms (single, double or family) from £12. Less for 7 nights. Rooms have central heating; armchairs; tea/coffee facilities.
Dinner £7.50 for 3 courses and coffee, at 7pm. Special diets if ordered. Drinks can be ordered.
Sitting-room   with central heating, open fire, TV, books.
Nearest main road A28 from Hastings to Canterbury.
Closed in winter

At the quieter end of the street stands this small Georgian house furnished with antiques, oriental carpets and well chosen wallpapers. There are attractive details, such as fanlight, arches and turned banisters – and a pretty garden of paved paths, flowers and a magnolia. The big sitting-room, which runs right through from front to back, has a huge log grate in a brick inglenook. Each bedroom is different. I particularly liked one with velvet chairs and Paisley wallpaper.

A typical menu cooked by Mrs May might comprise home-made celery soup, a trout or steak pie with fresh vegetables, and home-made ice cream. Dinner must be ordered in advance.

Tenterden, an interesting old town itself, is in the middle of an area full of things to see and do and is an agreeable place in which to shop. Within easy reach are the castles of Leeds, Chilham and Bodiam; Battle Abbey; Smallhythe (Ellen Terry's home); and stately homes such as Penshurst. Canterbury is 45 minutes away. All around are the pretty villages, ancient churches and rural views typical of Kent, 'the market-garden of England'. Seaside resorts and many of the historic Cinque Ports are easily reached. Elegant Tunbridge Wells and its shops (antiques, books, crafts, clothes boutiques) lies a few miles in the other direction. This is an area where there is always something interesting afoot – notices along the country roads announce events like ox roasts and country-and-steam fairs or invite you to buy Jersey cream or to pick your own strawberries. (My favourite simply read: 'Beware. Ducks crossing'.) Tenterden has a steam railway, the Romney Marsh churches are near, and fine gardens (Sissinghurst and Great Dixter among them) are too numerous to list – as are garden centres.

Readers' comments: Excellent standards.

Single people may find more company in houses that have a shared dining-table, a bar, and no TV in the sitting-room. As my descriptions indicate, some owners mingle more with their guests than others do. Houses marked **S** charge singles little or no more than half a double.

There is no point in turning up with a dog or child in tow if the description does not say these are accepted; nor in expecting a garden, or alcoholic drinks, if these are not indicated.

WEST HOUSE C(6) **D PT S**
12 West Street, Warminster, Wiltshire, BA12 8JJ Tel: 0985 213936

2 bedrooms (single or double) from £16. Less for 3 nights. Rooms have central heating or electric heaters; shower or bathroom; armchairs; views of country or garden; tea/coffee facilities.
Dinner £11 for 3 courses with wine and coffee, at 8pm. Vegetarian or special diets if ordered. Lunches, packed lunches, snacks.
2 sitting-rooms with central heating, open fire, TV, books, piano, record-player.
Large garden
Nearest main road A36 from Salisbury to Bath.

A very graceful sitting-room extends from front to back of the 18th-century stone house: soft pink sofas and armchairs contrast with a celadon carpet, their colours complemented by those of handsome chinoiserie curtains with pheasants. White-shuttered windows are at each end. On the walls of this and other rooms are some of the sporting prints and watercolours which Charles Lane collects (and writes about). A fine staircase leads to charming bedrooms: I particularly liked one with rosebud wallpaper matching the pink slub spread on the cane-headed bed. Flowers and fruit are put in each room.

In the equally attractive dining-room, Celia Lane uses cordon bleu recipes for such meals as salmon mousse, chicken bonne femme, and the best raspberry pavlova I've ever tasted.

At the back are two large walled gardens with old-fashioned roses, herbaceous beds and an immense tulip tree (it flowers late in July).

Charles is, incidentally, a descendant of the celebrated Jane Lane whose story is told elsewhere (see King's Lodge).

The Lanes love to tell their guests of good places to explore – not just the famous sights (Salisbury, Bath, Glastonbury and Wells) but delightful spots such as Shaftesbury, Frome, Devizes or Bruton, for instance. Quite close by are Amesbury, Avebury ring, Stonehenge, Longleat and its famous lions, the lovely Vale of Pewsey, Wilton House, Stourhead and many beautiful but lesser known gardens. Plenty of antique shops in and around Warminster.

Book well ahead: many of these houses have few rooms. Do not expect dinner if you have not booked it.

If you have not arrived by, perhaps, 6pm your room may be let to someone else – unless you telephone to say you are on your way.

Unless otherwise agreed, send a 10% deposit when confirming your booking.

WESTERN HOUSE C S X
Cavendish, north-west of Sudbury, Suffolk, CO10 8AR Tel: 0787 280550

4 bedrooms (single, double or family) from £10. Rooms have central heating or electric heaters; views of country or garden.
Large garden
Nearest main road A1092 from Clare to Long Melford.

Twice made redundant, Peter Marshall decided he had had enough of industry and – his children now being grown up – would instead make a living from his best asset: his attractive 400-year-old house in the historic village of Cavendish.

He and his wife Jean (who teaches singing) are vegetarians, so at one end they started a wholefood shop, full of the good smells of dried fruit and fresh herbs, and refurnished several bedrooms to take bed-and-breakfast guests. Breakfast is served in bedrooms. Options include all kinds of good things (such as their own muesli, eggs, mushrooms, tomatoes and home-made bread) but no bacon. They are prepared to provide meatless evening meals, or will recommend good restaurants of all kinds in the village, at Long Melford or in Sudbury.

Each beamed bedroom, reached via zigzag corridors, is very pretty, and spacious – well equipped with chairs, table etc. One at the front (double-glazed, because it looks onto the main road through the village) has a fresh white-and-green colour scheme extending even to the sheets.

One of the nicest features is the large and informal garden where paved paths wander between old-fashioned flowers, elderly fruit trees, and plant troughs.

Cavendish is one of a string of mediaeval villages described elsewhere. Clare is close, so is Sudbury town, Bury St Edmunds and Long Melford – very long indeed, lined with dignified houses and antique shops. Its church and its great mansions (Melford Hall and Kentwell Hall) are well worth seeing. So are Lavenham, Kersey, East Bergholt, Dedham (Alfred Munnings exhibition), the Romano-Norman city of Colchester (with castle), Castle Hedingham, a steam railway and Beth Chatto's garden.

Readers' comments: Excellent, with very good breakfasts. Much enjoyed it; and the shop is excellent. Extremely comfortable; warm welcome. Absolutely excellent, high standard.

When to go? Seaside resorts or other places suitable for children will be at their busiest (and dearest) in July–August and during half-term holidays (especially, in late May, which is also a bank holiday period). Other peak periods are, of course, Easter, Christmas, New Year and the bank holiday in late August. (The bank holiday in early May is not usually a peak, because it comes rather soon after Easter, but much depends on the weather.) There are local peaks, too (the Gold Cup races at Cheltenham or the regatta at Henley, for instance, are apt to fill hotels for miles around), and local troughs (Brighton, a conference centre, is least busy in high summer). You won't get much personal attention when hotels are full to bursting.

WESTERN HOUSE

Winchelsea Road, Rye, East Sussex, TN31 7EL   Tel: 0797 223419

C PT X

3 bedrooms (double or family) from £12. Much less for 2 nights or bargain breaks. Rooms have central heating or electric heaters; shower and wc; armchairs; views of country or garden; tea/coffee facilities. Coffee, tea, for a charge.
Large garden
Nearest main road A259 from Dover to the west.

The mediaeval port of Rye was perched high on a thumb of land (almost an island) projecting into the sea. But centuries ago the sea receded, leaving behind dry land which became ideal pasturage for sheep. It is here, at the foot of Rye town, that tile-hung Western House was built in the 18th century, commanding far views – you can even see Hastings in clear weather – from its cobbled terrace (with working pump) where tea may be taken, or from the huge lawn surrounded by brilliant flowerbeds set against mellow stone walls. On summer evenings, the terrace is lit by old Victorian street-lamps.

Artist Ron Dellar is the present owner of Western House, and his paintings fill the dining-room walls. Up the staircase, and in the bedrooms are all manner of 'finds' he has amassed over the years: African masks, a parrot in a glass dome, an 1820 box of paints ('Constable was alive then', he comments), Rupert Bear books, antique toys. Melanie, his wife, sells Victorian lace, linen, baby-gowns and books which are laid out in the big entrance hall.

This is a house of character, as befits its long history. A boat-builder lived here and, later on, members of Parliament. Among its visitors (in 1913) was the impressionist artist Pissarro; and Ron has incorporated him in a mural featuring Rye church which he painted for one of the bedrooms. All these rooms are attractively decorated, with interesting wallpapers and fresh flowers, and have good views of the marshes across which you can walk to Winchelsea. There's a moated Martello tower out there, giant marsh-frogs croak throatily, you may see herons or marsh harriers flying overhead. (Although the house is on the road to Winchelsea I slept undisturbed.)

Around Rye are Camber sands, Bodiam Castle, Battle Abbey, Winchelsea and gardens at Sissinghurst and Great Dixter.

Dinner is not usually served because Rye has so many good inns and restaurants such as the Old Forge or Flushing Inn.

Readers' comments: We were particularly delighted. View magnificent.

Houses which do *not* take children tend to have vacancies in July and August.

No one in this book insists that you stay out all day. But do not necessarily expect heating to be on, drinks available, etc.

WESTLEA *New*   **C(2) D H PT S**

29 Riverside Road, Alnmouth, south-east of Alnwick, Northumberland, NE66 2SD   Tel: 0665 830730

7 bedrooms (single, twin, double or family) from £12. Less for bargain breaks. Some have own bath/shower; TV; tea/coffee facilities; central heating; views of river, country or garden; balcony. No smoking. (Washing-machine on request.)
Dinner £6.50 for 4 courses (with some choice) and coffee, at 7pm. Non-residents not admitted. Vegetarian or special diets if ordered. Lunches, packed lunches, snacks. Tea, coffee, free. Drinks can be brought in.
Sitting-room with central heating, TV, books, record-player, video.
Small garden
Nearest main road A1 from Newcastle to Edinburgh.

This is a very comfortable modern guest-house facing the Aln estuary, immaculately kept by Janice Edwards. One attractive bedroom (wildflower fabrics and cane bedheads) opens onto the sunny front garden; others vary in size and style but all are well equipped. The upstairs sitting-room has a balcony from which to enjoy the river view.

Breakfasts are imaginative; and for dinner (4 courses) there may be such dishes as beef, salmon, Cheviot lamb (with Northumbrian baked suet-puddings) or game pie. With coffee come home-made truffles.

Nearby Alnwick is the seat of the Duke of Northumberland (and the historic Percy family whose deeds feature in so many of Shakespeare's plays), who lives in Alnwick Castle – ruined but then restored in the 18th century. This area is a good place in which to follow riverside walks; to explore the dramatic coastline and its many castles – particularly Warkworth at daffodil-time; to visit Craster for its succulent kippers (the ancient smoke-house is a listed building); and to walk to the romantic clifftop ruins of Dunstanburgh which Turner painted many times; or little Amble for its sandy beaches and island of eiderducks. Alnmouth itself is a picturesque yachting resort and has one of England's oldest golf courses (1869).

Visitors enjoy trips to the Farne Islands to watch seals and puffins, to Holy Island and to the Scottish borders. At Bamburgh is the Grace Darling museum as well as a theatrically sited castle and golden sands; inland are Rothbury and the mansion of Cragside. Although scenery – free from crowds – is the area's greatest attraction, there are plenty of other interesting things to see, such as the wild white cattle, a rare survival, at Chillingham; the farm park at Embleton; or the World Bird Research Station (very tame birds in 17th-century buildings, and an arboretum). Blyth has one of the county's several railway museums, there are a great many country parks, and this is a good area in which to seek out craft workshops.

Take the trouble to get free booklets about the area before you set off. Every habitual traveller should keep a copy of the booklet of local Tourist Information Centres issued free by the English Tourist Board (Thames Tower, Blacks Road, London W6; tel: 01-846 9000) for this purpose.

WHEATHILL FARM

C

Church Lane, Shearsby, north-west of Market Harborough, Leicestershire, LE17 6PG   Tel: 053758 663

4 bedrooms (single or double) from £10. Less for 7 nights. Rooms have central heating; one has shower; armchairs; views of farmland or garden; tea/coffee facilities. No smoking.

Dinner £6 for 3 courses and coffee, at 6.30pm. Vegetarian or special diets if ordered. Packed lunches. Coffee, tea, free. Drinks can be brought in.

Sitting-room with central heating, open fire, TV, books.

Large garden with boules and croquet.

Nearest main road A50 from Leicester to Northampton.

In 1823, the owners of this cottage (part Saxon, part mediaeval) put a new façade on the front: brick, with trim white paintwork. But behind this the old beamed rooms remained unchanged, with huge inglenook housing a log stove, and a twisting stair.

Sue Timms has a decorative touch, and uses pretty fabrics or beribboned net in cottage-style bedrooms (even in one of the bathrooms too). The house is full of unusual heirlooms, including a 100-year-old pot-plant which originally belonged to a lighthouse-keeper (her great-uncle) on the wild Farne Islands off the Northumberland coast. Outside is an attractive garden with lily-pool and lake.

Home-produced meat and eggs go into the meals which Sue prepares. A typical example: grapefruit grilled with brown sugar, sirloin of beef with Yorkshire pudding and garden vegetables, summer pudding with cream.

Shearsby is, like many others around here, a particularly pretty village, not far from Georgian Market Harborough (its lively markets date from 1200) and at the centre of rich grazing country – a tranquil region threaded by waterways with, at Foxton, ten locks packed in a tier to raise boats up a 75-foot incline.

Further north is the scenic Charnwood Forest area – a mixture of heath, crags, ridges and remnants of oak forest with fine views from its hilltops. Within a short distance are Anstey's mediaeval packhorse bridge, the pretty little spa town of Ashby de la Zouch, a particularly interesting church at Breedon-on-the-Hill, and Loughborough which has a carillon of 47 bells in a high tower in the park. Other sights include Birdland, Twycross Zoo and Stanford Hall.

Single people may find more company in houses that have a shared dining-table, a bar, and no TV in the sitting-room. As my descriptions indicate, some owners mingle more with their guests than others do. Houses marked **S** charge singles little or no more than half a double.

Families which pick establishments with plenty of games, swimming-pool, animals, etc., or that are near free museums, parks and walks, can save a lot on keeping youngsters entertained.

WHICHAM OLD RECTORY
Silecroft, west of Millom, Cumbria, LA18 5LS   Tel: 0657 2954

4 bedrooms (single, double or family) from £11.50. Less for 2 nights. Rooms have central heating; armchairs; views of country or garden; tea/coffee facilities.
Dinner £5.50 for 3 courses (some choices) and coffee, at a time to suit guests. Vegetarian or special diets if ordered. Packed lunches, snacks. Tea, free. Drinks can be brought in.
Sitting-room with central heating, log fire, TV, books.
Large garden with clock golf.
Nearest main road A595 from Greenodd to Workington.

So many people head for the heart of the Lake District that the outlying areas of the National Park remain uncrowded and uncommercialized. The south-west corner in particular is often overlooked, even though it is within an easy drive of famous beauty-spots and has its own particular attractions – uncrowded beaches, for example, and a mild maritime climate. The last accounts for the peaches and mulberries that flourish in the garden of the Old Rectory – the one appearing on the dinner-table, the other going into the wine which guests usually sample.

The house is typical of those Victorian rectories built for Trollope-size clerical families with domestic staff in proportion. David Kitchener – an ex-RAF supply officer and an accomplished woodworker – has put a lot of work into the spacious house, some of it to display intriguing family possessions – Victorian dish-covers, an ancient cast-iron pressure cooker – and other interesting bric-à-brac: a big model of a dhow he bought when on service in the Middle East, a fairground flare, woodwork from a Warwickshire church, a collection of kukris and other weapons.

He and Judy Kitchener also find time to grow most of the vegetables which she uses in her enthusiastic cooking. There is always a home-made soup, with alternative first courses, then for example coq au vin (which may be half a chicken per head), with at least three vegetables, to which guests help themselves, and a sweet such as raspberry mousse, to which the garden is likely to have contributed too. The freshly baked bread is the speciality of Judy's mother – who worries if dishes come back from the table empty, in case guests had not been offered enough.

All the bedrooms overlook the lawn, next to which is a small semi-circular conservatory which David has built onto the end of the stable, so that guests can enjoy the garden even when a sea breeze is blowing. The energetic can take a footpath to the top of Black Combe (2000 feet) for views of Scotland and Wales. The less energetic can explore the beach at Silecroft, with its sands and rock-pools. Up the coast are mansions and gardens, a narrow-gauge railway, and old seaports. Eastward are pleasant market towns, Morecambe Bay and the seabird reserve of Walney Island. Inland is, of course, the Lake District.

Two-thirds of the houses in this book have bargain breaks or other discounts on offer, some exclusive to readers. Only a third raise prices at the peak of summer.

WHITE BARN

Crede Lane, Bosham, west of Chichester, West Sussex, PO18 8NX
Tel: 0243 573113

rear view

6 bedrooms (single, double or family) from £16. Less for 7 nights or bargain breaks. Rooms have central heating or electric heaters; shower or bathroom; armchairs; views of garden; tea/coffee facilities.
Dinner 4 courses (with choices) and coffee, at 7pm. Special diets if ordered. Snacks.

Non-residents not admitted. Drinks can be brought in. No meals in August.
2 sitting-rooms with central heating, open fire, TV, books.
Garden
Nearest main road A27 from Chichester to Portsmouth.

As interesting architecturally as any house in this book, White Barn is no barn but a very modern house indeed (single storey), designed by architect Frank Guy, and standing in the seclusion of a former orchard.

The dining-room is impressive: its principal features are a roof of exposed boards, a vast glass wall on one side (opening onto a red-tiled terrace and lawn), and a circular brick-edged flowerbed half indoors and half out.

This room is open to the big kitchen with its scarlet Aga cooker, pans hanging from brass hooks, and solid beech work-counter with old brass grocery-scales.

Then there is an oddly-shaped sitting-room, built all around the circular brick hearth on which a modern log stove stands. Its huge sofas face a narrow window 20 feet high. Throughout there are white walls and glossy scarlet doors.

Few visitors prefer a separate table for meals but join all the others at a huge pine refectory table, laid with flowery Portmeirion pottery, where Susan Trotman serves such appetite-whetting meals as curried parsnip soup (or some very original salad or pâté) before, perhaps, pork cooked with ginger (and four vegetables), then a pavlova topped with lemon curd and Jersey cream, or a Bakewell tart.

Bedrooms open onto the garden, or overlook it. One is an imaginatively planned family suite: the room with children's bunk beds is like a cabin.

Not far away is the Saxon harbour of Bosham (its church is depicted in the Bayeux tapestry), thronged with little boats. Chichester, described elsewhere, lies in one direction and the historic naval waterfront of Portsmouth in the other – where you can visit HMS *Victory*, the *Mary Rose*, the dockyard museum, old bastions and byways, Southsea Castle, and the ring of high Victorian forts. The colossal, ironclad HMS *Warrior* is the latest attraction.

Readers' comments: Very comfortable, food superb. Excellent value, memorable – not to be missed! Wonderful. Warm and welcoming. A memorable stay; outstanding. Food is out of this world. Top class! Comfortable, restful, very good food in ample quantity.

WHITE BEAR INN
Shipston-on-Stour, Warwickshire, CV36 4AJ   Tel: 0608 61558

9 bedrooms (single, double or family) from £19 **to readers of this book**. Less for 7 nights or bargain breaks. Rooms have gas heaters; shower, or bathroom; TV, armchairs; tea/coffee facilities.

Dinner A la carte, from 7.30pm. Special diets if ordered. Lunches, packed lunches, snacks. Drinks can be ordered.

Nearest main road A34 from Oxford to Stratford-upon-Avon.

In the centre of Shipston – a quiet little town on the edge of the Cotswolds – is this typical old inn. Typical except for the food, which Hugh and Suzanne Roberts have made exceptional. Even the snacks served in the beamed bar are well above the ordinary (delicious stuffed mushrooms, for instance, with a topping of melted cheese). At dinner, one chooses from a lengthy à la carte menu that includes such things as mussel chowder or salmon-and-prawn pâté for starters; beef en croûte with Madeira sauce or veal provençale (cooked with aubergine, tomato, garlic and wine); then perhaps an apricot soufflé or chocolate sponge sandwiched with maple cream and chocolate mousse.

Upstairs are pine-doored bedrooms pleasantly decorated – I particularly liked a blue attic room with leafy view; others overlook road or roofs. Fresh flowers and good pictures are everywhere. (No sitting-room.)

Shipston (itself an attractive town, with interesting little shops) lies conveniently between Oxford and Stratford-upon-Avon. Within easy motoring distance are Warwick Castle, the Cotswold towns, Cheltenham Spa, Woodstock (for Blenheim Palace), the famous gardens of Hidcote and Kiftsgate, and the lovely Vale of Evesham from which come the White Bear's fruit and vegetables.

When writing to me, if you want a reply please enclose a stamped addressed envelope.

There is no point in turning up with a dog or child in tow if the description does not say these are accepted; nor in expecting a garden, or alcoholic drinks, if these are not indicated.

If, when touring, you ask a host to book your next stop – at another *Staying Off the Beaten Track* house – remember to pay the cost of the telephone call.

WHITE HOUSE

Grindon, east of Leek, Staffordshire, ST13 7TP   Tel: 053 88 250

3 bedrooms (double) from £12. Less for 2 nights. Rooms have central heating; TV, armchairs; views of country or garden; tea/coffee facilities. No smoking. Shower in one. **Dinner** £10 for 4 courses and coffee, at 7.30pm. Drinks can be brought in.

Sitting-room with central heating, open fire, books.
Garden
Nearest main road A523 from Macclesfield to Ashbourne.

In the 17th century, this sparkling white cottage was a little inn, in a beautiful part of the Peak District (1000 feet up, it overlooks the very lovely valley of the River Manifold). Philomena Bunce used to teach crafts and needlework, and every bedroom reflects this – the pretty, fresh colour schemes and the hand-made lampshades, cushions and padded bedheads are her work.

Outside is a very pleasant garden with seats on a paved area with roses and cottage flowers. Drink in hand, one can watch the sunlight fading and, over a mossy wall, cows ambling on their way to be milked, while the swifts dart low.

Philomena serves dinner in her pine dining-room only at weekends (at other times, visitors walk to the nearby Cavalier Inn). She is an excellent cook. On the night when I stayed, she served a very good pâté, chicken in a sauce of apples and cream (the accompanying mange-touts and other vegetables were lightly cooked), and a feather-light raspberry pavlova – on white-and-gold china, with quilted placemats. Breakfasts include several out-of-the-ordinary options, such as kippers delivered from Craster in Northumberland or a Staffordshire oatcake (like a pancake) topped with a tasty mushroom, mustard and egg mixture.

Apart from visiting the Peak District, Dovedale and the Manifold Valley from here, you can explore lesser-known Derbyshire and the much underrated north of Staffordshire. In the south the scenery is pastoral, with calm rivers. Derby city has an 18th-century quarter and other historic buildings, many parks, and Kedleston Hall – an Adam mansion. Alton Towers – an exceptional leisure park – is near. There are markets and impressive mediaeval churches in this area, fine gardens, riverside walks and pretty villages (Marston and Swarkestone, for instance), Melbourne Hall (art treasures, fine formal gardens and lake), ancient Repton with a church over 1000 years old, and the show village of Sudbury.

Readers' comments: Furnishings outstanding; highest standard of comfort, good food and warm welcome. Our stay one of the pleasantest ever. Absolutely superb – perfection! A wonderful find, and very reasonably priced. One of the best weekends we can remember; perfect comfort, lovely surroundings, delectable meals. A gem! Made to feel part of the family. Excellent, comfortable, friendly, a beautiful spot. Excellent accommodation, peaceful.

WHITE HOUSE *New*   **C PT**
10 High Street South, Olney, east of Milton Keynes, Buckinghamshire,
MK46 4AA   Tel: 0234 711478

8 bedrooms (single or double) from £16.25. Less for 7 nights. Some have own shower; tea/coffee facilities: central heating. (Washing-machine on request.)
Sitting-room with central heating, TV, books.
Small garden
Nearest main road A509 from Olney to Milton Keynes.

Although this house, dating from 1802, is on a busy road, there are quiet, modern bedrooms at the back – all immaculate. The breakfast-room overlooks a lily-pond in a small rock garden; and there is a comfortable sitting-room with big velvet armchairs. Right opposite is a good wine bar for evening meals: Ken and June Roberts serve only breakfasts (but with a varied choice). Unlimited help-yourself tea and coffee are available all day, free.

Olney is a very attractive little town with 18th-century and other old buildings, including an elaborately carved Lace Hall (Buckinghamshire was famous for its hand-made lace). The unusually wide High Street is where, every Shrove Tuesday, women race along tossing pancakes as they go. Off it are passages with antique shops open even on Sundays. As Olney is close to junction 14 of the M1, it is a useful place for a stopover (or when visiting nearby Milton Keynes) but it deserves a longer stay for in the vicinity are bird gardens, Stevington windmill and Bromham watermill on the beautiful Ouse (with milling, wildlife and art exhibits). Historic Bedford is near, described elsewhere, and there is fine scenery, particularly among the riverside villages north of the road to Bedford – Harrold has a country park, village green and lock-up; and Turvey a statue of Jonah, in the river.

When to go? Seaside resorts or other places suitable for children will be at their busiest (and dearest) in July–August and during half-term holidays (especially, in late May, which is also a bank holiday period). Other peak periods are, of course, Easter, Christmas, New Year and the bank holiday in late August. (The bank holiday in early May is not usually a peak, because it comes rather soon after Easter, but much depends on the weather.) There are local peaks, too (the Gold Cup races at Cheltenham or the regatta at Henley, for instance, are apt to fill hotels for miles around), and local troughs (Brighton, a conference centre, is least busy in high summer). You won't get much personal attention when hotels are full to bursting.

In holiday areas, travel on any day other than a summer Saturday if you can. Make ferry, Motorail or coach/train reservations well in advance if travelling at such periods.

WHITE LODGE

Grosvenor Road, Swanage, Dorset, BH19 2DD   Tel: 0929 422696

C(4) **PT S**

11 bedrooms (single, double or family) from £12. Less for 6 nights. Rooms have central heating or electric heaters; shower and wc; armchairs; views of sea, country or garden; tea/coffee facilities.
Dinner £6.50 for 4 courses (with choices) and coffee, at 6.30pm. Special diets if ordered. Packed lunches. Coffee, tea, for a charge. Non-residents not admitted. Drinks can be ordered.
2 sitting-rooms with central heating, TV, books, piano; and a bar.
Garden
Nearest main road A35 from Poole to Dorchester.
Closed in winter

In one of those steep, quiet streets which encircle Swanage and its bay stands a good, solid home of seventy years ago built, I would guess, by some architect influenced a little by Lutyens. In its white walls are stone-mullioned windows of generous size, with leaded panes. The staircase is solid oak, with a striking stained-glass window rising up two floors. Some of the bedrooms have magnificent views over the rooftops to the sea with its boats and water-skiers, while the big bay window of the sitting-room looks onto a flowery little garden. A homely little guest house, for a traditional seaside holiday.

Bill and Beverley Ashton serve generous meals: a help-yourself casserole may be placed on each table, and there are second helpings available from a choice of puddings (the pear and mincemeat flan is particularly good).

The safe, sandy beach and the shops are just down the hill, and within a short distance are all the other beauty-spots and sights of the Purbeck area. The Dorset coastal path appeals to walkers, but there are plenty of other scenic walks elsewhere too – to places like Durdle Door and Old Harry rocks, or Lulworth Cove. Brownsea Island and Kingston Lacey house are popular outings.

If you go further west you will be in 'Hardy country', designated an area of outstanding beauty, and protected as such. Along the coast, cliffs and sands alternate (a good fossil-hunting area). Inland are picturesque thatched villages with mediaeval churches to explore, many stately homes, heaths, woods and well waymarked footpaths. You can go on wagon-rides from Bridport as a change from motoring or walking. Popular sights include West Bay harbour, Parnham House, Forde Abbey, Bridport Museum, Abbotsbury swannery and gardens, and the gardens at Clapton Court.

Just as this book was going to press, I learned that the Hutchins family are taking over. Readers' reports welcome, please.

WHITESTONE FARMHOUSE *New*   C D PT S
Staintondale, north of Scarborough, North Yorkshire, YO13 0EZ
Tel: 0723 870612

rear view

4 bedrooms (single, double or family) from £8.50. All have central heating; views of sea, country or garden. No smoking. (Washing-machine on request.)
Dinner £5 for 4 courses and coffee, at 6.30pm. Non-residents not admitted. Vegetarian or special diets if ordered. Snacks. Tea, coffee, free. Drinks can be brought in.
2 sitting-rooms with central heating, open fire, TV, books, record-player.
Small garden
Nearest main road A171 from Scarborough to Whitby.

'I like my guests to feel they are having a dinner-party every night!' says Pat Angus, which is one reason why many return again.

That and the position of the stone-built farmhouse just south of Robin Hood's Bay (famous for its three-mile sweep, and the constant erosion which has caused many cottages to tumble into the sea) and near National Trust coastal scenery, all with spectacular views.

There is a glass-walled sun-lounge so that you can see meadows with goats, cows and lambs in one direction and the sea in the other – from the comfort of the large curved sofa or an armchair. A steep staircase leads up to neat bedrooms which enjoy similar views.

Adjoining the farmland are woods and Hayburn Wyke nature reserve – roe deer occasionally wander in from the reserve. There are footpaths down to the rocky shore and along a disused rail track; the long-distance Cleveland Way passes by.

As to Pat's dinner-parties, here is an idea of the kind of thing she prepares for her guests: fruit juice; tomato stuffed with walnuts, raisins, cheese and chives in mayonnaise – served with a salad and home-baked wholemeal roll; turkey breast in breadcrumbs with cranberry sauce and four vegetables; sherry trifle. Exceptional value.

Staintondale's attractions include not only the coast but also the North York Moors. To the north is Whitby (described elsewhere) and to the south Scarborough – a huge mixture of resort, fishing harbour and historic town, with superb scenery around (both cliffs and sandy bays). Some of it is now garish; but the harbour and fishmarket are as they always were, and dramatically positioned on a headland are the remains of a Norman castle overlooking Scarborough's superb bay.

Anne Brontë died and is buried at Scarborough. She wrote about 'the deep, clear azure of the sky and ocean, the bright morning sunshine on the semicircular barrier of craggy cliffs surmounted by green swelling hills, and on the smooth, wide sands, and the low rocks out at sea – looking, with their clothing of weeds and moss, like little grass-grown islands – and above all, on the brilliant, sparkling waves. And then the unspeakable purity and freshness of the air!'

Readers' comments: A lovely atmosphere, food excellent in content, presentation and quantity. A caring couple.

WHYKE HOUSE

C PT S S-C X

13 Whyke Lane, Chichester, West Sussex, PO19 2JR   Tel: 0243 788767

rear view

4 bedrooms (single, double or family) from £12.50. Less for 3 nights. Rooms have central heating; TV, armchairs; views of garden; tea-making facilities.
Sitting-room with central heating, books. No smoking.
Small garden
Nearest main road A27 from Worthing to Portsmouth.

In an ordinary suburban cul-de-sac, very close to the historic centre of Chichester (and overlooking a grassy Roman site at the back, where children now play) is an unusual bed-and-breakfast house, ideal for families.

Here Tony and Lydia Hollis cook their guests' breakfasts (and service their rooms), give advice on sightseeing, then depart to their own home next door. There is a fully equipped kitchen which guests are then welcome to use to prepare other meals, if they do not wish to go to Chichester's many restaurants and cafés (the Nags is popular). Unlimited tea etc. is provided. Guests can also use sitting-room and back garden (with croquet), glimpsed in the drawing. It is almost like being in a home of your own, with complete freedom – except that smoking is restricted.

The furnishings, though homely, have individuality. Family antiques mingle with Russian folk art, local paintings (you may meet the artist) with soft furnishings made by Lydia – who also has a flair for painting furniture decoratively.

For some older guests, the ground-floor bedroom and shower are particularly convenient. Guests can be met by car at the station. Bicycle and tandem for hire.

Other entries describe the cathedral city of Chichester and its environs, which include Arundel Castle, Fishbourne Roman palace, Bosham waterfront village, Goodwood House, the open-air museum of ancient buildings and West Dean gardens. Tony, once in the antiques trade, is a good adviser on the best shops locally.

Readers' comments: The Hollises are so kind and helpful. Very comfortable; the Hollises are charming and very helpful; unpretentious and suited to young families. What good value. Comfortable and enjoyable. Comfortable, quiet, convenient; most welcoming. Pleasant weekend, comfortable; so helpful and welcoming; a real treat to stay.

Inclusive terms for dinner, bed-and-breakfast (particularly for a week) can be much lower than those quoted here for these items taken separately. For short-notice bookings you may be able to get a reduction.

No proprietor wants to have a room standing empty. This particularly applies to Sunday nights. Some hotels make a discount if you want only two courses from a three-course menu.

---

17 Carr Hill Lane, Briggswath, Sleights, south-west of Whitby, North Yorkshire, YO21 1RS   Tel: 0947 810525

3 bedrooms (double) from £11. Less for 7 nights and bargain breaks. Some have own bath/shower; TV; tea/coffee facilities; central heating; views of country or garden. No smoking. (Washing-machine on request.)
Dinner £8 for 4 courses (with choices) and coffee, at 7pm. Non-residents not admitted. Tea, coffee, free. Drinks can be ordered.
Sitting-room with central heating, books, record-player. No smoking.
Small garden
Nearest main road A169 from Whitby to Pickering.
Closed from October–March

Bountiful Roman goddesses Flora and Pomona adorn the sitting-room door, with swags of fruit; the front hall has stained glass; there are big sash windows throughout and handsome fireplaces of marble or decorative tiles: all redolent of the Edwardian era when this house was built. Surrounded by gardens, it looks down over the quiet Esk valley (yet busy Whitby is quite close).

Judy Potts has boldly decorated the dining-room with a striking gold Chinese wallpaper and tasselled pelmet, while in the sitting-room comfortable leather chairs and sofa surround the log fire. One bedroom has a brass bed, festoon curtains, rosebud bedlinen and pink corduroy sofa (and a really beautiful shower). The mulberry room has a frilled four-poster and an excellent bathroom with bidet.

Visitors help themselves from a drinks tray before dinner – which might, for instance, be smoked trout, chicken (with stuffing, broccoli, red cabbage Austrian-style, and jacket potatoes with cream cheese), Malvern pudding (an egg-custard and apple dish), then cheeses with celery. Wine is included.

Whitby is both fishing port and seaside resort, overlooked by the dramatic ruins of its 13th-century abbey on a high headland. The old part of the town is a place of steep byways, craft workshops and Captain Cook's house. There are sandy beaches further along. Briggswath is on the edge of the North York Moors (described elsewhere); and from nearby Sleights there is a picturesque steam railway line which goes right across the moors to Pickering. If you go up the coast you come to the fishing village of Staithes (more Cook connections).

On the other side of Whitby is 17th-century **Cross Butts Farm** which is truly magnificent. Not only is it handsomely panelled but it has an immense four-poster, seven feet wide, with barleysugar posts. Long hours went into the making of its crochet bedspread. Other rooms are attractive: Eileen Morley has used rosebud fabrics and broderie anglaise, for instance; and, in the beamed breakfast-room, willow-pattern curtains to match the china on the dresser that stands against

one of the stone walls. For dinner, many visitors go to the Magpie. The farm is near sandy beaches.

WINCHELSEA TEA ROOM *New* C PT
Hiham Green, Winchelsea, south of Rye, East Sussex, TN36 4HB
Tel: 0797 22679

3 bedrooms (single, double or family) from £13. Less for 7 nights. All have own bath or shower; TV; tea/coffee facilities; central heating.
Dinner £6.50 for 3 courses and coffee, at 7.15pm. Non-residents not admitted. Vegetarian or special diets if ordered. Lunches, packed lunches, snacks. Tea, coffee, free. Drinks can be ordered.
Sitting-room with central heating, books.
Small garden
Nearest main road A259 from Dover to Brighton.

Beyond a modest exterior and Edwardian-style tea-room, a surprise awaits. Fred and Linda Rankin's home is larger than it looks, rooms are spacious and immaculate, and they have furnished them with considerable style – aiming to combine modern comfort with Edwardian antiques and colour schemes.

There is a large upstairs sitting-room for visitors with pink curvaceous sofas and a handsome but ancient (1919) sewing machine – on which Linda made all the curtains in the house. Bedrooms (and bathrooms) are of a high standard. Two open onto a little garden, others are upstairs; one is virtually a suite, with kettle and refrigerator for snacks. Lace spreads, buttoned velvet bedheads and wild-flower wallpapers are typical of the style of each.

Dinners, too, are above average. As a change from more traditional dishes, you may be offered tuna and water-chestnut puffs for a starter, then chicken breast stuffed with mushroom and ham, followed by apricot and almond upside-down pudding.

Unlike its neighbour, Rye, Winchelsea is not particularly famous and I have always found it quiet when Rye was thronged with tourists. It is a delightful, unspoilt little town in which to wander, with beautiful countryside and coast nearby.

On the road to Hastings is 18th-century **Winchelsea Farmhouse** (tel: 0797 226669), surrounded by a National Trust landscape. Mary Carmichael's decorative touches include festoon blinds and cane bedheads with flowery duvets; padded blue velvet with pine bedroom furniture (this room has a sofa); white voile contrasted with poppy plates; in yet another room, a fabric patterned with garlands and bows. Many rooms have garden or hill views. Flowering shrubs surround a lawn and brick terrace, and an adjoining brick barn is smothered in a mass of

wisteria blossom every summer. A typical meal: fish chowder, lamb in sauce with asparagus and mushrooms, baked Alaska. (There is a pool table.)

Hazleton, west of Northleach, Gloucestershire, GL54 4EB   Tel: 0451 60364

4 **bedrooms** (single or double) from £15.
Bargain breaks. Rooms have central heating

or electric heaters; shower and wc (bathroom available); armchairs; views of country and garden.
Dinner £12.50 for 4 courses and coffee, at 7.30pm. Packed lunches. Coffee, tea, for a charge. Drinks can be ordered or brought in. Sunday lunches in winter only.
2 **sitting-rooms** with central heating, open fire, TV, books, piano, record-player.
Large garden
Nearest main road A40 from London to Wales.

After Mr Harrison retired from business, he and his wife Sydney extended their 1960s home of Cotswold stone in order to turn it into a small guest-house. This was only a few years ago, but already many visitors have been back several times. The greatest attraction is Mrs Harrison's outstanding cooking (though she serves dinner on only three days a week). Not only is everything impeccably prepared – vegetables delicately sliced and lightly cooked, bread home-baked, breakfast orange juice freshly squeezed, kippers sent from Craster – but she has a repertoire of imaginative dishes that puts many an expensive restaurant in the shade. With your breakfast porridge you will be offered whisky. And all the food is served on Royal Worcester porcelain. On nights when dinner is not served, she recommends the Fosse Bridge, Frog Mill or the Mill at Withington.

The Harrisons are modest, unassuming people whose only aim is to make their visitors feel at home. The friendly welcome is manifest the moment you arrive and a free glass of sherry awaits you in your room.

As to the house itself, this is furnished with much attention to comfort, and in tranquil colours. All the rooms are immaculate, and the furnishings (conventional in style) are of high quality. The house stands in a quiet spot some 500 feet up in the Cotswold hills, where the air is bracing and the views are of far fields and grazing sheep. It is on the outskirts of a rambling village of old stone farmhouses with a small church nearby – part of it Saxon.

Hazleton – under 2 hours from London – is close to beautiful Northleach, which has a mediaeval church of great splendour and an excellent museum of country life; Cirencester, a lovely market town with the outstanding Corinium museum, crafts, another church as grand as a cathedral and a great park; Burford; and Cheltenham, with all the elegance of a spa, particularly at the Montpelier end of the great Promenade (another good museum and fine church). The beauty of the Cotswold hills needs no describing, nor its showpiece villages like Bourton-on-the-Water, Bibury and Stow-on-the-Wold. There is a Roman villa at Chedworth, butterfly and bird gardens, folk and farm museums, wildlife and rare breeds parks, stately homes and gardens, castles (such as Sudeley), abbeys and walks.

Readers' comments: Food absolutely outstanding, even for a spoiled Swiss! Absolute calm. First-rate; inventive menu; highly recommended. Excellent food and genial hosts. Food outstanding; what a find! Superb cooking. The best meal we'd had – highly recommended. Excellent in every way, especially food and wine. The best cook we've found in England. Excellent food; very comfortable; welcoming. Our third visit. Excellent cook and hostess; very comfortable. One of the nicest people; outstanding cook.

WOLD FARM

C D PT S

Old, west of Kettering, Northamptonshire, NN6 9RJ Tel: 0604 781258

7 bedrooms (single or double) from £12.50. Less for 3 nights. Some have own bath/shower; central heating; views of country or garden. (Washing-machine on request.)
Dinner £8 for 4 courses and coffee, at 7pm. Vegetarian diets if ordered. Packed lunches, snacks. Tea, coffee, free.
2 sitting-rooms with central heating, open fire, TV, books, record-player.
Small garden
Nearest main road A43 from Northampton to Kettering.

This 18th-century house has particularly attractive and spacious rooms, and golden pheasants in a delightful garden. A garden-house has recently been converted to provide more bedrooms, one of which is on the ground floor.

For dinner, Ann Engler serves – in an oak-beamed dining-room with inglenook fireplace – such meals as a quiche or fish salad followed by a roast joint and then perhaps profiteroles or lemon meringue pie, and cheeses – with a sherry, wine or beer included.

A feature of the rolling agricultural landscape round here is the network of 18th- and 19th-century canals, and the reservoirs (now naturalized) that were built to top up the water in these. At Stoke Bruerne a waterways museum tells the whole story of the canals, and you can take boat trips. The many stately homes include Althorp (childhood home of the Princess of Wales) and Boughton House (modelled on Versailles). There are Saxon churches at Brixworth and Earls Barton. The county is famous for its high-spired churches and for its many historical associations: it has two 'Eleanor Crosses' erected in the 13th century by Edward I wherever his wife's coffin rested on its journey to burial in Westminster Abbey; Fotheringhay is where Mary Queen of Scots was executed; Cromwell defeated Charles I's army at Naseby in 1645 (good bar food at the Fitzgerald Arms, and a museum of the battle). In the Nene Valley is a scenic steam railway.

Looking at all the things there are to see and do – interesting to children and adults alike – it seemed to me that staying here would be a very good all-weather alternative to a traditional seaside holiday for the family. There's a live museum of roundabouts and organs, for instance, near Northampton; several water gardens and bird gardens; Wicksteed Park, famous for its playground amusements, at Kettering.

In autumn Blakesley village has a soap-box 'grand prix' and Ashton world conker championships.

Northamptonshire is at the centre of England, with motorways making it quickly accessible from almost anywhere.

Inclusive terms for dinner, bed-and-breakfast (particularly for a week) can be much lower than those quoted here for these items taken separately. For short-notice bookings you may be able to get a reduction.

No proprietor wants to have a room standing empty. This particularly applies to Sunday nights. Some hotels make a discount if you want only two courses from a three-course menu.

THE WOOD *New*   **C PT S**
De Courcy Road, Moult Hill, Salcombe, south-east of Plymouth, Devon
TQ8 8LQ   Tel: 054884 2778

rear view

6 bedrooms (single, double or family) from £13. Less for 7 nights and bargain breaks. Some have own bath/shower; TV; tea/coffee facilities; central heating, views of sea, country or garden; balcony. (Washing-machine on request.)
Dinner £10 for 4 courses (with choices) and coffee, at 7.30pm. Vegetarian or special diets if ordered. Lunches, packed lunches, snacks. Tea, coffee, free. Drinks can be ordered.
Sitting-room with central heating, open fire, TV, books, piano, record-player.
Small garden
Nearest main road A38 from Exeter to Plymouth.

One of the most spectacular sites in this book is occupied by a turn-of-the-century house which seems almost to hang in the air, so steep is the wooded cliff below it. One looks straight down onto the pale golden beach of South Sands (a small cove), and the blue waters of Salcombe estuary with the English Channel beyond. Rocky headlands stretch into the distance. To make the most of this exceptional view, some bedrooms have balconies and the elegant L-shaped sitting-room has huge windows that open onto a paved terrace (sometimes meals are served on a verandah). One can walk through the garden to a steep woodland footpath which goes down to the sands – but what a climb up again! – and from there take the ferry to Salcombe. Sometimes visitors can borrow a boat.

Bedrooms, on two floors, have different styles. No. 1 is all white with rosebuds on everything from walls to windowseat. No. 2 has a sensational bay window framing a view of the estuary. No. 3, a single, is very pretty: Laura Ashley festoon blinds and wallpaper, pine panelled doors. No. 4, with bamboo furniture and a turquoise-and-cream colour scheme, has a verandah; as does No. 5, with four-poster and outsize bathroom. No. 6 is level with a small lawn.

In the dining-room (handsomely furnished with velvet chairs, white-gold Minton china and linen napkins), Pat Vaissière serves candlelit dinners that use much local produce – such as cheese-filled eggs, lamb with apricot-and-almond stuffing, chocolate rum trifle, and cheeses. Rolls are home-baked.

Salcombe is Devon's southernmost resort, and arguably its most beautiful one. Even orange and lemon trees grow here which, together with palms, remind one of parts of the Mediterranean. The estuary is very popular for sailing, garden-lovers come to see Sharpitor (NT), walkers make for the viewpoints of Bolbery Down and Bolt Head. All along the coast from here to Plymouth are picturesque waterfront villages, such as Bantham and Newton Ferrers, described elsewhere. In the opposite direction are Kingsbridge (old market town), the long stretch of Slapton Sands (nature reserve, with lagoons), picturesque Dartmouth (of outstanding historical interest – two castles, quaint quays, elaborately carved woodwork on buildings, the Royal Naval College, river trips, two ferries).

Readers' comments: Outstanding standards. They go out of their way to provide that little bit extra at every turn. Made to feel so much at home. Worth coming for the food alone!

322

WOODY BANK

St Lawrence, west of Ventnor, Isle of Wight, PO38 1XF   Tel: 0983 852610

C(10) **D PT S X**

8 bedrooms (single or double) from £25 with dinner. Less for 7 nights. Rooms have electric heaters; shower or bathroom; armchairs; views of sea, country or garden.
Dinner 4 courses (with choices) and coffee, at 7pm. Vegetarian or special diets if ordered. Packed lunches, snacks. Coffee, tea, for a charge. Non-residents not admitted. Drinks can be ordered.
2 sitting-rooms with electric heating, open fire, TV, books; bar.
Terraced garden
Nearest main road A3055 (coastal road round island).

This 1840 house is set among terraced gardens on a steep slope leading down towards the sea – one of many such mansions which wealthy Victorians built along a coast they called 'the English Madeira'. In its grounds are mimosa, figs, vines and palms.

Shirley and Geoffrey Wilson have furnished the sitting-room in Victorian style; but the dining-room is in complete contrast with bamboo chairs and sliding glass walls that can be opened wide to the garden. The cellar bar, too, opens onto the garden. Bedrooms vary greatly in size and style: the best has fine walnut beds and a huge mahogany wardrobe, plus capacious armchairs from which to enjoy the sea view. Bedrooms at the front have a sea view; those at the back overlook a road (little used at night) and a nature reserve.

As to dinner, there are choices at every course – lentil soup or egg bouchées, for instance; venison or mullet with anchovy sauce; queen of puddings or bananas in rum-and-lemon sauce; cheeses.

St Lawrence has not only the tiniest church in England (12th century) but another with exceptional pre-Raphaelite stained glass. It has a tropical bird park, glass-making studios, and a network of undercliff footpaths among rocks where subtropical plants grow wild, with small bays and coves down below. Most visitors make for Queen Victoria's Osborne House, Carisbrooke Castle, the Botanical Gardens, Arreton Manor, St Catherine's lighthouse and the gardens at Barton Manor vineyard. Those who prefer the quieter west end of the island head for Freshwater Bay, Tennyson Downs, the wildlife reserve at Newtown, the Needles fort and Alum Bay with its sands in a myriad of colours.

Some readers tell me they have stayed at lots of places from *Staying Off the Beaten Track*. I wonder who has stayed at most? A free copy of the next edition awaits the reader who sends me his/her comments on the greatest number!

Some hotels and even farms offer special Christmas holidays; but, unless otherwise indicated (by the code letter X at top of entry), those in this book will then be closed.

WYKEHAM ARMS *New*   D PT
Kingsgate Street, Winchester, Hampshire, SO23 9PE Tel: 0962 53834

rear view

7 bedrooms (single, double or family) from £13.75. Some have own bath/shower; TV; tea/coffee facilities; phone; central heating. No smoking in one of the bedrooms. (Washing-machine on request.)
Dinner A la carte or £6 for 3 courses (with choices) and coffee, at 6.45pm. Vegetarian or special diets if ordered. Lunches, packed lunches, snacks. Tea, coffee, extra. Drinks can be ordered.
Sitting-room with central heating, open fire, TV, books. No smoking.
Small garden
Nearest main road M3 from London.

It would be easy to pass this by without a second glance, a seemingly ordinary pub in a quiet side street near the cathedral. But ordinary it is not. Despite its Victorian-looking frontage it is one of Winchester's oldest inns, dating from 1760. (It is named after William of Wykeham, the mediaeval founder of Winchester College.)

Inside, is a series of traditional bars where real ales and malt whiskies are served, log fires blazing on chilly days ('We get through 40 tons of logs a year'), old Windsor chairs drawn up to pine tables with candles lit at night – also, a comfort which coaching travellers did not enjoy two centuries ago, thick blue carpet underfoot. There is a breakfast-room for guests, with sprigged tablecloths, large windows and (as in all room) flowers, and an upstairs sitting-room with pine panelled fireplace and grandfather clock. In the attic is – surprise! – a sauna. The small lawn at the back has hanging baskets of lobelias and petunias around.

Bedrooms have been attractively furnished: for instance, with Laura Ashley fabrics, antiques, pot-plants and Jane Austen pictures (and mini-bars). From some there are roofscape views with glimpses of the cathedral beyond the chimney-pots. (A family room is supplied with toys.) And I found total silence at night.

Graeme and Anne Jameson have given the inn a reputation for excellent food (served in the bars), using fresh ingredients. On the menu, which constantly changes, you might find such unusual things as sea bass soufflé, courgette and thyme soup, monkfish provençale, venison steak au poivre, honey and walnut tart and cider bavarois among more conventional dishes – all cooked by Joanne Docherty.

Winchester (so soon reached by motorway from London or Heathrow; or from Southampton or the New Forest) was once, in Saxon and early Norman times, the capital of England: it was old even then, as prehistoric and Roman finds have shown. The Norman cathedral is one of the longest in Europe, and it has seven elaborately carved chapels, royal tombs, mediaeval wall paintings. Unlike many, it is well sited on lawns that allow an unimpeded view of it. In the city itself, there are a great many old buildings, mediaeval to 18th-century, including a watermill; and there are pleasing walks not only through its lanes but on the banks of the River Itchen. Some of the ancient city walls and gates still survive, and in Castle Hall is a replica of King Arthur's round table as envisaged by Tudor antiquaries. Another survival to be seen in the streets: elderly men in gowns and ruffs. They are pensioners from the Holy Cross almshouses south of the city.

TOURING
WALES

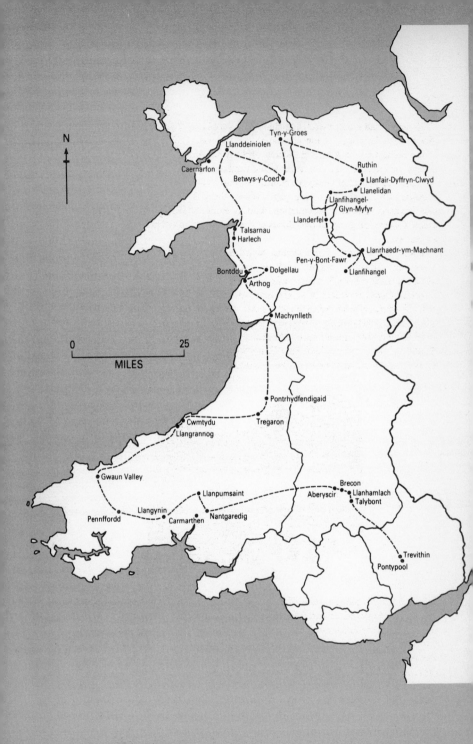

'You won't find much there', armchair critics told me. 'Poor food [wrong] . . . it always rains [wrong] . . . low standards [yes and no].'

We ate not one bad meal in Wales, and several outstandingly good ones; and except for half a day the sun shone while England remained grey as a floorcloth. I found many houses of very poor standards: tawdry, dingy or (in one case) smelly. Nevertheless, as the following pages show, there is an ample choice of really excellent and varied accommodation. And accommodation prices are substantially below those in England: at two-thirds of the houses described here you can stay for £12 or less.

Wales is a country of superb and varied scenery, too, with glorious beaches. There are plenty of 'sights' such as castles, steam railways, award-winning museums and so forth. Yet, even when travelling during the August Bank Holiday weekend (easily avoiding 'A' roads, large towns and the main seaside resorts), we found it mercifully free of cars and crowds. An ideal choice for an 'off the beaten track' holiday at moderate cost and with truly hospitable hosts.

The M4 from London enters Wales through the county of Gwent. Beyond Pontypool and over the 1200-foot Garn Wen mountain by a rough and lengthy track – superb views, but not a drive for the timid! – is **Ty'r Ywen**, 'house of yews',

Ty'r Ywen

at Trevithin (Mamhilad, NP4 8TT; tel: 049528 200), which young Susan Armitage and her husband laboured for three years to transform from a derelict state to the present very attractive home. Every guest room has a four-poster (one has two), made by David with pretty draperies by Susan, and the en suite bathrooms are luxurious. Across the inglenook fireplace is a massive 2-foot beam. In the huge dining-kitchen, fiddleback chairs surrounding two refectory tables, Susan serves (with the help of their vegetable garden and Jersey cows) such meals as: melon salad, chicken legs with stuffed courgettes and blackcurrant gâteau. David, a hospital engineer, drives a vintage car to and from his work, the long track notwithstanding.

Next, into the large county of Powys and following the Usk still further upstream one comes to the inexpensive 17th-century **Llanddetty Hall Farm**

Llanddetty Hall Farm

(Talybont, LD3 7YR; tel: 087487 267), in the heart of the Brecon Beacons National Park. All bedrooms have Welsh tapestry bedspreads and some have views of the river, while at the back runs the historic Brecon and Monmouth canal, with narrow-boats passing by (boat trips and tow-path walks are two of many local diversions and visitors can borrow the farm's canoe). Marjorie Morris is an accomplished cook: a typical menu is salmon mousse, chicken and mushrooms in wine sauce, and Eve's pudding made with Llanddetty's own raspberries or gooseberries. Just outside Brecon itself is a great 18th-century stone mansion, **Peterstone Court** (Llanhamlach, LD3 7YB; tel: 087486 666), log fires within and

Peterstone Court

a heated swimming-pool without. The rooms here are exceptionally spacious and Jean Abbot, who likes bright colours and flowery fabrics, keeps them immaculate. Plain home cooking – for instance: melon, roast lamb, charlotte russe, Welsh cheeses. On the other side of Brecon is the Victorian **Old Rectory** (Aberyscir, LD3 9NP; tel: 0874 3457), well tucked away in the hills, which Elizabeth Gould has furnished to high standards of comfort and solid quality – but prices are modest. A

Old Rectory

horse, ram and squirrel greeted our arrival, and there is poultry too. I particularly liked the pink bedroom which has windows on two sides through which to enjoy very lovely views of the Brecon Beacons. Imaginative dinners include such dishes as smoked haddock ramekins, beef Stroganoff and Elizabeth's Malibu dessert – coconut liqueur combined with tropical fruits and whipped cream. (Bicycles and pony rides available.)

Travelling westward towards Carmarthen, in the county of Dyfed, I found one of the very best places of all: **Cwmtwrch Farmhouse Hotel** – its name means 'valley of the wild boar' (Nantgaredig, SA32 7NY; tel: 026788 238). Jenny Willmott and her husband have transformed a group of old farm buildings with great sensitivity. The dining-room (open to non-residents) has stone walls painted white, slate floor, boarded roof above, and grey Paisley cloths on the tables. At one side, her kitchen is open to view; on the other is a glass wall overlooking the courtyard, pots of begonias and busy-Lizzies, and sheep fields beyond. The food is exceptional. Stuffed mushrooms (with garlic and cheese), followed by individual fish pies (salmon etc. under puff-pastry) or very tender venison, with vegetables imaginatively cooked; and a flan of grapes with sponge and almond topping were among the varied choices when we stayed, all cooked to perfection. There are a small bar and two sitting-rooms: all with interesting and lovely objects, paintings and pottery (for sale). Some bedrooms (full of character) are in the old farmhouse and others (all at ground level) in a recent conversion of stables: whitewashed stone walls contrast with antique beds, colour schemes of pale blue and grey echoing the colours of the local stone.

Also in this area is **Fferm-y-Felin** or 'mill farm' – the mill is nearby (Llanpumsaint, SA33 6DA; tel: 026784 498 after 7pm), the 18th-century home of Anne and David Ryder-Owen: a place of particular interest to birdwatchers. David, a keen ornithologist, can tell you where to spot pied fly-catchers, buzzards and even the rare red kite. He has created a small lake for emperor geese and black swans; and throughout the house are Victorian stuffed birds and badgers. Beyond the dining-room (furnished with antiques and with a spiral stair in one corner) is a sitting-room so large that it has a fireplace at each end; pink buttoned velvet sofas and a walnut piano contrast with rugged stone walls. Anne serves such meals as corn-on-the cob, wild trout with home-grown vegetables, and apple crumble. This would be a good place for a family holiday: the children's bedroom (with toys) has a picture-window overlooking the lake and its waterfowl, and there is a pet donkey as well as other livestock.

During the Roman occupation, wherever there was a ford to be guarded along the River Ginning a camp (castra) was built; hence the origin of **Castell Gorfod** (Llangynin, SA33 4JU; tel: 0994 230835), the home and farm of the Harvey-Smiths. A very long and hilly track leads through oak and larch woods to the suntrapping valley where it is hidden, a Swiss-style façade of 1874 concealing older parts behind. Roses and clematis climb up iron pillars to the verandah's glass roof, and the surrounding lawn where peacocks roam is punctuated by great redwoods, Wellingtonias and an immense tulip tree. There is a pool with a series of waterfalls. Rooms are very spacious, with solid old-fashioned furniture, and include a family suite with its own sitting-room. Carol uses home-grown produce for such meals as pancakes with shrimp sauce, roast lamb and raspberry mousse, followed by Welsh cheeses.

For anyone tracing their family history, I recommend a stay at inexpensive **Mount Pleasant Farm** (Penffordd, SA66 7HY; tel: 09916 447) because Pauline Bowen is an expert in the subject, while Peter collects vintage cars and bygones. A

Mount Pleasant Farm

warm, hospitable couple, their small beamed farmhouse has been immaculately modernized and is very comfortable. Good home cooking. Further north, in the heart of the Pembrokeshire National Park and near Fishguard, is something quite exceptional: **Tregynon Farmhouse Hotel** (Gwaun Valley, SA65 9TU; tel: 0239

Tregynon Farmhouse Hotel

820531). Of all the places I stayed at in Wales, this remote 16th-century house had the most spectacular scenery around it, including an Ice Age ravine with waterfall, ancient oak woods, countryside where badgers and polecats or buzzards and red kites are sometimes spotted, wild moorland and a prehistoric fort. From nearby peaks of the Preselli mountains, one can sometimes see Ireland and Snowdon. Not far away are some of the sunniest sandy beaches in the country, renowned for their pure air. The meals, too, are exceptional with much emphasis on wholefood. The Heards grow vegetables organically, keep a variety of livestock, and have their own trout ponds. Their speciality breads, sausages, traditionally smoked ham, cheeses and even their own spring water contribute to the very special experience of eating at Tregynon, and you can relax afterwards by a log fire in the beamed sitting-room.

Hendre Farm

On Cardigan Bay is a picturesque sandy cove over-popular in high summer, but set aside from the throng here is quiet **Hendre Farm** (Llangrannog, SA44 6AP; tel: 0239878 342), unpretentious but very comfortable and with good home cooking by Bethan Williams, using the farm's own fruit, vegetables and other produce: a good choice for a traditional farmhouse holiday, particularly with children. Just a little further, in a wooded valley protected by the National Trust is **Park Hall** (Cwmtydu, SA44 6LG; tel: 0545 560306), one of the most interesting

Park Hall

'finds' that I made; a quite exceptional guest-house has been created in this turn-of-the-century mansion which is decorated with flair, using much Victoriana – the table linen and silver, the brass beds, the leather chesterfields and even the bath with brass claw feet are in period. Antique lace has been used quite a lot, and Laura Ashley Victorian-style fabrics. From pine-panelled bay windows, there are views of Cardigan Bay between the hills and of the picturesque valley running down to it. Dinners here are of a high order. A popular starter is, after soup such as vichyssoise, a prawn and avocado salad; main courses can include salmon poached in vermouth; with such puddings as profiteroles – and then cheeses. Just as this book was going to press, I heard that Chris Macdonnell had taken over: readers' reports welcome, please.

Inland lies the quiet little market town of Tregaron and an unspoilt inn, the **Talbot Hotel** (Tregaron, SY25 6XX; tel: 09744 208) with bars dating back to the 13th century when drovers used to pause here while their herds of cattle filled the square outside. These days, the square is busy only when the opening-day of the pony-trekking season is marked by a gathering of riders, overlooked by the big

Talbot Hotel

statue of Henry Richard whose 1840 Peace Society was a precursor of the United Nations. The one-time coach-house is now the dining-room; of the Victorian bedrooms, I preferred those at the back – overlooking a garden where a circus elephant was buried in 1848, not long before George Borrow stayed here ('Excellent supper and a very comfortable bed', he wrote in, *Wild Wales*: still true, I found, under Sally Williams' management today; and a very unfrequented spot even on August Bank Holiday).

A little to the north of this is 17th-century **Pantyfedwen** (Pontrhydfendigaid, SY25 6EN; tel: 09745 358) home of two teachers, Ceri and Siân Davies. This is in

Pantyfedwen

the Strata Florida, 'flowery vale', just beyond very lovely abbey ruins. Behind its sparkling white façade are ancient inglenook fireplaces, a curious spiral staircase of stone and other ancient features preserved when the house was recently modernized. Siân has used attractive fabrics, white flokati rugs on board floors and furniture in keeping with the house (refectory tables, for example). There is one of the most luxurious bathrooms in this book. As to meals, which include home-grown vegetables, a typical dinner might be leek soup, carbonnade of beef and orange mousse.

Another totally different experience awaited us near Machynlleth, at **Talbont-drain** (Uwychygarreg, SY20 8RR; tel: 0654 2192). Hilary Matthews abandoned a London career as a social worker to restore this remote house, high in the hills, furnishing it simply but with attractive colours and textures. Inexpensive walking holidays are a principal attraction here (no car is needed: Hilary will pick you up at Machynlleth station and drive you up her long, twisting lane); and once a year there are weekends of guided walks with – surprise! – authentic Indian food at the end of the day, cooked by Umsie Pillay (a doctor from south India). At other times, Hilary serves such 2-course meals as bacon-and-leek flan with vegetables, followed by nectarines in a creamy sauce. Occasionally she does fungus identifying (and cooking) weekends. Her breakfasts feature Welsh specialities: I recommend 'Glamorgan sausage', a type of cheese croquette. Some guests enjoy her excellent pianola as an after-dinner treat. Talbontdrain is in a varied area of woodland, waterfalls, moors and sheep pastures; utterly peaceful.

And so into the county of Gwynedd and the Snowdonia National Park. Of Wales' many lovely estuaries, the Mawddach (near Dolgellau), is perhaps the most beautiful: 'No finer view of sea and mountains', wrote Wordsworth. On the south bank, beyond a craggy oak glade, I found a very modestly priced 'b & b' house, **Herongate** (Arthog, LL39 1BJ; tel: 0341 250349), the simple but pleasant home of Pat Mallatratt whose late husband's paintings line the walls of the small sitting-room. Herons, oystercatchers and tame sheep seeking titbits can be seen from the bay windows. The house is in a small, isolated terrace built by a Victorian entrepreneur as part of a grander plan that never materialized. (B & b only: one can dine in Dolgellau or at Borthwnog Hall). For something much grander, cross to the other side of the estuary where **Borthwnog Hall** (Bontddu, LL40 2TT; tel: 034149 271) is now a small hotel of distinction, with fine gardens along the

Borthwnog Hall

waterfront: palms flourish in this mild region. In the handsome dining-room, its tables laid with damask and silver, Derek and Vicki Hawes serve excellent meals (such main courses as steak with a sauce of whisky-and-cream, chicken breast stuffed with crab, or duckling roasted in honey). The sitting-room is elegant, in traditional 'country house' style, with French doors opening onto the verandah; and above this is the finest of the bedrooms, its three windows opening onto a balcony from which to enjoy the view of the Mawddach. Pretty carpets and fine antique beds are features of all the bedrooms. Downstairs, the library is used as an art gallery with Welsh landscapes for sale at very reasonable prices. Naturally, charges here are a bit higher than at houses previously described, but ask for their bargain-break terms.

Harlech's tremendous castle is perched high up, and in one of the steep lanes behind it is little 16th-century **Castle Cottage** (Harlech, LL46 2YL; tel: 0766 780479), clematis growing up its white walls – a notable restaurant run by Jim and Betty Yuile with good but small bedrooms above (again, slightly dearer than most so far described). There's a snug bar with white stone walls and log fire in winter and a miniscule rock garden with chairs beyond a small sitting-room. Light colours and (on the top floor) views of old roofs, castle and sea make the little

Castle Cottage

rooms attractive. Jim, a much-travelled economics lecturer, has collected recipes from all over the world, and so the à la carte menu includes such unusual starters as stuffed sardines or grilled goat's cheese, guinea-fowl with bacon-and-chestnut sauce or chicken and leek croquettes; pears in cassis.

Set on a trim lawn with flowerbeds and pines, is Edwardian **Gwrach Ynys**, 'dwarf island' (Talsarnau, LL47 6TS; tel: 0766 780742), surrounded by reclaimed saltmarshes over which the sea once swept and by the paddock of Melys, a friendly white pony. Gwynfor and Deborah Williams have restored and furnished the house to much of its original standard of handsome comfort, with open fires in marble or stone fireplaces, big sash windows with green views and Portmeirion's pretty botanical pottery on the tables. Much local produce is used for traditional meals that may start with home-made soups, pâté or salmon mousse; usually followed by a roast, beef olives or chicken pie; with puddings such as chocolate soufflé, pavlova or trifle.

Just beyond Caernarfon, **Ty'n Rhos Farm** (Llanddeiniolen, LL55 3AE; tel: 0248 670489) is now almost a hotel (priced accordingly), run in a very professional

Ty'n Rhos Farm

way by Nigel and Lynda Kettle. A wing of modern, well-equipped bedrooms and en suite bathrooms has been added. This is nevertheless still a working farm, which supplies produce for the table (and cheese to take home). Lynda is an excellent cook of such meals as beef soup, salmon with Hollandaise sauce, and chocolate sponge with brandy sauce.

From here it is not far to the heart of Snowdonia and to the pleasant mountain resort of Betwys-y-Coed amongst the many guest-houses of which I thought two were particularly interesting – especially a small watermill, partly 14th-century and with its wheel awaiting restoration, hidden away near the museum of vintage motors (both owned by the Houghton family): **Royal Oak Farmhouse** (Betwys-y-Coed, LL28 0AH; tel: 06902 427/632). Although so central, the mill is hidden in a little valley with a deep salmon pool close by. The lattice-paned windows, great stone fireplace, carved oak settle and small but very pretty bedrooms give this inexpensive guest-house great character (very good bathroom, incidentally). It was once the home of the painter David Cox, when (in the late 18th century) Betwys was an artists' colony, and his studio still stands in the garden. Elsie Houghton serves only breakfast, but there are good eating-places in Betwys – including a former coaching inn called **Ty Gwyn**, 'white house' which, although on a road, has quiet bedrooms at the back (Betwys-y-Coed, LL24 0SG; tel: 06902 383). Sheila Ratcliffe has a flair for interior decoration, and every bedroom – small or large – is beautiful, many with en suite bathrooms (a fact reflected in the prices).

The most impressive is an attic suite with four-poster and sitting-room; the most convenient for anyone disabled, a pretty ground-floor room. Even in the ancient, beamed bar (fire glowing in the old black range, copper pots, carved oak settle) her colourful patchwork cushions are everywhere; and at the back is a very comfortable sitting-room and then another where she sells antiques and old prints. Cooking is done by chef Martin, the Ratcliffes' son, whose specialities include exotic dishes like lamb flamed in crème-de-menthe or pork in an apple and ginger sauce (the table d'hôte menu is simpler). Even the bar snacks include such imaginative options as shark with garlic butter, bulghar wheat and walnut casserole or homely rabbit pie. Trout comes from the River Conwy, which flows by the other side of the road.

Further down the River Conwy, one can head for the hills and **Cefn** (Tyn-y-Groes, LL32 8TA; tel: 0492 650233), well secluded. The white, 17th-century house is surrounded by lawns with camelias and magnolias from which to enjoy superb views of Snowdonia and of the valley below (there is also a glass-roofed verandah, and a summer house). Sitting/dining-room (with inglenook fireplace), handsome bathrooms and most bedrooms are exceptionally spacious, well decorated and with thick carpets. Margaret Waddingham produces such meals as egg mayonnaise, roast Welsh lamb, gooseberry meringue tart and cheeses. Very good value indeed.

I, like many people, had underestimated the county of Clwyd. No national park here, but superlative scenery nevertheless in the range of Clwydian hills running south. Ruthin is an attractive little town (at its castle, really good mediaeval banquests are held). Just south of here, a disused railway station is now an unusual – and unusually excellent – guest-house; **Eyarth Station** (Llanfair-Dyffryn-Clwyd, LL15 2EE; tel: 08242 3643). It has been imaginatively converted and furnished by Jen Spencer. Ground-floor bedrooms have such touches as broderie anglaise festoon blinds and canopied bedheads with Dollymixtures fabrics; some (more simply furnished) are in what were the porters' rooms and, having a kitchen attached, are ideal for families wanting a semi-self-catering holiday. Excellent bathrooms (even a bidet), and a sauna. What was once the waiting-room is now a very large sitting-room with balcony just above the fields: big sofas, modern marble fireplace and thick carpet make this particularly comfortable. The dining-room – once the station platform – has sliding glass doors to a terrace and small, well-heated swimming pool. Jen offers several choices for dinner, from which one might choose (for instance) tomato-and-basil soup,

Leyland Arms

335

chicken risotto and a gâteau. All this for very moderate prices. Also in this area of superb scenery is a picturesque old inn with good food: the **Leyland Arms** (Llanelidan, LL15 2DT; tel: 082 45 20), run by Jennifer Street. Its stone walls are an ideal backdrop to the tubs of brilliant flowers outside, and an exterior stone stair leads up to bedrooms furnished in cottage style. The food here is extremely good, with bar meals of gourmet standard – excellent seafood pancakes, for example. (The Streets also run a restaurant in Chester, called Porters.) Very much homelier but in a wonderful position is Allan Stevenson's 17th-century **Crown Inn** (Llanfihangel-Glyn-Myfyr, LL21 9UL; tel: 049082 209) perched on the bank of the bubbling River Alwen. Tucked under a jutting crag, the inn's little beer-garden is on a series of small terraces down to the water's edge. Though bedrooms are simple (and inexpensive), there are en suite bathrooms and colour televisions. The Stevensons cook whatever you request. There is free fishing for brown trout, and a nature trail in the grounds.

Just across the border into Gwynedd again is beautiful Lake Bala on the way to which is one of the most attractive houses I found in Wales, **Dewis Cyfarfod** – 'the chosen meeting-place' (Llanderfel, LL23 7DR; tel: 06783 243). Drovers used to meet at this spot where road and river converge, a convenient place to water their livestock. Now the pair of 17th-century cottages is the elegant home of Peter and Barbara Reynolds, furnished with antiques and pretty chintzes, good paintings and well-chosen colour schemes. The spacious sitting-room has groups of comfortable armchairs, a log fire, and panoramic valley views through its picture-windows, with the chance to spot squirrels, foxes and a great variety of birds. In one bedroom, William Morris's 'strawberry thief' fabric complements a white wallpaper with cherries, and other rooms are equally pretty – one with a walnut bed and wildflower fabric, another (in a ground-floor cottage close by) with an oyster and charcoal colour scheme. One bathroom is particularly sumptuous (two basins, royal blue and gold fittings), another has swags of flowers painted by Barbara. The Reynolds, too, own a celebrated restaurant in Chester (Abbey Green), and so it is not surprising that meals here comprise such feasts as celery and lemon soup, beef braised with oranges and wine (accompanied by savoyard potatoes, Polish cauliflower and mange-tout peas), fromage frais with strawberries and then farmhouse cheeses – unless you prefer a light supper. One can eat on the terrace in fine weather, surrounded by pots and baskets brimming with flowers, or in the elegant dining-room; with silver, crystal and candles on the table.

There is an especially lovely drive through hills, moors and woods to the

Dewis Cyfarfod

beautiful and little-known Tanat Valley where Enid Henderson and her niece run the **Glyndwr Tearoom** (Pen-y-Bont-Fawr, SY10 0NT; tel: 069174 430) in what was once a slate-miner's cottage: the slate floor and little black cooking-range are still there. Behind is a pretty riverside garden. All rooms are homely but pleasant, there is good home cooking, and where else but in Wales would you find bedrooms

Glyndwr Tearoom

with their own bathrooms for a mere £9 a head? A similar price is charged at **Bron Heniog** on the way to the country's highest waterfall (Waterfall Road, Llanrhaedr-ym-Machnant, SY10 0JX, tel: 069189 521), the handsome stone house of 1861 to which the Australian-born Pashens retired from London, filling it with their collection of antiques, oil-paintings and Blüthner grand piano: the curving staircase is almost an art gallery. One bedroom, with prettily draped bedhead, looks onto the unusual tortuosa willow (as depicted on willow-pattern plates). Lorraine's dinners include dishes like avocado mousse, sweet/sour pork, and home-made rum-and-raisin ice cream. (Free admission to the family's nearby Rare Breeds Farm.)

Bron Heniog

Finally, close to the English (Shropshire) border, and once more in Powys, is **Cyfie Farm** (Llanfihangel, SY22 5JE; tel: 069184 451), a picturesque hillside house of stone with a very pretty garden: as romantic a place as you could wish and near scenic Lake Vyrnwy. Inside, all is low beams, narrow stairs, nooks and crannies (except in the spacious stable suite, a more modern conversion, with its

Cyfie Farm

own sitting/dining-room). This is a beautifully kept house, which Lynn Jenkins has furnished attractively, with pleasant fabrics and wallpapers, pewter plates arrayed on the old dresser, pot-plants and antiques in the sitting-room. She is an excellent cook of traditional meals. Visitors have been known to stay three weeks at Cyfie – not once but repeatedly – in this surprisingly little-known part of Wales.

Special needs catered for as follows (for explanation of code letters, see page **xxviii**)*.
Establishments marked with a star will accept the discount vouchers from page* **ii**.

Borthwnog Hall	C				S-C	
Bron Heniog★	C	D	PT	S		X
Castell Gorfod★	C	D			S-C	
Castle Cottage	C	D	PT	S		X
Cefn					S-C	
Crown Inn	C			S		X
Cwmtwrch Farmhouse Hotel★	C	D	H			X
Cyfie Farm	C					
Dewis Cyfarfod	C(8)	D		S		
Eyarth Station★	C	D	H		S-C	X
Fferm-y-Felin★	C	D	PT	S	S-C	X
Glyndwr Tearoom★	C					
Gwrach Ynys★	C	D				
Hendre Farm	C		PT			
Herongate				S		
Llanddetty Hall Farm	C	D	PT			
Mount Pleasant Farm★	C		PT	S		X
Old Rectory	C	D		S		
Pantyfedwen	C			S		
Park Hall★	C	D	PT	S		
Peterstone Court	C			S	S-C	
Royal Oak Farmhouse		D	PT			
Talbontdrain★	C			S		
Tregynon Farmhouse Hotel	C	D	H	S		X
Ty Gwyn★	C	D	H	PT	S	S-C	X
Ty'n Rhos Farm	C(5)		H			
Ty'r Ywen	C	D				X

TOURING
SCOTLAND

Contin
Kirkhill
Croy
Westhill
INVERNESS
Daviot
Drumnadrochit
Farr
Foyers
Kincraig
Banavie
Spean Bridge
FORT WILLIAM
Onich
Kentallen
Glencoe
Milton Morenish
Connel
Killin
Lochearnhead
OBAN
Balquhidder
St Fillans
Seil
Cladich
Callander
Kilmelford
INVERARY
STIRLING
Arrochar
Denny
GLASGOW
EDINBURGH

N

0   50
MILES

The Highlands, with their long history of hardship and strife, have relatively few guest-houses or small hotels of architectural distinction, attractively furnished, to compare with the great many found in England. But what so many of Scotland's hotels do have instead are outstanding sites with superb views of mountains or valleys (glens), sea or lakes (lochs), and access to country and water sports, birdwatching and good walking in wild country. As to food, cooking is usually very traditional but, even in the least expensive farmhouses or smallholdings (crofts), you may be served salmon or other fish straight from the sea, game (including venison) or Aberdeen Angus beef. Home baking flourishes, too. As to prices, some thirty hotels or houses described below not only have good standards but come within the average price-range of this book (Coul House and the Moorings are a bit dearer).

I arrived in the Highlands at Inverness (on the north-east coast) by Motorail and journeyed across to the west coast at Fort William, then south via Oban and Inverary, returning home by Motorail from historic Stirling, where Highlands turn to Lowlands: a route chosen for its scenic contrasts, its spectacular mountains, lochs and coastline, almost untouched by commercialism or so-called 'development'.

AROUND INVERNESS   To the north-west of the town is the sunny region of Easter Ross where **Coul House Hotel** (Contin, IV14 9EY; tel: 0997 21487) is a

Coul House Hotel

typical Scottish country hotel, much used by salmon-fishers. Anne Bryan and Martyn Hill have preserved its atmosphere of traditional dignity. There are elaborately decorated ceilings; an octagonal sitting-room with large windows overlooking the rhododendrons and lawn where a piper plays every summer Friday evening; and, in the entrance hall, logs crackle on a raised granite hearth. Very good Scottish food (bar meals too), with choices at each of the four courses – some of the specialities are trout en croûte, cullen skink (smoked haddock soup) and chicken cooked with smoked salmon in brandy cream. There is a holiday

341

package which includes free entry to many local sights; ordinary b & b prices are a little high.

If you prefer a more homely atmosphere, I recommend **Wester Moniack Farm** (Kirkhill, IV5 7PQ; tel: 046383 237). It has very neat bedrooms, and an attractive setting beside a mediaeval castle that is now a winery. Mrs Munro is a good cook.

To the east of Inverness, I was very impressed by the standard of bedrooms at a little cottage built shortly before the windswept moor nearby was the scene of the Battle of Culloden, 1746 (the defeat of Bonnie Prince Charlie). These rooms, equal to many modern hotels', are in a new extension; the stone-walled sitting-room and boarded dining-room are the original part. Through picture-windows is a panoramic view of the Moray Firth. Gai Hornby provides dinner as well as b & b at **Drumbuie** (Westhill, IV1 2BX; tel: 0463 791591).

Nothing could be more different from this little house than **Kilravock Castle** (Croy, IV1 2PJ; tel: 06678 258), home of the Rose family since 1460. Some of the

Kilravock Castle

historic bedrooms are quite exceptional – one, stone-arched, has a half-tester bed, prettily draped; others are in a country-style wing. Ancestral portraits, antiques and chintzes give the dining- and sitting-rooms traditional style; the library is panelled. Dinner on Sunday evening is a help-yourself buffet in the old banqueting hall. (This is an actively Christian household, with a short grace before each meal.) There are many sports facilities in the extensive grounds; and guided tours of the castle. Very good value.

My other choice in this area is **Daviot Mains Farm** (Daviot, IV1 2ER; tel: 046385 215), built in courtyard style over a century ago. The accommodation is simple but pretty, there are log fires, and Margaret Hutcheson's cooking is

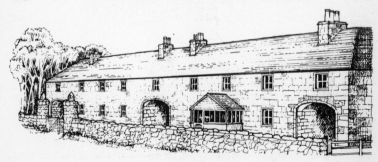

Daviot Mains Farm

exceptional: a typical meal might include Stilton-and-onion quiche as a starter; chicken with mushroom and almond sauce, crisp topping; and a pudding made with yogurt, cream and strawberries.

A few miles away is one of the most elegant (and secluded) houses I found in Scotland, pink-walled **Dunlichity Lodge** (Farr, IV1 2AN; tel: 08083 282), home of Commander and Mrs Ian Wedderburn. Dinner is served at a Regency table; the carpet and hessian-covered walls of the dining-room are dark brown, contrasting with coral chintz curtains; alcoves display cut-glass decanters and silver. In the sitting-room, pink and green cretonne chairs are grouped round a fireplace of unusual green marble where logs blaze. Stripped-pine doors line the corridor in a ground-floor wing of excellent bedrooms and bathrooms. Desirée Wedderburn makes and sells little découpage boxes and miniature tapestries depicting local scenes or wildlife.

Dunlichity Lodge

INVERNESS TO FORT WILLIAM The most direct route is through the Great Glen, where the Caledonian Canal links east coast to west via Loch Ness and Loch Lochy. Just above the west side of Loch Ness (by Urquhart Castle) is a farmhouse quite unlike any other I found, for young Vanessa Macdonald-Haig has a flair for interior decoration – and for finding unsuspected treasures at sales and in junkshops. As a result, this is the most imaginative and attractive of houses: **Borlum Farmhouse** (Drumnadrochit, IV3 6XN; tel: 04562 220). The sitting-room has many horse paintings (Borlum has 40 horses and a riding-centre) on ochre walls which match the carpet, silk curtains on a gilt pole, and a mustard-yellow Knole sofa. Through a board-floored room lined with books one reaches the unusual dining-room: a Victorian-style conservatory, with superb views down

Borlum Farmhouse

to the loch. A staircase with twirly iron banisters leads up to very pretty bedrooms and bathrooms – one bedroom, for instance, is white and green, with white lace on the bed and pink lampshades; in another, decorative touches include Japanese fans and ribbons; embroidered hangings are the focal point of a third; rosebuds on white fabrics and a moss-green carpet feature in another. At present, visitors dine at the Lewiston Arms, or one of several other hotels in the village, but Vanessa plans later to offer dinners (the best of Scottish recipes).

On the opposite side of the loch, where there is an alternative route along it, I found a traditional hotel, perched high above the loch-side and with fine views: **Foyers Hotel** (Foyers, IV1 2XT; tel: 04563 216) where Stewart MacDougall has achieved a reputation for good food, using the best Scottish produce, from Moray

Foyers Hotel

Firth sole to Aberdeen Angus beef. There is a third route, longer but very beautiful indeed, which veers east towards the Cairngorms, along which I found the **Ossian Hotel** (Kincraig, PH21 1NA; tel: 05404 242), run by John Ramage and his family. Apart from adding some handsome items he brought from India

Ossian Hotel

and a sideboard topped with a single 12-foot slab of marble (from Carlisle Castle), he has retained much of the solid, old-fashioned dignity that was established during the hotel's Victorian heyday. A la carte meals (steaks, trout, salmon and game predominate) are served at tables laid with damask and silver – some tables are in a big bay window surrounded by trees. Bedrooms vary: no. 4 is the most

Invergloy House

interesting, for it has a 'Gothick'-style bed of carved pine and, very different, a
Sheraton loveseat. Nearer to Fort William is Loch Lochy and **Invergloy House**
(Spean Bridge, PH34 4DY; tel: 039781 681), hidden away in a loch-side wilderness of flowering shrubs and varied trees – for once it was the coach-house of a
long-gone mansion belonging to a centenarian suffragette who employed six
gardeners (also long gone – which is why the 50-acre garden is now wild, and home
to a family of roe deer). One steps into a white, light dining-hall with grand piano –
Margaret Cairns is a musician as well as a good home cook – off which is a
sitting-room (and another piano) with a picture-window from which to enjoy the
35-mile view across lawn and loch to mountains behind which there are sometimes
fiery sunsets. One bedroom, with floor-to-ceiling window, also faces this way. (No
smoking.)

Rather than stay in busy Fort William itself I recommend Banavie, which
almost adjoins it, and the modern **Moorings Hotel** (Banavie, PH33 7LY; tel:
03977 550), beside 'Neptune's staircase', a flight of locks on the Caledonian Canal,

Moorings Hotel

overlooked by Ben Nevis. On the way to Glen Finnan, it is well placed for touring
not only among the mountains of the west Highlands but the island of Skye, too.
The Sinclair family employ a French chef and he prepares traditional Scottish
specialities with flourishes of his own – tarragon sauce accompanies the Mallaig
turbot, for instance; Black Isle duck comes with peach-and-port sauce; scallops
from Loch Eil are cooked with prawns in wine and then toasted with Gruyère
cheese.

Further along the leafy glen is a secluded guest-house, **Glen Loy Lodge**
(Banavie, PH33 7PD; tel: 039781 700) run by the Ward family. I particularly

345

liked bedroom 9 because it has a door straight into the 4-acre wild garden through which the River Loy runs. The Lodge has its own boat on Loch Arkaig. Once a week there is smoked salmon and/or salmon on the menu which typically may include such other dishes as leek soup to start with and rhubarb mousse as a pudding.

FORT WILLIAM TO OBAN   The road south runs alongside Loch Linnhe and the Atlantic coast on the edge of which is **Cuilcheanna House** (Onich, PH33 6SD; tel: 08553 226), at the heart of a 100-acre cattle farm. Parts are five centuries old.

Cuilcheanna House

Not only is its setting superb, with loch views in one direction and the Glen Coe mountains in the other, but Margaret Dewar's reputation for good food is well known. After a home-made soup, she may serve lamb chops with garlic potatoes and other vegetables, then a Norwegian cream soufflé. If you prefer the lively bustle of a traditional inn (frequented by mountaineers, particularly in February and March) press on a little to awesome Glen Coe itself, scene of the treacherous massacre of the Macdonalds by Campbells who were billeted on them in 1692. At the **Clachaig Inn** (Glencoe, PA39 4HX; tel: 08552 252), run by Peter Daynes, there still hangs a notice 'No hawkers or Campbells'. The services of a mountain guide are available if you want to climb, walk or ski over the hilltops; in winter, there are illustrated lectures by famous mountaineers; in summer, exhibitions of

Clachaig Inn

local landscape artists; and on every Saturday night, folk music. But some people come mainly for the food, particularly rump steaks served sizzling on an iron platter and Ecclefechan tart in which honey, fruit and nuts combine (served with cream). Accommodation is simple but comfortable.

Also in this area, down a very long, ferny track, is **Ardsheal Home Farm** (Kentallen, tel: 063174 229) which Mrs MacArthur has furnished attractively – for instance, antiques in the white-walled sitting-room, country pine furniture in a

Ardsheal Home Farm

former kitchen (now dining-room), Stag furniture and tulip bedspread in a large downstairs bedroom. She provides dinner only for those who stay at least a week; others go to the Holly Tree or the Duror Inn. This is a hill farm with cattle and sheep, surrounded by glorious scenery and wildlife (best in May or June), and with its own private beach.

Southward again, where Loch Etive joins the sea, is the big **Falls of Lora Hotel** (Connel, PA37 1PB; tel: 063171 483), owned by two sisters – Sandra Innes and Catherine Webster. It's a large hotel, built a century ago when Victorian tourists first came here by rail, and still with many features redolent of that period – sideboards loaded with Sheffield plate, stags' heads in the hall. But some rooms have been completely modernized. For instance, the bar is now all bamboo and orange plush and one bedroom has a circular bed and its own jacuzzi – others differ greatly, from small-and-simple to spacious rooms with prettily draped four-posters. Prices vary accordingly (if you don't mind the stairs, I recommend no. 59 for its loch view and low price; if you want a private bathroom, no. 53). There are plenty of choices on the conventional 4-course menu cooked by Colin Felgate but

Falls of Lora Hotel

347

if you stay on a Thursday you will be offered (at no extra charge) a special 'Taste of Scotland' dinner of 7 courses: smoked trout, leek soup, haggis, smoked haddock in cheese sauce, roast venison, Glayva mist, Scottish cheeses.

OBAN TO INVERARY The only bridge across the Atlantic, built in 1792, brings you to the little island of Seil, south of Oban, and the **Willowburn Hotel** (Seil, PA34 4TJ; tel: 08523 276). It stands right on the shore, facing the mainland, an unassuming white building run by a hospitable young couple, Archie and Maureen Todd. The food is well cooked, with choices at each course – a delicious pâté might be followed by Atlantic salmon and a very light lemon mousse, for

Willowburn Hotel

example. Much of the island is a conservation area, with buildings from the times when Seil slate was quarried to send all over the world. At the other end is **North Cuan Croft** (Seil, PA34 4RB; tel: 08523 367), the cottage home of woodturner Len Skeels who migrated here from London. Tucked under an overhanging cliff, the little house is something of a surprise for inside are rather elegant furnishings: bedrooms have velvet bedheads and large colour TVs, for instance, and Maureen's meals are served on bone china, with silver.

Back on the mainland the road south runs past the **Cuilfail Hotel** (Kilmelford, PA34 4XA; tel: 08522 274), its name meaning 'sheltered corner'. Its garden (brilliant with azaleas and daffodils in spring) lies across the road, running downhill to a stream. It was a drovers' and coaching inn when Keats stayed here, dining 'tolerably well on fowl' and watching women spinning wool. Rooms are pleasant, if unassuming (those at the back have hill views) and there is an

Cuilfail Hotel

interesting bar, stone-walled and with pews around the log fire, leading to a flagstoned dining-room with pine tables and chairs. Hilary McFadyen serves good bar snacks as well as a 3-course dinner with imaginative choices at each course which may include courgette-and-rosemary soup, rabbit and mustard casserole and brown sugar chestnut meringues. There is a separate 2-room wing for families. This is a sparsely populated part of the country, known both for its wildlife and for several great gardens (warmed by the proximity of the Gulf Stream) which are open to the public. From nearby Oban there are sea trips to the Western Isles.

Inverary, at the head of Loch Fyne (famous for its kippers), is an attractive little resort of white houses and small shops. For a rural ambience, however, it is worth detouring to Cladich on Loch Awe, and **Rockhill Farm Guesthouse** (Ardbreck-nish, PA33 1BH; tel: 08663 218). The 17th-century accommodation is homely in

Rockhill Farm Guesthouse

style but well equipped and the loch-side setting is idyllic. Helen Whalley is a good cook of such meals as watercress soup, Loch Awe fish pie (it includes salmon and pike from the loch as well as other fish) and amaretto trifle or raspberries from the garden with cream from Rockhill's cows. Loch Awe's sheltered bays and its islands are accessible, there are ruined castles, and on the farm Hanoverian foals are bred – there are also sheep, goats, donkeys and a St Bernard.

AND SO TO STIRLING   Alternatively, to the south-east there is Loch Long and the Firth of Clyde. On the shores of Loch Long is a modest little guest-house-cum-boatyard, **Rossmay** (Arrochar, G83 7AH; tel: 03012 250), almost with its

Rossmay

feet in the water. Peggy Rose (who teaches Scottish dancing) has chosen tartan carpets, and crisp, light colour schemes for the bedrooms and family suite; there's a glass verandah from which to enjoy the view; and simple meals are available – as inexpensive as the accommodation.

Yet another loch, Tay, is at the foot of the steep, beautifully landscaped garden of **Mill House** (Milton Morenish, near Killin, FK21 8TY; tel: 056 72 228). The

Mill House

house is modern, rather like a Scandinavian timber chalet, but furnished with fine antiques and Jean Anderson's own handiwork – a scrap-screen, Berlin-work bedheads and so forth. From the large sitting/dining-room one steps onto a wood verandah overlooking the loch. To one side of the house is a waterfall and crags where wildflowers grow. Dinner (served by Roye in his Anderson kilt) may comprise grapefruit with crème de menthe, lamb casseroled with wine, and a fruit soufflé, for example – all served on Susie Cooper china. A pre-dinner sherry is included in the price. Jean used to be a headmistress, in England, and it speaks volumes for her that a few years ago one of her former pupils chose Mill House for her honeymoon.

Loch Earn has many hotels: I recommend **Mansewood** at one end (Lochearn-

Mansewood

head, FK19 8NS; tel: 05673 213) or **Achray House** at the other (St Fillans, PH6 2NF; tel: 076485 231). At Mansewood, Hank and Maureen Clare do all the cooking themselves. A platter of fried seafood might be followed by chicken Savoy with imaginatively prepared vegetables and creamy puddings or Scottish cheeses. I had a very pretty bedroom with flowery white voile giving it a crisp and delicate air. Maureen collects pictures of poppies – I counted over 100 in the dining-room,

Achray House

their colour complemented by the scarlet tablecloths. A comfortable sitting-room (with log fire) leads through to a sun lounge full of pot-plants and a bar with aeronautical mementoes of Maureen's previous career. Achray House, run by the young Ross family, has very pleasantly furnished rooms – a tartan and pine dining-room (flowers, silver candelabra and cut-glass on the tables) and pretty bedrooms, many with loch views. There is a family suite. The bar leads to a verandah and the garden overlooking the loch, where the hotel has a private jetty. There is a good choice on the evening menu (and good bar meals as an alternative): things like melon with prawns in a cream-and-curry sauce as a starter; venison cooked with brandy and mushrooms or lamb cutlets with Pernod; and apricot/almond meringue or chocolate-and-Cointreau flan.

Travelling further south one can detour to the little village of Balquhidder and the grave of outlaw Rob Roy. On the way is **Auchtubhmor House** (Balquhidder, FK19 8NZ; tel: 08774 632), once the home of a descendant of Rob Roy, Sir

Auchtubhmor House

Gregor McGregor, and now of young Virginia Pickering who has furnished it with great individuality – bedrooms verge on the luxurious. Its setting is superb, high up and with dramatic views of Glen Leny from the terraced lawns. In the big sitting-room, large sofas and chairs are grouped around the open fire. All the bedrooms are excellent (my favourite is no. 3: blue-and-white Laura Ashley fabrics, cane bedhead, rocking-chair, pine bathroom and a fine view). All bathrooms are excellent – one with long, garlanded curtains; another with oval bath and bidet. For dinner, Virginia may serve (for instance) watercress soup, chicken in a yogurt-and-curry sauce, and a home-made gâteau. Turreted **Leny House**, a baronial pile, is nearer to Callander – the setting for 'Dr Finlay's Casebook' (Kilmahog, FK17 8HA; tel: 0877 31078). It stands in its own park-like grounds, looking towards one of Scotland's most famous beauty-spots, the woods and hills of the Trossachs, and to Glen Leny, a region of waterfalls and wildlife. From about the year 900 this site was the ancestral home of the Buchanans; the part of the house dating from 1513 was originally their fortress. This was enlarged in 1691, and again in 1845 when the handsome sitting-room was built, with pine-shuttered

Leny House

bay windows facing south – pale green and creamy pink predominate here, and big U-shaped sofas almost fill the room. From the tartan-carpeted hall (with concert piano) a great staircase rises to big light bedrooms, all well carpeted but varying in style. In some of the older rooms Jacobite plotters held secret meetings or stored illegal arms. (Only b & b is provided, but very good meals can be had at the nearby Lade Inn or in Callander.)

Last but far from least: **Topps Farm** (Denny, south of Stirling, FK6 5JF; tel: 0324 822471), a surprising discovery for this peaceful 1000-acre farm is in fact not far from the M80 motorway – Glasgow is less than half an hour away and Edinburgh three-quarters of an hour in the opposite direction. The house itself is modern, completely comfortable and with picture-windows from which to enjoy the views (it is on a high and breezy site). But the big attraction is Jennifer Steel's cooking. Starting as an enthusiastic amateur, she later did a chef's training – and then a special course on wild mushrooms, one of her specialities (from which she makes 'fairy hoosie soup' among other things). Her research into traditional Scottish dishes means you may be offered such a menu as 'nun beads' (cheese, herbs and cream in pastry), 'wee grumphies' (pork balls made with cheese and apples), 'chappit neeps' (turnips mashed with cream), 'lillylyn pudding' (rhubarb, cream and custard). Wine is often included in the very moderate price of such meals – and then for breakfast trout or haggis will be among the many choices on offer. What better way to end a tour of Scotland?

Special needs catered for as follows (for explanation of code letters, see page **xxviii**).
Establishments marked with a star will accept the discount vouchers (see page **ii**).

	C	D	H	PT	S	S-C	X
Achray House	C						
Auchtubhmor House	C						
Borlum Farm	C	D		PT		S-C	X
Clachaig Inn	C		H	PT	S	S-C	X
Coul House Hotel★	C	D	H	PT			
Cuilcheanna House	C	D				S-C	
Cuilfail Hotel★	C	D			S		
Daviot Mains Farm★				PT	S		
Drumbuie	C						
Dunlichity Lodge	C	D	H				
Falls of Lora Hotel★	C	D	H	PT			
Foyers Hotel★	C	D		PT			
Glen Loy Lodge	C	D			S		
Invergloy House	C(8)				S		
Kilravock Castle	C		H	PT	S		
Leny House★	C			PT		S-C	
Mansewood	C	D			S		
Mill House★							X
Moorings Hotel★				PT			
Ossian Hotel	C	D		PT			
Rockhill Farm	C(6)	D			S	S-C	
Rossmay	C	D		PT	S		
(Sundays free to over-60s)							
Topps Farm★	C		H				
Wester Moniack Farm	C	D			S		
Willowburn Hotel	C	D		PT			X

A major promotion this year is focusing attention on the best of home-produced food – something which already features strongly in most of the hotels and houses (especially farms) which are in *Staying Off the Beaten Track*. A great many use home-grown or local produce, either in traditional dishes or for recipes that are their own speciality – like Avonside's raspberry brûlée, Martlemas beef at Beehive Cottage, pigeon with juniper berries at Butchers Arms, Buttons Green Farm's asparagus mousse, rhubarb and orange pudding at Cove House, lobster 'Auld Reekie' at the Crab & Lobster, Church House's sorrel soup, and the hazelnut ice cream served with damson sauce at the Coach House, Crookham – but this list could go on and on.

Many houses in this book are in the vicinity of pick-your-own fruit fields, or farms where produce can be bought at farm-gate shops, to take home; and in the sightseeing notes of many entries you will find references to these.

At different seasons, there may be open days on local farms; livestock markets; agricultural shows; and rural displays (sheepdogs in action, ploughing contests, cheesemaking, crafts etc.).

There will be such a huge number of special food, farming and countryside attractions on the go that there is being produced a new *Countryside Directory* (Sphere), to be available in 1989 for the first time. This is a guide to farm shops, country parks, farm museums, craft workshops, farm or nature trails and speciality food producers – a first-rate reference book to keep in the car, with over 2000 entries.

It will even tell you where to find forestry centres, farm interpretation centres, country walks, gardens open to the public, vineyards, herb gardens, trout farms, butterfly gardens . . . Everything you can imagine that adds pleasure to a day in the country will be covered, with full details of how to get there (with maps), when it's open, admission charges (if any), and whether you can take your dog or someone in a wheelchair.

The *Directory* will be available from March 1989 at bookshops.

ENGLISH HERITAGE MEMBERSHIP

If you appreciate England's historic monuments, it's worth joining a special 'club' by becoming a member of English Heritage.

A membership card entitles you to visit English Heritage properties without payment – Hampton Court and the Tower of London, too; half-price admission to many buildings in Wales and Scotland; a beautifully produced quarterly magazine, (with articles by experts, colour photographs, details of forthcoming events in English Heritage properties ranging from concerts to mediaeval jousts, book reviews, and even a children's page – children are enrolled in the junior section, Keep, with its own events, badges, etc.); an illustrated handbook describing all the sites, worth £2; a map of England showing where they all are; guided tours and talks exclusive to members, particularly where local branches flourish; and the offer of books and souvenirs by post, at special prices.

To join, either call at an English Heritage property or post this coupon to English Heritage, Box 43, Ruislip HA4 0XW. If applying for more than one person, send list of names (IN CAPITALS) with children's birth dates.

☐　**Individual:** £10 a year
☐　**Family groups:** £20 for two parents and all children under 16, who will be enrolled in KEEP. Each receives a card.
☐　**Senior Citizen:** £6 for people qualifying for the state pension.
£ _____ is enclosed*/may be debited to the credit card shown below.
*Cheques should be made payable to ENGLISH HERITAGE.
Access/Amex/
Barclaycard No　☐☐☐☐☐☐☐☐☐☐☐☐☐☐☐☐☐☐☐☐☐
Mr/Mrs/Ms (initials): ___ Surname (capitals): _____
Address: _____
_____ Postcode: _____

YOU AND THE LAW

Once your booking has been confirmed – orally or in writing – a contract exists between you and the proprietor. He is legally bound to provide accommodation as booked; and you are legally bound to pay for this accommodation. If you are unable to take up the booking – even if through sickness – you still remain liable for a very substantial proportion of the charges (in addition to losing your deposit).

If you have to cancel, let the proprietor know as soon as possible; then he may be able to re-let the accommodation (in which case you would be liable to pay only a re-letting cost or forfeit your deposit).

A note to American readers. It may be an acceptable practice elsewhere to make bookings at several houses for the same date, choosing only later which one to patronize; but this way of doing things is not the British practice and you are legally liable to compensate any proprietors whom you let down in this way – see above.